Powerful PERENNIALS

Enduring Flower Gardens That Thrive in Any Climate

NEDRA SECRIST

Hobble Creek Press | An Imprint of Cedar Fort, Inc. | Springville, Utah

© 2015 Nedra Secrist
All rights reserved.

Front cover photo courtesy of Miranda Dejarnett. Back cover photos (hens and chicks, aconitum, and peonies) courtesy of Walters Gardens. United States Frost Areas map reprinted with permission from *Compton's by Britannica*, ©2011 by Encyclopaedia Britannica, Inc.

ISBN 13: 978-1-4621-1635-5

Published by Hobble Creek Press,
an imprint of Cedar Fort, Inc.
2373 W. 700 S., Springville; UT, 84663

Distributed by Cedar Fort, Inc.,
www.cedarfort.com

LIBRARY OF CONGRESS CATALOGING-IN-PUBLICATION DATA

Secrist, Nedra, 1936- author.
Powerful perennials / Nedra Secrist.
   pages cm
Includes bibliographical references and index.

Summary: Discusses why gardening is different in the western United States than it is in the eastern United States and suggests solutions for challenges such as dry, rocky soil, intense sunlight, high elevations, and lack of water.

ISBN 978-1-4621-1635-5 (alk. paper)

1. Perennials--Great Basin. 2. Flower gardening--Great Basin. I. Title.

SB434.S44 2015

635.9'32097924--dc23

2014033201

Cover and page design by Angela D. Baxter
and M. Shaun McMurdie
Cover design © 2015 by Lyle Mortimer
Edited by Eileen Leavitt

Printed in the United States of America

10 9 8 7 6 5 4 3 2 1

Printed on acid-free paper.

DEDICATION

Dedicated to every gardener with imperfect soil who can't figure out why their garden doesn't look like some English garden on the cover of a magazine.

CONTENTS

POWERFUL PERENNIALS

The reward is in the process, not the destination.

ANY GARDENER WILL admit that gardening in the Rocky Mountains is like attending a school of "hard rocks." But in spite of everything, we grow amazing gardens because we use perennials. The fact of the matter is, perennials are easy to grow!

I'm always disappointed that the Rocky Mountains are left out of most gardening books, with only a side comment about how appropriate our climate is for alpine or rock garden perennials. We do grow these tough, small, drought-tolerant perennials, but why is it assumed that because of our hot and cold climate extremes and the lack of good soil and water, not much in the way of gardening goes on here? Well it does! We do garden! Our mountains are a majestic backdrop, and while it's a daunting task for any gardener to try to compete with their natural beauty, we do garden here in the western United States.

WHY WE GARDEN

At gardening seminar presentations, I always start out the discussion by asking the students why they garden. They invariably frown at me like it's a dumb question, but as they stop to think, awareness dawns on them, and they realize it is actually a multilayered question. When the answers start coming, they are as delightfully different and surprising as the students. Most answers fall into the categories of well-being and physical, mental, financial, and even creative health. A few of these delightful responses explain why gardeners, with their muddy knees, dirty fingernails, aching backs, and butts stuck in the air, slave in the heat of the sun during all of daylight hours and wish they could keep gardening long after night falls.

UNCONDITIONAL LOVE

I want to start with my own answer as to why I garden: I garden because flowers, more than anything on earth, teach unconditional love. All they require is a little nurturing, and they lift their beautiful flower faces to smile at you!

My husband's Grandma Louise, a strong and self-reliant lady, was my gardening mentor. Her life was difficult. She lost her husband when he was only twenty-nine. Grandpa Ed was killed when he was scalded by hot syrup in an accident at a sugar factory, and Louise was left with two small sons to raise. Women at this time rarely worked. Nevertheless, she "made do." When I was a young bride, my husband and I built a home on the same street as Grandma. When we arrived home from work each day, we could hardly get the door unlocked before the phone rang with a request from Grandma to take her to the grocery store where she could get her daily Coke and socialize with the neighbors.

One spring afternoon, as Louise and I returned from the store, my curiosity couldn't be stopped. In her hands she gently held her usual package of bedding plants. Grandma would, without fail, purchase a six-pack of bedding plants and a six-pack of Coke. I knew the flowers were her only extravagance, and I finally had to say, "You must really love those flowers!"

"I do love them! Furthermore, they love me back!" she answered, and then she gave me a long look that questioned if I was old or wise enough to understand her reply. After a long, poignant pause she continued: "Flowers are the one thing in life that I can love and trust that they will never hurt me!"

STRESS RELIEF

My student Leah agrees with this reason. She returned from a stressful day at work with a pounding tension headache. Rather than taking medication, however, she headed outside. "I slipped out back to my flower garden and began deadheading and pulling a few weeds. I've found that if I'm weeding, no one comes around to bother me. They probably think I'll put them to work. If only they knew the truth. I putter around in my garden for some alone time. Within an hour, my headache had evaporated."

Afton, another avid gardener, agrees. "If there were more weeding, there would be less road rage!"

FITNESS AND WEIGHT CONTROL

"When I'm outside in the garden, I don't stop to eat," says Marlene. "It must be plain distraction because I'm so happily involved when I'm gardening that I won't stop and don't bother to eat. I always lose weight during the summer. I suppose I haven't mastered eating and pulling weeds at the same time."

Our lake neighbors Brian and Sherry have perfected the art of mountain fitness. Instead of pounding the pavement and sweating as they run around the mountain roads surrounding Bear Lake, where we spend our summers, they go outside and work in the garden. Sherry says, "My health fitness is 'playing' in my garden. When I quit for the day, I gaze back at how nice the garden looks and feel contentment at the lovely living space I've created. I'm happy because everything looks so fine. A little labor was involved, but just being outside with the flowers and sun all around keeps me healthy."

"My doctor doesn't seem to realize that gardening is a true exercise," adds Brian. "He is always prescribing a regular exercise program. Physically for my age, I can still work [like the] young'uns. The doctor just hasn't seen me shovel truckloads of manure for her garden," he grins, pointing at Sherry.

My husband, Donrey, and I are somewhat older than Brian and Sherry, but we're still gardening. Donrey says he has never met a retired gardener. He thinks gardening has helped us stay young.

If you take into account joint flexibility, osteoporosis prevention, and calories burned, gardening provides significant health benefits. "Two separate studies that followed seniors in their sixties and seventies for up to sixteen years found, respectively, that those who gardened regularly had a thirty-six percent and a forty-seven percent lower risk of dementia than non-gardeners, even when a range of other health factors were taken into account."[1]

PHYSICAL AND EMOTIONAL THERAPY

Marilyn teaches physical education to seventh graders and is thrilled to have her summers free to garden. "I've always hated going to the gym. Gym clothes are so annoying. I just love my old, scruffy, hole-in-the-knees, dirt-stained gardening clothes. I garden so I can dodge the day-in, day-out housework and get out of the house." Then she laughs, finally hearing what she had just said. "It's ridiculous. Can you believe a gym teacher who can't stand gym clothes and going to the gym?"

This comment from a not-so-avid gardener, Pauline, is a classic: "Somewhere I read that technically you're not considered a couch potato if you're sitting outside," she wrote.

Colleen, a quiet kind of gal, opened up and told me about her mother who was recovering from a stroke by exercising in the hospital's therapy gardens. "The nursing home used the back section of their garden as a place to help Mother recover her balance, muscles, coordination, and strength," Colleen explained. "She was required to navigate sloping pathways through perennial gardens, up and down, back and forth, twice a day. At first she couldn't do it, but eventually she was able to go partway with help. In addition to [her] being able to walk again, [her] doctor explained that simply spending time in nature lowered her blood pressure better than meds."

Bodie, a talented and very creative young man, has been so badly broken in multiple car accidents that he has difficulty caring for himself and is homebound. However, through the pain, he somehow still cares for his yard and garden, which is the most original and attractive in his neighborhood. He says that when the sun comes out, the neighbors come out and will stop to talk gardening or ask his advice with gardening questions. Many of his friends and neighbors have him help design their flower beds. Other times of the year, Bodie feels so isolated that he finds it hard to fight off pity parties and can fall easily into depression. "I just need to focus on the sun coming out again," Bodie admits. "The garden is always open!"

Arlene, president of the local gardening club, explained her appreciation for gardening this way: "My brother started using drugs after returning from Afghanistan. He was a mess! Finally, he got a job tending the city's gardens. Now he is a productive human being. He has always been sort of an introvert and says the gardens give him the quiet and peace he craves. He now has a sense of purpose and says the soil has a restorative effect. He explains it as an energy transfer from the earth. He has married, and he and his wife enjoy gardening together. In the summer they sell their fresh produce at the farmers market."

My long-term gardening friend Cleo stopped by one late-spring evening to visit. Cleo is a highly respected mental health council and probation officer for the juvenile court system and uses gardening to balance out the stress the job causes. One time, she came over, and I showed off my newly planted hybrids, complained about all the perennials that winter had killed because our winter was so dry, and then I dug a few starts for her to take home. It was almost dark, so I cautioned her about keeping them moist until they could be planted.

"No worries," she grinned. "My son gave me a new shovel for Mother's Day with a flashlight attached. He did it as a joke, but I use it. I'll stick these in when I get home."

I had to laugh, and then I paused and looking at her seriously and asked, "Why do you do it, Cleo? Why are you so avid about gardening?"

Her answer was quick and to the point, "It's cheaper than Prozac!"

RECREATION AND LIFESTYLE

Robin, another gardening friend, came to me for advice on planting the huge landscape of a very wealthy homeowner. The woman did not want her planting done by a landscaping firm whose style was to cover the grounds with shrubs that the homeowner detested and the deer loved! She wanted flowers. Tons and tons of flowers. I was so envious of the fun Robin would have planting this landscape that I asked how her business got started. Robin explained that she had been earning good money at an extremely responsible administrative job.

"The long hours and high pressure got to me! Then my husband left, and in my misery I walked off the job. Losing my husband, my income, work friends, and lifestyle were depressing and I sank deeper and deeper. I knew I was a total failure! My only relief was when I worked in my garden. It's pretty hard to be a failure in a garden. Every single year, gardens give us a second chance to start new and correct our last year's mistakes."

Robin called again last fall to ask about deer-proof perennials. She was planting the Grand America Hotel gardens in the resort community of Sun Valley, Idaho. I asked how things were going, and she said that she had been able to find peace, wholeness, and an element of financial security by doing what she loved.

"Besides, I don't want things," she explained. "I tried that, and it didn't work. I want the serenity and happiness that gardening furnishes. When I'm inspired with flowers and creating beauty, my spirit sings."

FINANCIAL HEALTH

Angie had worked at a garden nursery before, and she knew that it was what her heart wanted her to do. She came to Secrist Gardens and asked me for a job.

"I'll even work for free," she pleaded. "I just have to get my hands in the dirt and be around the flowers!" I grinned back at her, sensing I had just met a kindred spirit, and hired her.

"You don't have to pay me; honestly, I'll just work for flowers. We've bought a home, and the yard is nothing but rocks and dirt."

Every Saturday when her husband came to pick her up, they would stay late and excitedly shop for flowers, filling up a pick-up truck.

I moved to Bear Lake for the summer, and the next spring, I called Angie to see if she might want to help me again. Angie started to cry and said her husband's job hadn't worked out, and they were moving back to Sugar City.

"My main problem," she tried to explain, "is that with the business cutting back so many jobs, there are so many houses up for sale that I don't think there is much hope of selling ours. There are three houses with *For Sale* signs on our street alone."

I commiserated and asked her to keep me posted. Not even a week later, Angie called me with good news.

"We've sold our home!" she eagerly cried. "And you won't believe it; we got more than we had planned on asking. I made much better than good wages from you last year! I made a fortune! Not another home in our division has sold except ours! We know it sold because of our landscaping! Our beautiful flowers sold our home!"

FAMILY CONNECTIONS & WORK ETHIC

Laurie, a self-made and overworked CEO who operates her own company, thinks obsessive gardening is genetic brain damage and is ridiculous! As she planted her 137th pot of sedum to edge and stabilize a steep, clay-soil flower bed, she looked up at me pointedly with a scowl between her eyebrows and asked, "Why did you give me these genes, Mother?"

My son Don gardens entirely differently from his sister. Don does quality control for the government and is precise in everything he does, including yard work. I asked him one day why he didn't get some help in his perfect, there's-a-place-for-everything backyard. "You don't hire a pizza cutter to do a surgeon's job," he stated as he turned the lawn mower to cut his lawn the second time, in the opposite diagonal direction.

This next story is about Dirk, a single parent with three sons. I visited Dirk's yard when he was honored with the prestigious Yard of the Month award.

"Why do you garden, Dirk?" I asked as I looked around his lush, immaculate, professionally landscaped–looking grounds.

He stopped the hoe that was seeking the only weed in the entire place and looked at me for several minutes. Then, realizing it was a fair question, he replied, "The boys and I [were living] in a rental when we bought this property and house. It was the first dirt we could really call our own. The place had never had any care, but my boys and I had hope and started back at square one. The lot had to be stripped, leveled, and amended, and we did it together. After we installed the sprinkling system, my oldest son was so good at it that he was hired by a landscaper to install sprinklers as a summer job.

HOPE

Rose and Bob were a loving couple who were connected heart and soul for fifty-five years. When Bob passed during winter, Rose was devastated. As soon as the weather warmed, I visited Rose and took her a potted bleeding heart flower that was just breaking dormancy.

She smiled her thanks, saying, "Flowers have the power to express caring more than anything else. For this reason I love and appreciate them back."

We went out onto the patio to enjoy the spring sunshine's warmth, and I asked how she was doing.

"I'm lonely," she replied, "but now that I can be outside, I'll be fine. Everything in the garden brings Bob back. I remember when we installed the arbor and the fence, poured the walks, and planned and planted the gardens. It was so exciting and satisfying a time—our happiest time, in fact. I can still feel the joy of all the brides who had their weddings here and all the cookouts and family reunions we hosted."

She was silent for a while and then looked at me with a long, slow, enlightened look and whispered, "He is here with me now. His body might be gone, but he is here watching the spring awaken. The garden teaches that life follows death. Just look at those crocuses blooming. Anyone but a gardener would have sworn they were dead last summer, and they returned. Bob knew this garden would bear fruit long after he had worn out, and I know it's true!"

I also know it is true and it's only a mystery to those who do not garden. Valuable life lessons where families bond through work, play, and laughter are taught gently in the garden. Gardens teach the very basic elements of life—from food production to creativity. The natural cycles of a garden are like metaphors for life. Our gardens show the perfection of all existing Earth creatures and teach healing powers and life-enhancing qualities. They make homes look appealing, but they also give a home a connection to the past—a sense of having put down roots. Whenever the primroses or campanulas in my garden start to bloom, I think about my mother-in-law's smile when she brought me these perennials as starts many years ago.

To own your own plot of ground, till it, plant seeds, and watch life renew itself is the most satisfactory thing a man or woman can do. But now, finally, it's time to garden!

Happy gardening!

AUTHOR'S NOTE

This book is organized into four sections highlighting different challenges we face as gardeners. Within each section are a variety of perennials that will help you navigate each of these challenges. Even though I've organized these into the four sections, you should know that every perennial has its own personality and style of growing. I've tried to make it easier for you to get acquainted with the flowers by writing the flower descriptions from each perennial's point of view. A side sketch narrated by me will follow each description to give you some tips and provide you with more information.

My experience comes from years of gardening in the Rocky Mountain area, so I will use examples from that area throughout this book to illustrate my points. However, the principles of gardening in cold climates, in dry climates, with hungry wildlife, and with poor soils can apply in many different locations. Learn from my examples and apply them to your own garden.

NOTES

1.   Anne Harding, "Why Gardening Is Good for Your Health," Health.com, last modified July 8, 2011, accessed December 9, 2014, http://www.cnn.com/2011/HEALTH/07/08/why.gardening.good/

DIFFERENT GARDENING

Two tectonic plates collide
Thrusting high a rocky divide.
Glaciers level as they slide
Creating mountains with valleys inside.

Would any gardener choose this site—
Bitter winters and sunlight too bright?

Temperatures erratic, like elevations,
Snow sporadic, due to locations.

But a mountain fortress protects four seasons,
Halting flood or tornado collisions.

Worst pests and weeds feel alienation
So "what's not to love?" is their reason.

COLD-HARDY PERENNIALS

IN A COLDER climate, perennials really have to fight to grow. In warmer, wetter, more consistent climates, flowers fight not to grow! The answer to a successful perennial garden in a tough climate is simple: plant only cold-climate perennials. One of the first steps to becoming a gardener is becoming familiar with hardiness zones.

Today is June 4. My local news station just forecast freezing temperatures for tonight! Yesterday, June 3, the temperature went as high as 88°F in Salt Lake City, Utah. The announcer quipped, "We have winter and then the Fourth of July!" When you garden under conditions like these, you garden differently. Consequently, a cold-hardy perennial garden is a far cry from the textbook-variety fancy garden shown in most books, magazines, and catalogs. This is epsecially true where I garden, in the Rocky Mountains. Our cold, snowy winters and sizzling, dry summers present unique gardening challenges, but perennials are up to it!

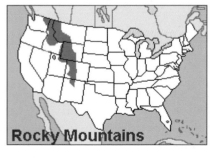

This map of the Rocky Mountains in western North America shows the most difficult area in the United States to grow perennials. Most gardening here occurs in the high mountain valleys or along the benches at the base of the mountains. Notice how the orange area of the map curves into an elongated *s* shape. It is this curve that provides protection for gardeners who live in the mountains. Polar air masses from the Artic move east into Montana instead of down the Rocky Mountain range. The frigidly cold air from the Great Plains is blocked by the mountains to the east and northeast, and Pacific storms must first cross the Sierra Nevada mountain ranges before reaching our inner continental position. The Rocky Mountains, with their high-reaching barriers of stone, protect the inhabitants from winds or floods from all points of the compass.

To succeed at growing perennials, it's important that you understand how differences in temperature, elevation, location, snowpack, short growing seasons, and freeze and thaw fluctuations may affect the success of your garden.

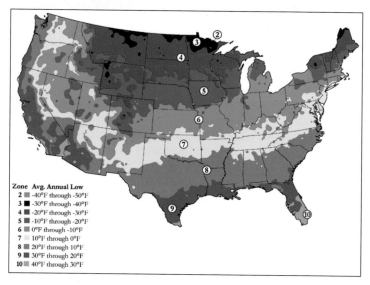

Zone	Avg. Annual Low
2	-40°F through -50°F
3	-30°F through -40°F
4	-20°F through -30°F
5	-10°F through -20°F
6	0°F through -10°F
7	10°F through 0°F
8	20°F through 10°F
9	30°F through 20°F
10	40°F through 30°F

DIFFERENT GARDENING DUE TO TEMPERATURE

Cold temperatures affect the hardiness of plants, so choosing perennials that are considered cold-hardy is a top priority for western gardeners. A useful tool for selecting these perennials is to use a USDA Zone Hardiness Map, as shown above. Plant specialists and meteorologists have mapped North America into ten bands or zones of average, minimum, and maximum temperatures. Zone 1 is the coldest, and Zone 10 is the warmest, so choose perennials that match your area's temperature zone. Potted plants are required to be labeled with their hardiness zone as well as their light and water requirements. Any blue (Zone 4) or green (Zone 5) areas in the northern United States can successfully grow the cold-hardy perennials introduced in *Powerful Perennials,* excluding the East and West Coast acidic soil areas.

This area graph gives a quick view of the lowest hardiness zone temperatures in which a perennial will survive in different locations. This data has been calculated using nearly thirty years of local data and is more accurate for gardeners to use. Notice the wide variations in average temperatures and elevations and how they correlate.

In your geography class, you learned that the further north you go on the globe, and the higher the elevation, the colder the winters are. If you were to draw a line between Boise, Idaho, and Jackson, Wyoming, the line would be almost horizontal. The two locations are at a similar latitude, so it's easy to assume that their growing conditions would be similar. However Boise, Idaho (elevation of about 2,840 feet), and Jackson, Wyoming (elevation of about 6,230 feet), have drastically different growing conditions. In Boise, gardeners grow perennials that will winter easily down to -10°F or a Zone 6. Gardeners in Jackson, Wyoming, however, must plant perennials that can tolerate temperatures of -50°F. Here, gardeners need to plant Zone 2 perennials if they don't want their gardens to winter-kill. At the southern tip of Utah is St. George, a winter sunbelt area that sits at an elevation of approximately 2,800 feet and seldom drops below freezing. Southern Utah has more success with growing perennials suitable for drought and hot sun areas, so even though its elevation is similar to Boise, the same plants that thrive in one location will suffer in the other.

All of these communities are very different from each other, thus the gardening must be different. If you are worried that a perennial you want for your garden will not survive, plant a lower-zoned perennial.

For more information on the entire area, from the top of Idaho to the bottom of Utah, plus Montana, Wyoming, Colorado, and Nevada, please visit forestry.usu.edu, then keyword search "hardiness."

DIFFERENT GARDENING DUE TO ELEVATION

The terrain of the West is the most diverse in the United States. The Rocky Mountains climb to the top of the Tetons at about 13,700 feet and then drop to the Great Salt Lake level of 4,200 feet. Because temperature and elevation are connected, a savvy gardener must first look at elevations to understand temperatures. An interesting example is the Wellsville Mountains and the Peter Sinks areas. These two are barely twenty-five miles apart, and yet are worlds apart in climate due to elevation.

HIGH ELEVATION: WELLSVILLE MOUNTAINS

The Wellsville Mountains are located in Northern Utah. They separate the Cache Valley from the Wasatch Front. At 9,372 feet, they are only moderately tall but are narrow. For this reason, they are claimed as one of the steepest mountain ranges in North America. The growing season is expected to be shorter in the coolness of the mountains, but it is also shorter in the valley bottoms.

LOW ELEVATION: PETER SINKS

Peter Sinks, an uninhabited portion of Logan Canyon, holds the honor of producing the all-time coldest temperatures recorded. According to the local weather station on February 2, 2011, the temperature was -49°F. The same day in 1985, the temperature was -69°F. Peter Sinks is a tub-shaped valley over a mile long and about as wide. Cold air is denser and heavier and runs downhill. It can be 15°F to 20°F colder at the bottom than the top.

ROCKY MOUNTAIN
WEATHER STATIONS STATISTICS

STATE	COUNTY	WEATHER STATION	ELEVATION	ABSOLUTE MINIMUM TEMPERATURE (F°)	AVERAGE MINIMUM HARDINESS		YEARS OF DATA
Utah	Box Elder	Bear River Refuge	4,210 ft.	-21°	Zone 6	Zone 4	21
Utah	Cache	Logan Radio KVNU	4,490 ft.	-30°	Zone 5	Zone 4	30
Utah	Daggett	Flaming Gorge	6,270 ft.	-38°	Zone 5	Zone 3	30
Utah	Rich	Laketown	5,980 ft.	-37°	Zone 5	Zone 3	30
Utah	Weber	Pine View Dam	4,940 ft.	-39°	Zone 4	Zone 3	30
Utah	Washington	St. George	2,762 ft.	12°	Zone 8	Zone 7	30
Colorado	Moffat	Dinosaur National Monument	5,920 ft.	-29°	Zone 5	Zone 4	25
Idaho	Bear Lake	Lifton Pumping Station	5,930 ft.	-41°	Zone 4	Zone 2	30
Idaho	Bonneville	Idaho Falls Airport	4,730 ft.	-38°	Zone 5	Zone 3	30
Idaho	Power	Pocatello Airport	4,450 ft.	-33°	Zone 5	Zone 3	30
Idaho	Boise	Boise Airport	2,840 ft.	-25°	Zone 6	Zone 4	30
Wyoming	Teton	Jackson	6,230 ft.	-50°	Zone 3	Zone 1	30
Wyoming	Uintah	Evanston 1-E	6,810 ft.	-35°	Zone 4	Zone 3	29

Information courtesy of Utah State University

DIFFERENT GARDENING DUE TO LOCATION

Location can cause wild fluctuations in temperatures—often called microclimates.

Brigham City, Utah, is nestled along the west-facing bench of the Wasatch Front mountain range. This area is known for having mild winters and is often called "the Banana Belt." With the protection of the mountains on the east and the Great Salt Lake (which never freezes, due to its high salt content) on the west, Brigham City's lowest recorded temperature is -25°F. Zone 6 perennials would probably overwinter here, but a standard rule of thumb for gardeners is to drop the hardiness zone to one lower, so Zones 3, 4, and 5 are safer. May 1 is typically a safe planting date.

The location of Laketown, Utah, also sits on the edge of a large body of water, but Bear Lake is fed by a mountain spring and freezes when winters get cold. Mountain snowpack usually lasts from November to May, so planting before June 1 is a risky gamble in the Bear Lake Valley. A gardener's location plays an important part in the hardiness of perennials. When in doubt, it is wise to begin by observing what grows well in other local gardens. You will waste a lot of time and money if you insist on planting perennials that will not tolerate the temperature conditions in your area.

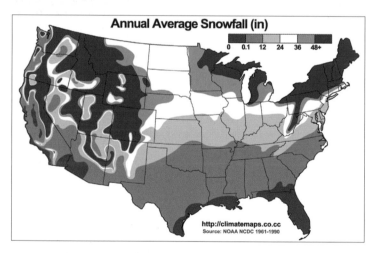

Annual Average Snowfall (in)

0 0.1 12 24 36 48+

http://climatemaps.co.cc
Source: NOAA NCDC 1961-1990

DIFFERENT GARDENING DUE TO SNOWFALL

Perennials without winter moisture are doomed. Without water, the roots of dormant plants lose the resiliency that gives the plant the ability to withstand cold. Surprisingly, snow cover in winter is the greatest asset a gardener can have to protect perennials. Soil under snow may freeze only an inch deep, so it will not affect a plant's roots. Winter air fluctuates immensely, and snow cover helps soil temperature stay constant. A layer of dry, fluffy snow is best. For example, Utah's "greatest snow on Earth," contains between 50 to 90 percent air and transmits an amazing amount

of light. Just like the wild ups and downs of western topography and temperatures, snowfall west of the Rocky Mountains varies from more than two hundred inches to less than ten inches. High elevations can receive more than seven hundred inches while west- and south-facing slopes may get only ten inches.

If your winters are arid, irrigation is a must. Because of freezing temperatures, irrigation systems must be drained in winter. A deep soaking of gardens in the fall, before freezing, provides some insurance. Be especially careful to saturate areas under pine trees. Snow doesn't penetrate the dense boughs and sometimes even leaves a snow-free nest for deer to sleep under. Another problem area is a garden that faces south, because its snow cover melts in winter.

July the previous year. The gardens are lush.

January the following year. The gardens are without snow.

June the following year. Many perennials died without snow cover.

Solution. Plant something other than perennials. Without snow cover, perennials can be lost.

SOUTH-FACING PERENNIAL BORDER PROBLEMS

This picture series shows the same perennial border in summer when packed with all kinds of cold-hardy perennials. The next photo shows the same garden the following January without snow cover.

Sadly, about all that survived are the amazing indestructible sedums and the creeping baby's breath. When my gardens suffer heavy winter losses, one quick solution has been to plant fast-growing annuals to fill in the empty spaces. Dinner-plate dahlias are a favorite. Dahlias can be harvested after fall's first freezing nip and be stored for winter in a basement area. They multiply nicely, giving a gardener twice as many for the next year.

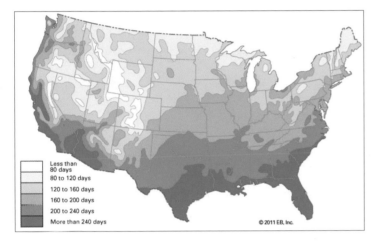

Less than 80 days
80 to 120 days
120 to 160 days
160 to 200 days
200 to 240 days
More than 240 days

© 2011 EB, Inc.

DIFFERENT GARDENING DUE TO SHORT GROWING SEASONS

The map above shows the growing season for various areas of North America. The short growing seasons are another deterrent to gardening. Cold-climate perennials all have the survival skills of being able to move from growth to a period of dormancy. Tissues harden as days grow short. The prime trigger that starts this hardening process is not falling temperatures but the shortening of days and the lengthening of nights. The number of hours of daylight is consistent year after year, while temperatures can fluctuate wildly. Unfortunately, when an early frost hits, plants are not ready and haven't started the hardening process. This is why so many perennials in areas prone to killing frosts do not survive in winter.

TRICKS FOR GROWING PERENNIALS IN SHORT-SEASON AREAS

- Eliminate the really early-blooming perennials like rock cresses.
- Bulbs are safer to use—especially the daffodils, which are weatherproof—and the small early-blooming bulbs such as snowdrops. Bulbs can be trusted not to break dormancy too soon.

- For early-spring perennial color, plant early-blooming flowers like soapwort, geraniums, or centaurea.
- Plant flowers that bloom midsummer, like Zone 3 delphiniums, maltese cross, or daylilies.
- Fall-blooming perennials need to be well chosen. The earlier blooming asters like 'Alma Potschke' will go easily through a snowstorm if you rinse off late snows with a hose. Later asters may not get to bloom.
- Chrysanthemums are a waste of time, blooming way too late for short-season gardeners.
- Do not fertilize after the first of August. Fertilizer causes the plant to put on a new flush of foliage. Without fertilizer, the roots push down to gain extra strength that will help them winter.
- After the first freeze, cut perennials back, but leave the trimmings on top of flower beds for added winter insulation, or wait to trim your gardens until spring. The dead foliage acts as a snow trap for more cover.

DIFFERENT GARDENING DUE TO FREEZE AND THAW FLUCTUATIONS

Freeze and thaw fluctuations are another one of the major reasons gardeners lose plants in winter. A January thaw will not only damage perennials but will kill shrubs and trees. If the down comforter of snow melts, perennials like coral bells will heave right out of the ground. Late frosts can occur the entire month of April and often in May and June. Asters, the easiest plant available, are a late-emerging and hardy Zone 3 perennial, so they should be safe in a freeze-thaw situation, but they're not! Asters, like most other perennials, take so much energy to break dormancy that a late frost will kill them.

The best solution for protecting perennials from freeze-thaw cycles is to bury them deeper than suggested when planting and to place a layer of compost over the garden after a fall freeze. Wait until the ground freezes to place the compost, or it will invite small critters to tunnel under the soft mulch for winter cover. By the time the ground freezes, most critters are safely tucked somewhere other than our gardens.

The early spring thaws bring so much delight to gardeners that they often flock to the garden centers, not being able to resist planting. I have a dear gardening friend who works in a local box store nursery. One very early, warm spring morning, I asked how business was.

"Packed," she replied. "We are selling annuals faster than we can get them delivered in from California!"

We both knew that the warm temperatures were a sucker hole for gardeners, and when I raised my eyebrows, she replied, "The store's policy is to sell them once. And if the plants freeze? Oh well. Just sell them again."

Planting the powerful perennials introduced in this section will ease the urge to buy impulsively! *Powerful Perennials* offers the answer to cold-climate gardening.

Achillea filipendulina
(ak-i-LEE-uh)
'Coronation Gold'
YARROW

SHAPE	Sturdy bush, flattop flowers
HEIGHT	Thirty to thirty-five inches tall
WIDTH	Thirty by thirty inches
BLOOM TIME	June through September or October
COLORS	Gold
SITE	Lean soils
LIGHT	Full sun
HARDINESS	Zones 3–8
COMMENTS	Long blooming with attractive, deer-resistant foliage

In late summer, achillea blooms with phlox and lilium.

Achillea and white anthemis light up a June garden. Achillea enhances every perennial color but yellow.

In early summer, achillea blooms with nepeta and orange poppies.

The brilliant scarlet red of *Lychnis*, or Maltese cross, backs up the flat-topped blooms of achillea.

GREETINGS FROM A powerful flower whose healing abilities have been documented since the Trojan War. I feel very proud of my lengthy list of powerful credentials. My name probably came from the healer Achillea who used my foliage to heal wounds and stop the bleeding of the Trojan soldiers. Legend has it that the druids and Chinese somehow used my power to predict the future. Even the early settlers and fur trappers of the American West knew of my ability to heal.

Today, my healing powers are used more for shaving cuts and toothaches. More important to gardeners is that if my leaves are added to a compost pile, I will speed up the decomposition and infuse a copper fertilizer into the mulch.

Historical data is nice, but I'm much, much more than an ancient reference. I'm proud to say that I'm the modern hybrid A. 'Coronation Gold'. I'm truly the queen of the summer garden. I was even named 'Coronation Gold' to commemorate the 1953 crowning of Britain's Queen Elizabeth II. Queens are powerful, and so am I!

First, I'm hardy and easy to grow, always returning after a harsh winter. Next, I'm easy to propagate. Spring is the best time to divide and start perennials. This gives me the entire summer to develop my strong root system. Simply dig the new shoots formed around my base or dig and split my tough root ball into smaller sections and replant. I'll grow and quickly form a dense mound of herbal, aromatic foliage.

My foliage is bushy and thick with straight, thirty-inch long stems that never flop or need staking. The silvery-green foliage is a perfect combination with masses of tiny, bright gold flowers that cluster on top like flat plates. I'm a rich gold color so powerful that neighboring flowers need to contrast rather than blend.

A. 'Coronation Gold' and 'Moonshine' are two of the longest-blooming perennials for the Rocky Mountains. Both of us are sterile hybrids, meaning we do not waste energy setting seed, but rather use it to bloom and bloom and bloom. Our brilliant yellow-gold flat-topped flowers never look tired or bedraggled. They remain fresh until almost the end of the growing season.

Only a handful of other perennials are capable of our bloom power, but none are as carefree as we are. Most will require a haircut or deadheading after our initial flowering to bloom again. Our close relative, the A. millefolium, blooms in various colors, but at the end of its flowering, it turns an unsightly white that is very unattractive.

Other perennials that have a reputation as "long blooming" in a garden are the perennials with excellent foliage. In other words, their foliage remains good looking, but they do not have flowers. Silver-foliaged artemisias; bergenias, or heartleaf; *Heucheras*, or coral bells; and *Helleborus*, or Lenten roses, hold their beautiful foliage even through winter. Grasses are known for season-long interest, as are sedums with their interesting silvery rosettes in spring to their clumps of unique flowers that distinguish a fall garden. *Iris pallida*, or striped iris, is also nonstop color in a perennial garden with its eye-catching foliage. Foliage is very important, but when a gardener wants season-long color, we are the best perennials to have.

BOTANICAL PRONUNCIATIONS: CALISTHENICS FOR THE TONGUE

PERHAPS YOU NOTICED the two different pronunciations for *Achillea* 'Coronation Gold': (uh-KILL-ee-uh) or (ak-i-LEE-uh). I prefer the second pronunciation. It is much more musical. Whichever pronunciation a gardener uses is correct as long as the listener understands. In other words, never allow botanical pronunciations to cause shyness. Pronounce the names as if they are your native language.

When I first practiced the name of *Aquilegia,* or columbine, (ak-wih-LEE-jee-uh) it sounded so beautiful that I just kept repeating the word.

To be able to communicate, start at the beginning with pronunciations. Names are how you know a plant. Our perennials have so many different common names due to regional areas and different pronunciations, even within the plant trade, that without the botanical name, a gardener could end up buying alchemilla instead of aquilegia. This is why it is important to use the consistency of a universal plant language, or Botanical Latin. Practice makes perfect! Remember, knowing the perennials' names is just like knowing the name of a good friend.

In traditional English pronunciations, the uppercase letters in each word are the accented syllables. If you are looking for a perennial not listed, perhaps the plant is not zoned for our western climate or it may not like our alkaline soils. Hopefully this chart will help you feel more comfortable.

One good thing about Botanical Latin is that Latin is a dead language, meaning the names of the perennials will not change. However, many great gardens have been grown by gardeners who never called a plant by its Latin name. These gardens were grown with hard work, creative dedication, and perhaps, a green thumb!

BOTANICAL PRONUNCIATION GUIDE

ae	Pronounce as *ea* in *meat*	Example: *Paeonia*
c	Pronounce as *c* in *cat* before a, o, u (hard *c*)	Example: *Catananche*
c	Pronounce as *c* in *center* before e, I, y (soft *c*)	Example: *Centaurea*
ch	Pronounce as *k*	Example: *Achillea*
e	Pronounce as *e* in *me*	Example: *Verbena*
g	Pronounce as *g* in *gap* before a, o, u, (hard *g*)	Example: *Gallium*
g	Pronounce as *g* in *gem* before e, I, y (soft *g*)	Example: *Geum*
oe	Pronounce as *ee* in *bee*	Example: *Oenothera*

A

ACHILLEA
(ak-i-LEE-a)
(uh-KILL-ee-uh)

ACONITUM
(ack-oh-NEYE-tum)

AJUGA
(uh-JOO-guh)

ALCEA
(al-SEE-a)

ALCHEMILLA
(al-keh-MILL-uh)

ANCHUSE
(*an-CHOO-sah*)

ANEMONE
(uh-NEM-oh-nee)

ANTHEMIS
(an-THEME-is)

AQUILEGIA
(ak-wih-LEE-jee-uh)

ARABIS
(AR-uh-biss)

ARENARIA
(ah-ray-NAH-ree-uh)

ARMERIA
(ar-MAIR-ree-uh)

ARTEMISIA
(ar-te-MEEZ-ee-uh)

ARUNCUS
(uh-RUN-kus)

ASCLEPIAS
(as-KLEE-pea-us)

ASPARAGUS
(as-PAIR-uh-gus)

ASTER
(AS-ter)

AURINIA
(aw-RIN-ee-uh)

B

BERGENIA
(ber-GEN-ee-uh)

BRUNNERA
(BROON-er-uh)

C

CALAMAGROSTIS
(cal-a-ma-GROS-tis)

CALAMINTHA
(kal-ah-MIN-tha)

CAMPANULA
(kam-PAN-yew-luh)

CENTAUREA
(sen-TOR-ree-uh)

CENTRANTHUS
(sen-TRAN-thus)

CERASTIUM
(ser-AS-te um)*A*

CIMICIFUGA
(sim-i-si-FUG-a)

CLEMATIS
(KLEM-at-is)

COREOPSIS
(cor-ee-OP-sis)

CORYDALIS
(ko-RID-a-lis)

D

DELOSPERMA
(del-o-SPER-muh)

DELPHINIUM
(del-FIN-ee-um)

DENDRANTHEMA
(den-ran-TEEM-uh)

DIANTHUS
(dye-AN-thus)

DICENTRA
(dye-SEN-tra)

DIGITALIS
(dij-uh-TAL-lis)

DORONICUM
(dor-ON-ih-kum)

E

ECHINACEA
(eck-i-NAY-see-uh)

EUONYMUS
(yew-ON-i-mus)

EUPATORIUM
(yew-pah-TOR-ee-um)

EUPHORBIA
(yew-FOR-bee-uh)

F

FESTUCA
(fes-TU-ka)

G

GAILLARDIA
(gay-LAR-dee-uh)

GALIUM
(GAL-lee-um)

GENTIANA
(jen-shi-AH-na)

GERANIUM
(jer-AY-nee-um)

GEUM
(JEE-um)

GYPSOPHILA
(jip-SOF-i-la)

H

HELENIUM
(HEL-ee-nee-um)

HELIOPSIS
(hee-lee-OP-sis)

HELLEBORUS
(hell-e-BOR-us)

HEMEROCALLIS
(hem-er-oh-KAL-iss)

HEUCHERA
(HEW-ker-a)

HEUCHERELLA
(hew-ke-REL-a)

HIBISCUS
(hy-BIS-kus)

HOSTA
(HOS-tuh)

HOUTTUYNIA
(hoo-TOE-nee-uh)

I

IBERIS
(cyc-BEER-is)

IRIS
(EYE-ris)

K

KNIPHOFIA
(ny-FO-fee-uh)

L

LAMIUM
(LAY-me-um)

LAVANDULA
(lav-AN-djew-luh)

LEUCANTHEMUM
(leu-CAN-the-mum)

LIATRIS
(ly-AY-tris)

LIGULARIA
(lig-you-LAIR-ee-uh)

LINUM
(LI-num)

LIRIOPE
(lih-RYE-oh-pea)

LOBELIA
(low-BEE-lee-uh)

LUPINUS
(loo-PY-nus)

LYCHNIS
(LICK-nis)

LYSIMACHIA
(ly-sih-MAH-kee-uh)

M

MALVA
(MAL-va)

MATTEUCCIA
(mat-TEW-shee-uh)

MONARDA
(mow-NAR-duh)

MYOSOTIS
(my-o-SO-tis)

N

NEPETA
(NEP-uh-tuh)

O

OENOTHERA
(*ee-noth-eh-ruh*)

P

PACHYSANDRA
(pak-i-SAND-dra)

PAEONIA
(pay-OH-nee-uh)

PAPAVER
(pa-PAY-ver)

PENSTEMON
(PEN-steh-mon)

PEROVSKIA
(per-OFF-ski-uh)

PHLOX
(floks)

PLATYCODON
(plat-ee-KO-don)

POLEMONIUM
(pol-ee-MO-ni-um)

POTENTILLA
(poh-ten-TILL-uh)

PRIMULA
(PRIM-yew-la)

PULMONARIA
(pul-mo-NAY-ri-a)

R

RUDBECKIA
(rud-BEK-ee-uh)

S

SALVIA
(SAL-vi-a)

SAPONARIA
(sap-o-NAY-ree-uh)

SCABIOSA
(ska-bee-OH-suh)

SEDUM
(SEE-dum)

SEMPERVIVUM
(sem-per-VY-vum)

SIDALCEA
(sy-DAL-see-uh)

SISYRINCHIUM
(sis-i-RING-ki-um)

STACHYS
(STAY-kis)

T

TANACETUM
(tan-a-SEE-tum)

THALICTRUM
(tha-LIK-trum)

THYMUS
(TY-mus)

TIARELLA
(tee-uh-RELL-uh)

TRADESCANTIA
(trad-ess-KANT-ee-uh)

TROLLIUS
(TROLL-ee-us)

V

VERONICA
(ver-ON-ih-kuh)

VINCA
(VIN-ka)

Y

YUCCA
(YUK-uh)

Aconitum
(ack-oh-NEYE-tum)
WOLFSBANE

SHAPE	Mound, spike with plume flowers
HEIGHT	Twelve to thirty inches
WIDTH	Fifteen inches around
BLOOM TIME	Early fall to frost
COLORS	Shades of blues
SITE	Alkaline soils
LIGHT	Shade or partial shade
HARDINESS	Zones 3–8
COMMENTS	No serious problems

Aconitum is extremely long-lived when it is planted in a cool, shady spot.

Aconitum plants have extremely long lives, but their bloom power may weaken. If this happens, restore the perennial by dividing.

A. *fischeri* produces upright spikes of lavender-blue flowers. The foliage is dark green, glossy, and divided deeply.

A. *napellus,* commonly known as monkshood, is right at home in a midsummer shade garden.

I AM A MAGNIFICENT specimen, and you would think that with my stunning beauty I would have been given a more alluring name than "wolfsbane," but the common name stuck. Think of me saying "good eeevenink," with a Transylvanian accent, and that may help you remember that I got my name because I have a reputation for repelling werewolves and vampires. Native Americans also used me to coat the tips of their arrows. *Bane* means a curse or poison, and I am poisonous—especially in my sap and roots. They are lethal! Deer, pests, and diseases never dare to bother me. Aconitum is also known as woman's bane, devil's helmet, blue rocket, helmet head, monkshood, friar's cap, aconite, and leopard's bane.

I'm an extremely hardy, long-lived perennial when I'm planted in a cool, shady spot. I will beautify the perennial garden every late summer through fall for at least twenty-five years. If I am divided, I'll last even longer.

Division is best done in early spring, but I admit my oval-shaped, fleshy, brittle tubers don't appreciate being disturbed. Be sure to wear gloves when you work with me! Remember, I'm poisonous. Dig the entire root ball. Pull apart the short, carrot-like tubers, making sure that a nice little green-crowned tuft tops each of my starts. Then quickly tuck me into a composted, manure-enriched soil. A composted soil keeps me cooler. Step back and allow me two to three years to grow undisturbed, and the reward will be a tall, vertical accent to the partially shaded fall garden. I'll delight all who gaze at me with my unique little face-like blooms that are massed on top of my tall, straight stems. Pointy hoods cover each face, and when the hoods are lifted, funny little wolf eyes will smile back.

Plant me with three or more other aconitums for a dynamic display. In the mountains, we grow shorter and sturdier, but should we need a little extra support, a group is easier to stake. An early trim in spring will also keep us thicker and stronger.

The soothing blue colors I add to the garden tone down the rich impact of the fall colors in the landscape, but some of us differ from each other in color, growth, and bloom time.

- *A. napellus,* or common monkshood, has been around the longest, is the tallest at three feet, and is the earliest bloomer. *Napellus* may need to be staked.
- *A. fischeri* blooms lavender-blue and grows eighteen to twenty inches tall with stronger stems and glossier foliage.

I come in a variety of hybrids and several bicolored plants, like the exquisite 'Eleanor', who is near white with a narrow purple edge. The flowers of 'Stainless Steel' are a metallic blue, and 'Blue Lagoon' is a dwarf hybrid with more fernlike foliage. The larger flowers of 'Blue Lagoon' start blooming lower on the stalk for a top-to-bottom display.

Other friendly companion perennials that unite the fall shade garden are *Phlox paniculata*, which blooms the same time as *A. napellus*. Phlox blooms in every color, but blue or yellow is more attractive when I add in my blues. *Physostegia*'s pink or white spikes are a nice contrast, and chocolate-foliaged *Eupatorium*, with its white lacy sprays, will nicely light up my blue spikes. See how important blue is to the garden?

Planting shorter perennials in front of me in case I show some sparseness at the base of my tall stems is a safeguard. The short asters like 'Aster Alert' or the 'Woods' pink, blue, or purple are ideal short companions for me and will usually bloom in a partially shaded garden.

Because of my height and similar foliage, I'm often compared to delphiniums. My foliage is a richer, glossier, deeper green with narrow leaves. My flower stems are stronger and not hollow inside, so I rarely need to be staked. Delphiniums will snap off in the wind, but I won't! I also live longer than delphiniums.

I make a lovely addition to any garden. Just be careful not to mistake me for a snack!

COMMON NAME CONFUSION

LIKE THE ACONITUM (with its seven or more other names), many of our most popular perennials have names that go way back in folklore. Plants were often given descriptive names like goat's beard, red hot poker, 'Silver Mound', and Jacob's ladder. Sometimes the common name tells about a plant's character. Dianthuses are called pinks because they bloom in all shades of pink. The coneflower gets its name from the distinctive dark cone they have in the middle.

Let's say that you saw a white flower in a neighbor's yard that would be perfect in your garden. You visit the local box store nursery and look for this flower. There are white Shasta daisies called 'Snowcap', a soapwort named 'Snow Tips', a *Physostegia* 'Summer Snow', and spring-blooming *Anemone* 'Snow Drops'. Don't forget about the silver-foliaged *Cerastium,* which is called snow-in-summer! The box store might not have a clue as to what white plant you are looking for, and your visit would be in vain. Worse, you might take home the invasive and dreaded snow-on-the-mountain!

Perennials are also called different names in different localities. *Centranthus ruber* has many names, including red valerian, red spur valerian, or Jupiter's beard. Each spring when the preschoolers come to the garden to see the flowers, using the common name is what makes their tour delightful. They easily remember basket-of-gold, forget-me-not, and bleeding heart. One overactive four-year-old holding a heart off the plant, decided that bleeding hearts should be called "someone in a bathtub." That was a good for a laugh, but the perennial that the kids laughed the hardest at is the stinking hellebore, which they love to pick blooms off of to take home to mom. It really does stink! Never would these children remember the Latin or botanical names, so there is always a place to use the entertaining old-fashioned common names.

To avoid the confusion, the following list of common names is cross-referenced to help gardeners know what perennial they are both asking and looking for.

Note: If a perennial is not listed here, the reason may be that it does not grow well in our area due to the zone or soils.

COMMON	LATIN
Allwood pinks	*Dianthus*
Alpine aster	*Aster alpinus*
Alumroot	*Heuchera*
Avens	*Geum chiloense*
Baby's breath	*Gypsophila paniculata*
Balloon flower	*Platycodon grandiflorus*
Basket-of-gold	*Aurinia saxatilis*
Beardtongue	*Penstemon*
Bee balm	*Monarda didyma*
Black-eyed Susan	*Rudbeckia hirta*
Blanket flower	*Gaillardia*
Blazing stars	*Liatris spicata*
Bluebells of Scotland	*Campanula rotundifolia*
Blue fescue	*Festuca ovina*
Blue flax	*Linum perenne*
Bugleweed	*Ajuga Reptans*
Butterfly bush	*Buddleia davidii*
Butterfly weed	*Asclepias tuberosa*
Canadian goldenrod	*Solidago Canadensis*
Candytuft	*Iberis sempervirens*
Carnation	*Dianthus caryophyllus*
Carpathian bellflower	*Campanula carpatica*

COMMON	LATIN
Catchfly	*Lychnis viscaria*
Catmint	*Nepeta mussinii*
Checkerbloom	*Sidalcea malviflora*
Cheddar pink	*Dianthus gratianopolitanus*
Chinese Larkspur	*Delphinium grandiflorum*
Chives	*Allium schoenoprasum*
Cinquefoil	*Potentilla nepalensis*
Clove pink	*Dianthus plumarius*
Columbine	*Aquilegia*
Columbine meadow rue	*Thalictrum aquilegifolium*
Coral bells	*Heuchera*
Cottage pink	*Dianthus plumarius nummularia*
Creeping baby's breath	*Gypsophila repens*
Creeping Jenny	*Lysimachia*
Creeping phlox	*Phlox subulata*
Creeping speedwell	*Veronica repens*
Creeping thyme	*Thymus serpyllum*
Cupid's dart	*Catananche caerulea*
Cushion spurge	*Euphorbia polychroma*
Daisy	*Leucanthemum*

COMMON	LATIN
Dead nettle	*Lamium*
Dollar plant	*Lunaria annua*
Donkey-tail spurge	*Euphorbia myrsinites*
Drumstick primrose	*Primula denticulata*
English daisy	*Bellis perennis*
English lavender	*Lavandula angustifolia*
Fernleaf yarrow	*Achillea filipendulina*
Figleaf hollyhock	*Alcea ficifolia*
Flowering sage	*Salvia × sylvestris*
Forget-me-not	*Myosotis sylvatica*
Foxglove	*Digitalis purpurea*
French tarragon	*Artemisia dracunculus*
Garden phlox	*Phlox paniculata*
Garlic chives	*Allium tuberosum*
Gas plant	*Dictamnus*
German catchfly	*Lychnis viscaria*
German statice	*Limonium tataricum*
Globe thistle	*Echinops ritro*
Gold dust	*Aurinia saxatilis*
Golden Marguerite	*Anthemis tinctoria*
Goldmoss stonecrop	*Sedum acre*
Harebell	*Campanula rotundifolia*

COMMON	LATIN	COMMON	LATIN	COMMON	LATIN
Heartleaf	*Bergenia cordifolia*	Painted daisy	*Tanacetum coccineum*	Spike speedwell	*Veronica spicata*
Helen's flower	*Helenium autumnale*	Pasqueflower	*Pulsatilla vulgaris*	Spotted dead nettle	*Lamium maculatum*
Hens and chicks	*Sempervivum*	Peachleaf bellflower	*Campanula persicifolia*	Spurge	*Euphorbia*
Hollyhock	*Alcea rosea*	Perennial cornflower	*Centaurea Montana*	Statice	*Limonium latifolium*
Honesty	*Lunaria Annua*	Perennial flax	*Linum perenne*	Stonecrop	*Sedum*
Iceland poppy	*Papaver nudicaule*	Persian cornflower	*Centaurea dealbata*	Strawberry foxglove	*Digitalis × mertonensis*
Jacob's ladder	*Polemonium caeruleum*	Pincushion flower	*Scabiosa caucasica*	Sunflower heliopsis	*Heliopsis helianthoides*
Jupiter's beard	*Centranthus ruber*	Pink	*Dianthus*	Sweet William	*Dianthus barbatus*
Kenilworth ivy	*Cymbalaria muralis*	Prarie mallow	*Sidalcea malviflora*	Sweet woodruff	*Galium odoratum*
Lady's mantle	*Alchemilla mollis*	Primrose	*Primula*	Tall speedwell	*Veronica longifolia*
Lamb's ears	*Stachys byzantina*	Purple coneflower	*Echinacea purpurea*	Thread-leaf coreopsis	*Coreopsis verticillata*
Lemon thyme	*Thymus citriodorus*	Purple rock cress	*Aubrieta × hybrida*	Thrift	*Armenia hybrida*
Leopard's bane	*Doronicum orientale*	Pyrethrum	*Tanacetum coccineum*	Tickseed	*Coreopsis grandiflora*
Lupine	*Lupinus × hybrida*	Red hot poker	*Kniphofia uvaria*	Torchlily	*Kniphofia uvaria*
Maiden pink	*Dianthus deltoides*	Red valerian	*Centranthus ruber*	Trailing rosemary	*Rosmarinus officinalis prostratus*
Mallow rose	*Hibiscus*	Rock cress	*Arabis caucasica*	Wallflower	*Cheiranthus, Erysimum*
Maltese cross	*Lychnis chalcedonica*	Rock rose	*Helianthemum nummularium*	Whorled tickseed	*Coreopsis verticillata*
Meadow rue	*Thalictrum aquilegifolium*	Rock soapwort	*Saponaria ocymoides*	Wild pansy	*Viola tricolor*
Michalmas daisy	*Aster novi-belgii*	Rose campion	*Lychnis coronaria*	Windflower	*Anemone sylvestris*
Miniature hollyhock	*Sidalcea malviflora*	Rose mallow	*Hibiscus*	Wolfsbane	*Aconitum*
Missouri primrose	*Oenothera missouriensis*	Rose of Sharon	*Hypericum calycinum*	Woodland forget-me-not	*Myosotis sylvatica*
Moss campion	*Silene schafta*	Russian sage	*Perovskia atriplicifolia*	Woodruff	*Galium odoratum*
Moss phlox	*Phlox subulata*	Sandwort	*Arenaria montana*	Wooly yarrow	*Achillea tomentosa*
Mother-of-thyme	*Thymus serpyllum*	Schafta campion	*Silene schafta*	Wormwood	*Artemisia*
Mountain bluet	*Centaurea montana*	Sea lavender	*Limonium latifolium*	Yarrow	*Achillea millefolium*
Nepal cinquefoil	*Potentilla nepalensis*	Sea thrift	*Armeria maritima, A. pseudarmeria*	Yellow archangel	*Lamiastrum galeobdolon*
New England aster	*Aster novae-angliae*	Shasta daisy	*Leucanthemum × superbum*	Yellow foxglove	*Digitalis grandiflora*
New York aster	*Aster novi-belgii*	Sneezeweed	*Helenium autumnale*	Yellow oxeye daisy	*Rudbeckia hirta*
Obedient plant	*Physostegia virginiana*	Snowdrop anemone	*Anemone sylvestris*	Yellow stonecrop	*Sedum acre*
Orange sneeze weed	*Helenium Hoopesii*	Snow-in-summer	*Cerastium tomentosum*		
Oriental poppy	*Papaver orientale*				

PERENNIALS THAT MAY BE TOXIC

Aconitum is so exquisite in both flower and foliage that it is irresistible to gardeners.

However gardeners need to be aware that aconitum is poisonous if eaten and will cause skin irritation if touched by sensitive-skinned gardeners. Other perennials that gardeners need to be cautious of are *Convallaria*, or lily-of-the-valley; iris; and *Digitalis*, or foxglove.

Many of our common perennials are only harmful if eaten in sufficient quantities. Parents of children need to be cautioned and so do pet owners.

PERENNIALS THAT ARE ONLY HARMFUL IF INGESTED

- *Anemone*, windflower
- *Aquilegia*, columbine
- *Chrysanthemum*, Hardy Mum
- *Clematis*
- *Delphinium*, Larkspur
- *Dianthus*, Sweet William
- *Euphorbia*, Spurge
- *Eupatorium*, Joe-pye Weed
- *Hedera*, English Ivy
- *Gypsophila*, Baby's Breath
- *Iberis*, Candytuft
- *Iris*
- *Lillium*, Lily
- *Lupinus*, Lupine
- *Narcissus*, Daffodil
- *Paeonia*, Peony
- *Papaver*, Poppy
- *Ranunculus*, Buttercup
- *Sedum*, Stonecrop
- *Thalictrum*, Meadow Rue
- *Vinca*, Periwinkle

13

Alcea rosea
(al-SEE-a)
HOLLYHOCKS

SHAPE	Tall spires with trumpet flowers
HEIGHT	Three to seven feet tall
WIDTH	Two feet by two feet
BLOOM TIME	Midsummer
COLORS	Bright pink, red, maroon, yellow, light pink, and white
SITE	Regular soil
LIGHT	Full sun
HARDINESS	Zones 2–8
COMMENTS	Hollyhocks are considered a biennial

Alcea, or hollyhocks, are usually considered a biennial flower, meaning they only live for two years. The ones pictured have lived in this same spot for over twenty-five years. Go figure!

Each seed pod holds so many large seeds that a successful germination is a given, and this success makes gardening a fun childhood experience.

All that's needed for hollyhock dancing dolls are the brightly colored blooms, a toothpick, and a wooden clothespin. What fun for little girls to create a chorus line of cancan dancers!

The screening ability and whimsy of hollyhocks makes them the perfect perennial for a children's garden.

GOOD MORNING! I'M a traditional perennial/biennial with charm. I have a nostalgic old-time cottage garden appeal that's hard to match. I'm a species plant, so my seed is produced freely, generating future hollyhocks that will bring a riot of color to the summer garden, with minimal care required. To grow me is to love me!

I've been around for centuries, and the combination of my height (six to seven feet) and the fact that I'm easy to propagate gives me a special charm. Many of my new hybrids are double ruffled in mixed or eye-catching single colors. A few, like the 'Ficifolia', or fig-leaf, and the yellow 'Rugosa' hollyhocks are classified as true perennials and are fragrant. All hollyhocks send up sturdy, strong stems and magnificent spires of ruffled blooms in shades of red, maroon, pink, yellow, and white. I'm more perennial that biennial because I stand in the same spot and bloom year after year.

I reseed readily. Simply cut my stock when the frilly blooms reach the top of my stem and stop blooming. The stock will be lined with flowerless, rounded, pie-shaped pods. Using pruners, cut the heavy hollyhock stem, leaving about ten inches at ground level. Lay the stock with its seed pods at the foot of the mother plant, and allow the pods to naturally open and self-seed. Not every seed will germinate, but enough will that summer weeding must be done carefully so as not to disturb the seedlings. Be prepared. I just might cross-pollinate and produce flowers that are different than my mother's, but I promise I'll be an impressive sight in the landscape. Even better, not one plant costs a cent, and the mother plant was likely a gift from a neighbor. Now how's that for old-time thriftiness?

Because of my height, I look especially handsome planted along a sunny wall or fence line that provides a little support. In a western climate, we are not prone to flopping and usually do not require staking.

CHILDREN'S GARDEN

My screening ability makes me a perfect candidate for creating a children's garden. Have the child plant me back in a corner of the garden where I'll become the walls for a secret hiding place. Help the child harvest a handful of my dried blooms and open the seed pods. Because my seeds are large, small hands can easily shake them loose. Using a sturdy stick or hoe, help the child draw the outline of the playhouse walls. Sprinkle my seeds along or in the outline. I am an edible flower, but it's best not to teach children to taste me until they can distinguish between flowers that are edible and those that are toxic.

An attractive stand of hollyhocks will entice hummingbirds and butterflies to the playhouse. The reds and pinks and the open shape of my blooms cause an automatic response in these miraculous pollinators.

Because hollyhocks also attract every garden pest there is, my large palmate leaves are a salad bar for insects. My bottom leaves have a tendency to look tattered, so trim me up to thin out any damaged leaves and to improve circulation. Spider mites love me! For these and most any other hollyhock problems, spray us regularly with a strong stream of water. To help prevent rust, water me at ground level or use a soaker hose. Keep the soil moist.

Don't let the child panic at the sight of a slug or ragged leaf on my stem. Just like everything in life, I'm not perfect. Gardens are natural systems, and natural systems always have flaws. Did I just teach another life lesson that nothing and no one is perfect?

All in all, planting robust old-fashion hollyhocks is very rewarding, especially for a children's garden. We hollyhocks have lots to share and teach about life, and we can do this for the cost of only a few seeds. May every garden grow hollyhocks!

TALL PERENNIALS IN THE GARDEN: HEADS ABOVE THE REST

*A*LCEA ROSEA, or the hollyhock, is a tall, stately, "heads above the rest" perennial. Tall perennials in the garden serve two main purposes. The first is providing the necessary structure and height in both the back of a perennial border and the center of an island bed. Second is that tall perennials, with their imposing sizes, grab the viewer's attention and become garden focal points, adding an element of zing to the garden.

In the language of gardening, the terms *borders* and *beds* are simply the location of a planting area. Borders are planted in front of or along a type of horizontal structure (a fence line, a hedge, a wall, or the foundation of a home). Border-type planting areas are always viewed from the front. Tall perennials should be planted first to provide an outline or the highest horizontal layer. Once these are planted, the rest of the flower border is simple to fill in with medium-sized and short perennials. One caution: planting tall, then medium, then short perennials in tight rows looks unnatural, so break up this military look with a tall focal point in front, or move into the width of the border with a flat, short ground cover.

A flower bed is usually an island type of bed that can be viewed on all sides and is planted differently from a structure-backed border. In an island bed, the tall perennials are planted in the middle or center stage of the bed. The height of the tall perennials needs to be in proportion with the size of the bed, or approximately half the width of the island.

A mounded or raised island bed adds a dimension to the garden that promises to become a favorite section. Planting the tallest perennials on the high point of the mound will accent the island for a stunning display. Raising the flower's height also increases the color impact. Perennials used in island beds are more visible than border-planted flowers, so excellent foliage that stays attractive even when not in bloom is a must.

Along with hollyhocks, the following perennials are an introductory sampling of tall perennials. The hardiness zone listed with the plant indicates where the perennial will perform best. The lower the zone, the more sustainable the perennial will be in higher elevations. Milder valley gardens can enjoy all of the following tall focal-point perennials.

Achillea 'Coronation Gold' blooms throughout the summer months. Achillea, with its flat, rounded golden flower heads and gray-green foliage is tolerant of a wide range of conditions and is sterile and dependable. Zone 3.

Eremurus, foxtail lily, sends up its lacy, colorful spires to three or four feet tall. The bulb puts on a stunning show and then goes dormant. Zone 4.

Calamagrostis 'Karl Foerster' reaches a height of 5–6 feet. It grows tall and slim, doesn't flop, and won't reseed. Zones 4 or 5.

Allium grows from a bulb and reaches 2–4 feet tall. Purple ball shapes bloom in late spring. Goes dormant after blooming. Zone 3.

Eupatorium rugosum 'Chocolate' grows up to 30 inches tall and is covered with white pearl-like flowers in fall. Zone 4.

Helianthus 'Summer Sun' produces a mass of golden, daisy-like flowers that bloom all summer, creating a 3-foot-tall focal point. Zone 3.

Delphinium 'Summer Skies' add an exciting summer focus but will need staking and go dormant after blooming. Zone 3.

Eupatorium purpureum, or Joe-pye weed, is a huge 4–6 foot late summer bloomer. It boasts pink lacy blooms. Zone 3.

Hibiscus 'Lord Baltimore' is a late-season 30-inch tall perennial. It has huge 10-inch rounded flowers that are long blooming. Zone 5.

Iris spuria has sword-like foliage. It grows to 30 inches tall and blooms in early summer. Zone 4.

Lilium tigrinum blooms later than Asiatic lily, giving another season of color. They reach up to 5 feet in height and are long lived. Zone 3.

Phlox paniculata, or tall garden phlox, is extremely colorful and showy when it blooms midsummer. Phlox grows 3–4 feet tall. Zone 3.

Kniphofia, or red hot poker, has unique torch-like blooms in glowing scarlet, orange, gold, and ivory. 3-foot-tall spiky foliage. Zone 5.

Yucca, or Adam's needle, brings architectural form to any garden in both winter and summer. Zone 4.

Lilium asiatic is an elegant perennial that blooms during summer in every possible color but blue. Zone 3.

Perovskia, Russian sage, produces a cloud of lacy blue flowers on silvery foliage that towers 4 feet and is nearly as wide. Zone 4.

SUMMARY

All of the above perennials have excellent, long-lasting foliage. Allium and foxtail lilies are the exception. Their foliage goes dormant after blooming, so plant these where removal of their leaves will not detract as a focal point.

Tall perennials offer a wide variety of choices that will provide structure and dimension to the garden. Adding height to flower beds and borders can be the key for excellent design.

Aquilegia
(ak-wih-LEE-jee-uh)
COLUMBINE

SHAPE	Clump foliage, cuplike blooms
HEIGHT	One to two feet tall
WIDTH	Depends on the variety
BLOOM TIME	Late spring to late summer
COLORS	Every color, often bicolor
SITE	Thrives in .06 to .07 alkaline soil
LIGHT	Partial shade
HARDINESS	Zones 3–7
COMMENTS	Will not perform well in southern area gardens

A. 'Cardinal'

A. 'Blue Bird' from the 'Songbird' series is a charming, upright facing, sky-blue and white columbine. *Aquilegias* are native perennials that prefer the cooler high elevations.

'Music' series columbines are brightly colored and are a standard in woodland and cottage gardens. They are the most colorful of all columbines. This bloom of color is from a dropped seed.

A. 'Origami' with its extra-long spurs is the longest-blooming of the aquilegias.

WHEN SPRING SHOWERS start and I am bending my head in the rain, it will be worth a trip to the garden to let me say good morning. I'm a favorite of gardeners because I look so unique. My fairy-like blossoms consist of five petals that form a bowl or cup. When this cup is inverted, it looks like a little nest of doves. The Latin word for dove is *columba,* so my common name means "dove." Attached to the back of my cup are five prominent spurs that resemble the outstretched talons of an eagle. These projecting spurs are how I got my Latin name, *Aquilegia,* from the Latin word meaning "eagle." The cup and spurs give my flowers a unique beauty that is matchless in the garden and holds sweet nectar for the hummingbirds.

My exceptional blossoms come in every imaginable shade and bicolor combination. When my flowers dance on the tip-top of the stem, they bring magic to the garden. My foliage is finely divided, sometimes bright green but often blue-green. I form a tidy and appealing clump of foliage with clover-shaped leaves.

My history isn't long. I'm a native North American perennial found throughout the Northern Hemisphere, but cultivation has been only about three hundred years. The Native Americans used me medically as a tranquilizer and added my flowers to their salads. The flowers are safe, but my seeds and roots are poisonous.

In the coolness of my native mountain home, I function at my best even blooming through two seasons. I need a cold period of eight to twelve weeks for my plants to be robust and free flowering. Even my seeds need a winter cold treatment, or vernalization, before they will germinate.

My seeds are the best method of propagating more plants. I reseed readily, and if my seeds are left on my stems to dry, I'll sprinkle them like fairy dust all over the garden. My seeds tend to cross-pollinate, and often seedlings revert to yellow. In some cases, this is good. A grower needs to know that hybridized columbine varieties such as 'McKana's Giants' have a tendency to be short-lived perennials, but when their seedlings naturalize they are more robust and endure forever. When hybrid seeds germinate, they don't always resemble their parents. In the case of the 'McKana's Giants', all of the seedlings will turn out blue, purple, or white. Most of the other hybrids will surprise a gardener with a vast array of colors, but yellow will dominate. Seed production is what shortens the life of a columbine to only two or three years. It saps the strength of the mother plant, who will lose her vibrant colors and turn a muddy color. To prolong the mother columbine's life, it's wise to trim her back before she sets seeds.

I'm extremely easy to grow. I grow in average soil, and once I'm established I become very drought tolerant. I like cool weather, so plant me in a partial-shade garden where I'll bloom longer, sometimes up to the Fourth of July.

Through hybridizing, many superior members of my family have expanded. The 'McKana's Giants' were one of the first hybrids and are the tallest (up to 30 inches tall). The 'Origami' series is the longest blooming and has extra-long spurs. 'Origami Red and White' and 'Rose and White' won the prestigious Royal Horticultural Society Award. The 'Winky' series are small and petite, with compact, blue-shaded, tight mounds of foliage that hold upward-facing blooms of colors mixed with white. 'Winkys' are adorable. The 'Music' series of columbines grow to only fifteen inches and do not require staking. These are all exceptionally special, but the A. 'Songbird' series has it all. We share a sturdy compact habit with extra-large, showy flowers that measure up to three inches in length.

The 'Songbirds' are named to match the color of a bird:

- 'Blue Bird' is sky blue and white.
- 'Blue Jay' blooms dark blue and white.
- 'Cardinal' is red and white and is an award-winning perennial.
- 'Dove' has very large, pure-white flowers.
- 'Goldfinch' is outstanding with its bright shades of yellow.

Hybrids rarely self-sow true to the mother plant, so expect a variety.

It's understandable why I'm such a favorite in gardens. I bring a colorful freshness, so harvest my seeds and sprinkle your own magic!

Heuchera, or coral bells, blooms for over six weeks, and the hummingbird bill fits nicely into its bells.

Daylilies bloom in hummingbirds' favorite colors of red, orange, and pink. The colors, along with the open, well-spaced flowers make it easy sipping.

Crocosmia 'Lucifer' is not really zoned for the areas covered in this book, but it's such a fine hummingbird plant that I grow it on the south foundation of my home.

HUMMINGBIRDS IN THE PERENNIAL GARDEN

FLOWERS WITH CUPS or bells like columbines are magnets for hummingbirds. Aquilegia's cups and spurs make it easy for a humming bird to sip from it. If the flowers happen to bloom in red or orange, the hummingbirds will be more attracted. Hummingbirds are on the top of the list of God's miracles. Weighing in at an eighth of an ounce or less, with wings that beat seventy-five times a second and propel at thirty miles an hour, this bird is held in awe. A human would have to consume 155,000 calories to maintain a hummingbird's metabolism!

Our favorite hummingbird is the rufous hummingbird. We named it Rufus. It has a long, straight, and very slender bill just right for sipping columbines. The female is slightly larger than the male, and both seem to be in shades of brown. They may not be brightly colored, but their feistiness makes up for it. Rufus is only a visitor and passes through on its journey southward to Mexico.

Lounging on our deck where the bird feeders hang and watching Rufus is one of our ultimate summer pleasures. Rufus is so territorial and pugnacious that he does aerial flips and dives to drive away other hummingbirds.

We hang birdfeeders with sugar water on tree branches for the hummingbirds. The feeders are a lot of time-consuming work because if they're left too long, they can ferment and become toxic. Filling them is worth it, but I must admit that as August begins and cooler weather starts its arrival, I breathe a sigh of relief because I won't have to sterilize bird feeders every morning. Rufus also eats insects, and we have watched him take them from spider webs or catch them in midflight.

The bird feeders are more for our entertainment than they are nectar for Rufus because we have tons of flowers. The extremely high metabolism of hummingbirds requires the richer nectar of flowers, and the sugar syrup of the feeders just won't cut it. More important to gardeners is that the flowers need Rufus for pollination, so it's a two-way deal.

Open-faced flowers like columbine are structured to accommodate hummingbirds. In an aquilegia's bloom, the bird's bill fits neatly into the long tube shape of the flower. The bird's tongue laps up the nectar at the lowest place in the spurs. As the hummingbird takes in nectar, the bird's forehead rubs against the flowers stamens and pistils and does its pollination work.

Hummingbird plants are not attractive to bees. These flowers usually have no platform where a bee can land. The fast beating wings of hummingbirds hold them aloft while they sip, so they have no need for a landing spot. Hummingbirds prefer red flowers, a color that bees have a difficult time seeing. Insects are attracted by smell and birds by vision. Hummingbird flowers need little or no scent. Nature is incredible; the flowers that are difficult for bees and insects to pollinate have been covered by hummingbird visitors.

Hummingbird flowers that bloom need to be spaced apart to give room for the whirring wings. These perennials need to bloom longer and during daylight hours. In our gardens, we make sure to plant seasonal flower nectar for Rufus. Our hummingbirds show up the last week of June. Here are a few of the preferred perennials in bloom at that time:

- *Heuchera,* coral bells, blooms in all sorts of red shades. The tiny bells fit all the criteria of what a hummingbird wants, and so do these.
- *Aquilegia,* columbine.
- *Lychnis* 'Lumina' and Maltese cross are both red-orange.
- *Papaver,* Iceland or oriental poppies are popular because of their colors and wide, open centers.

In early summer, the delphiniums and digitalis in their rosy colors and nepeta satisfy the nectar requirement of the hummingbirds. In midsummer, they flock to the local garden pub where they serve clematis and penstemon. Late-summer drinks include alcea (hollyhocks); hibiscus; monarda (bee balm); and the warm colors of the tall garden phlox.

By August, all of the annuals are at their high point of blooming, and the choice is enormous. The best annuals for hummingbirds are petunias, snapdragons, and zinnias, especially if they are red.

One last important point: all birds require a source of water. Bird baths, ponds, fountains—any of these will keep the birds in your garden happy.

Planting these types of perennials will bring in the hummingbird entertainment and add to the enjoyment of your garden.

Rufous, a species of hummingbird native to my garden, is attracted to Indian paintbrush and to the hummingbird feeders.

Sidalcea is an elegant, tiny hollyhock that hummingbirds flock to so they can enjoy a "sippy cup" from this 'Party Girl'.

Late summer before the "hummers" start their migration, they need to stoke up on calories from all of the red annuals in full bloom. Lilium, cannas, and dahlias are favorites.

Centaurea montana
(SEN-TOR-EE-UH)
MOUNTAIN BLUET

SHAPE	Unbranched stems with daisy-shaped, elaborate blooms
HEIGHT	Twenty-four inches
WIDTH	Twenty-four inches
BLOOM TIME	Late spring through June and again in fall.
COLORS	Usually blue with violet-red highlights
SITE	Rocky mountain soil, alkaline soil, and drought-tolerant gardens
LIGHT	Full sun
HARDINESS	Zone 3
COMMENTS	Deer resistant, invasive

C. 'Amethyst in Snow' is a new hybrid centaurea that is incredible. The flower blooms in May, and then with a little deadheading, it will bloom again in June and again in the fall.

Mountain bluet's frilly blossoms attract butterflies and provide seeds that birds enjoy. It's often called "bachelor's button" due to its large, showy, deeply fringed flowers.

C. 'Amethyst in Snow' has unusual buds with ornamental, pineapple-like scales. Their pure-white petals radiate in an intricate starburst from a dark royal purple center.

C. 'Amethyst Dream' has the same pinwheel flowers as 'Amethyst in Snow', but the colors of the large blossoms are a deep royal purple tinged with red on the petals.

HOWDY, GARDENING GUYS and gals! *Centaurea* may be my Latin name, but mountain bluet is the name that tells who I really am. I'm a wide-open-space kind of flower. I grow everywhere in the western states, and I'm pleased to be included on lists of popular wildflowers.

There's no other way to say it, my flowers are flamboyant. With my true-blue blooms that shoot out from my reddish highlighted center, I'm a blue ribbon winner! My petals shoot out, around, and under, and have black tips. They can be harvested as cut flowers or dried for floral arrangements, making me a favorite for gardeners.

I'm vigorous and can be rampant, so I hope you won't fence me in. I just naturally want to grow and roam my garden home. If a gardener really wants me to stay put, then I must be cut back to the ground as soon as I stop blooming. A good layer of mulch as a winter bedroll will also curb my spreading.

In spring, it's easy to start a new "spread" by division with a shovel, or you can just wait until my seeds fall and let Mother Nature do the germinating. The cold winters will see to it that my seed puffs get their required cold treatment so they will germinate, grow, and bloom.

By next spring, there will be a whole passel of mountain bluet all over the homestead. This self-seeding ability is probably why I won a spot on the western wildflower list.

I know you will be pleased to meet my little sister, *C. dealbata*, or Persian cornflower, and my big brother, *C. macrocephala*. So as not to slight my high-flaunting hybrid cousins *C.* 'Amethyst in Snow' and 'Amethyst Dream', I'll mention them also.

Persian cornflower is a frilly little filly. Her fringed, bushy one-and-one-half-inch flower surrounds a paler, almost white center. Her foliage is better than mine and holds up nicely all summer. It is darker green on top but silvery and hairy underneath. The bottom branches grow longer and shorten toward the top in a divided triangular shape. Persian cornflower blooms for a full four weeks and reaches several feet high and several feet wide. Like her big sis, she loves cold climates and high mountains.

My big brother *C. macrocephala*, or Armenian basket flower, is a massive four-foot dude who dominates the garden when in bloom. His leaves are huge, rough textured, strap shaped, and imposing. In bloom, he rules the roost with his huge mop head cluster of unusual golden flowers from early to late summer. Basket flower, with thistle-like petals, can be wild in appearance. He might look tough, but my brother is well mannered and easy to grow. He's another long bloomer, flowering through June and July, but unlike me he will not bloom again if deadheaded.

My high-flaunting cousin 'Amethyst in Snow' is a thorou-bred. She is the first bicolor centaurea cultivar to be introduced to gardeners. Her flowers bloom solitary on top of lance-shaped stems, twelve to eighteen inches high. Her pure-white petals radiate outward from a deep-blue center like a pinwheel. Plant this showy perennial in masses in the middle of a sunny border for a May-through-June show. 'Amethyst', like all centaureas, will attract birds and butterflies, is drought tolerant, and will naturalize.

The color of 'Amethyst Dream' will knock your boots off. The bloom is the deepest, darkest purple—as dark as the shadows at dusk. The color is intensified by a deep-red center. Yep, both 'Amethyst Snow' and 'Amethyst Dream' are pretty fancy. But all of us are wonderful.

INVASIVE PERENNIALS:
THE ORIGINAL MARATHONERS

CENTAUREAS ARE REFERRED to as stoloniferous plants. The botanical Latin root meaning of *stolon* is "branch." Thus centaurea's stoloniferous root systems are underground branches that generate new shoots at the end. Many stoloniferous perennials are called "runners."

"Runners" in a perennial garden become invasive weeds when the environment is within the plant's comfort zone. My first "runner" experience was a gift from a gardening neighbor. She proudly brought me a newspaper-lined box filled with this attractive green and white variegated perennial ground cover. Delighted, I quickly planted this gift into four different sections of my garden. Within a couple of years, this gift had spread everywhere, and I realized that it wanted to take over the yard and maybe even the world! For many summers, I dug the tiny white roots and strained the dirt through a repurposed old screen door. Now, fifty years later, I'm still fighting the hated "runner" *Aegopodium*, or bishop's weed. I must not be the only gardener who

Campanula, clustered bellflower, with its intense deep-purple flowers, is so attractive that is tempting to plant it! Using a rock wall barrier to keep its stolons in check is an excellent method of enjoying a beautiful perennial.

detests this plant. Bishop's weed has obtained legal status in the state of Idaho as a noxious weed.

Fortunately, centaureas are better mannered than bishop's weed. A simple barrier buried underground will curb its underground stolons from spreading. Linear root barrier rolls made of high-density polyethylene are available in many garden centers. The rolls come in thicknesses of either forty millimeters or sixty millimeters and are sold in twenty-foot lengths. Depending on how deep gardeners need the barrier, they can choose from twelve, eighteen, or twenty-four inches in height. Installation is easy. Dig a trench surrounding the perennial "runner," and place the polyethylene inside the trench. Refill the trench. Keep the blooms deadheaded if the perennial is one that will reseed. A layer of mulch after the garden has frozen in fall is always a deterrent to seeding.

Other barriers can be used. A concrete curbing helps keep "runners" from spreading. A block wall or rocked edge will also help hold the perennials in check.

New barrier products such as a fabric with a copper latex coating on one side can be installed to stop the underground branches from spreading. Once the strip is buried, root growth will stop when it comes into contact with the copper.

These barriers are helpful when a perennial has other fine qualities, but a sounder method of controlling "runners" is to not introduce them into the garden. Number one on my invasive list is the hated bishop's weed.

Number two is *Asclepias tuberosa*. The plant's common name is butterfly weed because it's related to milkweed. This family of plants is the only place where monarch butterflies will propagate. I wanted monarchs in the garden. Also, the catalog picture showed butterfly weed as a bright orange color. Orange is in direct contrast to all of the greens in the garden and a color not as plentiful in many other perennials. I really had to have this plant, so I sent for it!

Excitedly, I planted it in my garden. It ran like crazy in my amended soil! Another disappointment—it blooms a sort of yellow and not the bright orange so attractively pictured in the catalog.

Now I'm forced to dig up my most prized perennials *Phlox* 'David', *Iris* 'Argentia', *Sedum* 'Red Emperor', and my beloved lilium to remove the roots that have spread from the single asclepias plant that was left in the flower bed into the roots of these other fine perennials. In our climate and in amended soil, it's an invasive "runner." However, in order to provide a host plant for the monarch butterflies, it was transplanted into lean soil behind the shade shed and is now surrounded by a heavy sixty-millimeter, eighteen-inch polyethylene barrier where it blooms contentedly, and the monarchs get to continue enjoying the garden.

If a catalog plant description uses the words *vigorous*, *spreading*, or

Asclepias, butterfly weed, is a dud in my garden and had to be removed. Digging up plants from my garden feels like an immoral or illegal act, so out of pity, one bush was left. Big mistake! Now the roots have moved into other perennials.

aggressive, gardeners beware! Asking questions of other gardeners also saves grief. Other "runners" to beware of that are impossible to cradicate even with yearly doses of weed spray and a sharp shovel are listed below:

- *Adenophora*: This tall, narrow late-summer bloomer has long white radish roots. It multiplies thickly over winter. Lilybells consider weed killer as a fertilizer.

- *Hemerocallis fulva*: Often called tawny or roadside lily. Once this daylily is planted, it is "signed in cement" forever.

- *Physalis*: Chinese lantern. This is an orange, ball-shaped unique-looking plant I started from seed. It grew in gallon pots over winter so vigorously that its roots broke out of the bottom.

- *Polygonum*: Jerusalem artichoke. Believe me, this is not an artichoke! It's more of a tall sunflower-looking weed. Perennial vegetables are few and far between, so I planted it. The roots are edible if a person is starving, but perennial asparagus is much better.

- *Ranunculus repens*: Creeping buttercups. The foliage of buttercups is dark green and shiny. Yellow buttons completely cover the foliage in springtime. When blooming, creeping buttercups are so pretty in the garden that they are hard to resist, but resist you must! They will take over your entire garden.

- *Sedum acre*: Goldmoss stonecrop. In Idaho, this plant's nickname is star-of-Idaho. In Utah, it's called star-of Utah. Just one tiny piece of goldmoss dropped in shade, sun, road base, or any place in the garden will grow. Every spring, I bury it deep in the flower bed and use it as underground compost. Even then it grows!

Delphinium elatum
(del-FIN-ee-um)
LARKSPUR

SHAPE	Tall and elegant spike with clustered flowers
HEIGHT	Up to six feet
WIDTH	About twenty-four inches
BLOOM TIME	Midsummer
COLORS	Rare shades of blue, also whites, pinks, and purples
SITE	Cool summers in alkaline soils
LIGHT	Full sun
HARDINESS	Zones 2–5
COMMENTS	Brings elegance and blue colors to the garden; deer resistant

Delphiniums, with their summer sky colors, are the most beloved perennials in the garden.

Notice the distinct palm-shaped leaves of this 'Magic Fountain' blue with dark bee delphinium.

An up-close glimpse of a delphinium's bee, or center, shows the hollow where bees climb into when pollinating.

D. 'Magic Fountain' delphiniums are more dwarf-sized, growing 20–30 inches in height. This mauve is just one of the rare shades of blue that they bring to the summer garden.

I'M THE BELOVED favorite in the summer perennial garden, and since my tall showy spires highlight glamour photos all over in garden magazines, books, and catalogs, I almost need no introduction. Like a high-fashion runway model, I strut my stuff in midsummer when gardens are at peak performance for photo shoots, but I choose to believe I'm loved because of my elegant vertical accents of blue that showcase the other perennials so well. My colorful spikes are densely packed with a double row of petals. At the center they form a fuzzy hollow for bumblebees and butterflies to pollinate. I suppose this is why my center petals, in either contrasting or blending shades, are referred to as bees. A curved spur on the top was thought to resemble the bottle-like nose of a dolphin. This is how I got my Latin name of *Delphinium*, or "dolphin." The Latin *elatum* part of my name means "tall."

My showy blue flowers rise up from a rosette of deeply cut *palmatus*-shaped leaves (Latin for "palm"). My thick stems are hollow, so care must be provided to not allow my heavy blooms to snap off in the wind. Using single stakes of bamboo or metal along with stretchy ties to attach it to my stem will keep me erect. Thinning my blooms for cut flowers makes for a stronger delphinium and a wonderful arrangement for the church or home.

Delphiniums in lower, warmer regions are often planted as annuals, but when I'm planted in the cool summers and deep-snow winters, I'm in my comfort zone and can be long-lived and healthy.

My size seems to require a steady supply of rich compost tucked around my base. It's a well-known fact that when outhouses are moved in the Yellowstone Park area, delphiniums are the first wildflower to move into the newly cleared, nitrogen-enriched area. We are native to the high mountains in the Northern Hemisphere and thrive in the mineral-rich alkaline soils of that area.

Propagation is simple too. To promote blooming, remove my spent stems. New shoots will form around my root clump. These new side shoots are the most dependable method of propagation. Gently remove my new offspring and replant wherever the garden needs a touch of elegant class. Seed pods from my cut stems can be sprinkled right into the flower beds. In three years, my little ones will be blooming in their own spotlight.

As with other perfectly beautiful specimens, I have a protective patron or guardian. All parts of me contain an alkaloid delphinium, which is toxic. Cattle ranchers will delay moving their herds onto wild delphinium ranges until late summer when the flowers have finished blooming and plant toxicity is reduced. Deer avoid me, intuitively aware that I can cause cardio-toxin and neuromuscular-blocking effects.

In the West, we grow shorter and sturdier, and we bloom and live longer. This doesn't hold true of the hotter, dryer, lower valley regions.

D. grandiflorum is a shorter, bushier perennial, bred for the lower, warmer elevations. Gardeners in warmer southern locations can still have the true blues of delphiniums by planting this compact series, which is long blooming. *D. grandiflorum* grows to two feet with thread-like, deeply divided leaves and loose flower heads. It blooms in the same beloved colors. It is a considered perennial but is usually short lived, almost like an annual, and it reseeds prolifically. 'Blue Butterfly' and 'Blue Mirror' along with the 'Summer' series ('Summer Blues', a soft sky blue; 'Summer Morning', a clear pink; and 'Summer Nights', a deep blue) are gorgeous wherever they grow.

Add me to your perennial garden for my height, midsummer bloom, color, elegance, and of course because I'm so very, very beloved by every gardener.

These round tomato baskets make nice supports for perennials. Cut off the wire spikes that are usually sunk into the ground. Bend the cutoff spikes into a hook. To stabilize, place the cage "big circle" down.

Bamboo stakes are lightweight, strong, attractive, and completely biodegradable.

STAKING PERENNIALS

S TAKING PERENNIALS is a real pain in the butt. Sometimes it's not until the poor perennial is lying in the mud that a gardener decides to stake. In the West, where plants grow shorter and sturdier due to poor soils and arid climates, gardeners need to stake delphiniums due to their hollow stems and heavy blossoms. They also need to stake peonies to show off the great foliage and hold up the huge blooms and to stake dahlias—a nonwinter hardy tuber. No garden would be complete without delphiniums, peonies, and dahlias, so stake we must.

An interesting variety of staking materials is available, but I think my secret staking solution is the best. First, here are a few of the most entertaining solutions:

FORTY-EIGHT-INCH TOMATO BASKETS

These cages are fifteen by fifteen inches wide. To use, stick the bottom spikes into the ground and square up the huge cage. Then stand back and see how your delphinium looks standing in jail.

POLYPROPYLENE SPIRALS

These spirals have a pointed end to anchor in the ground and uncoil into a seven-foot spiral, which is attached to a wooden stake at the top. Seven-foot plastic spirals attached to seven-foot wooden stakes sticking up all over perennials flower beds are not a pretty picture.

FROG VINE HOLDER

Another staking technique—which, if it would have worked, might have been delightfully whimsical—is Gumby-like frogs. They were advertised in a magazine, and when they arrived and were tried, the arms and legs were much too short to wrap around anything larger than a pencil. They would not even hold a clematis vine to an arch. My grandsons got caught placing the frogs in an obscene chain, and getting them grounded was all the frogs were really good for.

ROUND TOMATO CAGES

Another traditional staking method is the round cage tomato baskets. Blooming perennials always topple these baskets just when the flowers reach their peak of performance. However, tomato cages with a little adjustment are my number one secret staking solution. First, cut off the puny wire stakes that are to be pushed into the ground. Then bend one end of the cut wire into a crook to be used later to securely anchor the cage. Place the large ring end of the tomato cage upside down over the plant, and then anchor the ring with the bent hook supports. The attractive peony foliage fills this shorter ring quickly and gives the perennial a tidy vase-shaped appearance and lasts until after frost. At fall cleanup time, the removal of the obnoxious wire legs, which have a tendency to poke out eyes, makes stacking of the baskets quick and easy for storing.

Next is the secret staking solution for showing off the elegant blooms of delphiniums. This method is so simple, so inexpensive, and so totally natural that most gardeners will wonder why they didn't think of it. Use the stretchy mesh bandage tape used by hospitals, a material we call "horse-wrap," to secure the plant. This material comes in different widths that can be sliced into an appropriate size such as two inches. Use biodegradable bamboo stakes that come in either green or tan, and stick them deep into the ground for a camouflaged cage around the delphinium bush. Then wrap the bamboo with a double twist of horse-wrap to give a totally solid foundation for the height and width of these beloved garden perennials. Delphiniums wrapped this way have a strong tendency to bloom again in August and September. The stress of being snapped off in a wind, just at June bloom time, must weaken the plant and cause it to be short lived. This staking technique eliminates that stress and gives the delphinium more strength to return year after year. The mesh tape is a great improvement over using ridiculous old panty hose for a stake wrap.

OTHER TIPS FOR SUCCESSFUL STAKING

- Get it done early. As the plant fills out, the staking will disappear into the foliage.
- Choose perennials that have strong stems. *Aconitum*, monkshood; *Aruncus*, goat's beard; Heliopsis 'Summer Sun'; and *Echinacea*, coneflower; are typical of perennials that will not flop. Tall flowers with spikes or heavy flowers are the most prone to toppling.
- Choose sturdy cultivars of perennials. For example the Shasta daisy 'Becky' is one of the tallest daisies and has huge blooms but has been bred with stronger stems.
- If staking is not an option, do not plant clematis, chrysanthemums, *Delphinium* × *elatum* hybrids, *Digitalis* (foxglove), tall asters, or *Campanula lactiflora*. Select low-growing varieties of these perennials that will not fall over. For example, *Delphinium* 'Magic Fountain' and 'Guardian Mix' are only thirty to thirty-five inches tall, so they are not as prone to breaking.
- Plant an informal garden called a "cottage garden" that allows perennials to weave and sprawl in the garden.
- Overwatering or overfertilizing causes perennials to grow tall and leggy, and so will planting sun-loving perennials in a shade garden.
- Plant your perennials in a location not susceptible to wind to save them from breaking.
- Divide older perennials when they show a tendency to flop open in the middle.

Using these tips plus horse-wrap with bamboo stakes and revised tomato cages will make staking a much easier, simpler task. A gardener just might decide they like staking.

Winding horse-wrap or stretchy bandage tape around bamboo stakes makes an easy, stable cage for tall plants with heavy flowers like delphiniums. The wrap holds solid until fall clean-up when it starts deteriorating, making it easy to remove.

String or twine or even pony-tail clips can be used, but the stretchy hospital tape sticks to the bamboo spikes and will not slip. The bandage wrap will not cut the stems.

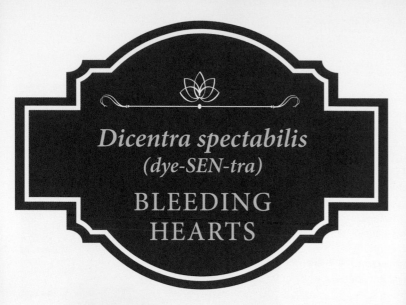

Dicentra spectabilis
(dye-SEN-tra)
BLEEDING HEARTS

SHAPE	Shrub with long stems and heart-plume flowers
HEIGHT	Thirty inches
WIDTH	Thirty inches
BLOOM TIME	May to June
COLORS	Pink
SITE	Alkaline soils, cool climate
LIGHT	Partial/Full shade
HARDINESS	Zone 2
COMMENTS	Ephemeral perennial, deer resistant

Bleeding hearts requires a cold winter to set their graceful blooms, and will go dormant in the he of our summer temperatures.

D. spectabilis is a timeless perennial with heart-shaped flowers and fern-like foliage.

Bleeding hearts get better as they get older. Give a potted bleeding heart plant to a grieving gardener who has lost someone dear to them. Every spring this living valentine will remind them of their loved one.

The slightly toxic nature of bleeding heart blooms mean that wildlife avoids them.

ONJOUR, MON AMI! Timeless and ethereal, I am a living valentine, and my spectacular beauty prompted my Latin name, *Spectabilis*, meaning "spectacular" or "worthy of notice." When my rosy pink sentimental hearts bloom, I'm noticed! Even my charming blue-green compound foliage is worthy of notice. Growing approximately thirty inches tall, my leaves are deeply divided. Thin stems shoot up and then bend gracefully, weighed down with numerous heart-shaped drops. I make a heartfelt gift for any sweetheart, or even for a grieving friend, and I add a delicate, ethereal, living valentine to every garden.

I'm a native perennial and have been around for a long, long time, probably growing in your grandparent's garden. I grow best in a cool, sheltered garden spot that has been enriched with manure. Planting me on the east side of the house or in a woodland-type setting will help prevent strong winds from snapping my hollow stems. Cold, snowy winters aid my blooming and increase my size. One caution concerning late-spring freezes; I break dormancy early, pushing my reddish stems up out of the ground. Should a late snow storm or freezing temperatures damage my shoots, simply cut the stems. I'll reemerge thicker, stronger stemmed, and will produce more of my delightful blooms. Also, when summer heats up or if my soil dries out, I'll go dormant until the next spring. Because of this I'm often called an ephemeral perennial.

Propagating me with seed is tedious and complicated. It can take up to six months going in and out of refrigeration for germination to occur.

Division is also difficult because my roots are long and brittle. Fall dividing is recommended, but I need time to establish my new roots before winter. Spring is not good because that's when I'm blooming. Hesitate before you decide to divide me. It will take several years for me to get established and for a mother plant to recover.

If you must divide me, however, here are a few pointers:

- Wait until I go dormant, and then dig a circle around me. My roots grow horizontally, and butchering these thick fleshy roots is damaging.
- Discard my old, hollow stems with a sharp pruner, and then cut me into pieces, making sure that each division has a root and a pointy eye growth.
- Plant me quickly, not letting my roots dry out. Make sure the space is plenty wide for my roots. My crown needs to be able to peek out, so don't plant me too deep.
- Water me, remembering that I'll always need adequate moisture to keep my roots cool.
- A thin layer of compost, at least two inches deep, placed around me each fall will help keep me moist and vigorous.

Little kids are attracted to my fascinating flowers. One little girl sighed as she looked at me and decided I was a necklace. Her brother gave her a disgusted look and argued, "A necklace? Silly, it's a big fish eating a little fish." Children make everything fun, but watch that they do not eat my hearts, because they can have toxins. If that little girl had decided to place a necklace of my hearts around her neck, it could have caused dermatitis. My toxins are relatively mild, but this is why deer will not bother me.

Planting companion perennials that grow in the same shady environment I do will help cover any bare spots left after my foliage goes dormant. The best choice of all other shade perennials is the hosta. Late-breaking hosta, with its perfect foliage, will come up and fill in the area until first frost, giving me a chance to rest. Shade-loving ground covers like wild geranium or lamium will weave through the border, covering my dormant spot. Another fine fall-blooming shade plant, *Physostegia* 'Miss Manners', would make an excellent companion. 'Miss Manners' is either pink or white, and it grows in a fifteen-inch spike similar to a snapdragon. Most any late-blooming perennial will make a good companion plant.

GERMINATION OF BLEEDING HEARTS

I T'S BEEN SAID that bleeding heart seeds are tedious and complicated to propagate. Gardeners always want to know why, so here it is. The following numbered information is from the Ball Seed Company "Bible" of germination by Jim Nau.[1]

1. *DICENTRA SPECTABILIS* SEEDS GERMINATE BEST WHEN USING FRESH SEED.
    Translation: Fresh seed is mandatory; otherwise seeds will take a year to germinate. *That's longer than a pregnancy!*

2. COLLECT THE BLEEDING HEARTS' SEED IN AUGUST AND SEPTEMBER.
    In hot, dry summers, the bleeding heart has already gone into dormancy and been cut back. *Where are the seeds?*

3. SOW SEEDS IMMEDIATELY INTO A GERMINATION TRAY.
    Is a germination tray something like a petri dish?

4. PRETREAT *DICENTRA* SEEDS.
    Translation: Two pretreatments are required. Warm-moist and cold-moist. *Where's Betty Crocker when you need her?*

5. BLEEDING HEARTS' SEEDS ARE DOUBLE DORMANT.
    Translation: Until the seed can absorb water, it will not germinate and must be kept moist. The seed coat is impermeable. *Where's the closest fertilization clinic?*

6. PLACE SEED INTO THE GERMINATION TRAY OF MOISTENED PEAT MOSS.
    Translation: Place repeated layers of seed between moistened peat moss. *Just like lasagna.*

7. EXPOSE SEED TO DAILY TEMPERATURES OF 68°F TO 86°F UNTIL THE END OF SUMMER.
    What if it rains? *Better learn to control the weather.*

8. EXPOSE MOISTENED SEED TO A PERIOD OF COOL/MOIST TEMPERATURES TO AID IN THE GERMINATION PROCESS.
    Translation: Place the germination tray full of seeds out in the garden and bury it as soon as fall and cool temperatures arrive. *Bury it in sun or shade?*

9. KEEP THE SEEDS AT A TEMPERATURE RANGE OF 35°F TO 40°F FOR THE WINTER.
    Translation: Hope it's a mild winter so temperatures don't get to single digits. *What if it doesn't snow? Again, to germinate bleeding hearts, a gardener better learn to control the weather.*

10. A REVERSE PROCEDURE FOR *DICENTRA* SEEDS MAY BE USED.
    Translation: Do the cold-moist procedure first and the warm-moist second. *Shift into reverse.*

11. PLACE THE FRESH-SOWN SEED THAT IS IN THE GERMINATION TRAY INTO YOUR REFRIGERATOR FOR A MONTH AND A HALF.
    Translation: Put the box of dirt and seeds in your fridge for a month and a half. *Be sure to remove it in time for the Thanksgiving turkey!*

12. FOLLOWING THIS, REMOVE THE GERMINATION TRAY FROM THE REFRIGERATOR AND PLACE IN A WARM SPOT, 60°F TO 65°F FOR SEVEN TO TEN WEEKS.
    Translation: Set the tray on your kitchen table in the sun. *Set it with or without napkins?*

13. TRANSPLANT OVER A PERIOD OF TIME.
    Translation: Seeds germinate erratically, one or two at a time. *Just like eating an elephant. One bite at a time.*

14. IF GERMINATION IS LOW (20–40 PERCENT), RETURN THE GERMINATION TRAY TO THE REFRIGERATOR FOR ANOTHER TWO TO FOUR WEEKS AND REPEAT THE ABOVE.
    Translation: Start over. *Note that seeds collected and stored dry until February or March give 0 percent germination.*

All kidding aside, the *Ball Perennial Manual: Propagation and Production* by Jim Nau is an excellent tool for gardeners. Any flower that blooms will set seed, so germination should simply be discovering the correct sequence or environment the seed requires. Seed propagation is a fascinating and miraculous act that involves many different seed germination techniques.

My gardening friends shared a few interesting points concerning the challenge of germinating bleeding hearts: none, not even the "green thumbers," had ever successfully germinated bleeding heart seeds. One thought is that two plants for pollination are necessary to produce viable seed. Another said the seed was so small that the entire plant had to be put in a paper bag just before it goes dormant in order to collect the seed. One more said it would take ten years before the plant would bloom. These could be truth or fiction, but for certain, bleeding hearts are difficult to germinate.

One important note pertaining to a bleedings heart's germination is that it is a native North American perennial. This means that bleeding hearts have been doing a self-seeding germination for thousands of years before we came along. Mother Nature grew bleeding hearts without even knowing about the fourteen-step process.

Iberis sempervirens
(eye-BER-iss)
CANDYTUFT

SHAPE	Small shrub with filler clusters of flowers
HEIGHT	Twelve inches tall
WIDTH	Will spread to about twenty-four inches
BLOOM TIME	May to June
COLORS	Pure white, lavender, pink
SITE	Well-drained soils
LIGHT	Full or part shade
HARDINESS	Zone 3
COMMENTS	Evergreen

A close-up of candytuft's blooms show their resemblance to a white, lacy doily.

When candytuft is through blooming, the stems elongate and start to look untidy. A quick haircut will help it hold its shape the entire season through winter until it blooms again in spring.

Candytuft is now available in a color other than white. *I.* 'Absolutely Amethyst' light lavender clusters bloom a month later and are not as hardy as white candytuft.

Candytuft is so well behaved, even after blooming, that it makes an attractive perennial for a container.

YOU CAN CALL me "Perfection," and I'll tell you why. My frothy white masses of circular flowers completely envelope my dark green foliage. My leaves are narrow, shiny, and waxy. I'm a small-sized perennial, only about twelve inches tall, but my stems will spread nicely. My form is a tight mound that stays evergreen year-round, so I always look perfect.

My size makes me the consummate edging plant for planting along stairs or pathways. I'm often considered an alpine perennial and used as a drought-tolerant ground cover. I look lovely when seen cascading over walls or rocks.

Because a garden never has enough white, and white makes everything "pop," I give a white-collar crispness to neighboring perennials. I look especially nice planted in front of columbine or in the dense foliage of tulips. Adding me as filler to a vase of cut tulips gives the perfect finishing touch to a spring bouquet. My neatness gives taller perennials a classic completed look. A clump of lilium or the red foliage of *Penstemon* 'Husker Red' looks exceptional planted behind me because my nice foliage fills in at their feet.

I'm very comfortable planted in partial shade or shade. A flat mat of ajuga planted in front of me is a lovely contrast of color and leaf texture. Physostegia also grows well in partial shade and blooms late summer, adding a touch of color for later on. Fall asters are attractive in back of me if the spot is not too shady. A partial-shade garden keeps my foliage fresher and shinier. I bloom heavier in full sun, but my foliage stays nicer in a shadier area.

I'm hardy in every way. I'm drought tolerant, needing just regular watering due mainly to a strong taproot. I'm comfortable in most soils, even in the lean Rocky Mountain soil that usually provides good drainage or clay soil that holds water.

My Zone 3 hardiness is assurance that I'll get through winter. My beautiful evergreen foliage comes through fine even when covered in deep snow. When the spring weather stays cool, I'll bloom longer than my full four weeks. In the chill of the upper elevations, my bloom time sometimes extends into July.

It's appreciated when a perennial stays right where it's planted, and I do. I seldom need division, but prostrate stems may root and can easily be dug and transplanted. A haircut and shaping after blooming will not only keep me vigorous and promote next year's flower production, but it will also provide stem cuttings that are easily rooted. Propagation with my stem cuttings is the best way to obtain more free-flowering and uniform perennials. Seed-propagated candytuft just isn't as perfect. That doesn't mean my seeds are not acceptable, it's just that cuttings are more consistent. The seeds are great and contain many medicinal properties. The ancients used them for rheumatism and gout. Nowadays, we are useful in cardiac hypertension, asthma, and bronchitis in doses of one to three seeds at a time, twice a day.

My two best candytufts are *I. sempervirens* 'Snowflake' and 'Little Gem'. 'Snowflake' is vegetative, meaning it is produced from cuttings or starts. 'Snowflake' is an attractive easy-to-find perennial that forms a perfect cushion of narrow, dark green leaves that are smothered in clusters of snow-white flowers. 'Snowflake' received the Royal Horticulture Society Award for excellence.

I. sempervirens 'Little Gem' only differs from 'Snowflake' in that it's smaller, growing five to eight inches and is not as vigorous. This dwarf selection forms a small, dense mound of evergreen leaves that are more compact than the species typical is. The small size of 'Little Gem' makes it an excellent choice for edging or planters.

Disease and pests usually don't bother me, except in the higher elevations of the Rockies where there are herds of deer looking for food in winter. They will "scarf" down anything evergreen and think I'm candy!

The ancients named me candytuft, not because I smell like candy (that's my annual cousin) but because my name derives from a place once called Candia on the island of Crete. The Latin adjective part of my name is *sempervirens,* which means "forever" or "evergreen." I really am evergreen, and I really am "Perfect."

WINTER PERENNIALS: NATURE'S FOURTH-SEASON MIRACLE

Bergenia's luscious heart-shaped leaves are surrounded by a colorful hyacinth-like bloom in the early spring. Bergenia stays short and evergreen and always looks classy.

Bergenia cordifolia has thick, leathery leaves that turn an attractive burgundy in winter. Its tattered leaves may be in need of a trim because of a thick blanket of snow.

Grasses in winter blow gracefully in the wind. Fountain grass provides an element of entertainment in the winter landscape.

CANDYTUFT'S LUSTROUS, "PERFECT" foliage stays evergreen in winter. How can this be? Candytuft, like other evergreen perennials, gives gardeners a fourth-season gardening miracle.

The first miracle occurred when plants evolved from their tropical beginnings and became hardy in another environment. Perennials with winter hardiness developed a compact covering of bud or bulb. These coverings contain a hormone that helps maintain a necessary water balance. The water, along with the plant's chemical components such as proteins, sugars, and fats act like antifreeze in the cells. Dehydration is what causes the most winter damage in plants because the cell loses its antifreeze properties.

It's logical that candytuft's waxy-leafed foliage inhibits water loss and increases hardiness, especially when planted in a protected or shady area, but winter perennials can be looked at in different ways. First are perennials that go dormant but maintain pleasing winter foliage. These perennials need not be cut back in fall. One of the best of these is ornamental grasses. These grasses stand tall above the snow, and the wind plays on their soft golden stems. A frothy wheatlike seed pod on the tip attracts birds to the garden. The birds are entertainment for the long-suffering gardener who watches, rests, and browses the plant catalogs, all the while dreaming up a new, creative project for the garden come spring.

Another perennial attractive to birds in wintertime is the coneflower. Birds land on the chocolate buttons on top of stiff stems and act like they are sipping hot chocolate. The tall sedums and the strong arching stems of the goldenrod also invite the birds to lunch. Adding winter-interest perennials to a landscape is not only good for the landscape but also good for the birds.

The second group of winter-interest perennials is considered evergreen, like candytuft:

- *Ajuga*, bugleweed, has bluish, flat leaves that will stay evergreen but will look somewhat dormant until May.
- *Armeria*, thrift, has a short mound of grasslike foliage that stays attractive throughout every season.

Hellebores peeks through the snow early, usually in March, so it has been nicknamed "Christmas rose."

- *Bergenia's* thick, leathery leaves turn a rich burgundy in winter. Planting it along a front porch or walkway welcomes guests to a front door. When this plant winters under a deep blanket of snow, its leaves will need a trim.
- *Delosperma*, hardy yellow ice plant, has flat succulent leaves that turn rosy-red in winter.
- *Dianthus*, pinks, has silvery foliage that winters well as long as it received a fall haircut.
- *Helleborus* are sometimes called Christmas roses because they bloom incredibly early on thick, leathery foliage. They are difficult to start but once established are long-lived and hardy. This plant is infamous for not surviving transplanting, so purchase potted plants.
- *Heuchera,* coral bells, has exceptional color of foliage that has a tendency to stay evergreen. It might need to be replanted as soon as the snow melts if it has pushed its shallow root up and out of the ground due to freezing and thawing temperatures.
- *Phlox,* creeping phlox, has foliage that resembles a pine tree and, like a pine tree, it stays evergreen.
- *Sempervivums*, hens and chicks, are a favorite in every season. Their thick succulent rosettes hold moisture and turn shades of bronze in wintertime.
- *Sedum,* stonecrop, persists in winter, meaning it is somewhat evergreen. It will look sort of dormant in early spring but will snap back as soon as temperatures rise.
- *Yucca*, Adam's needle, is totally evergreen. The sword-like foliage on this plant is thick and tough, covered with hair along the edges. A native desert plant, yucca knows how to retain its antifreeze moisture. When the snow melts, yucca will be just as distinguished as it was last fall. A few yellowed stems at the base of the plant will need removing.

The leathery leaves of hens and chicks ignores any and all kinds weather. This perennial's foliage looks excellent, always.

Evergreen perennials are an amazing example of how nature evolves to provide hardiness. All of these plants have waxy or thick succulent types of leaves so they can hold the water that will keep their cells making their personal antifreeze. The thinner-skinned evergreens usually do better in a shady spot in the garden and will appreciate a little protection of leaves or compost.

Winter gardening may be a new concept for a gardener to think about, but adding a few winter-interest perennials into the landscape may soothe a gardener's obsession. Or . . . skip the frostbite and gaze out of the warm kitchen window, knowing that the gardens are fine because the winter-interest perennials are keeping you entertained and the rest are sleeping. After all, without winter there would never be columbines, peonies, poppies, daffodils, or tulips to welcome a gardener back into the outside sunshine again.

Yucca is easy to start by splitting the mother plant in spring. However, be aware that once a yucca is introduced into a garden, it will always remain an evergreen year in and year out as a permanent addition to the landscape.

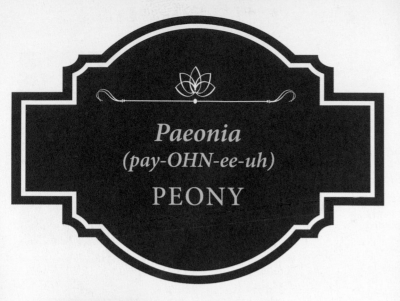

Paeonia
(pay-OHN-ee-uh)
PEONY

SHAPE	Shrub with globe flowers
HEIGHT	About twenty-four inches
WIDTH	About twenty-four inches
BLOOM TIME	Around Memorial Day
COLORS	Shades of red, pink, and white
SITE	Intermountain soil
LIGHT	Full sun in higher elevations, afternoon shade in valleys
HARDINESS	Zone 2
COMMENTS	Plant peonies in a permanent place

Memorial Day is the day we remember our military heroes who have preserved our way of life. Peonies are a fitting tribute to our fallen soldiers.

P. 'Bowl of Beauty' blooms later than other peonies, usually in mid-June. Their open, five-inch, hot pink bowl holds a smaller peony nestled inside.

P. 'Sarah Bernhardt' has enormous pink flowers that bloom in late spring or early summer.

P. 'Karl Rosenfield', with its deep, rich red colors is considered the workhorse of the summer garden.

AUTHOR'S NOTE

I AM NOT A peony. In fact, I'm the gardener, but because I grow and love peonies, I've chosen to narrate this section.

My Grandma Belva was not a gardener. The only flowers she grew were peonies and lilac bushes. Her sole purpose in growing these was to be able to fill her recycled paper-mâché baskets to decorate the graves on Memorial Day.

Filling the baskets was a yearly extravaganza, and she always asked me to help. As we stripped the lilac bush and the peony blooms from along the driveway, she would, year after year, always pull the same corny joke on me:

"Knock, Knock?"

"Who's there?" I'd reply.

"Peony."

"Peony who?"

"Pee only when you have to!"

Then she'd laugh so hard that I couldn't help but laugh too.

Now, peonies always bring back these happy memories, and I think lovingly of Grandma Belva. Grandma didn't know a great deal about these dependable plants. She wasn't aware that peonies had been around for thousands of years. She had never heard the legends of how Paeon, a physician to the gods, was turned into a peony to be able to stay immortal. Could this be why they are so long-lived?

She only knew that the scrumptious pink or red blooms curled into a huge and beautiful ball and that they smelled good. She also knew that her peonies' dark-green glossy foliage, even after all the blooms were stripped, would create an attractive green hedge along the driveway.

Intuitively, Grandma had planted her peonies in an ideal spot, between the driveway and a cement edge on the lawn side. Peonies are snobs and prefer to live solo in their own beds rather than be squashed into a perennial bed with other flowers.

Later, these same peonies were passed down to my mother along with Grandma Belva's home. After breaking her pelvis at age ninety, Mother was moved to a nursing home. From her bed, she expressed concern not about her home, but about her mother's peonies. She was afraid she might die and that her home could be sold before spring, peonies and all. I offered to dig them.

The weather was cold for mid-October, but the peonies, with a lot of labor, were dug and potted into two-gallon-size pots. The soil was plain old garden soil, probably alkaline, clay-like, rocky, and quite heavy. The roots were huge and had to be trimmed to fit into the pots. I made sure each root had five or more of the buds called eyes, which looked exactly like the tip of my little finger. These were planted right at soil level. I ended up with forty-three nice potted peonies. I placed them in a dry irrigation ditch under the cherry trees for winter.

Their only blanket was the leaves and snow. I had no idea that peonies required a winter chilling of -40°F to break dormancy and bloom the following season or that propagating peonies was considered risky and that it would take three years before they would bloom. Nor did I know that they required a bushel-sized hole filled with amendments to be planted in.

It was either blind luck or divine intervention, but by the next Mother's Day I had thirty-seven nicely growing—not huge, but nice—potted perennial peonies that had belonged to my grandmother. I was more than pleased to give these to all the cousins, nieces, sisters, daughters (and sons) for Mother's Day. Those peonies are a living souvenir of Grandma Belva. A peony's multigenerational strength is why this plant is so treasured, and each season of bloom brings back fond memories.

Should your peonies stop blooming, check out the following possible reasons:

- If the initial planting site was conditioned with compost or manure, a peony will hardly require any additional fertilizer. (But in the Rockies, nitrogen is always needed.)
- Due to a peony's longevity, its soil can become depleted.
- Too hot or cold temperatures will kill buds.
- Peonies usually take three years to establish before they bloom.
- Peonies may be rootbound and need dividing.
- Peony foliage should be left on the plant until after frost.
- Peonies might be getting too much or too little water.
- When adding compost in the fall, leave the peony's center crown exposed. Peonies planted too deep will not bloom. Two inches of compost every year will eventually bury the peonies so deep that they will stop blooming.

BOTANICAL LATIN: DECODING PLANT NAMES

WHEN PLANTS WERE first named, their Latin names were clues about where they originated and the color, shape, and size of blooms and foliage. Both their family genus and a specific descriptive word were also included. The adjective singles out that specific perennial almost like our social security numbers or passwords on wireless connections do now. The aster is a good starting point to show how to decode the Latin names of perennials.

- **Family genus:** *Aster*—meaning "star-like"
- **Descriptive words:** *Aster Symphyotrichum novae-angliae*—*Angliae* meaning "England" and *novae* meaning "new"
- **Desriptive words, or adjectives:** *Aster novi-belgii*—*Novi* meaning "New York" and *Belgii* meaning "Belgium"
- *Aster × dumosus*—meaning hybrid or cross between two species and *dumosus* meaning "bushy"

Now you know everything about asters? Ha! Not quite, but every little bit helps. The botanical meanings tucked inside the words can help identify traits. There is a secret key to perennials if you look at the Latin word or the phrase hidden within the perennial's Latin name.

Hint: Latin words are always written in italics. Latin can be annoying when browsing plant catalogs but enlightening if you can decode the names. The challenge of using botanical terms to decode characteristics and descriptions might just be fun!

PLANT NAME	BOTANICAL LATIN	MEANING
Achillea 'Coronation Gold'	*Coron*	Crown-like
Acorus gramineus variegatum	*Variegatum*	Variegated leaves
Ajuga reptans	*Reptans*	Creeping on the ground
Alchemilla mollis	*Moll*	Hairy leaves
Alpine Aster	*Alp*	Alpine regions
Aquilegia	*Aquil*	Eagle-like
Armeria maritima	*Maritima*	Of water, beach
Astilbe chinensis	*Chinensis*	From China
Bergenia cordifolia	*Folia*	Referring to foliage
Brunnera macrophylla	*Macr*	Large flowers
Calamagrostis acutiflora	*Acut*	Pointed and sharp
Campanula carpatica	*Campan* and *carpatica*	Bell shaped and on the ground
Campanula glomerata	*Glom*	A cluster
Catananche caerulea	*Caerul*	Dark blue
Centranthus alba	*Alba*	White
Centranthus ruber	*Ruber*	Red
Cerastium tomentosum	*Tomentosum*	Densely wooly

PLANT NAME	BOTANICAL LATIN	MEANING
Coreopsis grandiflora	*Grand*	Large
Delosperma floribundum	*Floribundum*	Free-flowering
Dianthus deltoides	*Deltoides*	Triangular
Digitalis purpurea	*Purpurea*	Purple
Echinacea	*Echin*	Bristle-like cone
Eupatorium rugosum	*Rugosum*	Dark-red color
Festuca ovina	*Festuca*	Grasslike
Gaillardia grandiflora	*Grand* and *flori*	Large and flowers
Helianthus 'Summer Sun'	*Heli*	Referring to the sun
Hemerocallis	*Hemero*	Beautiful for a day
Hosta aureo-variegata	*Aureo, auri*	Golden or golden varigation
Hosta undulata albomarginata	*Albo* and *marginata*	White and margin
Iberis candytuft	*Iber*	Referring to Spain
Iris sibirica	*Siberica*	Referring to Siberia
Leucanthemum	*Leuc*	White
Lilium	*Liliflorus*	Lily flowered
Malva moschata	*Moschatus*	Musky
Papaver orientale	*Orientalis*	Eastern
Physostegia virginiana	*Virginianus, virginicus, virginensis*	Specifically native of Virginia but often used to mean North America
Saponaria ocymoides	*Sap*	Soap made out of roots
Saxifraga	*Sax*	From rocky area
Scabiosa japonica var. alpina	*Japonica* and *alpina*	From the mountains of Japan
Sedum spectabile	*Spect*	Spectacular, showy
Sedum spurium coccineum	*Coccin*	Red
Sempervivum	*Glauci, glauco*	Gray-green, Powdered foliage
Sempervivum red rubin	*Semper*	Evergreen
Solidago canadensis	*Canadensis*	Referring to Canada
Thymus citriodorus	*Citri*	Citrus
Trumpet vine flava	*Flava*	Yellow
Veronica austriaca	*Austr*	Referring to Austria

Papaver orientale
(pa-PAH-ver)
POPPY

SHAPE	Big bulky clump, Flowers cup shaped
HEIGHT	Three feet when in bloom
WIDTH	Thirty inches
BLOOM TIME	June
COLORS	Red, scarlet, orange, salmon, pink, or white
SITE	Neutral-to-alkaline soil
LIGHT	Full sun
HARDINESS	Zone 3
COMMENTS	Not for southern gardens

The scarlet-red feather petals of 'Turkenlouise' poppies are indeed flamboyant. This poppy has stronger, sturdier stems and never gets damaged in wind or rain.

P. 'Brilliant' is just beginning to open its enormous red, oval-shaped heads of eye-catching color.

P. 'Royal Wedding' has white crêpe paper flowers with a black center and is gorgeous in the garden.

P. 'Prinzessin Viktoria Luise', or 'Princess Victoria Louise', has such delicate, elegant salmon coloring that it really is fitting for a princess.

LET ME INTRODUCE myself. I am the magnificent and fantastic *Papaver orientale*. My history is a long, long tale of seduction and intrigue. Poppy seeds have been found in Egyptian tombs; a fertility poppy goddess figurine was found in Crete; and the ancient Greeks portrayed me as the symbol of sleep, night, and death. Hippocrates (460–377 BC) emphasized my medicinal properties as being narcotic and cathartic. Pliny the Elder, a Roman historian, mentioned that I am able to promote sleep and relieve indigestion and respiratory problems. A century later, Galen wrote that I am the strongest known drug for dulling the senses and inducing sleep.

Just kidding! As *P. orientale*, I really wanted to be the seductive perennial, but—actually—I'm not. My older sister *P. somniferum* is the seductive one. *P. Somniferum* is the annual with the long, long history of narcotic sleep, who sometimes gets into legal trouble. She is also the poppy that provides dried poppy seeds for pastries. For her, large-scale production began, and she became important for creating drugs like morphine and codeine.

My only history is having vivid, upward-facing, six-inch blooms that are almost like a flamboyant flamenco dancer. The skirts are my bright petals in spectacular shades of red, scarlet, orange, salmon, pink, and white. These enormous ruffled crêpe-paper-like petals attach to my sultry dark-haired center in a twirling circle of gaudy color.

I dance on sturdy pale-green stems that hold me firm unless I'm caught up in strong winds. I need to avoid open windy locations or my blooms will get battered and my dark stamen center will stain my skirt.

Should my stem break, gather me for cut flowers. Clean slice my stem. Using a match or lighter to sear the stem will keep my milky latex sap from seeping out into the vase.

I belong in full sun where I'll shine. Planted in intermountain soil with its coarser, drier texture and alkalinity is my ideal situation. Plus, these mountains satisfy my native requirement for cold winters. This is everything I need to ensure a long and productive life.

Several weeks after my spectacular performance, I need to rest. It's time for me to go dormant. My foliage will look ratty, so cut me back to the ground. Next year's flowering depends on the warm season dormancy of July and August, but not to worry, in September I'll return as a small green tuft. After winter's vernalization or period of chilling, I'll again return to dance my wild, flamboyant, pleasing performance. I will not bloom in areas with warm winters and most likely won't survive.

Gardeners are never pleased with a big bare spot in their gardens after I go dormant, so it's important that I recommend a follow-up number. Hardy hibiscus is a late-season-breaking perennial that will camouflage my dormancy. It has almost equal stature, bloom size, and color and does not bloom until July. It will do a fine job except it's a Zone 5 and will winter-kill in the colder, higher elevations of the intermountain area. If that's the case, use an annual like a dahlia. Dinner-plate dahlias give such a bloom-filled performance that I fear I may be replaced.

Propagating my deep taproots is tricky and not too successful. I detest being moved and will take at least two years before I'll be ready to dance again. If a gardener chooses not to purchase garden-center-potted poppies, which can be planted successfully at any time, they must wait until I'm dormant to divide me. New sprouts will have started around my clump. Carefully remove the sprouts and quickly replant the root vertically in a deep hole. My crown must be at soil level. Reseeding can happen, but be prepared—my seeds will revert to my original orange poppies.

Here is a convenient list of easy-to-grow species and cultivars:

- 'Beauty of Livermore' blooms are ox-blood red
- 'Helen Elizabeth' has crinkled, salmon-pink blooms and shorter stems.
- 'Prince of Orange' is tangerine orange.
- 'Royal Wedding' has clean white petals with a black eye.
- 'Turkenlouise' blooms on thirty-inch stems in fringed, red-orange flowers.
- 'Brilliant' blooms a vibrant red with enormous oval-shaped heads.

I may not be called seductive like my older sister, but because I'm so eye-catching and saturated with hot colors, it's natural to call me at least flamboyant.

Bulbs like allium go dormant right after they bloom, leaving ball-shaped seed heads like those pictured here of *Allium* 'Purple Sensations'. Mixing this perennial in with the lilium creates another full season of color in the garden.

Snowdrop anemones prefer to be in a shady rock garden.

PERENNIALS THAT GO DORMANT

PERENNIALS ARE FASCINATING! Some stay evergreen, like candytuft. Others go dormant, like bleeding heart when summer heats up, and oriental poppies do a double dormancy of three months warm, six months cold. Another intriguing group of perennials are the early-spring bloomers, which are marked by short life cycles. The plants pop up almost out of the snow and bloom, reproduce, and then go dormant again.

Plants that go dormant are sometimes referred to as ephemerals. Many of them grow in woodland-type settings where sunlight is void. The perennials bloom in the new sunlight of early spring before the canopy of trees and shrubs leaf out, then return to dormancy when the shade again envelopes them. Woodland ephemerals are usually acid-soil lovers, but there are still a few that grow well in the arid, alkaline soil of the Rocky Mountains.

Spring bulbs like alliums, daffodils, and tulips move toward dormancy right after they bloom. It seems as if they are programmed to conserve energy in preparation for next spring's show.

It's fascinating the way perennials have evolved, but what's a gardener to do when these perennials go dormant and leave a big blank spot in the garden? It would be wise for a gardener to prepare by knowing which perennials go underground to rest. Here are a few examples.

Starting in spring are the snowdrop anemones. These exquisite white single-flowered little darlings have bright yellow centers. Snowdrops grow in a clump of deep-green foliage that sends up an erect stem to hold the two-inch flower heads.

Dodecatheon, or shooting star, is another interesting ephemeral. Its surprising appearance in the early spring garden is a thrill to a gardener who has forgotten all about this little sweetheart's existence. It grows to twelve inches tall over rosettes of broad, lance-shaped leaves. Its flowers are rose-colored clusters that supposedly shoot their seeds all over the garden.

I had never grown shooting star, but it sounded so fascinating in the catalog that I sent for it. When the plants arrived, they were a big disappointment. The roots were like a piece of string with hardly a trace of crown. I potted them anyway, but it took two years before they bloomed. Out of the twenty-five plants that I purchased, only three grew. I would have complained to the catalog company, but when the shooting star bloomed, it was so beautiful that the cost didn't matter.

Doronicum, leopard's bane, grows easily in intermountain gardens. Depending on the variety, it will grow from one to two feet. 'Little Leo' is the shortest, and 'Magnificum' is the tallest. Leopard's bane's foliage is one of its best features. Its dark green heart-shaped leaves resemble prickly holly foliage, but it is soft and pliable. Gardeners can't help but welcome the first daisy-like bloom of the summer, especially when these flowers bloom in a profusion of bright yellow.

Matteuccias, ostrich ferns, are a natural for cold-climate shade gardens. Massed under high-canopied trees, they add drama and elegance to any garden. When summers heat up, ferns in the intermountain valleys will turn brown, collapse, and move underground. In the coolness of the mountains, they hold their magnificent vase shaped fronds all summer. Ostrich ferns are dependable native Alaskan perennials.

The shade-loving perennials of spring are a necessity in any garden, but for an all-season display, plant the dependable hosta as a companion. You can also use shade annuals like begonias, coleus, or impatiens to change those dormant spots to a summer season of beauty.

Pulsatilla resembles woodland plants but prefers full sun. Often called pasque-flower because its bloom time corresponds to the Passover and Easter, this perennial stays small and has delicate-looking, fernlike foliage that hides Easter eggs perfectly. It is a hardy perennial and is therefore a must for early spring color. Surprisingly, this plant does not go dormant in the coolness of the Bear Lake gardens. Planting sun-loving, later-blooming *Monarda* 'Petite Bouquet' or *Rudbeckia fulgida* around it will let the spring bloomer rest without leaving a blank spot in the garden.

Early-blooming bulbs like alliums, daffodils, and tulips die back after blooming, leaving an untidy spot in the garden. Always plant these perennials toward the middle or back of a flower bed so their yellowing foliage is disguised. Surround them with perennials like daylilies, whose foliage corresponds nicely.

The previously mentioned perennials, along with bleeding hearts and oriental poppies all go underground. They are not dead; they are sleeping. All are attractive and important to the spring garden but should be used sparingly.

Planting perennial partners around these plants helps, but my very best tip for hiding the blank spots is adding snapdragons to the garden. A magnificent stand of snapdragons comes in every color except blue and provides masses of color the entire season. Snapdragons love intermountain soil, and the variety of climate conditions. They can be easily started as seed and will reseed in your garden year after year. Most importantly, snapdragons will turn a dormant spot into the most eye-catching part of the garden.

Doronicum is so lovely that gardeners can't help but wish that it lasted longer.

Ostrich ferns, with their two-to-three foot height, add a special dimension to the shade garden.

Pulsatilla, or pasqueflower, blooms at Easter—thus the common name *Pasque,* which means "Passover." It's also the perfect size for hiding Easter eggs for children to find.

Saponaria ocymoides
(sap-o-NAY-ree-uh)
SOAPWORT

SHAPE	Low cascading mound, filler-type clusters of flowers
HEIGHT	Eight inches
WIDTH	About twenty-four inches
BLOOM TIME	Late May through June
COLORS	Shades of pink
SITE	Alkaline soil
LIGHT	Full sun
HARDINESS	Zones 2–7
COMMENTS	Considered a cleaning agent

Soapwort is right at home in rock gardens, bringing a softer element to them..

A young seedling forms a neat tight ball a year after it germinates. This is a reseeded soapwort plant.

An excellent companion plant for soapwort is its close relative *Silene schafta*. It blooms in late summer, adding another season of color to rock walls.

Soapwort will naturally reseed in a rock garden or rock wall because it grows well in the alkaline soil furnished by the limestone and minerals in the rocks.

I'M AN OLD-WORLD wildflower that is delicately beautiful, but I'm also tough. I grow well in alkaline soils, cold climates, and high elevations. My taproots grow deep, giving me drought tolerance even when planted in sand. I'm vigorous but never aggressive. My pink masses of tiny two-inch blooms will completely cover or cascade down rock walls. I soften the front edges of flower beds or walkways with masses of exquisite pink color.

My foliage, with its ruddy-red stems and small dark-green leaves, is a complement to my clusters of pink flowers. When my spent blooms are cut back after they finish flowering, my small, tight mound of waxy leaves fills back in and stays neat all season long. I stay evergreen in mild winters, but in the colder regions, I might go dormant. I'm really an attractive plant, but more important, I'm much more than a pretty face.

First of all, I'm an easy-care, rugged perennial that outblooms and outspreads most other flowers, and I'm easy to propagate! After trimming my spent blooms at the end of June, take the cuttings (with seeds intact), and place these stems along rock walls or anyplace that needs a softening beauty. These stems will drop their seeds, and by spring a myriad of baby soapworts will appear at absolutely no cost. Because my seed requires a chilling before it germinates, I'll look a little scrawny the first year. All I will need is another winter's cold treatment in order to bloom, and I'll carpet the garden with color.

While it's true that I am very attractive and easy to care for, my most distinguishing feature is that I'm a powerful herb rich in saponins, nature's cleansing agents. Both my Latin name, *Saponaria*, and my common name, *soapwort*, are derived from my cleaning abilities. Museums use my thick, soapy roots to clean heirlooms such as handmade lace because I'm so gentle. In the New England textile industry, I was used not only for cleaning but also as a thickening agent. Soapwort shampoo is all natural and cleans gently, making it good for hair. The shampoo is simple to make, requiring only two ingredients:

- Two cups of distilled water
- 1½ tablespoons chopped or dried soapwort

Add me to the water and let the mixture soak overnight. Then place in an enamel or glass saucepan and bring to a boil. Cover the pan and simmer on low heat for twenty minutes. Remove from heat. Allow mixture to cool to room temperature and strain using a nylon or muslin strainer (no metal). Pour strained liquid into a clean bottle. The shampoo must be used in eight to ten days or it may spoil. A few drops of additional herbs such as lemon verbena, lavender, or rosemary can be added for scent, but I naturally exude a delicious raspberry smell with a hint of clove.

Soapwort has been used for people externally, both as a cleansing agent and medical herb for skin problems (eczema, acne, boils, and so on). For emergency cases such as contact with poison ivy, the parts of the leaves above ground will soothe the burning rash. Herbal medical practitioners recommend my use to cure bronchitis, coughs, and even asthma, but my seeds are poisonous, so a home gardener should be cautious before using internally. Collect my flowers in summer and dig my roots in fall. Dehydrate them in the sun for further use.

A cleansing agent like me is an important survival necessity in case we don't always have supermarkets to count on, so please put me in your garden. I come back each year, but I'm not persistent, so always allow some reseeding. Mulching will prevent seeding, and cutting me back after I bloom will help if I overseed. Remember, less seeding means less weeding.

Many gardeners consider my graceful foliage to be my most outstanding feature. This is why I'm great in containers. I'll give three weeks of trailing, abundant blooms, and then after cutting back my stems, stunning foliage will spill over the edges of the pot or planter the rest of the season. I'll probably over-winter in the container because many gardeners swear I'm a Zone 2 perennial, and I'm very drought tolerant. I'm a valuable perennial with many talents—much more than just a pretty face.

PERENNIALS AS HERBS IN THE GARDEN

A DEEP CONCERN ABOUT side effects from the multitude of synthetic drugs on the market has revived the use of herbal remedies such as the use of saponaria for skin healing purposes. I have no claim at being a healer—I'm only the messenger—but I know that perennial herbs are not only a fine addition to gardens because of their beauty but also because of their convenience. It's not always feasible to run to the pharmacy. Below are introductory tidbits on perennial herbs.

HARVESTING YOUR HERBS

The quality of the herb is most important when it's used for healing. Pick perfect leaves at the plant's prime, and harvest in early morning. Dry and then store the herbs carefully in glass jars with labels and dates. Dried green herbs lose their medicinal potency after six to seven months. Roots and seeds are effective for up to three years.

INTERNAL USE

Herbal infusions are teas that are taken internally. Generally a tea or infusion can use either fresh or dried herbs. Fresh herbs have a higher medicinal value, but dried herbs are available year-round, so more recipes call for dried herbs. Use distilled water. A usual dosage is eight fluid ounces to two teaspoons of herbs. Drink an infusion three times a day. (Half the amount for children and the elderly.) *Any internal use needs doctor approval!*

DECOCTIONS

Decoctions are similar to teas but are used mainly with hard materials like roots and seeds. If green parts are used, bruise and crush them to help release their active principles. The recipe is the same as for an infusion but needs to simmer longer until the mixture has been reduced to one fourth of the original volume. Honey can be used as a sweetener.

Refrigerated decoctions should keep for up to three days. *Doctor approval required!*

EXTERNAL USE

External herb uses include hot or cold compresses or poultices. Soak a clean cotton cloth in a hot infusion or decoction and apply to an infected area. Wrap the area with plastic and then apply a folded towel to maintain the heat. A cold compress is the same but with cold ice water. A poultice differs only in that crushed plant parts are used to make a thick paste with boiling water and then applied.

Here are a few perennial plants with a reputation for healing:

ACHILLEA, YARROW
- Chew fresh leaves to aid a toothache.
- Make a decoction for wounds, chapped skin, or a rash.
- Use an infusion for a mouthwash for inflamed gums.

AJUGA REPTANS, BUGLEWEED
- An infusion of dried leaves and boiling water is thought to lower blood pressure.
- Has a mild narcotic effect.

ALCHEMILLA, LADY'S MANTLE
- Use only green parts. Drink an infusion during pregnancy and for ten days after giving birth to help the womb contract.
- Regulates the menstrual cycle in young women and relieves menopausal discomfort in older females.

ALLIUM, GARLIC
- Contains some iron and vitamins and acts as a mild antibiotic.
- Will cleanse the blood and reduce blood pressure. Will protect against the common cold.

ARTEMISIA, WORMWOOD
- Is for external use only because it's toxic.
- Leaves placed on the skin give a deep penetrating heat to soothe rheumatism.

CENTRANTHUS, VALERIAN
- Used for the treatment of restlessness and sleep disorders.
- Has generally fewer side effects than narcotic drugs and does not produce a hangover.

CONVALLARIA, LILY-OF-THE-VALLEY
- Lily-of-the-valley has been used to slow the pace of the heart. However, the entire plant is poisonous and can only be used by a professional herbalist.

DIGITALIS, FOXGLOVE
- Provides the main drug for treating heart failure, but should not be used in home remedies because of toxins.

ECHINACEA, PURPLE CONEFLOWER
- Used for just about everything, including toothaches, sore throats, snakebites, rabies, and blood poisoning. My personal experience with echinacea as a healing herb was for a toothache. I couldn't get to a dentist, so I went into the garden and dug around an echinacea plant. I exposed the fleshy roots and broke two of them off. After replacing the soil, I washed and cut the roots into pellets. I held the pellets directly on the pained tooth, and in no time it stopped aching! Echinacea in the perennial garden is an absolute must!
- Echinacea infusions are believed to stimulate the immune system.

EUPATORIUM, JOE-PYE WEED
- Use dried eupatorium in small doses. An infusion will induce perspiration, relieve gout, and rheumatism. (Plants can be poisonous.)
- Can help remove stones in the bladder.

FILIPENDULA ULMARIA, MEADOWSWEET
- The buds were the first discovered source of salicylic acid from which aspirin was later made. It can be used for whatever aspirin is used for, such as fevers, colds, headaches, and as a mild sedative.

FRAGARIA, WILD STRAWBERRY
- Infuse it as a tea for urinary disorders and as a tonic for kidneys.

GALLIUM, SWEET WOODRUFF
- Bruise fresh leaves and apply to wounds.
- Infuse dried leaves for a tea to relieve stomach pains.

HELENIUM, HELEN'S FLOWER
- Decoct roots as a general tonic and as an expectorant to ease bronchitis and coughs.

HELIANTHUS, SUNFLOWER
- Eat a handful of the sunflower's seeds for vitamins that will benefit the skin.
- Boil seeds for twenty minutes and drink to relieve coughs and inflammation of the kidneys.

HESPERIS, SWEET ROCKET
- These have been used to prevent and cure scurvy.
- A strong dose may induce vomiting.

LAMIUM, DEAD NETTLE
- Has astringent properties.
- Bruised leaves applied directly to the skin are said to staunch bleeding.

LAVANDULA, LAVENDER
- Infuse flowers into a tea to soothe headaches, calm nerves, ease gas, and relieve fainting and dizziness.
- Distill as a massage oil for skin sores, inflammation, rheumatic aches, anxiety, insomnia, and depression.

LONICERA, HONEYSUCKLE
- Use the flower in an infusion for treating coughs and asthma.
- It has a diuretic and laxative property, and contains salicylic acid.

MALVA, MARSHMALLOW
- Infuse the root as a tea for coughs, diarrhea, and insomnia.
- Add to ointment for burns.
- A poultice treats inflammation.

MELISSA OFFICINALIS, LEMON BALM
- Place fresh leaves directly on insect bites and sores.
- Infuse as a tea for relief from chronic bronchitis, feverish colds, headaches, and to calm tension.

MONARDA, BEE BALM
- Infuse leaves as a tea to relive nausea, gas, menstrual pain, and insomnia.

MYOSOTIS SYLVATICA, FORGET-ME-NOT
- Used in homeopathic remedies for respiratory problems.

NEPETA, CATMINT
- Contains vitamin C.
- Infuse nepeta to relieve colds, fevers, and colic in children. It is also a cure for headaches, upset stomachs, and it can be used as a mild sedative.
- Apply infusion externally to sooth scalp irritations.

OENOTHERA, EVENING PRIMROSE
- Seed capsules can be taken for female tension, menopausal discomfort, and psoriasis.
- Contains gamma-linoleic acid, which seems to relieve multiple sclerosis and other degenerative diseases.

PAPAVER, POPPY
- The opium poppy gives us morphine and codeine, which are important painkillers.

PULMONARIA, LUNGWORT
- Chest coughs, wheezing, and shortness of breath are thought to benefit from an infusion of dried leaves.

PYRETHRUM, PAINTED DAISY
- The dried flowers will deter all common insects. It is now being used as a new, environmentally safe substitute for chemical sprays.
- Pyrethrum is not to be ingested!

SALVIA, SAGE
- Leaves aid digestion and are an antiseptic, an antifungal, and contain estrogen.

- Teas are nerve and blood tonics. Soothes coughs and colds.
- Also helps assuage irregular menstruation and menopause.

SEMPERVIVUM, HENS AND CHICKS
- Sempervivum is a great first aid herb because of similar but reduced healing abilities typical of aloe vera.
- Slice open a fresh leaf and apply directly to the skin for minor burns, wasp stings, or insect bites.

SOLIDAGO, GOLDENROD
- Flowerets can be used fresh or dried in a tea to relieve kidney and bladder issues.
- Aids in control of the urinary organs.

THYMUS, THYME
- The leaf has the strongest medicinal qualities.
- Infuse a tea for a digestive tonic and for hangovers.
- Sweeten the tea with honey for convulsive coughs, colds, or sore throats.

VERBENA, VERVAIN
- Use the entire plant as a tea to aid digestion, for a sedative nightcap, or for after nervous exhaustion.
- Verbena can also be used as an anticoagulant.

USE WITH CAUTION!

Although herbs do not have the side effects of drugs, they do affect major organs within the body and should not be taken unnecessarily. Do not self-prescribe! Researching and discussing with your physician is always prudent.

Perennials are like an insurance policy against a mega disaster or the world imploding. That is a lot to expect from something gardeners plant, because they know their perennials will bring them joy. Perennials are truly amazing.

Scabiosa caucasica
(ska-bee-OH-sa)
PINCUSHION

SHAPE	Mound with wiry stems and flat-topped flowers
HEIGHT	Fifteen inches tall
WIDTH	Fifteen inches around
BLOOM TIME	June to August
COLORS	Blue, violet, and white
SITE	The alkaline side of neutral
LIGHT	Full sun
HARDINESS	Zones 3–7
COMMENTS	Butterfly magnet, deer resistant

S. caucasica produces a rich nectar that attracts butterflies and bees to the garden.

Butterflies are good indicators of what is happening in the environment. When plants are sick, butterflies are sick.

'Fama' Alba is fabulous for its unique, complex blooms that attract pollinators to dine at this high-class restaurant

A side view of scabiosa's intricate pincushions on the top of the flower appears as a work of art.

I FEEL SO SHY about introducing myself because of the negative connotation my name *Scabiosa* gives. I'm a high-quality, fabulous perennial that got dubbed *Scabiosa* because it was believed I could cure the skin disease scabies. My adjective, *caucasica*, is a botanical Latin word that indicates where I originated from. I came from the Caucus Mountains located between the Black sea and the Caspian Sea in Europe. I also question my common name of pincushion. I am studded with white pearl corsage pins in the center of my blooms, but the name pincushion? Does anyone nowadays even know what a pincushion is? I think my name should hint at what a natural beauty I am.

I add an airy appearance to the garden. My fabulous blooms stretch up to three inches across and dance above wiry stems. My flat domed flowers are richly textured and far more complex when viewed up close than they seem at a distance. I'm the largest, darkest blue scabiosa available. White 'Fama', with their flat petals at the outer margins and a tightly tufted center cluster, are incredible. My flowers float on fifteen-inch stems that rise from a tidy rosette dome of narrow, green leaves. As my leaves develop along the stems, they become more lobed than the basal leaves and bend nicely.

I start blooming in June with a dazzling display of abundant flowers that lasts until August. If I'm not allowed to set seed by diligent deadheading, I will bloom continuously into September. Not only am I a long-blooming perennial, but I last almost as long as a cut flower due to my stem strength and flower quality. The best time to cut me for a flower arrangement is when my bloom is just opening.

After about three years, I may start to produce fewer blooms. If this is the case, it's time to divide. Spring is the best time to dig me for propagation or to take basal cuttings. Seed production is tricky because I need light to germinate and can't be covered. Unless you have a greenhouse that can maintain sixty-five to seventy-degree temperatures to start my seeds, stick with division. Replant my new starts in a mass planting in the garden where the clear blue and white blooms will attract butterflies. I'm a nectar-producing machine for flying garden friends, so plan on bees and butterflies visiting your garden when I'm around.

I'm easy to grow. My hardiness is a Zone 3, and a little afternoon shade can help ease me through the hotter summer temperatures of the lower elevations. A cover of leaf mulch or compost will help me stay cool. Keep the leaf mulch from crowding over my crown, for I'm prone to crown rot if kept too wet. I survive winter easily, even without snow cover.

My little cousins, 'Butterfly Blue' and 'Pink Mist' often don't last through cold winters, but the winter season suits me fine. 'Butterfly Blue' won the Perennial Plant of the Year Award for 2000, so it could be assumed that she should be hardier. Perhaps she has been weakened by hybridization. 'Pink Mist' is a seedling from 'Butterfly Blue' and is even wimpier.

I add a romantic or informal look to a garden. I do not require staking, and I bend with the wind, so any substantial companion perennials that give me a little more structure will add to my attractiveness. Plant short evergreen candytuft for spring, the tight solid foliage of *Monarda* 'Petite Bouquet' for summer, and a short *Aster* 'Alert' for fall. Behind my airy foliage, plant delphiniums in corresponding shades of blue and white, or pink *Nepeta*'s 'Sweet Dreams' for an eye-stopping display. For more intense drama, plant the bright-colored *Phlox paniculata* that blooms purples, corals, hot pinks, and fuchsia. Phlox will back me until the end of summer.

Also, all of these perennials are first-choice menu items for butterflies. I'm sure any gardener is now convinced that I am a fabulous flower. Please agree with me and instead of *scabiosa*, please call me *fabulous*!

Monarchs require milkweeds as their host plant but will use *Asclepias* as a substitute. Asters and other fall-blooming flowers help with nourishment for their long migration to Mexico.

Swallowtails will use herbs like parsley, dill, or citrus as the caterpillar host plant and asters, alfalfa, and Joe-pye weed for their dining.

BUTTERFLIES IN THE PERENNIAL GARDEN

S*CABIOSA* 'FAMA' IS a nectar-producing fast-food stop for butterflies. Perennials that invite these enchanting visitors to the garden add another joyful dimension to gardening. My first real awareness of these lovely creatures came over twenty years ago in the tropical butterfly house at the Pacific Science Center in Seattle, Washington. It was winter, mid-February, and I was at a low point in my life. The conservatory was a balmy 80°F, and I went inside to warm myself, but to my surprise, it also helped warm the hurt in my heart. While observing the delicate, intricate perfection of these flitting, flying miracles, it was quite impossible to deny that God, the Great Creator, knew exactly the way things should be. Since then, the practice of planting nectar-rich perennials for butterflies in the garden became very important. They are my symbol to accept what is handed out, knowing it is what it is and that it is okay!

All it takes to bring butterflies to the garden is to provide a good source of nectar by planting these perennials.

- *Achillea,* yarrow: The flat, platelike blooms provide a secure landing pad for butterflies to rest. *A. millefolium* and *Asclepias tuberosa* are both good host plants for the butterfly's eggs, but they are both invasive, so plant them in lean soil with some type of root barrier.
- *Alcea,* hollyhocks: The mallow family of perennials also fits into this group of butterfly-preferred plants because of their height, bloom time, and open-faced flowers. I discovered several butterfly pupas along the stems of hollyhocks when I was cutting them back. The pupa cases seem to have a strong covering of superglue, because they are indestructible.
- *Aster*: The fall flowering time coincides with the Monarch butterflies' migration and provides the nutrition they need on their journey to and from Mexico. The Admiral butterfly's family also flocks to asters.
- *Chrysanthemum,* mums: Any open-type daisy bloom appeals to butterflies, even Shasta daisies. The Sulpher butterfly group uses apple trees as a host and chrysanthemums and daisies for a nectar source.
- *Coreopsis,* tickseed: Skippers and Whites are drawn to both the color and nectar of this flower.
- *Dianthus,* pinks: These are the earliest blooming perennials that attract butterflies. I found Spring Whites flitting around *Dianthus* and creeping phlox in an unheated greenhouse at Bear Lake in early March. This really made me smile.
- *Echinacea,* coneflower, and *Rudbeckia,* black-eyed Susan: The same groups of butterflies choose these flowers for lunch, which isn't surprising because they are sisters. Swallowtails and Monarchs like the open-daisy bloom, the long blooming period, and of course, the nectar from these two exceptional native perennials.

- *Eupatorium,* Joe-pye weed: A multipurpose habitat for butterflies, birds, and bees. Its height provides hiding spots from predators. (As a side note, butterfly spots that look like eyes on their wings confuse an attacker as to which way they are moving. All butterflies are poisonous and foul tasting. The more colorful the butterfly, the more toxins they exude. Ants, spiders, mites, and wasps will eat the eggs or larvae. Birds and wasps prey on adult butterflies, so between hiding in thick foliage, eye spots, and poison, butterflies are not as susceptible as their fragile appearance indicates.)

- *Gaillardia,* blanket flower: Look for Sulphers, Whites, and Swallowtails once *Gaillardia* blooms.

- *Helenium,* sneezeweed and *Heliopsis,* sunflower: Both of these perennials are tall, so Checkerspots use them as a host where they lay their eggs and as a nectar source later.

- *Liatris,* gayfeather: Liatris is a native North American perennial. Late blooming natives are usually a choice habitat for butterflies.

- *Monarda,* bee balm: With a name like bee balm, it's obvious that bees are attracted to this plant, but so are butterflies. The Checkered White, Fritillaries, Blues, and Swallowtails can always be found sipping from the red shades of these blooms.

- *Phlox paniculata,* tall garden phlox: Its sweet fragrance is a favorite of the Checkerspots, Viceroys, and Fritillaries. The Whites enjoy the creeping phlox.

- *Sedums*: The taller varieties are always covered with both butterflies and bees of every kind. This is a must-have in the garden if you want to attract these visitors.

- *Verbena Canadensis* 'Homestead Purple': It is a nectar-producing machine and a Zone 6 perennial. It doesn't grow well in northern Utah, but I still plant it as an annual because it's an I-cannot-do-without-this type of plant. Butterflies feel the same way and use it as both a host and dinner. Two other annuals that serve this same purpose for butterflies are snapdragons and zinnias.

A few other tips to make your garden butterfly friendly:

Cautious use of insecticides is crucial. The caterpillar and butterflies are insects, and the sprays are lethal. If spraying is an absolute must, do it toward evening or in cool weather when butterflies are not as active.

Full-sun areas are best for butterflies, and all of the perennials they prefer are full-sun plants. Midsummer and fall-blooming perennials match the butterflies' life cycle, so plant late-season bloomers that produce abundant nectar.

Plant butterfly-attractive perennials in a area protected from the wind. These fragile but tough little garden delights need not fight the wind to feed. They are servicing our gardens by pollinating, so in return provide some protection. Also, butterflies need water (but not too much). A mud puddle suits them fine.

Last but not least is the need for a host plant on which they can lay their eggs. When the caterpillars hatch from the eggs, they eat the host plant for nourishment. Eventually the caterpillar will spin a chrysalis or pupa around itself. Depending on the type of butterfly, the caterpillar can remain in the chrysalis for as long as it naturally takes, from a month to a year, before it emerges as a butterfly. Provide a good source of nectar, and the butterflies will come!

Common branded Skippers are at home in the western mountains. One of their favorite restaurants is scabiosa.

A Swallowtail butterfly feeds on this delicious phlox.

Sedum
(SEE-dum)
STONECROP

SHAPE	Low ground cover
HEIGHT	Low-growing, six inches
WIDTH	Up to fifteen inches
BLOOM TIME	Summer through fall
COLORS	Bronze, variegated, and green foliage
SITE	Well-drained alkaline soils
LIGHT	Full or part sun
HARDINESS	Zones 3–9
COMMENTS	Suitable for rock gardens

Later in the season, S. 'Vera Jamison' is covered with vibrant rose stars.

Low-growing sedums like this S. 'Variegatum Kamtschaticum' are very popular in Rocky Mountain gardens because they thrive in our alkaline soils and hot sun environments.

S. 'Sunset Cloud' blooms in late summer. Because of its dark color, the unique foliage contrasts nicely as it cascades over rocks.

In late spring, the foliage of S. 'Vera Jamison' forms a perfect small clump for the front edge of the garden.

I'M A TOUGH GUY! You can even call me "the Great Stabilizer," because I hold the soil against rocky areas. If you garden in soil that is lean (meaning there's not a lot of nutrients), sandy (which won't hold water), or clay that won't drain, I'm the perennial that will grow there, or anywhere else for that matter. My leaves are considered succulent because they are thick, and their fleshiness helps store water. This makes me totally drought tolerant, which is even better in the dryness of the West. I also prefer the alkaline soil that is created by the weathering of rocks. Here I grow tighter and sturdier than in enriched garden soil where I may spread faster but will probably flop open later in the season.

Landscaping with the area's natural rocks is an economical and attractive alternative to poured concrete retaining walls and barriers. The rock walls hold the soil, and with the addition of my stabilizing power that spreads nicely but never invasively, we form a solid mat of foliage. I prevent washing or erosion, and the walls become a permanent work of art.

It's now trendy to use me as a roof covering for green roofs. I am superior to using grasses because of my easy, indestructible nature. The green plants lower energy consumption by increasing the insulation of the roof, and the plants filter pollutants. Planting a garden on the roof reduces storm water runoff, creates a wildlife habitat, and is very aesthetically pleasing.

S. 'Dragon's Blood' has rich, bronzed foliage with dark green leaves and red stems. My blooms will dry and persist through fall and winter. An easy way to propagate me is to pull the dry fall-bloom stems from the plant and stick a handful in a pot. Let the pot overwinter, and the following spring, almost like a miracle, I will have grown into a very nice pot of fully grown sedum at no cost.

S. 'Tricolor', another low-growing ground cover, has a band of creamy white around each leaf. Its stems and blooms are pink. Occasionally an all-green rosette will develop with the tricolored leaves. These should be removed; otherwise these vigorous, reverted stems could grow large enough to smother my unique foliage.

S. 'Vera Jamison' has the most elegant foliage of all low growers. It is somewhat taller, with larger leaves.

Two of my best sedums bloom with yellow stars. S. kamtschaticum 'Variegatum' grows in a semievergreen mound of scalloped leaves with creamy edges and blooms with orange centers surrounded by yellow, starlike petals. The other yellow flowered S. ellacombianum, often called Russian stonecrop, is a clean, low-growing spreader. As soon as summer arrives, hundreds of sunny yellow flowers will cover the succulent, triangular foliage.

Sedums are natives of Europe but have naturalized in America and grow well most anywhere we are planted. Our family contains over four hundred species, and about three-fourths of that number are ground-cover types. With our tendency toward drought tolerance, hot, sunny areas are natural places for us to grow, but we also do well in partial shade. We are among the most versatile of perennials.

We are the easiest perennials to start with vegetative cuttings. The odds of being successful in starting sedums are at least 95 percent. Sedums are forgiving of poor soil, lack of water, and even of tiny hands that have never planted before. You can pot my divisions, or it's also easy to take cuttings by using the following steps:

- Dip your sharp razor knife in alcohol before starting. Four-to-six-inch stem cuttings are taken in spring or any time the plant is not flowering.

- Let the cuttings rest in a cool, dry spot for two days so they can harden or form a callus on the end of the stem.

- Remove the bottom leaves and stick the cuttings about an inch into a well-draining medium. Press firmly. Root rot is about the only concern when starting sedums, and it's caused by overwatering.

And there you have it! It's as easy as one, two, and three. We root quickly from cuttings (within seven to ten days), but can be left in the pot longer for a stronger root ball. Do not fertilize until the plant is showing new growth.

This excellent ground cover provides not only a soil holding service but also a finished edge that keeps out weeds and makes the rest of the border look tidy. We are far more attractive and economical than bark. Divisions are a win-win solution.

Our common name is stonecrop, and sometimes we are called "lives-forever." The names are appropriate because only stones need less care and live longer than sedums.

Propagating sedum is done by potting cuttings. Here, starts of 'Vera Jamison' are cut from the mother plant and being stuck directly into a pot.

Here is a rooted 'Vera Jamison' after about six weeks. These cuttings are well rooted and are ready for potting or planting into the garden.

ROOFTOP GARDENS: SEDUM AS A MODEL FOR SUSTAINABILITY

OUR BELOVED EARTH is a magnificent model of sustainability. A simplified example of this is the oxygen cycle that sustains our life. Oxygen is created in plants and used as air for man. We breathe and return the air to the plants, such as sedums. This cycle is an easily understood model of meeting the needs of the present without compromising the needs of future generations. Planting perennials is a model for sustainability. They come up in the spring and bloom. The flower's blooms dry, and seeds are formed. The seeds drop and find a place to germinate, coming up in the spring to sustain the cycle. Gardening is a very important act of sustainability, and sedums—with their easy care, drought tolerance, and propagation abilities—are at the top of this act.

Sedums are being used to provide large, ecologically green rooftop gardens that reduce greenhouse gases and emit oxygen. Sedums are living purifiers that can replace the man-made footprint of miles and miles of commercial heat-sink with a natural habitat where wildlife can flock and nest.

Green roofs are changing the skylines. At the University of Wyoming, green roofs act as natural insulation and heat-sink modifiers in Laramie's high elevation and hot-sun environment.

The tri-leveled Student Union Building at the University of Idaho, as well as golf courses and hospitals all have green roofs. Even a public restroom at the Ruth Rowell Modie Wildlife Park in northern Idaho has a roof covered with sedums. They list the advantages of this green roof as storm water management, reduced heating and cooling, plus a longer roof life due to protection against damaging UV radiation. Below is listed the plants growing on the Modie Park restroom roof garden. All are drought-resistant sedums, which need only a computer-controlled irrigation system to help establish the plants after monthly rainfall.

RESTROOM ROOF

Visitors to the Ruth Rowell Modie Park are very curious about plants growing on the roof of the restroom.

The sustainable sedums planted on the rooftop provide storm water management, reduce energy costs, and curb the heat island effect—plus they extend the life of the roof.

MODIE PLANT LIST

S. spurium, 'Tricolor'
S. spurium, 'Dragon's Blood'
S. kamtschaticum, 'Variegatum'
S. rupestre
S. spurium, 'Fuldaglut'
S. spathulifolium, 'Carnea'
Sempervivum tectorum, 'Red Beauty'

In Montana, thousands of these sedums are grown on a small farm in Montana's Bitterroot Valley. The grower says that the minimum organic material that sedums produce makes them very maintence-free, so there is rarely a need for deadheading or cutting back. Often it can be a nuisance to climb up on a roof to garden, so these factors help make these successful for roof gardens.

The Denver Colorado Botanical Gardens have two green roofs, one in the York Street Gardens and the other in the Children's Garden. These roof gardens are used as a testing ground to determine sustainability, suitability, and performance of plants for green roofs in a semi-arid climate. The Botanical Gardens showcase over one hundred species of native and drought-tolerant plants that benefit both energy efficiency of the buildings and aesthetic amenities for the college and its students.

In Utah, The Church of Jesus Christ of Latter-day Saints has built one of the world's largest rooftop gardens. The gardens are not totally flat like many of the other roof gardens. They are designed to mimic the magnificent Wasatch Front Mountains that can be viewed east of the Conference Center. There are huge terraces and immense exterior stairs leading up to the rooftop meadow garden. All of these are landscaped with a variety of native perennials, shrubs, and trees. As the walkways lead a viewer up to the top, it feels like hiking up the mountains through groves of fragrant pines.

NOTE

Roof gardens have a long history. From the ancient hanging gardens of Babylon to the roof gardens found in the volcanic remains of Roman Pompeii, we realize roof gardens were a part of life. Thatched roofs were used later on European homes, and early American immigrants built sod roofs to protect themselves from the elements. Madison Square's name is because of its roof garden. When a gardener runs out of space, they can move to the roof.

The environmentally friendly, air-cleaning, five-acre alpine meadow rooftop gardens on the LDS Conference Center in Salt Lake City, Utah, won the 2003 Green Roofs for Healthy Cities Award of Excellence in the New Combination category.

COLD-HARDY PERENNIALS SUMMARY

GARDENING IN COLD areas is different and challenging. Choosing hardy perennials that will winter well in these regions is necessary. The following lists are perennials that have a reputation for being cold hardy. However, regional differences, including microclimates, must be accounted for. Any new gardener would be wise to find an experienced gardener in their area for mentoring; besides, gardeners are noted for sharing not only information but also plants and friendship.

The following lists are all zoned low; they're Zone 3, meaning perennials hardy to -40°F, and Zone 4, meaning perennials will survive winter to -30°F.

The cold-hardy perennials list, with their seasons, heights, and plants for sun or shade, gives a huge selection that will satisfy even the most discriminate gardener. Perennials showing up on both a tall and short list grow in different sizes. Within each perennial group, there will be a wide variety of flowers in that family to choose from. For example, Shasta daisies are tall, medium, and short.

You might see far different plants if you traveled the United States for a garden tour on the East and West Coasts, which receive tons of rain. However, all of these cold-hardy perennials like snow and will survive anywhere in the Zone 3 and 4 areas of the northern United States. They thrive up to Montana's northern border, and grow well across the Dakotas. These perennials really produce in the rich farmlands of Iowa's rolling hills and Nebraska's heartlands. Cold-hardy perennials even perform in the barren, oil-soaked, crater-shaped soils of Wyoming as it gradually lifts to join the Rocky Mountains.

Every property has climate limitations. In the West, our wild elevations, crazy temperatures, or erratic snow cover can be discouraging. When gardeners finds themselves sighing and wishing over a beautiful garden on a magazine cover, remember those perfect photos do not show the perennials that were tried and died. To stop the tried-and-died syndrome and change it to tried-and-survived, follow the suggestions in *Powerful Perennials* for creating a comfort zone for your perennials. Even more important is to get acquainted, and like old gardening friends, your perennials will be around for a long, long time.

NOTES

1. Jim Nau, *Ball Perennial Manual: Propagation and Production* (Chicago: Chicago Review Press, 1996).

SPRING-TO-SUMMER-BLOOMING PERENNIALS

SHORT–MEDIUM	MEDIUM–TALL
Alchemilla, lady's mantle	*Allium*
Anemone	*Aquilegia*, columbine
Arabis, rock cress	*Campanula*, bellflower
Artemisia, wormwood	*Centaurea*, mountain bluet
Aubrieta, rock cress	*Dicentra*, bleeding heart
Aurinia, basket-of-gold	*Iris*
Bellis, English daisy	*Papaver*, poppy
Bergenia	*Polemonium*, Jacob's ladder
Brunnera	*Penstemon*, beardtongue
Campanula, bellflower	*Salvia*, sage
Chives	*Tanacetum*, painted daisy
Dianthus, pinks	*Thalictrum*, meadow rue
Doronicum, leopard's bane	*Tradescantia*, spiderwort
Euphorbia, spurge	*Trollius*, globeflower
Galium, sweet woodruff	*Veronica*
Geranium, cranesbill	
Helleborus Lenton Rose	
Lamium, dead nettle	
Lewisia, bitterroot	
Lychnis, campion	
Myosotis, forget-me-not	
Papaver, poppy	
Phlox, creeping	
Primula, primrose	
Pulmonaria, lungwort	
Saponaria, soapwort	
Veronica	

SUMMER-TO-FALL-BLOOMING PERENNIALS

SHORT–MEDIUM

Artemisia, wormwood
Campanula, bellflower
Centaurea, mountain bluet
Cerastium, snow-in-summer
Coreopsis, tickseed
Dianthus, pinks
Ferns
Gaillardia, blanket flower
Grasses
Gypsophila, baby's breath
Hemerocallis, daylily
Heuchera, coral bells
Hosta
Lamiastrum
Lychnis, campion
Lysimachia, loosestrife
Monarda, bee balm
Nepeta, catmint
Oenothera, evening primrose
Penstemon, beartongue
Platycodon, balloon flower
Polemonium, Jacob's ladder
Potentilla, cinquefoil
Rudbeckia, black-eyed Susan
Salvia, Sage
Tiarella, foamflower
Thymus
Veronica

MEDIUM–TALL

Achillea, yarrow
Aconitum, wolfsbane
Anthemis, golden marguerite
Aruncus, goat's beard
Asclepias, butterfly weed
Malva, mallow
Nepeta, catmint
Penstemon, beardtongue
Phlox, tall garden phlox
Physostegia, obedient plant
Platycodon, balloon flower
Rudbeckia, black-eyed Susan
Scabiosa, pincushion
Yucca, Adam's needle
Veronica

FALL-BLOOMING PERENNIALS

SHORT–MEDIUM

Aster
Coreopsis, tickseed
Gaillardia, blanket flower
Gentiana
Sedum, stonecrop
Solidago, goldenrod
Veronica

MEDIUM–TALL

Aconitum, wolfsbane
Alcea, hollyhock
Aster
Helenium, Helen's flower
Hibiscus, rose mallow
Nepeta, catmint
Perovskia, Russian sage
Phlox, garden
Physostegia, obedient plant
Sedum, stonecrop
Veronica

POUNDING HEAT

Pounding heat
Won't let you work—
Won't let you sleep!

Cool canyons call
With welcome relief,
But it's really the mountains
Causing the grief.

Clouds lift over walls,
But no rain falls—
Giving air so arid
And sun so intense

Only a gardener
With more hope than sense
Would try to garden
A desert immense.

DROUGHT-TOLERANT PERENNIALS

THERE'S NO ONE better prepared to talk about drought-tolerant perennials than those of us in the West, but these principles will apply to any dry garden. Sitting atop the Continental Divide issues the ultimate challenge to western gardeners, but we grab our shovels and respond with determination and plant tough, drought-tolerant powerful perennials. We have learned to live with the land. Gardeners who experience drought in any location can learn from the techniques used by those of us who garden in the Rocky Mountains.

The Continental Divide, which follows the crest of the Rocky Mountains, reaches its highest point at Pikes Peak at about fourteen thousand feet and then drops steeply, sending its precipitation down to flow to the Pacific Ocean on its western side and to the Gulf of Mexico or the Atlantic Ocean on the eastern slopes. At the base of these slopes lies an expansive desert, waiting in vain for some Continental Divide moisture runoff. It doesn't happen! The Rocky Mountain region is surrounded by deserts!

The Great Basin Desert, on the west side of the Rocky Mountain chain, is an arid expanse of about 190,000 square miles and is the largest desert in the United States. A pattern called *the rain shadow effect* has been a player in creating this desert region. When moisture-laden prevailing winds are blocked by the high Sierra Nevada and Cascade mountain ranges, the moisture is dropped as the clouds climb to rise up over these mountains, leaving the Rockies with only leftover precipitation.

The Colorado Plateau, composed of dry alkaline lake beds and calcium carbonate dunes, lies along the eastern edge of the Rocky Mountains. High desert climates are harsh environments. Both deserts are known as cold winter deserts due to both the northern latitude and the low precipitation.

This is a harsh environment for growing gardens, but knowledge helps make everything more workable.

A quick look at the climate growing conditions of the experimental states shows why the enduring powerful perennials are needed in problematic areas. Gardeners who succeed are the ones who pay close attention to the climate and solve the puzzle of what will thrive in their environment before planting.

COLORADO'S GROWING CLIMATE

Colorado is always on the edge of a drought. Important to Colorado gardeners in the plains section of the state is a fortunate seasonal cycle, where 70 to 80 percent of the annual rainfall occurs during the April through September growing season. Near the foothills, where the majority of the population lives, gardeners are subject to winds and thunderstorm activity. Colorado's climate is relatively uniform across the state and is characterized by low relative humidity, abundant sunshine, infrequent rain and snow, and the addition of a large seasonal range in temperature. The temperature often climbs into the nineties, but the low humidity keeps even warm summer days reasonably comfortable. Winter temperatures are milder, requiring gardeners to only have to wear light jackets. Many years, the precipitation ranges from twelve to eighteen inches, but multiyear droughts are common. All of this presents a good reason for using drought-tolerant perennials.

IDAHO'S GROWING CLIMATE

Idaho has a very short growing season. Idaho lies entirely west of the Continental Divide, and, to a large extent, the source of its precipitation is the Pacific Ocean. Because of the diversity of Idaho's terrain, climatic conditions vary with elevation. Eighty percent of the time, the weather is sunny. Idaho has one golden day after another—a gardener's dream! Precipitation is around twelve to thirteen inches without snowfall. Irrigation and water supplies are nearly always plentiful, but Idaho adheres to a strict policy of protecting and keeping their water in Idaho.

In summer, periods of extreme heat extending beyond a week are rare, and the same can be said for low temperatures. However, in the higher mountain valleys, no month is without nighttime freezing temperatures. Even the hardiest, most drought-tolerant and cold-hardy perennials might struggle in Idaho's higher elevations.

MONTANA'S GROWING CLIMATE

Montana has two very different growing climates plus a very short growing season. Montana is the fourth largest state in the union, and climate variations are as widespread as the state is large. The Continental Divide traverses the western half of the state, so precipitation flows both west and south. West of the Divide, the climate is not unlike a that of the North Pacific Coast, with milder winters, cooler summers, and lighter winds. The eastern half of Montana holds the record for the some of the coldest temperatures in the United States, and this part of the state suffers from the rain shadow effect. Fortunately, most of the state has July temperatures around a steady 74°F that permits rapid plant development during the growing season. Precipitation varies depending on topographic influences. The lowest water average is 6.59 inches along the Clark Fork of the Yellowstone River and the highest is an average 34.70 percent at Heron on the northeastern border.

Gardeners appreciate that water supplies are available and drought in its severe form is practically unknown.

UTAH'S GROWING CLIMATE

Utah has adequate water only along the northern Wasatch Front and the Uinta northeastern Mountain ranges. Most of Utah is mountainous with crest lines above ten thousand feet. Gardeners must protect themselves with sunscreen and hats. The lowest area is Southern Utah and St. George, which is a winter retreat for "snowbirds" who prefer winter temperatures in the 50°F or 60°F ranges. Southern Utah is well known for its sunny days, averaging over three hundred annually. In St. George, gardens wait for rain and so do gardeners.

Utah is the one of the driest states in the US. Utah and Nevada both experience drought due to the rain shadow effect of the Sierra Nevadas. Precipitation varies greatly from less than five inches annually over the Great Salt Lake Desert to the ten to fifteen inches received by the leading agricultural areas. Irrigation is necessary for production.

When the first settlers arrived in Utah, their Mormon leader Brigham Young promised that the desert would blossom as the rose, and it does due to the foresight and irrigation techniques that were put in place early. Bear Lake, a natural lake with a storage reservoir fed by winter snowmelt and precipitation, is a choice example of the wisdom of these early settlers. A 5,902-foot level was legally filed and set as the lowest the lake could be pumped for irrigation and to generate hydroelectricity. Without this legal protection, greed could easily have drained this beautiful spring-fed lake.

WYOMING'S GROWING CLIMATE

Wyoming's constant wind erosion has left the state with poor soil. Wyoming is windy, and wintertime blizzards are common. Motels situated along Wyoming highways are often filled by snowbound motorists during winter months when roads must be closed. Most of the state has been subjected to erosion for thousands of years, and less than 10 percent of Wyoming has desirable soil. The lack of soil and adequate moisture limits even natural vegetation common to the west, like sagebrush and short grasses. The majority of the state is used for grazing and has a general appearance of dryness except in early spring when the landscape turns green. In summer, the grass and flowers have a tendency to turn brown. Most of the irrigated land is located along river systems like the Jackson Hole area. Wyoming has oil, but it is short on water, short on soil, and has lots of wind. What's a gardener to do?

LOW ON WATER, HIGH ON SUN

Every state in the Rocky Mountains has major limitations that make gardening very difficult. Many are too cold, while some are too hot. High elevations make seasons short, and all experience a lack of water. Compare our precipitation with the Pacific West Coast and the East

Coast that receive amounts to over thirty inches a year. Water like that is a gardener's dream.

Western gardens stop growing, stop blooming and almost go dormant in extreme heat because the photosynthesis and respiration cycle of plants cancel each other. Gardeners, in their wisdom, know they must slow the flow of H_2O and plant drought-tolerant perennials in their gardens. These types of plants are a responsible solution to our environment. They grow well in the West's poor soil, with its high alkaline pH and with a minimum of water.

WHAT ARE XERICS, OR DROUGHT-TOLERANT PERENNIALS?

Most perennials are fairly drought resistant once established, but perennials with the following traits are especially hardy.

DEEP ROOTS

Drought-tolerant perennials like *Papavers,* or poppies, have long taproots that reach deep underground into the soil to find moisture. To encourage perennials to grow deep root systems, you should water slowly and allow the water to sink deep. Soaker hoses provide this type of watering. Soil that has been loosened plus the addition of a few rocks or gravel and compost added to the bottom of a deeper-than-usual planting hole will also persuade roots to push down to where both nutrients and water are available. A few other examples of deep-root perennials are alceas, hibiscus, and yucca.

NATIVE PERENNIALS

Perennials native or naturalized to the Rocky Mountains are adapted to harsh climates, infertile alkaline clay soils, and intense sunlight, and they shrug off pests and wildlife. Not only do native plants have lower water needs, but they are also long lived, wind resistant, and are sustainably tough. *Guillardias,* or blanket flowers, are examples of native perennials so well adapted they are nearly as resilient as weeds!

Native grasses similar to those that covered the West are another example of perennials with drought abilities. Grasses easily survive long, dry summers and tolerate a wide range of soils. Grasses also prevent erosion and add an upright texture with graceful drama to a garden full of rounded shapes.

WATER-HOLDING FOLIAGE

Two examples of perennials that store water in their leaves are *Sempervivums,* or hens and chicks, and sedums. These plants have thick, succulent leaves with the ability to store moisture inside their foliage.

Waxy coated foliage like the dark green leaves of *Oenothera,* or evening primrose, and the swordlike leaves of yucca retain water. The waxy coating helps keep the moisture from evaporating.

Perennials with hairy leaves are protected from drying sun or winds. The soft, hairy foliage of *Salvia,* or meadow sage, and *Aurinia,* or basket-of-gold, gives these perennials drought tolerance.

Perennial foliage in shades of silver, blue, or even gray reflect the sun instead of absorbing it. *Stachys,* or lamb's ears, is very drought hardy and has both silver and hairy foliage. Due to the double drought-tolerant abilities of lamb's ears, too much water will be its death.

Narrow, finely textured, or even prickly-leafed perennials like cactus seem to take care of themselves during drought. Reduced leaf surfaces means less water loss. *Anthemis,* or the marguerite daisy, is an example of a finely textured perennial that is drought resistant. It could almost be called a weed if it wasn't so attractive, but once this flower enters your garden, it remains forever. They are persistent seeders and quickly grow into a three-foot mound that is attractive and covered with tiny white or yellow daisies. The ability to self-seed is another trait of drought-tolerant perennials, and it fits nicely into the self-sustaining survival of the fittest model. Cut it back before it sets seeds to save time. Less seeding, less weeding.

WHAT IS XERISCAPING

Gardening with perennials that require less water is called xeriscaping or water-wise gardening. The following pointers for successful growing of drought-tolerant perennials will explain how easy it is to grow these plants.

TRIMMING AND PRUNING

Xerics require little care. Wait to trim or prune these plants, allowing them to self-seed and self-mulch through winter.

ADDING ORGANIC MULCHES

Organic mulches fall into two main categories: rock mulches or compost mulches. A layer of either material will help the soil hold moisture.

ROCK MULCHES

Rocks and gravel are organic mulches that buffer soils against climate extremes. Rocks retain heat, so perennials mulched in this type of coverings will break dormancy earlier in spring and die back later in fall. Pea gravel or rocks are cheaper and provide a tidy, clean look to a garden. They are attractive and resistant to wind. A weed barrier under the rock mulch will help prevent weeds to an extent. Shallow weed seeds may still blow in and find a place to germinate, but they are easily removed from rock mulch over a weed barrier. This type of drought gardening is most often done in commercial parking lots to eliminate time-consuming plantings, high-maintenance care, and the excess use of water. A drip system located by the few perennials planted in this type of garden is a very efficient watering system. The addition of a few well-placed boulders act as focal points in rocked mulched gardens.

COMPOST MULCHES

Dark black soil compost mulches are the ultimate topping for a drought-tolerant garden. These mulches reduce soil temperatures, slow down moisture loss, control weeds and are a perfect spot for kids to play with their toy trucks.

Compost mulches are also very valuable in winter. Adding mulches in fall after the ground freezes helps prevent early freeze and thaw damage to perennials and the drying of soils. In winters without snow cover, should the temperatures reach 40°F, it would be wise to water monthly. Once-a-month watering is adequate, because overwatering in winter will add stress to weakened plants.

Compost mulches make flower gardens look superb with their dark soil as a background for perennials. Compost mulches do more than just make the flower beds look stunning. They also improve water drainage while still providing adequate water-holding capacity and nutritional balance to the soil. The poor soils of the Rocky Mountains can be changed to excellent soils by the addition of compost mulches.

FERTILIZING

The fertilizing of a drought-tolerant garden should be all but nonexistent. Xeric perennials that are fertilized will grow excessively lush foliage, which defeats the real purpose of this type of gardening, which is low-maintenance care. Drought-tolerant plants do better when they are allowed to do their own thing, but should they show signs of decline, then by all means fertilize and give some additional water.

FOLLOW WATERING RESTRICTIONS MANDATED BY THE COMMUNITY

Newly planted perennials, even those with a drought-tolerant reputation, will require two years of regular watering to get established. If the plants in your garden cannot take the drought, move or replace them with more water-wise types. Most gardens have a shady spot or an area that receives extra water, so stressed perennials can be moved. Any plant that is not doing well should be first cut back. If this doesn't help the plant, then move it to a more friendly location.

With water restrictions, forfeit the growing of annuals. Annuals require too much of everything: time, labor, fertilizer, and water. Any container pots should be huge so deep soaking can be done. The most efficient containers are cement retaining walls with a dripper-type soaker watering system installed to conserve not only the life of the plant but also time and money. Perennials are an excellent alternative to annuals in containers due to their drought-tolerant tendencies.

Sprinkling gardens with a hose in the middle of the afternoon wastes water and will only tighten a community's water restrictions. Water at night, slowly, letting the water soak deeply into the ground. This type of watering is beneficial for the plants as well as the water system. Be sure to follow any watering restrictions put into place by your community.

MODEL OF A NATIVE AND DROUGHT-TOLERANT LANDSCAPE

If you are baffled by the idea of a drought-tolerant garden, don't worry. They are livable and enjoyable gardens, despite the fact that they don't look quite like the lush Eastern gardens you may be used to seeing in magazines.

Jewel and Howard live in a multileveled villa that is nestled within a lush and stunning garden designed with drought-tolerant native plants. Jewel's garden's best feature is its carefree atmosphere. Energy seems to radiate from the plants in this garden, probably because they love where they are planted. Jewel and Howard installed a partial sprinkler system that waters the garden when they are away traveling. When native plants like silver-foilaged sagebrush, greasewood, and rabbit brush crowd the fence line at the border of the property, they are sometimes left to blend in to the natural landscape. Sometimes growing up to six feet in height, the natural sagebrush provides a protective border outside of the property line.

The couple's lot is enormous, and instead of using thirsty turf and hardscapes, they chose to incorporate winding sandstone pathways that wander through and around the entire property. Jewel expects any day to meet a deer along the trails. The paths are lined with native and drought-tolerant perennials, especially *Perovskia*, or Russian sage, for all-summer-long color and fragrance. Here and there, silver *Artemisia* 'Silver Mound' is tucked along the edges as well as *Aquilegia*, or columbine, and pink *Saponaria*, or soapwort, for springtime color.

A huge, five-foot-tall built-up berm lines the northern boundary between Jewel's property and the road to the beach. This berm is filled with a variety of perennials that bloom spring through frost. The color parade starts with the early-blooming *Papavers orientale*, or poppies, and *Aquilegia*, or columbines. Then the *Nepeta* 'Walker's Low' fills spots everywhere with its light blue, lacy flowers that, with one deadheading, will bloom until fall. Burgundy gaillardia mixes freely with the nepeta and the small *Gaillardia* 'Arizona Sun', blanket flower. Red or apricot edges everything. *Achillea* 'Coronation Gold' and 'Moonshine' have bright yellow and gold long-blooming flowers that show off among the sage and blues of the nepeta and its cousin *Achillea* 'Summer Berries'. The berm is Jewel's favorite part of the garden.

Genista 'Lydia', broom, is a Zone 4, two- to three-foot-tall mounding shrub covered with bright yellow pea blossoms. The Bear Lake natural sandstone paver patio, where the family enjoys grilling, has an overhead pergola covered with native Silver Lace vine that shades and protects an outdoor kitchen. A raised, walled flower bed on the east side of the patio is filled with a variety of short perennials, such as *Oenothera*, or evening primrose, that is a delight to watch open at dusk. Short *Gaillardia*, or the blanket flower, is allowed to reseed from year to year, so this spot is packed with an amazing display of hot colors. A relatively unknown perennial, *Genista*, or broom, a lacy-leafed, drought-tolerant, bright yellow blooming shrub encloses the ends of the patio. It can handsomely reach heights and widths of five feet. Some information hints that it is not hardy in the Rocky Mountains, but it certainly is!

The front fence line that looks toward the lake slopes downhill. At the top of the hill, spring-blooming long-tap-rooted, *Euphorbia polychroma*, or spurge, have grown to a perfect four-foot mound, a size that doesn't happen in other gardens. The spurge is attractive

all year, with almost eye-blinding bright yellow blooms in spring and then burgundy foliage in fall. It is surrounded with *Nepeta* 'Walker's Low', a soft-blue, tiny-foliaged, long-blooming perennial that is very drought tolerant. Below this massive planting are hundreds of *Alcea*, or hollyhock, plants that have been started from seed. Jewel cuts the hollyhock's spent blooms, still on the stock, in the fall and lays them along the fence line to reseed yearly. Now the fence is always covered from midsummer to fall with the tall, handsome, colorful blooms of these easy-care plants.

The end result of Jewel and Howard's landscaping is a multiuse garden that takes care of itself and uses almost zero water. They have created a garden that is a place of beauty, color, peace, and wildlife. The most important part of this garden to the couple is that they wanted a garden that resembled the naturalness of the mountains where they live, and they accomplished their goal beautifully!

Gardeners can feel uncomfortable when changing their tried-and-true successful gardens that they have grown for years into a drought-tolerant garden, but the water situation in the West is demanding that we pay attention. The first step in giving a gardener confidence to try a new type of gardening is awareness of what gives a perennial its drought tendencies. Notice if perennials have deep taproots, are natives with water-holding foliage, have a waxy coating on their leaves, or have small and finely textured foliage. All of these traits are an indicator that a perennial is drought tolerant.

Know also that drought gardening is simplified, having a crisper, cleaner, uncluttered look. Mulch is mandatory in this type of garden because of its moisture-holding abilities. Realize that drought gardens require low maintenance with minimal pruning, deadheading, or fertilizing. Now look further into this chapter of *Powerful Perennials*, and get acquainted with the water-wise perennials you can use in your own garden.

TIPS TO SLOW THE FLOW OF H_2O

- Plant drought-tolerant perennials.

- Take advantage of community resources. Most communities offer a free irrigation audit or a sprinkler system tune-up. This will help keep your lawn green and save money.

- Adjust your watering schedule to the season. July is usually the hottest month, but September cools down, and watering needs to be cut back.

- Turn off sprinklers during a rain storm.

- Repair water taps that drip. Add in a quick water turnoff between the end of the hose and the sprayer so water can be stopped before you reach the tap.

- Watch for rebates, which are often offered to water users.

- Use online resources to understand more about real-time watering or for a watering guide.

Artemisia
(ar-te-meez-ee-uh)
'SILVER MOUND' AND 'SILVER BROCADE'

SHAPE	Small shrub, filler flower
HEIGHT	Short dome, six to eight inches
WIDTH	Up to fifteen inches
BLOOM TIME	Insignificant flowers
COLORS	Silver, silky foliage
SITE	Hot sun, drought tolerant
LIGHT	Full sun
HARDINESS	Zones 3–8
COMMENTS	Too much fertilizer or water will cause dieback

The unique foliage of A. 'Silver Mound' is a soft silvery mound.

A. 'Silver Mound' is so soft and silky that it begs a gardener to touch or pat the mound.

The foliage of A. 'Silver Brocade' has brocade-shaped petals and grows more flat to the ground.

A. 'Silver Brocade' is an eye-catching addition to the front of any perennial garden.

MY FULL NAME is *Artemisia schmidtiana* 'Silver Mound'. My cousin and close buddy is 'Silver Brocade', or wormwood. We are so much alike with our outstanding silver foliage, small size, and easy dispositions that it's obvious we are related. The masses of tiny hairs covering our leaf surface reflect sunlight and give us our silvery sheen.

Our origins are similar to the native sagebrush that carpets the Rocky Mountains. Rich soil or overwatering will cause us to blacken, get floppy, get lanky, and require deadheading, It can also cause dieback.

Our flowers are even similar to sagebrush in the sense that they are very nondescript, in a washed-out, almost white, pale yellow. Most gardeners snip our blooms off because they look like weeds seeds. This isn't a put-down. We have no need for flowers.

One important tip most gardeners don't know about our flowers and foliage is that they have a clean, fresh fragrance. The smell is light and subtle, like the mountains after a summer rainstorm, but if our clipped-off panicle-type blooms are dried and added to potpourri, not only do they add touches of silver "bling" to the decorative mix but they help keep a room smelling fresh. Our leaves, placed in sachets, are often used as a deterrent to bugs and spiders in a room and will repel clothes moths when hung in a closet. The smell of our leaves has evolved as a defense mechanism that will keep insects, animals, and even deer and pets away, and has given us freedom from pests.

Artemesias are often classified as herbs and are referred to as the medicinal tonic called mugwort, which is used in antimicrobial remedies that soothe the intestinal tract and liver.

'Silver Brocade' and I also have differences: I'm very soft and feathery due to having lots of small silvery drought-tolerant leaves. Touching my leaves is like touching a velvety-soft stuffed toy animal. 'Silver Brocade' on the other hand has flat, rounded-lobe-type petals that feel like felt and resemble the pattern of an expensive brocade fabric.

It's this flatness of 'Silver Brocade' that gives it so many different ways to be used in flower beds. With its unique foliage, 'Silver Brocade' is a striking accent in a perennial garden. By forming an oval planting area resembling an expensive, silver picture frame, silver brocade can turn an overly busy perennial flower bed into a structured work of art.

As a 'Silver Mound', I'm especially useful when planted as a break between groups of perennials and will tie together diverse colors. Also, I'm a natural in a rock garden where the good drainage of the rocky soil will ensure my longevity. Planters or decorative containers give me a designer feel. My ability to cascade over the edges adds an eye-catching touch.

We are stunning with every other flower color in the garden and are easy additions to containers. We can survive even the coldest winter temperatures , which makes us excellent candidates for container gardening with perennials.

Division to propagate more of my special foliage is simple. Dig my entire fibrous root clump in early spring. Pull the root ball apart, being sure to maintain a stem for each root. Plant my starts, and be prepared to be delighted when practically every one of my divisions take hold and grows.

We are easy to mix with companion plants because of our with our neutral silver colors. Any companion planting needs to address our same growing requirements. You can plant me with salvias for spring and blue veronicas for late summer. I'm a perennial that is unseasonal. I'm attractive the entire year, especially when I get a haircut before July. Gather my stems and trim them off with scissors.

Other members of my clan that are taller and larger also add silvery contrasts to all the greens of the garden. These perennials are well suited to native or naturalized types of gardens, for they are tidier substitutes for sagebrush. A number of the larger varieties of artemisias spread rapidly or are aggressive, so limit your garden to the more well-behaved types.

SAGEBRUSH:
ROCKY MOUNTAIN CARPETING

BACK IN THE 1940s, when I was a kid, a traditional family outing that I hold dear in my memory was our annual pine nut harvest. Aunts, uncles, and cousins would gather to go on a late-fall escapade into the mountains to gather the nuts. These excursions occurred during late October, when the West was enjoying its favorite season of the year, a long Indian summer. On the long drive into the unpopulated mountains, where the pinion trees grew, I asked my dad why every square inch of the mountains was covered with ugly sagebrush. He glanced my way and explained that sagebrush was a North American native that liked our mountains so much that it spread quickly, covering all uncultivated areas. I shook my head with the arrogance of youth and demanded, "We should get rid of it. It's just so ugly!"

I assumed that because of the scruffy appearance of the sagebrush it should be removed from the mountains. Now I am much wiser and more observant as to how important sagebrush is to our environment. To know sagebrush is to love it.

Perennial sagebrush systems occur throughout the western states and are the dominant plant, covering miles and miles of our mountainous terrain. Sagebrush is even honored in Nevada by being named the state flower. The perennial shrub's leaves are covered with fine, silvery hairs, an indicator that it is drought hardy. Sagebrush can live well over a hundred years and has carpeted all uncultivated areas of the Rockies. It survives the western climate with a unique two-method system of collecting moisture: a taproot grows deep so it can reach a water table, and a shallow root system spreads out to gather any precipitation that falls. This and sagebrush's preference for alkaline soils are the primary reasons that it is so at home in the West.

In addition to the fact that it protects the soil from erosion and shelters native perennial grasses that are less prone to wildfire than invasive plants like cheatgrass, sagebrush has other great features: 40 percent of the chemical makeup of sagebrush is camphor oil, which is used in salves to ease joint pain and muscle aches. Adding camphor to lotions is not only an antiseptic but will also ease itching and irritation. Other volatile oils like turpentine make sagebrush toxic to internal parasites, so a mixture was used by early settlers to cure worms. All of the Native American tribes used sagebrush as an herbal medicine. For example, the Navajo used the vapors of sagebrush to cure headaches, and they powdered the leaves to use on rashes like diaper rash or cracks on the feet. The Cahuilla tribes would gather sagebrush seed and grind it to make flour. The Okanagan and Colville tribes used sagebrush to smoke their animal hides. Among the Zuni people, an infusion of the leaves was used externally for body aches and to cure colds. They placed ground sage between their toes to treat athlete's foot and as a foot deodorant. It seems that sagebrush was used from head to toe as a remedy for whatever it was needed for.

GREASEWOOD AND RABBITBRUSH

Sagebrush doesn't restore easily, but other look-alikes do. Greasewood and rabbit brush are often mistakenly called sagebrush. Both of these native perennials grow in the same environment with only a few differences. Greasewood's rigid stems terminate in cone-like spines and are green rather than silver. The root system of greasewood reaches down as far as fifty feet seeking groundwater, keeping its foliage lush-looking even in a severe drought. Greasewood prefers the lower elevation valleys and saline soils. Leaves that have fallen from greasewood have a salty taste. A stand of greasewood on the mountains will signal to an observer that the site has both salt and moisture. Unlike sagebrush, after a fire or scarring occurs, greasewood covers the site quickly. Seeds, cuttings, transplants, or even sprouts from the burned-over roots will grow and repopulate an area, acting as a major aid in controlling erosion.

Rabbitbrush is a fast-growing shrub that also helps heal the mountains after a fire, scarring, or the overgrazing of livestock. The shrub establishes quickly in similar ways to greasewood and will help prevent soil erosion until the slower-growing sagebrush can get reestablished and take over. Rabbitbrush is much more attractive than sagebrush and greasewood because of the energetic lime-green color of its foliage. It grows in a rounded form that is covered in a vibrant display of yellow flowers in the fall. This tough native shrub is so handsome that it makes an ideal foundation plant for a cultivated, drought-tolerant garden.

These three perennial shrubs need nothing—not fertilizer, deadheading, watering, or planting. They are totally self-sufficient, growing without any intervention from humans. They sustain each other in hard times. They provide food and shelter for wildlife, prevent erosion, and even have healing capabilities. Their roots grow deep, furnishing a type of cultivation to the soil that could never have been achieved in any other way.

The miles and miles of mountain terrain in the West would not be as satisfying if they were barren wasteland. Thankfully, sagebrush, rabbitbrush, and greasewood have provided a protective covering against wind, water, and heat erosion in our mountains.

Centranthus ruber
(sen-TRAN-thus)
RED VALERIAN

SHAPE	Bush, clump with flower filler, plumes
HEIGHT	Twenty inches
WIDTH	Eighteen to twenty-four inches
BLOOM TIME	Peaks in late spring, will bloom later in summer and again in fall
COLORS	Rusty-red, pink-red, white
SITE	Xeriscape and dry, alkaline, or sandy soil
LIGHT	Full sun
HARDINESS	Zones 3–8
COMMENTS	Reseeds in alkaline soil

Centranthus has a "tumbling tumbleweed" ability to self-seed. The garden is so colorful and lush looking that it is hard to believe it's also drought tolerant and long blooming.

A single start of centranthus left to set seed was all it took to fill this entire flower bed full of fine-looking, rosy-pink lacy colors set off with attractive blue-green lance-shaped leaves.

By shearing centranthus before it sets seed, the perennial will rebloom in July and again in September. This makes it a faultless plant even for a front-door garden.

The rosy-colored, lacy beauty of *C. ruber* adds an appealing open texture to any perennial garden.

I'M SO VERY, very pretty with my airy, rosy, star-shaped florets that I was even nicknamed Pretty Betsy. I've been tagged with so many nicknames that if my real or botanical name is unknown, confusion can occur. I'm called kiss-me-quick, scarlet lightning, Russian lilac, keys of heaven, bouncing Bess or delicate Bess, and Jupiter's beard for my dangling seed heads. A few of my names have a touch of the botanical, such as valerian, Greek valerian, spur valerian, Spanish valerian, pink valerian, and red valerian—the darkest red of any of the other varieties. I'm called valerian because I contain rich quantities of the herb valerian, which is used as a drug for managing anxiety, restlessness, insomnia, and emotional distress.

Centranthus came from the Greek word *kentron*, meaning "spur" and the word *anthos*, meaning "flower." Each of my tiny flowers has a spur, making me a favorite for butterflies to sip from, so *Centranthus* is an accurate description.

I'm one of the easiest and longest-blooming perennials to grow in cool summers and poor, even salty alkaline soil. I start to bloom heavily in late spring. By the end of June, I will need my fuzzy seed heads, which resemble dandelion seeds, cut back or deadheaded. By midsummer, I'll put on another flush of color that will need shearing by the end of August so that I will be able to bloom into fall. It is this repeat shearing that keeps my flowers flourishing.

My blossoms are massed so intensely that I remind gardeners of a red tumbleweed. I cover myself so completely with flowers that blooming and then blooming again can almost wear me out. When shearing me after my first blossoming, leave a few seed stems intact for propagation purposes. I'm not a long-lived perennial, and I often die after three years. Many gardeners mistakenly think I have been winter-killed, but really I've bloomed myself to death. All my seeds need are a winter's vernalization and Mother Nature's nurturing.

Seed-propagated starts may not be the same color as I am, but they are easy to weed out if a color does not appeal to a gardener. Dividing or moving established plants is the least efficient method of propagating me. My mortality rate when I'm dug and moved is extremely high. It is often easier and more dependable to just allow me to set seed.

I thrive so amazingly well in the poor, drier alkaline soils of the West that I'm sometimes called weedy. In the western environment, with its intense sun, I grow more compact and colorful, and I bloom longer. I don't even require fertilization. In fact, too much organic matter is a death sentence for me. What other perennial can be called invasive because they have a penchant for the difficult growing environment of rock gardens or salty soils? Gardeners need to know the value of deadheading so my reseeding doesn't become a problem for their gardens.

My lacy, see-through flowers make me an excellent midborder perennial. The slight variegation in my flower color makes me adaptable when mixing with other colors in the garden so I never clash with other plants. A white version of me, called *C. alba*, is shorter than I am but is extremely attractive.

My flowers have a fragrance that is appealing to some and a turnoff to others. They smell like musky perspiration. My waxy, fleshy leaves are a soft blue-green and are an oval–lance shape that maintains their good looks all summer. Everything about me adds beautifully to a garden. I'm easy to grow, and I don't require a lot of care. I have no pest problems. My water requirement is low. I bloom all summer in very unique colors. I grow in rocks where other perennials would refuse to grow.

LACY PERENNIALS: ADDING AN AIRY TEXTURE TO THE GARDEN

PERENNIALS WITH LACY flowers like *Centranthus ruber* are considered water-wise perennials because the smaller petal surface loses less water through evaporation. Incorporating lacy flowering plants into a drought-tolerant garden adds an element of beauty and a more airy and interesting texture.

The flower cycle of bud, bloom, and fade is fleeting, so foliage is just as important as the flowers. Considering foliage as a permanent landscape element, use lacy or airy foliaged perennials that conserve water in a water-wise garden. The following group of drought-tolerant perennials has the small lacy flowers and foliage that open up a garden with texture while allowing you to view what is growing behind them. The following plants are deer resistant and are ideally suited to the difficult Rocky Mountain growing environment.

ACHILLEA 'MOONSHINE'

'Moonshine' is a mainstay in the garden, blooming from June through September, and it always looks pristine. 'Moonshine' has flat-topped, bright lemon-colored flower clusters that form an upright fifteen-by-fifteen-inch clump that does not reseed.

ANTHEMIS 'CHARM'

'Charm' is a fresh, green, feathery-foliaged perennial that charmingly opens up the front edges of any flower bed. The clump forms a full fifteen-by-fifteen-inch plant. Susceptible to winterkill in cooler areas.

ASTER 'ALERT' AND A. 'WOODS'

The dark-green richness of both of these tiny-leafed dwarf perennials is open and lacy. The deep-fuchsia flowers of 'Alert' appear with the first cooling temperatures of September.

'Woods' asters bloom later and have a smaller, denser clump.

NEPETA 'KIT KAT'

The airy loveliness of its tubular-lipped flowers and knee-high, open, upright stems adds dimension, softness, and aroma to any garden site. 'Kit Kat' is a long-lived, long-blooming workhorse that can be sheared as a short shrub and does not self-seed.

COREOPSIS, THREADLEAF

Threadleaf is a small, finely foliaged perennial that opens up a garden with its lacy contrast. Threadleaf may be slow to break dormancy in spring but makes up for this by smothering itself with yellow, half-inch-sized daisies in the fall. Threadleaf is very well behaved and never aggressive, but it may not survive winter well in the higher elevations.

ERIGERON, FLEABANE

Fleabane is a carefree perennial that is native to the Rocky Mountains. The taller fleabanes are upright with small, narrow leaves that lessen as they reach the top, giving a very wispy, open look to the perennial border. Their aster-like flowers cluster at the tops of the stems in shades of blue and lavender and bloom late summer through frost.

FESTUCA IDAHOENSIS, IDAHO BLUE FESCUE

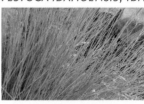

Native Idaho blue fescue is a fifteen-inch-tall, narrow, finely textured, powder-blue grass that adds a see-through appearance to the garden. Idaho blue is a top candidate for planting along an evergreen border, pathway, or container or as an accent plant. This slender, ornamental grass has blue-green flower spikes in summer that mature to tan in fall and persist through winter.

GAURA LINDHEIMERI, WHIRLING BUTTERFLIES

Whirling butterflies grows in a handsome vase shape with airy, arching, flowering stems. Butterfly-like flowers dance along the slender stalks, starting in summer and continuing their dance through fall. Its leafless, three-foot spikes are a unique accent to any garden where a lighter touch is needed. A reddish tinge to the leaves and stems adds another dimension to their beauty.

GENISTA LYDIA, BROOM

The tiny, elegant, oval-shaped leaves on broom give this shrub-like perennial an airy appearance in a garden. Broom will flower in summer and is covered with a profusion of yellow, pea-like blooms. The dark green, waxy, arching branches are strong and extremely attractive all season long, and the only attention required of broom is an occasional light pruning.

GEUM COCCINEUM, AVENS

Wiry stems rising from a basal six-inch mound of strawberry-like foliage furnishes texture to a perennial garden. The stems will be elongated to about twelve inches and bright orange-to-red blooms will explode on the tops in late spring. Avens is a Zone 4 perennial that really likes the intermountain dry soils and cool summers, but it may not winter well in the higher elevations.

GYPSOPHILA REPENS, CREEPING BABY'S BREATH

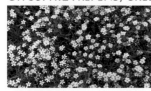

Creeping baby's breaths are petite. They are called either 'Rosea', a pink variety, or 'Alba', which bloom in white. They are both ground covers with fine gray-green foliage that grows six inches in height and spreads, cascading delightfully over walls. Clip off the dried blooms, and creeping baby's breath will reward the garden again and again.

LIMONIUM, STATICE

Statice, often called sea lavender, sends up slender stems massed on the top with lacy, sheer, papery blooms. Statice is a favorite filler for cut and dried flower arrangements. The most beautiful part of statice is the dark-green, leathery foliage that grows as a short, deer-resistant evergreen clump.

LINUM SAPPHIRE, FLAX

Flax blooms for a day and then drops her blue petals to the ground. The next day, the lovely flax will again cover itself with a mass of fresh blooms and will continue this blooming process for several months. Flax naturalizes in the western mountains by self-sowing.

PENSTEMON PINIFOLIUS, PINELEAF PENSTEMON

Native pineleaf penstemon adds an open, lacy look to a garden. In late spring, the unique stems will elongate and be topped with narrow, tubular blooms of a flame-red or orange that cover the entire plant. Pineleaf is a long-blooming perennial and is free of insects or disease problems, as most native plants are. Removing spent flowers will prolong blooming.

PULSATILLA VULGARIS, PASQUEFLOWER

For an all-year, delicate-looking, fernyfoliaged plant that is the first perennial to bloom in spring, pasqueflower is the answer. The word *pasque* means "Easter" in French. Thus, pulsatilla is called pasqueflower or Easter flower because its flower timing coincides with Easter. Pasqueflower blooms are exquisite bells in purple, white, or wine that precede the foliage and will eventually develop into attractive, wispy, ball-shaped seed heads.

SIDALCEA 'PARTY GIRL'

This plant is a thirty-inch-tall perennial with spikes of miniature hollyhock blooms. The narrow stems open in late summer with charming, unusual, one-inch funnels of rosy magenta with tiny white centers. It is a hybrid of native prairie mallow and is just as reliably trouble-free, coming back year after year. It will reseed lightly and make a classic cut flower.

Western gardens do not fit within the traditional perceptions of wet climate landscapes that are ingrained into our senses through literature, paintings, and photography. The dryness of our climate triggers an image of sparseness and empty space. But as the colletion above proves, growing with less water does not mean our gardens are lacking in color or beauty. Most of these plants will not tolerate wet soils, and they thrive in the intenseness of our sunlight and poor soils. Most are native or naturalized perennials that are sustainable through self-seeding. This being said, they are still beautifully lush, colorful, and very, very interesting.

Dianthus
(dye-AN-thus)
'FIREWITCH' AND 'FIRST LOVE'
PINKS

SHAPE	Low creeping mound or clump with flower cups
HEIGHT	Four to fifteen inches
WIDTH	Eight to fifteen inches
BLOOM TIME	Midbloom
COLORS	All shades of red, white, and pink
SITE	Well-drained alkaline soil
LIGHT	Full sun
HARDINESS	Zones 3–8
COMMENTS	Has a sweet, spicy fragrance

D. 'Firewitch' is a short, petite-sized dianthus with a cold Zone 3 hardiness and silvery-blue foliage that stays evergreen in winter.

D. 'Frosty Fire' has big double-frilled blooms in a pure, sensational red. *D.* 'Frosty Fire' is part of the allwoodii family, meaning it has been around for many years and proved its value.

D. 'Eastern Star' has the exotic colors of India. The center is white with a darker red rim that fans out to blend with a rich scarlet.

Add a touch of joy to your garden by adding the frilly, fragrant bicolored blooms of everyone's favorite flowers, *D.* 'First Love'.

YOUR GRANDMOTHER PROBABLY knew me by the name of "Pinks," and I hold a special place in gardeners' lives because I bloom in mid-June, just at the right time for Father's Day celebrations in the garden. My name is dianthus, and I've always been a gardener's favorite. My sweet fragrance, even without my compact dome of solid flowers, is a positive reminder of the love and joy that fathers bring to lives. I'm flawlessly beautiful with my small ideal size massed with brilliant blossoms of magenta, red, white, salmon, and pink in every form. But as the air becomes filled with my warm fragrance, it brings a reminder of happy times in the garden. Cookouts, games, laughter, and outdoor fun are memories attached to me, triggered by my clove-like spicy smell.

My name, *Dianthus*, originates from the Greek terms *dios* and *anthos*, meaning "the divine flower" or "the flower of God," and only God could have created the sweetness of my scent.

I'm also very useful. Traditionally, gardeners like to plant me in a rock garden because of my ability to flourish in a dry, sunny spot. I'm considered an alpine due to my hardiness and size, and I thrive in the limestone-rich soil of a rock garden. Historically, I've always been considered a cottage garden perennial that is very at home in the nostalgia-packed borders or beds of early gardeners. In cottage gardens I was tucked willy-nilly because of my easy disposition, perfume, and petite size.

I'm a favorite to plant along walls or rock pathways. As a border edger, my excellent form and shape, in addition to the masses of pinks and reds with bicolor accents are attractive. But more than that, I will surround a strolling gardener with my lingering aroma, which is a subconscious reminder that summertime joy lives right here in the garden.

I'm also a top-notch container plant. When I'm at peak bloom, no other perennial can compare with the compact intensity of my color. After a quick shearing of my spent blooms, I will sporadically bloom again in summer and fall. My silvery-blue grassy spiked foliage adds an interesting texture to a planter. As an added bonus, I stay evergreen even in colder gardening zones and actually prefer cooler climates.

I'm drought-tolerant, which simplifies caring for container plantings. Of interest is the fact that too much water will turn my foliage yellow, so plant me with other drought perennials like iris and sedum for any easy-care planter.

PROPAGATION OF DIANTHUS

I am not considered a long-lived perennial, so here are a few propagation tips for gardeners as an aid in ensuring my presence in their gardens.

Seeds can be purchased and started inside eight weeks before the last frost date. Plant the young seedlings into the ground as soon as they have two sets of leaves. We don't usually bloom the first year from seed.

I can be dug, pulled apart, and replanted. If the roots seem cemented together by soil, swish them in a bucket of water. Each division needs both roots with foliage attached, but the larger the start, the better we root. This rejuvenates an older nonproductive plant

Tip cuttings sheared from us after we bloom can be stuck into small nursery pots to root and then planted into the garden by fall. With early winters, we need adequate time for tiny fibrous roots to form, so check these before planting.

Layering our stems by pulling the stems over, pinning them to the ground and lightly covering them with soil is an effective way to gain more starts. The starts can remain attached to the mother plant until the next spring if they don't root early enough before winter sets in. A layer of mulch will help insulate the new babies until they are removed for planting.

DIANTHUS FAMILY TREE

There can be some confusion about the different names associated with dianthus A brief outline of the family might save a gardener some time:

- *D. chinensis,* or China pinks, are annuals. The ideal select hybrids perform uniformly and reliably, and telstars are early, vigorous bloomers.
- *D. caryophyllaceae,* or carnations, are grown mostly for the floral trade.
- *D. barbatus,* or sweet Williams, are biennials that need to be allowed to reseed.
- *D. Allwoodii,* or cottage pinks, are early hybrids with intricate blooms.
- *D. gratianopolitanus,* or cheddar pinks, are small, silver tufts with single or double flowers.
- *D. deltoides,* or maiden pinks, are the mat type dianthus for rock gardens.
- *D. plumarius,* or grass pinks, are taller with grassy-green foliage.

FLOWER FRAGRANCE: SMELL GOOD, FEEL GOOD

CATHERINE IS THE sweetest friend in the world. We met about seventeen years ago when she visited me at Secrist Gardens, and it's entirely due to her that I'm so enamored with dianthus. Catherine and her husband, Marcus, were newlyweds and had just bought a little house that they were trying to change into a home. Catherine was so delightfully young and fresh-faced with her rosy cheeks that I was attracted immediately, but I was more intrigued by the possessive way Marcus hung onto her hand than anything else. With a little curiosity I greeted them. Catherine didn't wait for any social discourse but excitedly blurted out, "Do you have any flowers that smell good?"

The question stunned me, and I had to think for a few minutes. Then I picked up the wonderfully fragrant D. 'Firewitch', that was just opening into full bloom and tried to hand it to the young girl. She fumbled as she tried to reach for the plant. It was then I realized that Catherine was blind!

Catherine groped for the plant, then taking a deep breath, she reached and was finally able to locate and grasp the pot into her hands. She lifted the pot to her nose, and I will never forget the look on her face as she smelled the fragrance that only dianthus can provide.

Catherine's beautiful face as she breathed in the spicy-clove smell was miraculous. Marcus's face was too! He grinned and said, "We'll take it!"

From that time, on these two have never missed a spring of visiting me to test a new smell.

Each year, I've tried to make sure there was a new and different fragrant perennial ready to surprise Catherine with. The perennial sweet peas I grew had no scent at all, and neither did the candytuft, even though they were advertised as being fragrant. Many of the newer roses are also scentless. I was forced to rely on the wide variety of hybridized dianthus, but even a few of these are without perfume. Why has this happened? Why are the old-fashioned species of perennials so much more fragrant, and why can't they be found in nurseries?

Consumers are the reason. They want perennials with larger, longer-blooming flowers in more unique colors, and they want them now! Consumers' desires have driven perennial hybridizers into breeding a diminished quality and quantity of fragrant plants.

Gardeners are hurting themselves by not adding more flowers with fragrance to their gardens. A flower's smell originates from glands in their petals. This is how flowers advertise their desire to be pollinated. Without fragrance, what's a plant to do?

Sometimes the plant's foliage is the attractor. The nepetas are members of the mint family, and their foliage has an aromatic mint smell. Artemesia's scented leaves smell clean. Salvias have a sage-like odor in their leaves, while monarda leaves have the orange smell of wild bergamot with a touch of mint. *Malva moschata alba* is fragrant in all of its parts, having a soft musky odor. Mock orange and 'Melissa', or lemon balm, has a citrus fragrance. Like 'Melissa', most herbs have strong-smelling foliage. *Filipendula ulmaria*, queen of the meadow, smells so pleasantly of wintergreen that it was strewn on the floors of the first Queen Elizabeth's rooms. *Perovskia atriplicifolia*, Russian sage, is an aromatic, long-blooming subshrub. Even *Thymus*, mother of thyme, the "walk-on-me" plant, sends up an aromatic cloud when it's walked on. All of these easily available perennials can become the platform for building a more fragrant garden.

Next, add in a few night-blooming perennials to attract night-time moths. These perennials usually bloom white so they show up better to the pollinators. White-blooming hosta is the only hosta that is fragrant. *Oenothera*, evening primrose, opens its trumpets wide at night, as does *Datura*, moonflower, as an invitation. Yucca has hardly any scent during the day, but sniff a creamy-white yucca bloom at night and be surprised at how powerfully it smells like an iris. The fragrance is enhanced in the evening or on a windless day.

Starting with early springtime, think of how happy you feel when a waft of the intense fragrance of hyacinths or sweet violets fills the air. By adding in the blooms of the intoxicating *Convallaria*, lily-of-the-valley; creeping phlox; and *Gallium*, sweet woodruff; another dimension of enjoyment becomes part of the garden, and the pollinators like it too!

Often a plant's fragrance is unpleasant, like the pungent smell of allium, which is so strong it chases deer away. *Dictamnus*, or gas plant's smell is a medicinal, rather offensive odor.

All of the sweet-smelling perennials add to the enjoyment of a garden, but the following listing of a few more fragrant perennials covers fragrance as the flowers bloom throughout the season:

- *Anthemis* 'Charm' has fine, aromatic foliage and blooms all summer. The plant smells like medicinal chamomile.

- *Hemerocallis,* lemon lily, has provided the genetic fragrance for many of the new hybrid daylilies, like 'Prairie Wildfire', which smells superb and has a pale yellow throat that attracts pollinators.

- *Iris* 'Immortality' not only smells delightful, but it is also an everblooming perennial. *I. pallida,* striped iris, smells just like grape KOOL-AID.

- *Lavandula,* lavender, is the ultimate in good clean smells.

- *Lilium* 'Casa Blanca' has an intense fragrance that carries a long way and can be overpowering in a closed area. Plan to cover your nose with golden pollen when you bend to sniff one of them.

- *Papaver alpinum,* alpine poppy, has an unexpected sweet smell.

- Peonies 'Karl Rosenfield' and 'Sarah Bernhart' are older species and are midly fragrant. Newer hybrids with fragrance usually have genes from tree peonies.

- *Phlox paniculata,* tall garden phloxes, are very fragrant—especially the 'David' and 'Laura' varieties.

- Penstemon native species are sweet-scented.

- *Scabiosa australis* is very sweetly scented and has flowers that keep coming all summer.

- Besides being so endearing, dianthus has the very unique fragrance of sweet cloves and spices, so add the above plants along with it, and the pollinators will flock to your garden as well as everyone else. A smell good is a feel good!

An interesting note that's hard to miss when looking over the above fragrant plants is that a high percentage of fragrant perennials are species of the original natives. As gardeners, let's hope that hybridizers find the secret code they seem to have missed and start breeding more smell-good perennials.

Gaillardia aristata
(gay-LAR-dee-a)
'Arizona Apricot', 'Arizona Red Shades', 'Arizona Sun'
INDIAN BLANKET FLOWER

SHAPE	Mound, daisy-shaped flowers
HEIGHT	Some are less than one foot, some are over two feet
WIDTH	Twelve inches
BLOOM TIME	Mid to late summer
COLORS	Yellow, red, gold, orange
SITE	Fast-draining, alkaline soil
LIGHT	Full sun
HARDINESS	Zones 2–10
COMMENTS	Native to the western United States

All three colors of the 'Arizona' series are in this pot and still blooming in mid October.

The height and loose shape of G. 'Burgundy' gives this unique wine-colored perennial a favored spot in a drought-tolerant or wildflower garden.

G. 'Arizona Sun' forms a neat mound of fiery-colored blossoms that will bloom for over four weeks. The seed heads that are left make high-quality bird seed and just may reseed for next year.

G. 'Arizona Apricot' has a softer apricot color palette. The flowers are the largest of the varieties and have an orange center.

AS A NATIVE perennial, I'm right at home in intense sunshine and lean, dry soils. I'll awaken you with all of the dazzling desert colors common in Southwestern textile arts, and that may be the source of my common name blanket flower, also known as *Gaillardia aristata*. My original height was just the right size to intermingle with the prairie and meadow grasses. With my colorful daisy blooms showing a touch above the turf, my red, orange, and yellow will bring these same dazzling hot desert colors to your garden.

My toughness and durability are established qualities, as shown by my Zone 2 hardiness and by my long-blooming and reseeding abilities. I'm one of the few perennials that prefers being started by seed. When a gardener gives me too much water, diseases like root or crown rot can occur. My daisy-like blooms, with their flat landing strips for birds and butterflies, bloom nonstop. This gives plenty of nectar for these garden guests. I'm also a deer- and rabbit-resistant perennial. My foliage may be nondescript in the shadows of my sizzling flower colors, but they are the hairy leaves of a drought-tolerant plant.

However, breeders did not appreciate the way my clumps of stems would bend, giving me a relaxed look, and they set out to breed me. Now I have three main sizes: tall, medium, and short.

TALL *G.* 'BURGUNDY'

The twenty-four-inch-tall G. 'Burgundy' is very popular because of its exceptional color. Wine-red petals surround a hairy center that emerges yellow and matures to a deep burgundy. 'Burgundy' is a Zone 5 perennial.

MEDIUM *G.* 'DAZZLER'

'Dazzler' is a medium-sized, sixteen-inch gaillardia that is primarily grown for its large, showy blooms. These blooms have taken a toll on the perennial's life span. Cutting 'Dazzler' back in September keeps it from blooming itself to death. The flowers are so distinctive that it received the Royal Horticultural Society's Award of Excellence.

Other varieties of medium-sized gaillardia include 'Oranges and Lemons', 'Commotion' series, and 'Fanfare'.

SHORT *GAILLARDIA × GRANDIFLORA* 'KOBOLD' OR 'GOBLIN'

'Kobold' is one of the first short hybrid gaillardias. 'Kobold' was a sensation with its twelve-by-twelve-inch dwarf size covered with scarlet petals and tipped with sunshine yellow. When 'Kobold' was added to the garden, its colors appeared garish, and because it never stayed put and the foliage sprawled, many gardeners refused to plant 'Kobold'. The hybridizing of 'Goblin' changed the hardiness from a Zone 2 plant to a Zone 5 plant.

At last! A drum roll is needed! The close-to-perfection, short G. *aristata*, named the 'Arizona' series, is now available in three different colors.

'ARIZONA' SERIES

'ARIZONA SUN'

'Arizona Sun' blooms profusely from seed the first year and does not require vernalization, meaning it does not need to go through winter temperatures in order to flower. This is important because the 'Arizona' series blooms a month earlier than other gaillardias. The large, three-inch, fiery orange-red blooms have the traditional yellow tips and bloom heavily all summer. The short, compact, petite perennial is smothered with flowers and is indifferent to heat or drought. It won both the prestigious European Fleuroselect Gold Medal Award for 2005, and the All-American Selections Award. Best of all, the 'Arizona Sun' plants are still hardy to Zone 3 temperatures and are deer and rabbit resistant.

'ARIZONA APRICOT'

'Arizona Apricot' is even more vigorous than my 'Arizona Sun' sibling and has a greater abundance of larger flowers and more attractive seed heads. Its foliage is a brighter green and is uniform, staying in a perfect mound the entire season. The elegant coloring of the flowers of 'Arizona Apricot' are showstoppers. The coloring is a subtle blend of deep orange at the center that radiates yellow outward to the tips. The center button is a mixture of both the tangerine and yellow shades, and the total effect is so brightly classy that apricot looks amazing any place it is planted. 'Arizona Apricot' also won the All-American Selections Award.

'ARIZONA RED SHADES'

'Arizona Red Shades' has the same elegant coloring as G. 'Burgundy', but it is so much more useable due to its compact, uniform size and hardiness. 'Arizona Red Shades', like my other siblings, make fine container plants because they bloom from midsummer through fall.

Thank you, hybridizers, for starting the breeding breakthrough in our blanket flower family.

HOT COLORS IN THE GARDEN: USING RED COLORS AS A DESIGN MODEL

GAILLARDIAS ARE DEFINITELY "hotties." Their hot colors of red, orange, and yellow are next to each other on the color chart and are called analogous colors.

A touch of hot colors grouped here and there in the garden is the easiest method of providing some key elements of design; color and contrast plus repetition and balance in a perennial garden.

COLOR

Color is frequently the first priority when gardeners choose perennials for their gardens, and this is how it should be. Planting flowers of favorite colors is satisfying, but it also tells something about the gardener. If you are a passionate gardener, you probably love the color red. Here is the side sketch you have been waiting for.

Choose red as an accent plant only. With the masses of green in the garden, using the opposite color wheel hue of red can feel chaotic. Clump the hot-toned perennials for color spots spring through fall. Their size is a key factor. Clump the tall perennials more to the back, medium perennials in the middle, and short ones along the edges or for filling in the front of the bed. Choose hot-colored perennials that have interesting foliage for most of the season for these accent plantings. Remember that perennials do not grow like lined-up school children. First off, the colors of perennials are very individualized; blues are usually lavender or violet, yellows are overwhelming; and the other colors are usually a tint either lighter or darker than pictured. Trying to design a garden using color may not turn out as visualized. Accent planting or clumping of three, five, or seven or more perennials creates a strong pattern that breaks up rigid rows, which brings us to the next design element.

CONTRAST

Contrast can be an element of color. Warm colors create feelings of excitement and passion, whereas cool colors like blues and violets seem to create peace and calmness. When mixing these for contrast, an awareness that warm colors dominate and cool colors recede into the background will give more cohesiveness along with the contrast.

Using a variety of foliage forms like vertical spikes, vase-shaped plants with strappy leaves, and rounded mounds or spreading perennials in a flower bed are an effective method of achieving contrast. For spring, try clumps of tulips that have the same bloom time and colors of a lilac bush. Tulips are short and lilacs are tall, but the contrast of the foliage and the repetition of the color is extremely effective in a garden. Planting strappy-leafed daylilies mixed with fountain grasses

of the same type of foliage makes the plant's original purpose obsolete by blending the two plants in one unattractive heap.

Foliage can also create contrast based on leaf size and texture. For example, planting a clump of fine feathery foliage like that of *Centranthus ruber* creates a calming effect similar to the colors of blues and lavenders. The medium-sized foliage of perennials like dark-red peonies and scarlet poppies act as midsection fillers. While the bold leaves of plants like hot-colored canna lilies or red-leafed ligularia are so dramatic, they should be used as an accent. Plant clumps of textures like you would plant clumps of colors instead of spreading them randomly throughout the garden.

REPETITION AND RHYTHM

Repetition and rhythm almost play the same role in tying the garden together by repeating plants or colors at several intervals in the garden, thus creating rhythm. Color is the most important element in rhythm, so the repetition of a red color will draw the eye to the first group and then to another red group farther away and then another red area will give attention-grabbing repetition or rhythm. Keep these elements simple by planting at least three clumps of a variety. Don't hodgepodge single varieties together unless the plant is massive, like a fountain grass, which creates its own rhythm. An edging planting of small mounds of hot-colored gaillardia would be a bust unless an odd number of three or five were used. Using repetition by staggering clumps of seasonal blooming perennials (like clumps of red tulips in spring, red flowering firefly and coral bells for midspring, red peonies and poppies for late spring, and so on through the seasons right up to the tall, rusty-colored flowers of helenium that bloom to frost) gives a satisfying rhythm of red shades to any garden.

BALANCE

Balance creates a feeling of harmony. Distributing the visual weight of perennials equally on opposite sides achieves balance. This design element can appear contrived, and even when the brain prefers it, perennials don't. For example, a set of steps in the middle of a garden area just begs for plants to be balanced on both sides. A gardener plans this focal point area with care. Striped iris, easily the most consistent and carefree perennial available, is planted in a nice clump of five on each side of the steps. The irises, with their eye-catching white stripes, look outstanding for the first two years. Then the worst thing that could happen to a clump of perennials happens! The iris on the right side of the stairs becomes full of grass. There is no other choice but to dig the entire clump out and remove the grass, one strand at a time, and replant. That's a big job. True balance on both sides of the steps is never achieved again.

Balance would have been easier to achieve by planting a clump of pink echinacea with phlox, which blooms at the same time with similar pink colors. For late spring, visually balance *Penstemon* 'Mystica' with *Lysimachia ciliate* 'Firecracker'. Both perennials have tall burgundy foliage, so balance would be achieved with height and the reddish hue.

RED PERENNIALS THROUGH THE SEASONS

SPRING

- *Armeria,* thrift, has 'Joystick Red', which is redder than other armerias. It's also taller, sturdier, and stands straight up in the midst of a small grassy clump that is short enough for the front border and stays evergreen in the winter.
- Daffodils bloom in the hot colors of 'Red Devon', 'Jetfire', and 'Scarlet O'Hara'.
- *Helleborus,* the earliest spring bloomer, now comes in the colors of 'Sunshine Ruffles' and 'Red Racer'.
- *Heuchera,* coral bells, not only have hot colors in their foliage but also have the cultivars 'Firefly', 'Melting Fires', and 'Ruby Bells'.
- *Pulsatilla rubra* also blooms early in warm red shades. The lacy foliage furnishes a nice contrast in the garden.
- Tulips outshine the sun with colors like 'Little Red Ridinghood', 'Sky-High Scarlet', and 'Sunlover'.

LATE SPRING

- *Avens, Geum* 'Mrs. Bradshaw', is a scarlet geum whose common name is 'Fireball'. 'Blazing sunset' is a true orange geum.
- *Centranthus,* red valerian, makes a top focal point, not only for its reddish color but also for its lacy foliage.
- *Dianthus* colors have red enticing names like 'Fire and Ice', 'Cranberry Ice', and 'Ruby Sparkles'.
- *Dianthus,* sweet William, has a new dark-red perennial called 'Heart Attack'.
- *Paeonia,* peony, has a new 'Bowl of Beauty'-type flower called 'Flame' with a yellow-orange center and scarlet petals.
- *Papaver,* the oriental poppy, always blooms in hot colors, and its nicknames describe it well: 'Prince of Orange', 'Brilliant', or 'Flamenco Dancer' have always been favorites of gardeners.

EARLY SUMMER

- *Iris* 'Raptor Red' and 'Tanzanian Tangerine' are hybrids that make a gardener hope that they are as hot as they sound.
- *Kniphofia,* red hot poker, comes in the heated-up colors of 'Fire Dance', First Sunrise', and 'Flamenco'. Their torches bloom in every shade of red, orange, cream, and yellow. Red hot pokers are Zone 5 perennials and are really suited to the lower elevations of Utah and the foothills of Colorado. Sadly, they do not thrive as well in the high, mountainous regions of the Rockies.

SUMMER

- *Coreopsis* gives the sun competition with the blooms of 'Early Sunrise', 'Sunshine Superman', 'Sunfire', and 'Rising Sun'.
- *Hemerocallis,* with its classy strap-like leaves, grows magnificent focal point clumps of hot colors. Red shades of daylilies are 'Funny Valentine', 'Prairie Wildflower', and the classic 'Bama Bound', 'Red-Hot Returns', and 'Ruby Sentinel'. Orange daylilies are come in the colors of 'Bright Sunset' and 'Mighty Chestnut', while yellow hues include 'Black-Eyed Susan' and 'Buttered Popcorn'.
- *Lilium,* which is a showstopping tall perennial, makes a stellar focal point. Huge clumps of these bright, gorgeous blooms will add not only color but also contrast with their unique, elegant foliage that stays a nice green until late fall. 'Red Velvet' tiger lily grows five feet in height. Its blooms won the North America Lily Society Hall of Fame Award. 'Firebolt', 'Gold Band', 'Orange Mountain', 'Orange Tiger', 'Royal Sunset', and 'Red Carpet' are just a few of these other hot beauties. Plant a clump of as many as can be financially afforded for a stunning accent in the garden.
- *Lychnis,* Maltese cross, flowers in true reds and oranges. The tall, up-to-thirty-inches Maltese cross is one of the brightest colors in the garden. Shorter Maltese crosses are twelve to fifteen inches tall with reddish-bronze leaves and flowers in both red and scarlet-red, making a very nice front-of-the-border perennial.
- *Tanacetum* 'Robinson's Red' (painted daisy) is a fuchsia red. This painted daisy makes a striking addition to the garden. The lacy, carrot-like foliage is a very handsome contrast perennial in the border. By cutting the daisy stem when it finishes blooming in June, painted daisies will bloom again. The rosier red of many flowers will look more comfortable planted away from the scarlet shades of reds.

LATE SUMMER INTO FALL

- *Alcea,* hollyhocks, are tall, warm spots in the garden, with names like sunshine and Chater's double red.
- *Monarda,* bee balm, has both a 'Cambridge Scarlet' and 'Gardenview Scarlet', but most monardas have red as their original basic color.

These hot choices should make it easy to add a little drama to the garden.

Hemerocallis
(hem-er-o-CAL-iss)
'Stella de Oro'
DAYLILY

SHAPE	Fountain, strap-like foliage, trumpet-shaped flowers
HEIGHT	Twelve to fifteen inches
WIDTH	Fifteen inches
BLOOM TIME	Peaks in June with sporadic flowers through fall
COLORS	Golden yellow
SITE	Well-drained soil
LIGHT	Full-to-partial shade
HARDINESS	Zones 2–9
COMMENTS	'Stella de Oro' is in a class of its own

'Stella de Oro' grows with such a matched precision that the perennial can be used confidently in public gardens all across the West.

The bright-yellow blooms of 'Stella de Oro' are delightful when mixed in with the blue shades of lavender.

There are over forty thousand named *Hemerocallis,* or daylily, cultivars noted by the American Daylily Society.

H. fulva was used in my first attempt at hybridizing, and this stunning double daylily shown above is the result. I call it 'Neon'.

HOLA, GARDENING AMIGOS! I'm *Hemerocallis*, and if you struggle with drought in your garden, you will be glad I have introduced myself. You may wonder why I would show up in a chapter about drought-tolerant plants since daylilies typically prefer average soil, water, and light. The answer is that unlike most daylilies, I'm very water wise. Part of the reason is because I'm a tiny, diminutive little plant with yellowish bulb-shaped roots that store water. However, it's more that that. I think it's because I'm flexible, tough, hardy, and I find it easy to ignore when I haven't been watered.

Of the forty thousand named hemerocallis, or daylily, cultivars noted by the American Daylily Society, I'm the most versatile and the easiest to grow. My optimal growing conditions are full-sun to partial-shade, but I even grow under pine trees. I thrive in every type of soil; normal, sandy, alkaline, or clay. My moisture requirements are average, dry, or moist. In other words, I grow delightfully whereever I am planted, and I'm planted in a wide variety of tough spots.

Not only am I an early-blooming daylily but I'm also an extended bloomer, which means I bloom for a full sixteen hours a day, and I'm often added to the list of nocturnal blooming perennials. Each of my blooms may last only a day, but my flowers cover every bit of me through June and then will show up a few at a time throughout the rest of the season. I multiply rapidly, but I have a noninvasive habit. I'm extremely hardy, and gardeners often remark that they think I'm really a Zone 2 perennial. This hardiness is why I'm a positive feature when used in planter containers. I winter well, so the next year, a gardener has a bigger, better planter at absolutely no cost.

I'm relatively pest-free, but if aphids do become a problem, try a strong stream of water to clean my foliage of them. If the aphids persist, spray me with an insecticidal soap, and as a last resort use a mild systemic pesticide that can be sprayed effectively. However, the use of any pesticide must be cautioned. Follow the instructions for tender and ornamental plants.

Deer will sometimes browse my new, tender lily shoots when the shoots break dormancy in the spring. This is a crucial hunger time for deer, especially for doe that are either carrying or nursing a new fawn. The deer nipping off my top shoots does no damage to me, but it has a tendency to thicken my stems, giving me more fullness. By the time I'm ready to set buds, the deer have moved into the mountains where food has become more plentiful. Planting daffodil bulbs in the same spot where I'm planted will quickly turn a deer away because they intuitively know that daffodils are poison. I pay it forward by hiding the daffodils' spent foliage with my fresh, green stems while the daffodils rest and collect their nutrients for next spring's flowers.

Should my blooming slow down, here are a couple of suggestions to encourage me to perform better. Do not let my seed pods develop. Setting seed takes huge amounts of my energy. In other words, the seed pods are replacing my flowers. Remove any bloomed-out buds before they start forming pods, and cut my flower stalks as they start to lose their color.

Another pointer is that even though I'm very drought-tolerant, sufficient water can increase the number and size of my blooms. Mulching also helps by improving the soil and encouraging it to retain moisture. Thus, mulch contributes to better blooming. Mulching is also the most effective method of weed control, and if a weed happens to show up, the mulch makes them easy to pull.

Another reason I may not bloom fully is that I might need dividing. I grow rapidly and need dividing about every five to seven years. For divisions, dig me in the early spring. A spring division gives me an entire summer to get my roots reestablished. Remove the entire clump and cut me into sections, making sure each section has a nice root ball and a top of at least three green fans. Laying my root ball on its side on the ground so the stems can be seen visually makes me easier to split. If pruners or a knife won't work, use a spade or two digging forks back-to-back to split my sections. Plant one daylily section back in the original spot and the others in another part of the garden, or share me with another gardener.

My hybridizer, Mr. Jablonski, who bred me back in 1970, choose to name me Stella because it means "star" in Italian. The phrase *de Oro* is Spanish and means "of gold." Adding this to the genus *Hemerocallis*, which derives from Greek *hemra* meaning "day" plus *kallos* for "beauty," and I become a beauty for a day that looks like a gold star. Excellent!

Gold stars are nice, but when I received the highest award given to a daylily, the Stout Silver Medal Award, I knew I had earned much more than a gold star. I knew I was a delightful and remarkable perennial.

'Always Afternoon' is one of my better reblooming daylilies. The word *always* in the name of a daylily is a signal that the lily is probably a hybrid rebloomer.

Hemerocallis 'Apricot Sparkles' looks and acts so much like 'Stella de Oro' that they could be twins. They have the same dwarf size and flawless form, but 'Sparkles' has a touch more apricot.

'Round Midnight' is the darkest, most richly colored Daylily imaginable. More than its unique beauty is the vitality of the perennial. It forms a thirty-inch tall clump with an abundance of well-branched scapes.

EVERBLOOMING HEMEROCALLIS: CONSTANT COLOR

IN MY IDAHO garden, I love 'Stella de Oro' not for its blooming ability but more for its trim shape, form, hardiness, and adaptability to our climate. Its delightful, golden-yellow blooms are small, but the color really stands out. Although being considered an ever-bloomer, 'Stella de Oro' blooms more like a regular hemerocallis in cooler, higher western elevations! In warmer climates, the reblooming tendency could be more prevalent.

I've tried intervention to lengthen 'Stella de Oro' blooming by removing the bud as soon as the bloom withers. I've upped the watering to see if that is the answer, knowing that it is very drought tolerant, but without adequate water, it may drop buds before it blooms. I mulch it every fall as soon as we get the first freeze and pull the mulch back in spring. I fertilize minimally, only when the lawns get their spring feeding, but the length of blooming stays the same. A gardener can't help but get excited at the prospect of a perennial that furnishes long seasonal color. Daylilies can be the most dependable flowers in dry gardens, and having these fine plants in bloom all summer is a gardener's dream come true.

However, here is the reality of how the new hybrid long-blooming daylilies perform in my experimental gardens. So far, only two have bloomed longer than the 'Stella de Oro', and those are 'Strawberry Candy' and 'Rosy Returns'. All everbloomers are very expensive and can cost much more than regular daylilies. These new hybrids have been bred using the recessive gene 'Stella de Oro', thus giving them a strong resemblance to the 'Stella de Oro' daylily. Many have the same small stature and flowers and are not the pictured perfection of marketing hype that is shown in catalogs and magazines. Gardening is different in dry areas, but listed below are my best everblooming or reblooming (the words seem synonymous in my garden) daylilies.

H. 'ALWAYS AFTERNOON'
'Always Afternoon' is one of my better reblooming daylilies. The word *always* in the name of a daylily is a signal that the lily is probably a hybrid rebloomer. The colors of 'Always Afternoon' are so beguiling that it is irresistible for many gardners. The dusky rose-frilled edges that surround a deep burgundy eye located between the throat and the tips of the flower segments or petals are stunning.

H. 'APRICOT SPARKLES'
H. 'Apricot Sparkles', looks and acts so much like 'Stella de Oro' that they could be twins. They have the same dwarf size and flawless form with the only exception

being that the two-inch blooms of 'Sparkles' have a touch more apricot than gold. The petals have fluted edges like on a pie crust, and are advertised as diamond dusted, meaning they are covered with iridescent dots.

H. 'DARING DECEPTION'

'Daring Deception' is my least favorite reblooming daylily. The strikingly different coloring of the mauve with the deep-burgundy eye pictured on the tag were impossible to resist; I had to have this dazzling lily in my garden. The reality was different! When 'Daring Deception' bloomed the first year, the colors looked washed out. The mauve is more lavender, and the center eye is a muddy shade of darker purple. This brings up a question. As a genetic tetraploid, 'Daring Deception' has an increased number of chromosomes, which increases the breeding possibilities. Could 'Daring' have been *too* daring?

H. 'HAPPY RETURNS'

'Happy Returns' is a 'Stella de Oro' hybrid that has been around since 1986. Any daylily with the word *returns* in the name is probably a child of 'Happy Returns', who is a child of 'Stella de Oro'. The soft lemon-yellow flowers all of the same color are eye catching and stand out in the garden. 'Happy Returns' is mildly fragrant and is compact, easy to grow, and has no insect or disease problems. This fine, dependable daylily stands eighteen inches tall over a clump of narrow blade-like arching green leaves. The blooms are up to four inches taller than those of 'Stella de Oro'.

H. 'JOAN SENIOR'

'Joan Senior' is an elegant, creamy-white daylily with curved segments or petals. This should give a more open-faced look, but mine are trumpet shaped. The segments are delicately ruffled. 'Joan Senior' is so pure looking with only a pale yellow watermark and a soft yellow-green throat that she adds an ethereal look to any flower bed. Her stems are twenty-four inches tall and have a heavy bud count, which probably won her the Award of Merit and the LAA award for the best performer.

H. 'PANDORA'S BOX'

'Pandora's Box' is similar in size and bloom time to 'Stella de Oro' and won the AGA Award for the best small flower. 'Pandora's Box' is elegantly beautiful with creamy flowers and a prominent burgundy eye at its center. It took almost five years in the garden before 'Pandora's

Box' decided to really bloom. It is planted in a west-facing garden spot with a touch of early morning shade, so it appears that 'Pandora's Box' did not inherit the vigorous growth habits of 'Stella de Oro', its mother.

H. 'PARDON ME'

'Pardon Me' was the first everblooming daylily in my garden. It is planted in full sun, and does not want to keep blooming. 'Pardon Me' is a replica of 'Stella de Oro' with the exception of having rusty-red flowers. The flowers are small, tight, and trumpet-shaped, and they thickly cover the entire perennial. I anticipated the blooms would be a true red and that the blooms would be open as advertised but they are not.

H. 'ROSY RETURNS'

'Rosy Returns' is a small charmer that cannot be propagated. 'Rosy Returns' is only fourteen inches tall, but her scapes carry loads of rose-pink flowers with a centered light stripe on the segments. 'Rosy Returns' has a rose purple eye and a yellow throat, which makes her stunning in a mass planting along the top of a wall.

H. 'ROUND MIDNIGHT'

'Round Midnight' is the darkest, most richly colored daylily imaginable. The colors of this stunning deep-burgundy, almost purple, flower simply sizzle! Adding to its beauty is a delicate, light-cream, wire-edged frame. More than its unique beauty is the vitality of the perennial. It forms a thirty-inch-tall clump with an abundance of well-branched scapes.

H. 'STRAWBERRY CANDY'

Finally, a new hybrid that gives 'Stella de Oro' some competition! 'Strawberry Candy' grows well in full sun to partial shade, in normal, sandy, or clay soil that can be average, dry, or moist. 'Strawberry Candy' is extremely cold hardy. In my garden, it is more of a salmon color than the advertised pink. Its ruffled petals or segments are edged with a coral band.

With the giant leaps made in hybridizing flowers, the day will soon arrive that gardeners will have a perennial that will bloom all summer. There is no doubt that this long-blooming perennial will be a hemerocallis. All this started with the first delightful little hybrid 'Stella de Oro'.

Iris pallida
(EYE-riss Pal-ih-duh)
'Aurea Variegata' and 'Argentea Variegata'
STRIPED IRIS

SHAPE	Fan-shaped foliage with trumpet blooms
HEIGHT	Fifteen inches of foliage
WIDTH	About eight inches around
BLOOM TIME	Late spring to early summer
COLORS	Cool blue
SITE	Perfect drainage, alkaline soil
LIGHT	Full sun
HARDINESS	Zones 3–8
COMMENTS	Looks excellent all season

I. 'Aurea Variegata' with its wide yellow stripe on each leaf is thriving on this hot south-facing foundation planting.

Rocks heat up the bed earlier in the season, so the *I.* 'Argentia' blooms early as the tanacetum or painted daisy. The lacy foliage of the daisy and thickness of the iris area clues that both perennials are drought tolerant and grow well in similar environments.

The blue spikes of *Veronica* 'Royal Candles' are into their second round of blooming and fuse elegantly with the blue and white stripes of *I.* 'Argentea' or 'Alba' in this fall-blooming container.

These iris rhizomes have been dug, divided, and trimmed and are now ready to plant. Iris is always planted close to the top soil surface.

MY COMMON NAME is sweet flag, and I'm one of the original ancestor parents of our modern-day irises. My unique vegetation is a particularly interesting variation of an old-fashioned favorite. My flowers are not the extravagant, huge, gaudy blooms of the hybrid bearded iris, but are cool blue with small, yellow fuzzy beards for pollination. My iris flowers are quite low-key but make up for that by blooming longer. Each flower has three petals called *standards* that grow upright and three petal-like sepals called *falls* that roll down. These simpler blooms stand up in mass on tall, twenty-five-inch stalks that look so clean and smell so wonderful that I easily become the favorite iris of the garden.

My rhizomes are also known as *orris root*, which is used as a perfumery base. The absolute oil extracted from my roots is coveted for its soft, sweet-clean fragrance and is used in expensive perfumes and as a fixative for potpourri. One ton of aged orris root produces only about seventy ounces of essential oil, so I'm one of the most prized and expensive perfumery materials on the market. The root has the smell of sweet violets, but my flowers smell exactly like grape KOOL-AID.

Both *I. pallidas* are very alike in our blooms but are somewhat different in our foliage. 'Aurea Variegata' has both golden and bright green stripes on strong, fanlike foliage that grow vigorous, robust, and well-branched plants. 'Argentea Variegata' grows slower and smaller with a creamy-white stripe accenting a more subtle coloring of grayish blue-green striped leaves. Everything about 'Argentea Variegata' is more delicate, and when divided it takes longer to recover, but this also gives a smaller-sized plant that in some ways makes it easier to use and care for. The robustness of 'Aurea Variegata', often called a 'Zebra Iris', dictates the need to be divided every three to five years when the quality and number of flowers decreases, while 'Argentea Variegata' rarely needs division.

If division is necessary, the best time of year to do this is when I go somewhat dormant, six weeks after blooming, or in the middle of August. This is early enough to ensure recovery time before freezing temperatures arrive. Dig my thick, fleshy stems, letting the rhizome structure dictate the division. Trim the stems or any part of the rhizome that does not look strong, but never cut into a solid clean rhizome with healthy growth. Trimmed rhizomes have the ability to self-heal and will recover. Leave a small fan of three or four of the overlaid leaves. Replant these close to the top of the ground surface. My roots will grow down from these rhizome stems while the same stems that grow straight up will form my leaves.

Too much water when I'm in my semidormant state can cause root rot, so only plant and water my starts enough to settle the soil around the fans. When I resume growing, start regular watering again. Moderate watering in the spring is helpful and is usually done by Mother Nature. My buds for the next year are formed as I complete my blooming, so water me for about six weeks after my flowers fade. I can easily go without water for two weeks in the heat of midsummer once I am established. This is why I'm an excellent drought-tolerant perennial for the fast draining soils like those in the Rocky Mountains.

My striped leaf variegation is probably a genetic or viral quirk. Mutations can change the green plant chlorophyll, leaving a yellow pigment called xanthophyll. Variegation is a different makeup of these two chemicals, and plants show up with golden edges or a dark center or vice versa. Sometimes the range of color variegation will be multiple shades of green, gold, yellow, cream, and even pink. Perennials will show up with stripes, spots, splotches, streaking or colored veins. When mutations happen, my exceptional foliage is an example of the end result. Plant growers are developing more and more variegation in perennials by taking the mutated foliage and furthering the colors and markings in the perennials. Variegation simply introduces an elegant and refined effect to the garden that stands as an accent or even replaces the short-term blooms of flowers.

Matching cultural perennial needs of sun and soil when planting striped iris into a perennial garden will keep me and my companion plants both happy. Choose full-sun perennials that do not require a lot of water. This is also a logical reason for choosing me as a perennial to plant in container pots. I do not require daily watering and I'm easier to care for. When I'm planted in the garden, my unusual foliage will accent other perennials as well as annuals, but overdoing with variegated foliage can also be a distraction in the garden. Too much of a good thing can ruin the good thing, so use my foliage with a fine touch and plant me as solo clumps, just here and there in the garden.

I'm an iris, but foliage is the name of my fame. Not only am I variegated but I'm also striped, giving me that extra kick in a garden of green. Adding this to the long-lasting good looks of my foliage, I become an indispensable element of the garden. Hopefully every gardener is enjoying me in his or her gardens by now, but if not, that gardener will have something exciting to look forward to.

"COOL" FOLIAGE IN THE GARDEN: FLOWERS ARE FINE, BUT FOLIAGE IS FABULOUS

IN NORTH AMERICA, gardeners get wound into a high state of exuberance when the months of June and July arrive. The skies are the bluest, the days the hottest, the sun the brightest, and the garden's flowers bloom with abandonment in every size, shape and color of the rainbow. An early summer garden is unequaled! . . . But then what?

I keep recalling the words of the famous TV star Judge Judy when she cautioned a young girl about the follies of thinking that her looks would get her whatever she desired: "Looks are temporary! Brains are forever!" Judge Judy explained in her very direct, down-to-earth style, and this philosophy easily applies to flowers.

Not many perennials bloom for more than a few weeks, so a flower, like beauty, is fleeting. Gardeners need to think beyond the flowers. Foliage carries the garden when flowers may not be at their best or there is a meltdown between seasons. Nature can slip up with inevitable weather changes and damage the flowers. Logic says foliage should be more important than flowers, but I don't know any gardener who uses logic when dealing with flowers. Variegated foliage like that of the striped iris, tells us that we don't have to think about logic in our gardens; just plant some great foliage!

Adding a touch of variegated foliage into our gardens is like adding a touch of foliar sophistication. The following perennials are a few of these eye catchers that are at home in our mountain environment:

AJUGA, BUGLEWEED
Bugleweed is an attractive, flat-growing ground cover that is now bred in near-black, rose, burgundy, and golden shades of foliage. Short spikes of blue flowers, bloom in midspring. Bugleweed prefers a partially shaded area of the garden and grows slower in alkaline soil. It is so indestructible that weeds rarely grow through it. Bugleweed looks excellent when planted in front or around the feet of hosta.

BRUNNERA, HEARTLEAF
Heartleaf foliage is stunning, with prominent outlined darker veins that form on a sturdy, shining, silvery clump of leaves. Forget-me-not, true-blue, wispy blooms hover for several months above the heart-shaped leaves during springtime.

DICENTRA, BLEEDING HEART
Old-fashioned bleeding heart, a perennial for shade, now has a radiant yellow-foliaged plant that adds light into the garden.

EUPHORBIA, CUSHION SPURGE
Cushion spurge's excellent foliage is now offered with cream margins, green and yellow variegated leaves, and deep colors like burgundy and red. The hybridizing and variegation has raised the zone of hardiness on many of these new perennials.

GRASSES
The cool-season grasses of calamagrostis are well suited to the Rocky Mountain areas. Their striking foliage now grows with a white stripe edge or a gold midrib stripe. It varies in size and is versatile as to growing conditions.

HEUCHERA, CORAL BELLS
Coral bells, with its mounding, heart-shaped leaves has been undergoing a massive introduction of sophisticated foliage. A partial-shade evergreen perennial, coral bells now has rich dark foliage with silver overlays, golden, lime, and even peach or caramel-colored leaves. A guest remarked when looking at a new coral bells in my garden that it looked as if it had been hit with herbicidal spray, so clearly not all of these colors are as attractive in the garden as they may be in a catalog.

HEUCHERELLA, FOAMY BELLS
Foamy bells is appropriate for partial-shade or shade gardens. This petite edging plant, with a separate colored center leaf, will change colors through its growing seasons.

HOSTA
This plant offers an amazing variegation of colors and textures. The cells mutate in different layers of the leaf, creating thousands of patterns of white, yellow, gold, and green by altering the number and type of plastids. For example, chloroplasts, which contain chlorophyll, are green. Chlorophyll reacts to sunshine and can stimulate the ratio of green plastids, thus getting a greener hosta. Sometimes the opposite can happen; the white edge on a hosta may burn due to the white color's lack of chlorophyll.

Hostas are the most popular perennial for shade and stay at a hardy Zone 3 no matter the variegation. They are so savvy that when their leaves start to unfurl, it's a sign that the early spring weather is safe for planting.

LAMIASTRUM, 'HERMAN'S PRIDE'

'Herman's Pride' grows in a perfectly mounded, silvery, variegated half-circle of elegant metallic-streaked foliage. I've renamed this striking shade plant "heavy metal," and the drier the garden spot, the brighter the foliage color glows.

LAMIUM, DEAD NETTLE

Lamium, with its silvery textured leaves, is a ground cover that lights up the dark areas of a shade garden.

LYSIMACHIA, LOOSESTRIFE

Loosestrife has always been a hardy perennial for western gardens and now has a variegated, lime-green leaf with wide ivory margins. The new spring growth is flushed pink and grows well in average sun, soil, and water.

PHLOX PANICULATA, TALL GARDEN PHLOX

Phlox has several variegated foliage cultivars. 'Nora Leigh' has variegated leaves that are creamy white with a green center line and 'Shockwave', has bright yellow and green foliage with creamy margins.

POLEMONIUM, JACOB'S LADDER

'Stairway to Heaven' is a variegated-foliaged Jacob's ladder that looks great all season long when planted in a partially shaded spot. The blue spikes that bloom in June are especially pretty with the variegated foliage.

PULMONARIA, LUNGWORT

Lungwort is an all-season spotted or silver-foliaged perennial for the early spring garden. Its flowers show up before the foliage and often change colors as they develop. Lungwort has long, pointed leaves that form a nice clump along the edges of the garden. New varieties like Diana Clare are totally silver.

SEDUM, STONECROP

Sedums have undergone tremendous changes in their sturdy foliages. Many are red, mauve or silver while some are bordered in a different color.

SEMPERVIVUM, HENS AND CHICKS

The new breeding of hens and chicks has given the gardener red, rosy, wine, silver, gray-green, and any other combination of colorful foliage rosettes.

YUCCA, ADAM'S NEEDLE

Yucca, with its architectural handsome foliage now sports golden edges or creamy centers that radiate upward from a central crown.

Looking over all of these foliage choices, it's hard not to notice that many are shade-preferring garden perennials. A full-shade area in a yard is a tough spot for a gardener to make look attractive. They always seem to have a "black hole." Using the cool-foliaged perennials from the above list will give an illusion of light in a dark area and the black hole will suddenly look brighter, larger, and more interesting.

Again, use variegated foliage sparingly. For example, if planting a striped grass that grows to six feet in height, one plant should certainly be enough. Variegated foliage is an accent and should be used only as an accent!

Pulmonaria, with its silver- or white-splotched leaves give drama to the garden.

Lavandula angustifolia
(*lav-AN-djew-luh*)
'MUNSTEAD' AND 'HIDCOTE'
ENGLISH LAVENDER

SHAPE	Compact, evergreen shrub clustered flowers
HEIGHT	'Munstead': twelve inches, 'Hidcote': fifteen inches
WIDTH	Twelve to fifteen inches
BLOOM TIME	June through August
COLORS	'Munstead' has blue flowers and 'Hidcote' is dark purple
SITE	Well-drained alkaline soil
LIGHT	Full sun
HARDINESS	Zones 5–8
COMMENTS	Very aromatic

In fall, the lavender can be sheared to form a neat hedge.

Hardy English lavender gives the garden much more than the beauty of its delightful flowers. From its crisp, clean fragrance and medicinal uses to its drought tolerance, lavender is a must-have perennial.

The comfortable, low-key shades of blue in 'Munstead' are attractive with every other color. Plus its compact growth and green shrub-like foliage make it a candidate for the center of a formal garden.

Lavender will winter easier when planted against the foundation of a building.

WELCOME TO MY world of lavender! I prefer to live in wide-open spaces with alkaline, rocky embankments and hot, sun-bleached days. I want my world to be natural, with soil that is not rich but lean sandy-gravel that drains well. I belong in harsh, exposed extremes of heat and wind. I need breathing room, and I'm even deer resistant! If this sounds like I belong somewhere like the Rocky Mountains, you are mistaken! Everything about the West is to my liking except for the bitter cold of the winters that move down from the north and do me in. I actually originated in the sun-filled mountainous regions of Europe and the Mediterranean, and this is where I really perform and should be grown. Perennials have a sense of home just like gardeners do.

SOLVING LAVENDER'S HARDINESS ISSUES

Here are a few pointers to help me with hardiness issues:

Plant me against the foundation of a building or wall. Foundations are usually somewhat protected in winter, especially if the spot is facing south or west where I can accumulate full sun heat. I need six hours of sun, or my branches become straggly.

Once I have matured, I'm a tough plant that is extremely drought-tolerant, but I will need regular watering for the first year until my roots get established. However, too much water will kill me off. I grow well in raised flower beds that detour excess moisture away. I appreciate gravel added to my planting hole and a fine layer of grit sprinkled around my crown. Dampness and humidity can take a bigger toll on me than cold, and I flat-out refuse to grow in the high humidity of the southern part of the United States. These small techniques will help with drainage so I'll stay healthier.

My stems can take a beating through winter, so gardeners are anxious to cut me back. Don't! Wait until new growth appears before any trimming is done. If absolutely necessary, prune out dead stems, but never cut into the older woody shrub stems at the base of the plant. I'm unlikely to regrow. Spring trimming is debatable. Most lavender is trimmed at the time of harvest just as the blooms start to open. Both my flowers and foliage are aromatic, so trim off the flower stems. Usually this cutting back is enough to give me denser, fuller foliage. Fall shaping isn't an option, for I'll need whatever I've got to help me through winter.

A lean soil will encourage a higher concentration of my valuable oils, and alkaline soils enhance my irresistible fragrance.

I can be grown as an annual or can be planted in containers and overwintered inside. The pot will need good drainage, so set it on an inch or so of rock gravel in the bottom of the container. Use a sandy soil mix with perlite that drains well. Nutrients will run quickly through this type of soil, so a slow-release fertilizer a few times during the growing season will make sure I get enough nutrition. Water me when the soil feels dry to touch, and water the soil—not my foliage. Damp foliage is an introduction to my decline that can lead to root rot.

Good air circulation when planting helps keep fungal diseases away. Space my plants a healthy distance apart so each mound can be clearly seen. Also, give me breathing room by keeping me weed free.

'MUNSTEAD' AND 'HIDCOTE'

'Munstead' English lavender is generally considered the hardiest, earliest blooming, and the most drought tolerant of the lavenders. My rich blue spikes group above my plant on slim stems. 'Munstead' is known for my compact shape and short stature that forms a uniform clump of aromatic foliage. I'm a refreshing green that displays the square-shaped stems that signal I belong to the mint family. My stems are clothed in needlelike leaves that stay evergreen. Propagate me by sticking cuttings taken before bloom time into small nursery pots filled with a loose medium mix plus perlite for extra drainage. Cover the pots with a clear plastic tent until they root. Self-seeding varieties will vary from the parents and take forever to germinate and grow, so seed propagation is not rewarding for gardeners.

'Hidcote' is also English lavender that is very similar to me but grows larger and has silvery foliage with rich dark purple flowers. Both of us are drought-tolerant perennials covered with fine hairs from stem to bloom, giving us extra water-wise qualities. Shiny oil glands that contain the renowned lavender oils are embedded among our tiny, star-shaped fine hairs. We both have been fortunate to have not been changed genetically through hybridization, so we are the best varieties of lavender for medicinal use. We are beloved perennials, famous for the high quality, easy harvesting and intensity of our perfumes, and we maintain our beautiful blue coloring when our flowers are dried. Start with either of us in your garden for the best success.

I'm such a romantic flower that most gardeners can't resist giving me a try.

LAVENDER AS A HEALER: LAVENDER ESSENTIAL OILS

LAVENDER IS PROBABLY the most enjoyable of all the perennial herbs. The composition of lavender, with its sweet, irresistible fragrance and its rich supply of volatile oils, gives lavender the ability to produce scented oils that are healing to the human body. Plants like lavender have been used through antiquity as natural remedies. We have become so dependent on prescription drugs that we often forget that growing in our own gardens is an amazing healer.

Lavender is considered a single essential oil because it can be used without any additions of other herbs. In other words, the oil is perfect as it is. Most essential oils require a combination of herbs, but not lavender. A gardener needs to understand the two major characteristics that give lavender oils their ability to be extracted. The first is a volatile nature. The oils must separate easily when exposed to air. Second, the oils must be hydrophobic, which means they do not mix with water. Lavender meets these requirements.

I grow lavender and was curious about essential oils. I wasn't interested in purchasing a "Frankenstein" type of distiller with all of its glass tubes and hoses, so I pulled the ancient juicer that my mom passed down to me off the shelf, cleaned it up, and harvested my newly opened lavender blooms.

The juicer was large enough to stuff a huge grocery sack full of lavender flowers into it. We have chlorinated water where I live, so I used distilled water to fill the heavy steamer bottom of the juicer pan. The middle section is composed of a huge twenty-inch-tall kettle with a center opening (similar to an angel food cake pan), which is fit over the bottom water container. Then the strainer full of lavender fits next, topped off with a close-fitting lid. The steam rose through the tube kettle, and as soon as the volatile oil started to drip, I turned off the heat. I let the lavender cool and drip overnight and easily skimmed the oil out of the tube pan the next morning. The oil was then bottled for future use into sterilized glass opaque jars at a ratio of eight drops of lavender oil to one-eighth cup of coconut oil. Two drops of vodka can be added per full four-ounce bottle for additional safe storage. An eyedropper easily measures the drops. Tightly cap the bottle and swirl the lavender clockwise. Store the oil away from heat, light, and moisture. Label and date the bottle so it is ready for use.

There wasn't a great deal of oil distilled, but the financial investment was all but zero, and doing this once a year when the lavender blooms is insignificant. However, when a grandchild comes to me with an "owie" and there is the healing power of lavender to rub on it, I'm thankful and realize it wasn't insignificant at all. Lavender is such a clean, refreshing oil that it seems to balance and heals wherever there is a need.

HOW TO USE ESSENTIAL OIL

Lavender essential oil's healing properties are legendary, but I only use it for the skin. Here are a few uses:

- A skin toner. Wet the cotton ball with the lavender oil and wipe over the skin after washing your face. The lavender will shrink pores while clarifying the skin.
- A healer. Itching skin, blisters, burns, dryness, rashes, and insect bites can be relieved by applying the oil directly on the inflamed area.
- A hair care product. The essential oil nourishes the hair and scalp follicles but also works as a cure for dandruff. Simply apply one-to-two drops on your hands and massage into the scalp before a shampoo. Then wash and rinse hair as usual.
- Tub therapy aid. The lavender oil moves to the upper water layer and will be quickly absorbed by the skin, the largest gland of the body. There it starts its miraculous healing.
- Massage therapy aid. Applying one to two drops straight from the bottle of lavender to a sensitive location of the skin and then massaging it will relieve pain.

All this power from a home-grown remedy makes me want to start growing more lavender.

Nepeta faassenii
(NEH-pe-tah)
'WALKER'S LOW'
CATMINT

SHAPE	Mound with spikes holding clusters of flowers
HEIGHT	Twenty-four to thirty inches
WIDTH	Up to twenty-four inches
BLOOM TIME	June to July
COLORS	Blue and lavender
SITE	Well-drained, ordinary soil
LIGHT	Full sun
HARDINESS	Zones 3–8
COMMENTS	Long blooming

Appearance wise, *N.* 'Walker's Low' makes an excellent substitute for the perennial herb lavender.

Planted in this full-sun, drought-tolerant garden helps nepeta maintain its nice compact size and profuse brilliant-blue blooms. Too much rich soil, water, or fertilizer will cause nepeta to splay.

This close-up of the two-lipped tubular flowers of *N.* 'Walker's Low' shows its misty masses of flowing energy.

Planted as a hedge, nepeta is dependable and will bloom most of the summer in brilliant blue flowers.

GOOD MORNING, GARDENING friends. My name is *Nepeta faassenii*. I'm an important but low-key perennial that is the backbone or spinal column of a perennial garden. Why? Well, mainly because I'm totally dependable! With my Zone 3 hardiness, I can be counted on to do my job and always return in spring more full and vigorous than ever. I thrive in drought-tolerant situations, but I'm okay with regular watering. I grow more compact in the lean soils of the West, and too much fertilizer or rich soil will cause me to splay or flop open. I'm so vigorous that no pests or diseases even attempt to bother me. In truth, I'm the dependable workhorse of the garden.

My size, with my compact flowering spikes, is not too big nor too small, but is just right to scatter bulk throughout the garden. I decorate the middle of the flower border as fillers with an almost watery shimmering-blue effect. I'm excellent growing along paths or edges of a border where my numerous masses of tiny flowers give texture and a touch of height to the garden. In a rock garden I'm probably the longest blooming of the other perennials. This and my drought tolerance is why I make such a lovely plant for containers or planters.

My dark-green, tight foliage makes an appealing foundation plant. The foliage stays nice, and when cut back around the end of July, as the blooms start to dry, I become a small compact mound only about a foot tall. Shear my fine-leafed foliage with hedge pruners or shears. Within three weeks, I assure you, I'll be blooming again and will continue until after frost, making me much more charming than shrubs. My stability also makes me maintenance-free (other than deadheading) when I'm planted as a hedge, and I will bloom most of the summer.

The lavender-blues of my flowers provide a feeling of space and distance that make a garden look and feel larger. My soft shades tone down exuberant reds and oranges and mellow the harshness of yellow. In fact, my blue-jean color will never clash with any other flower and is more visible to the human eye at twilight than other colors, with the exception of white. When planted in a private retreat, I will provide a calming place for a gardener who has had a busy day. Not only do my flowers calm, but my colors will also give a feeling of coolness.

Even my flowers and foliage can be trusted as good companions in the garden. Some of the members of my mint family spread voraciously, but I am very well behaved. Tiny flowers will fully envelope my dense aromatic foliage and attract butterflies and bees as if I was a popular eatery. Cats only like me if *N. cataria*, catnip, isn't around. Catnip gives cats a temporary high. It grows from seed, spreads uncontrollably, and is not suitable for perennial gardens.

While other flowers bloom and fade, I just keep adding the comfortable color of blue to the garden. Perennials that combine well with me in the spring are tall penstemons, like orange scarlet 'Jingle Bells' and the fat, flat foliage and blooms of bearded iris. The summer colors of *Achillea*, yarrow; any shade of *Lilium*, yellow coreopsis or tickseeds; and red *Tanacetum*, painted daisies and white daises, are improved alongside my flowers. I do a top job at softening the strappy structure of hemerocallis, and because I'm still blooming in fall, asters like 'Alma Potschke' look even classier with my tidy blue blooms filling in at their feet.

I'm not conceited, but what I do for the garden is what makes me valuable. Why would a gardener plant a difficult perennial when an easy, dependable plant like me is available? I'm not the only one to feel this way. Because of all of these qualities, I received the highest perennial award, the Perennial Plant of the Year for the year 2007.

My maintenance is minimal, and I really only require deadheading and dividing when I become overgrown. Life is too short to not enjoy the freedom that a perennial like me gives to the garden.

PERENNIAL PLANTS OF THE YEAR AWARDS

EACH YEAR, THE Perennial Plant Association, a trade group that works to educate gardeners on great performing perennial plants, selects their choice for the perennial plant of the year. *Nepeta* 'Walker's Low', received this award in 2007 by meeting all of the Association's requirements for selection. Any gardener shopping for an excellent perennial to add to their garden would benefit from looking over the list of winning perennials. The following criteria for being awarded the PPA award is used:

- suitable for a wide range of climatic conditions
- low maintenance
- pest and disease resistant
- readily available in the year of release
- multiple season interest or excellent foliage
- easily propagated by asexual (division or cuttings) or seed propagation

The limitless variety of regional climate conditions, elevations, available water, and sunshine are factors that need to be considered before every perennial plant of the year is embraced. Many of the awards have been given to perennials that prefer acidic soil or soil with a pH of less than 7.0, and some prefer alkaline soils, so this information needs to be known by a gardener before trying a new selection. Speaking as a gardener from the West, most of the award-winning perennials fit comfortably into the Zone 5, or a -20°F low, while the best perennials for our climate need to be in the Zone 4, -30°F, or a Zone 3 at a low of -40°F.

2014 *Panicum* v. 'Northwind'

2012 *Brunnera macrophylla* 'Jack Frost'

2008 *Geranium* 'Rozanne'

2005 *Helleborus* x *hybridus*

2003 Leucanthemum x *superbum* 'Becky'

The Perennial Plant Association's goal at its inception in 1990 was to bring awareness to gardeners of a variety of perennials. As a horticultural teaching tool, the PPA is now a highly-recognized resource for promoting perennial species in the green industry. The international trade organization is now two thousand members strong and is composed mainly of growers, gardeners, home owners, retailers, landscape designers, and educators. This huge group does the voting that introduces the next winning perennial.

The Perennial Plant Association's intention of teaching the public about perennials was the first of its kind, and now there are numerous copycat award programs around. A few of them are specifically for local areas and are usually administered through universities, cooperative extension services, or botanic gardens. The awards and recommendations of both new and old perennials from these plant trails assist gardeners in making educated decisions without the worry of the results being a marketing technique.

The daylilies, hostas, and irises all have individual awards. The American Daylily Society chooses a daylily each year to receive the Stout Silver Medal. The American Hosta Grower's Association presents a Hosta of the Year award, and the Iris Society gives the Dykes Medal.

Regional awards and recommendations of plants from all over the United States are also given not only to perennials but also to trees, shrubs, and annuals. The plants are tested to see how they perform in local region. Athens Select tests plants in Georgia for heat and humidity, and Texas Superstar testing is done by Texas A&M Agriculture Program.

The Missouri Botanical Gardens maintains a superb online database called Plantfinder, and it includes "plants of merit" or MOBOT awards. The plants of merit are tested on seventy-nine acres of gardens.

The MNLA or Minnesota Nursery and Landscape Association Awards are project awards given to new potential, outstanding landscapers working toward careers in the green industry.

Oklahoma Proven Selections are tested by every horticulture and landscape company in that state.

The American Garden Award is a North America popularity contest of flowers. Gardeners vote for the winner of this award on Facebook.

All American Selections, or the AAS, tests new varieties such as the *Gaillardia* 'Arizona Sun' and annuals and vegetables.

Closer to home in the intermountain area, Colorado University and the Denver Botanic Gardens have two fine perennial testing and awards programs. The famous Plant Select Award is presented to plants that help, change, or improve the environment. Water-wise plants are a big part of this program. Colorado also awards plants for longevity and survival in test gardens. This award is called the TOP award.

Utah's Choice is a program that tests plants native to Utah, and the best performers receive an award from the Intermountain Native Plant Growers Association.

All of these awards were kicked off initially by the Perennial Plant of the Year Award, and they have certainly helped gardeners everywhere. I probably would never have tried the beautiful nepeta because of its origins in the catmint family, which is infamous for its spreading and almost invasive abilities. Had it not been for the PPYA awards where I was introduced to *N.* 'Walker's Low', I would not be enjoying one of the finest perennials available. I'm thankful to PPYA for their educational help.

2000 *Scabiosa columbaria* 'Butterfly Blue'

1997 *Salvia* 'May Night'

1994 *Astilbe* 'Sprite'

1991 *Heuchera micrantha* 'Palace Purple'

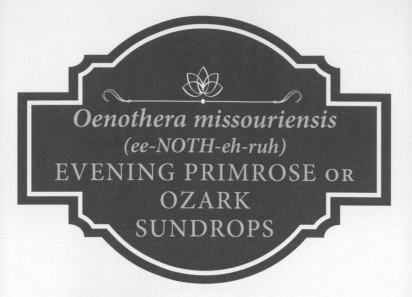

Oenothera missouriensis
(ee-NOTH-eh-ruh)
EVENING PRIMROSE OR OZARK SUNDROPS

SHAPE	Sprawling ground cover with trumpet shaped flowers
HEIGHT	About six inches
WIDTH	About fifteen inches
BLOOM TIME	Late June to frost
COLORS	Pale yellow
SITE	Well-drained soil
LIGHT	Full sun
HARDINESS	Zones 4–8
COMMENTS	Rock-garden or border perennial

The upturned stems of evening primrose almost give the feeling that the flower doesn't like sitting on the ground where it might get dirty.

Evening primrose is shown here with blue 'Sapphire' flax in a drought-tolerant garden.

Evening primrose has curious seed pods with round seeds sitting inside, waiting for their freedom to drop and germinate.

The delectable pale, lemon meringue color of evening primrose is so irresistible and delicious-looking that it's fortunate that it's edible.

GOOD AFTERNOON! I am *Oenothera missou-riensis*, but you may know me by my common name, evening primrose. I know you will find me fascinating because I'm so different from all of the spiky, mound types of perennials that surround me in the garden. My foliage sprawls over rock walls or tumbles over parking lot curbs and does it gracefully, because just as I'm about ready to touch the ground, the stem tip rises upward. I'm pleased with my three-to-four-inch, glossy, narrow lance-shaped leaves that are covered in fine velvety hairs, a sign of my drought tolerance. My unique stems and buds are brushed with red freckles that open on the tip ends for my clusters of flowers to emerge.

My flowers are spectacular! They are funnel-shaped with four petals and can be three to four inches across. As a high-light perennial, I break dormancy somewhat late in the season, waiting for longer, sunnier daylight hours, but I still have a long bloom time. On a late June afternoon, my flowers will start to open in real-time movement that can be enjoyed by an observant gardener. By evening, my flowers are fully open, with their delicate scent and prominent produc-tion structures on display. My enormous blooms have an unexplainable, phosphorescent light in the moonlight of the garden that attracts night moths for pollination purposes. My blooms persist all night and into morning. When my flowers' "one-night-stand" job is done, the fading petals start to fold protectively around a prospective seed pod. I repeat this performance nightly during my long spring to summer bloom period, forming seed pods until frost. I'm sure this is why I was tagged with the name evening primrose, I certainly look and act nothing like a primrose, so it has to be due to the late afternoon opening of my flowers that I got my name.

My seed pods are really unique and look like winged, minia-ture light-green pepper plants. If they are removed, I'll up my production of flowers, but if they are left on my stems, my energy goes into seed production. Leave a few of these pods to self-seed. The pod capsule splits into four sections at maturity and spills out the seed. The best germination occurs in light, loamy soil. Over the long summer, there will be ample seeds to germinate. My round, oily seeds are also used for primrose oil, which contains rare gamma-linolenic acid that is being used for medical research on heredity. I'm an edible perennial and was eaten like lettuce by Native Americans.

Two years will pass before my seeds will come into flower production. These naturalized stands of seeded plants surpass the original plantings by being healthier, happier, and more robust because they chose their own planting spots. The next generation seems better adjusted to the climate and environ-ment. An almost impossible planting area along the street and between the sidewalk is a good example of my second-genera-tion adaptability. I'm one of only a few perennials short enough and drought- and salt-tolerant enough to survive and look acceptable in a spot like this. *Armeria,* thrift; *Artemisia* 'Silver Mound'; *Iberis*, candytuft; *Heuchera,* coral bells; *Limonium,* sea lavender; and *Sedum*, stonecrop, will also tolerate the poor soil, lack of water, and snow salt thrown on the curb by snowplows in winter. I will not only tolerate these conditions but will also multiply into a larger healthy stand of superior oenotheras. I'm a hardy Zone 4 perennial, but I don't always live long, especially through extremely wet winters. This is another motive for encouraging seed reproduction.

I grow best in average-to-dry well-drained soil in full sun. My very favorite planting spots are rocky limestone bluffs or rock gardens. Traditional gardens are okay, but I'm suited to being planted in grasslands, in dry lands, and even along limy cement sidewalks, which are an ideal environment for my drought-resistant, woody roots and rhizomes to spread. My root system is shallow, so dividing is easy by lifting the roots with a shovel. Division of my thickened rootstock that forms small, hard, elongated brown rhizomes will keep me healthy, slow down spreading, and rejuvenate me. These divisions perform better when dug and replanted in spring.

I'll quickly die from rot in wet environments, especially in cold winter locations. Locate my plants with the crowns slightly raised so I'm allowed to dry out between watering. Because my root and rhizome system is close to the surface, I struggle through the cold of winter, so at least an inch of mulch will help me survive the harshness of that season.

My short size and long-blooming season gives me status as a perennial that covers the bare feet of taller plants. I really look cool planted in front of late-spring irises, blue nepetas in summer, and tall sedums and asters in fall. With my ability to sprawl over edges of rock gardens, plant me as the late-season shift. There are many spring rock-garden perennials like the rock cresses, soapworts, and veronicas to cover walls, but there are fewer like me for summer and fall gardens.

CURES FOR CURBSIDE QUANDARIES

LOCATED ALONG STREETS and between sidewalks is a nutrient-drained, compacted soil called the curbside, which is owned by the city but maintained by the homeowner. The soil has a high-alkaline pH from leaching of the limestone cement. The area is surrounded by baking asphalt, concrete, and car exhaust, and it is often hot enough to fry eggs in the summer. Many curb gardens are nutrient-depleted tree strips that create deep shade, which leaves the soil incapable of growing anything. The curb-strip is the recipient of snow-removal salt, dog doo-doo, kid's traffic, garbage can pickups, blown-in candy wrappers, and discarded pop cans. To make matters worse, it all sits in our front yards for everyone to see!

There has to be a more economical, water-saving way to improve these curbside quandaries. Water is the number one issue. These soil-compacted sidewalk strips surrounded by hard surfaces are hard to water. Most require hand watering because of the difficulty of tunneling under cement to install a sprinkler pipe. If the soil is built up with water-holding nutrient-rich compost, it will cause runoff. Wasted water running down the curb is not a pretty sight, and a gardener will be ousted from the neighbor social group because water conservation is on everyone's mind. What's a gardener to do?

We attended a funeral in the city center of Denver, Colorado, last year. I got lost in the city by straining to see all of the drought-tolerant curb-strip gardens where thirsty turf had been removed to make way for heat-loving native perennial gardens. The gardens were extremely attractive and nicely landscaped with wide-curving, raised flower beds. Gardens like these are showing up all across drought areas because most gardeners really do care about the environment. This is also happening because we're tired of browned and burnt grass across the front of their yards. Again, what's a gardener to do?

The first step is to check on city codes and ordinances. Do they allow roadside planting? Also know that snow removal using salt can destroy a garden, as can having it dug up to repair or install water systems and power lines that are buried there. Remember, the ground belongs to the city!

Next, turf will need to be removed to make a clean canvas. A gardener can use a shovel or rent a sod remover from a rental store, but removing grass is hard work. No matter how hard you try, there will be grass weeds in the garden left by the turf. Installation of a black plastic covering to cook the turf to death will work, but who wants their front yard curb strip covered with black plastic for a year?

Only the homeowner can decide to use their curb as something more than an unattractive eyesore. Wise judgment has to be used in the choice of plant materials. Cities can legally dictate the height and width of any perennials that may be planted there, and this is probably a good thing. A barrier of plants makes it difficult for a passenger in a car to find a place to open a car door to alight. A path between the curb and sidewalk will make it easier for passengers to exit and not have to traipse through a flower bed. Secure path rocks to the ground so they cannot be stolen or thrown by kids. The same goes for rock mulch or boulders used as focal points. Also, visual clearance is necessary when backing out of a driveway, and it's discourteous to both the mail carrier and homeowner to conceal the mailbox in a mass of perennials. Short or flat drought-tolerant perennials called step-on-me plants need consideration. They can withstand light foot traffic. Walk-on-me perennials include ajuga and *Lysimachia nummularia* for shade. *Callirhoe*, winecups; *Potentilla verna*; delosperma; low sedums; thyme, and *Veronica liwanensis* will carpet a sunny spot. All of these are low-water users and weed barriers.

Multibranched shrubs or trees that crowd sidewalk space and create hazards for foot traffic are inconsiderate. Trees planted in a curb median need to be limbed up high enough for cars to park under and give sunlight to plants beneath them. Low-growing native perennials are choices that are sturdy, hardy, and sustainable, so check these out first.

Bulbs are the answer for spring color in this type of drought-area garden. The small species tulips and early specialty bulbs like crocuses naturalize easy, as do the dwarf iris. Many of the specialty bulbs bloom before trees leaf out in a shady garden, so they will grow and bloom well in shaded tree strips. Daffodils are always useable, because like most bulbs, their dormant time during summer is when they appreciate heat and drought.

Many gardeners are using their curbs as an area to grow vegetables. There is nothing more attractive than a vigorous, healthy stand of tomatoes, peppers, cucumbers, and squash in a garden.

The first year or two, the gardener will have to make a commitment of time, labor, and soil improvements, but after that, the garden should take care of itself and have managed to crowd out weeds. Fall cleanup to prepare for the gigantic piles of cleared snow that will be thrown by snow plows onto the curb won't even be too difficult.

Initial planting of perennials with a natural salt tolerance and flushing the area to move the saline out of the plants' root zone area in early spring is another issue that needs to be addressed.

Many problem-solving, creative gardeners have come up with ideas for curb quandaries that are so simple and unique that they need to be seen to be really appreciated.

All of these hardscape curbs are the answer to snow removal. The snow will melt faster, and the salt will not damage perennials that aren't planted there. Plus, they are so attractive and creative that a neighboring gardener will wonder why he or she didn't think of it first.

Solving curb quandaries can bring a lot of initial hard work and require creative solutions of a homeowner. The first priority is getting rid of unhealthy, water-thirsty turf grass. The second is to replace this grass with a choice of drought-tolerant natives that are not too tall. Taking action to fix the problem of the curb also can encourage neighbors to ask questions, so be prepared for more social time. If you are successful, you'll also want to be prepared to see turf being removed from curbs up and down the street in preparation for neighborhood gardeners to create their own curbside gardens just like yours!

This huge corner lot solved its curb quandary with a variety of colored pavers, making it as bright and colorful as if they were flowers in bloom.

This curbside quandary is covered with clumps of drought-tolerant daylilies and the ground cover *Cerastium* 'Silver Carpet', making the meter easily available to the water meter reader.

A simple contrast of two different materials, brick and cement, in two different colors gives this curb as much class and color as any flower bed. The angled patterns create an interesting appearance.

A mulched curb is easy on the water budget allowance. A row of huge planters will need hand-watering but are well worth the time and cost by the effectiveness of how they soften the look of the long curb.

The simplicity of the three clumps of fountain grass looks amazing and is also drought tolerant and easy to maintain. The rocks and mulch areas add to the design but do not add to water use and labor.

The geometric patterns made by these white rocks set in cement are modern, clean, and appealing. This curb requires no water, no weeding, and no maintenance.

This corner wraparound curb was completely covered with an attractive hardscape rock-stamped cement design. The elegant foliage of fountain grass adds to the classy look.

Penstemon
(PEN-steh-mon)
'MYSTICA'
BEARDTONGUE

SHAPE	Clumps of spikes with trumpet plumes of flowers
HEIGHT	Up to thirty inches
WIDTH	Twenty-inch clump
BLOOM TIME	June
COLORS	White blushed with pink
SITE	Well drained
LIGHT	Full sun to partial shade
HARDINESS	Zone 3
COMMENTS	Bronze foliage

A close-up view of the 'Mystica' flowers show that the bloom is indeed pinkish and not white.

The remarkable foliage of P. 'Mystica' is as beautiful in bloom as in late fall when the fine perennial is a dark-foliaged accent.

'Elphin Pink', a *barbatus* cultivar with colorful coral blooms, is short enough for the front of the flower bed.

'Dark Towers' looks so much like its sibling 'Mystica' that it's hard to define the difference.

WHILE THE MIDDLE child in a family usually feels a little bit left out or passed over, you'll find that's not the case with me. My name is *Penstemon* 'Mystica', and I just happened to end up as the middle child of three new and improved penstemons that have been hybridized by mixing in digitalis or foxglove and me: The oldest sibling is 'Husker Red', I'm the middle child 'Mystica', and the youngest is called 'Dark Towers'.

First came the sensation caused by 'Husker Red'. Here was a penstemon that didn't really need to be grown in its native North American southwestern desert but could be grown in average gardens in average soils in both sun and partial shade. Here was a stronger, longer-blooming and longer-living penstemon with unbelievably beautiful red stems and bronzed foliage that stood out in the sea of green in a garden. And to top that, here was a penstemon that won the Perennial Plant of the Year Award for the year 1996.

And then I came along! It's not that I'm resentful or bitter; I really am a team player, and as the middle child I'm easier to get along with than most, but I want gardeners to understand my strong points and know that the amount of attention I receive doesn't necessarily have anything to do with how I'll turn out. I flourish without much care. First, my stronger stems of foliage stay faultless and neat until frost. The foliage of 'Husker Red' does better by being cut back, and this can leave holes in the border. Also, 'Husker Red' can tip over in a windstorm.

I stand taller and straighter, and I'm much bushier with a higher, fuller flower count. My flowers are not as white as 'Husker Red' but are blushed with a soft pale-pink, and my foliage is a more intense red that blends skillfully with my rosier flowers. The foliage of 'Husker Red' can easily revert to a standard green, while my color stays more stable. Also I'm easier to take cuttings from because my stems are thicker, and that makes me easier to propagate. I'm named the beautiful name of 'Mystica' for my mystical beauty. Poor 'Husker Red' got a seemingly curious name unless you know it was named for the Nebraska Corn Huskers, which is the university where it was developed.

Now we have a new younger sibling that is just too perfect in every way. 'Husker Red' and I will be pretty much ignored now. This more-than-perfect plant was also developed in Nebraska and is named 'Dark Towers'. All of our commendable perennial traits have been passed down to 'Dark Towers' but have been improved! The flowers of 'Dark Towers' are a richer pink with a touch of lavender and are larger. The foliage is taller, darker red, almost black, and is very vigorous. However, not all with this new perennial is as easy as I am, for 'Dark Towers' is patented (USPP#20013) and cannot be commercially propagated without paying royalties. Also, it can only be started from vegetative cuttings, while 'Husker Red' and I are seed-propagated perennials, which makes our cost much more reasonable. Any gardener can start our simple seeds by sowing them out in the winter garden so they will germinate. It helps that our seed has a long shelf life—up to ten years when kept dry.

Aside from this, the three of us are very much alike and are often indistinguishable in the garden. We are all hardy Zone 3 perennials. All three of us are favorites of hummingbirds and butterflies, probably due to the bell-like tubular shape of our flowers, and we are all deer and rabbit resistant.

Our blooms are excellent as cut flowers for a vase. Cut our blooms in the early morning and sear the stems with a match. We are very neat and tidy, lasting a good ten days in the vase without messing up a table top with dropped blooms.

Our striking burgundy foliage is even richer and darker when we are planted in full sun. Our flower stalks also like to worship the sun and will open charmingly to allow more sunshine in but will never need staking. In fall, our red foliage color deepens and becomes a commanding presence in the garden.

Arid western gardens with drought-type sandier soils are more comfortable for us to grow in. To prevent crown rot, plant us high, leaving the top edges of our root ball above the surrounding soil and do not mulch. Berms, raised beds, or along hillsides are planting spots where we will get good drainage.

When planting us in the garden border, consider our three-to-four week bloom time. Our height and width will require plenty of elbow room. The first year, we look small and insignificant, but our bronze rosettes will triple and reach our full amazing potential the following season. Penstemons are notorious for being short-lived perennials, so helping us shed viable seed is good insurance.

I'm guaranteed to bring joy to the garden and the gardener, so please don't ignore me, even if I am the middle child!

At least I got the perfect name, and I'm not going to change it.

TAGS FOR PERENNIALS: IDENTIFICATION CERTIFICATION

WITHOUT TAGS TO identify the three red-leafed cultivars of the hybrid mix of digitalis and penstemon, it would be very difficult to tell the plants apart other than 'Husker Red' has finer foliage. 'Mystica' and 'Dark Towers' are so much alike, with the exception of flower color, that it would be impossible to guess if the plants were not in bloom. This is why the tags and labels that come with the plant when it's purchased are important.

Last summer, very, very early in the morning, I was awakened by the harsh ringing of the telephone. I rolled out of bed and answered it.

A voice on the end of the line sounded relieved that I had answered and started to explain that she was up early, ready to do some weeding, and that she needed my help.

I groaned inwardly, hoping she didn't want me to come and help her weed, but I waited for her to continue.

"When I started to dig," she explained, "I just wasn't sure if I was digging a weed or a flower."

Understanding her quandary, I asked, "Has the plant started to bud or bloom yet?"

"No," she replied. "But it has really spread!"

"Can you describe how it looks?"

"Well," she hesitated, thinking hard, then said, "It's green!"

This is a common enough happening. We forget over the winter what we planted and feel frustrated when we can't remember. Perennials look entirely different in preseason bloom than when they flower, and so many have similar stem and leaf structures that a visual reminder is nearly impossible. This is where labels and tags become important. The hardest part is that labels rarely survive a season in the ground, so what's a gardener to do?

NAME THE FLOWER

Become acquainted with the flower. Knowing the name of the flower is not really different than knowing the names of friends. Check out the label. Notice the name printed on the top is usually the common name. Tag manufactures use this name first because they worry the botanical name might make gardeners uncomfortable.

The common name is listed at the top of the tag close to where the word *perennial* is written. Common names are often given to plants because of a character trait, like the daylily flower, which blooms only in the day. The name can also tell a plant's origins, like the English daisies. Sometimes the common name gives a clue to where the perennial will grow best. For example, rock cresses are rock-garden plants, and creeping phlox are ground covers that creep on the ground. Common names are important and even furnish a memory device to help gardeners remember their names.

The next word, *perennial* (meaning a plant that will survive winter and come back over the years), must be displayed on the tag by law. Impulse shoppers are prone to pick out a plant because the flower is so irresistible, but it may be only an annual, or a single season plant. The word *annual* is not required on a label, so if the tag is blank, then the consumer is safe to assume that the plant is an annual. When spring returns, gardeners feel frustrated at their loss of a plant they thought was a perennial, because they purchased an annual.

The next name on the tag will be the botanical name, which is usually written in italics. For an accurate identification of a perennial, the botanical and its specific adjective name is a must because it is universal. Please learn the Latin name!

New perennials may also have a cultivar name that is enclosed in apostrophes. Cultivars are creations of hybridizers but can also be a spontaneous genetic mutation that breeders will offer.

In summary, the cultivar name can be the first or given name, the botanical name is the last name, and the common name can be a nickname. The front part of the tag shows all this information.

SYMBOLS

As you look beyond the names, notice the symbols. Symbols are pictures that stands for a concept that is universally recognized. The sun symbols are easy to recognize.

FULL SUN, PARTIAL SUN, SHADE

The addition of other symbols on the front of the label is appreciated by customers who find the small print on the back of the tag hard to read. For example, notice the symbol for the perennial plant of the year on the *Nepeta* 'Walker's Low' tag.

Labels that show symbols of hummingbirds and butterflies quickly tell the gardener that these perennials attract pollinators.

Symbols of deer or rabbits with a diagonal line drawn through them on the labels are saying these perennials are deer resistant, but remember that these tags are made back east, where only white-tailed deer browse. Western mule deer have different appetites. The shoes indicate whether the plant is foot friendly and can be walked on.

Pictures of rocks on a tag are an indication that the perennial is good for growing in rock gardens. A covered wagon symbolizes a native perennial, and a green leaf or pine tree means the plant stays evergreen in winter.

Other symbols might include a nose for a fragrant perennial, scissors for a good cut flower, or a light bulb (meaning the plant requires the long daylight of summer to break dormancy).

Many growers like to donate to causes. The daylily 'Remember Me' is symbolized by a pink ribbon for the cancer society, and Habitat for Humanity and GreenCare are sent a portion of sales receipts of certain other plants.

Labels are like a catalog on a computer chip, and they are worth keeping. All of the above information on one small plastic card is quite a feat! So how can gardeners save these labels?

TAG SAVING TIPS

1. Used tags were scanned for this side sketch so a gardener can see that by being tech savvy, the information can be saved on your computer. It doesn't matter if the pictures aren't perfect or if they have soil spots. One tag per variety is adequate. A gardening friend of mine used a spreadsheet to document her tags. I suggested she market and sell her program, but she said she was far too busy gardening.

2. Another gardener punches holes on the end of the tags so they can be hung on a large key ring. She uses a separate ring for each flower bed section, which she numbers. Flower bed #1 is where she always starts gardening first.

3. Little plastic drawers keep the tags of a schoolteacher friend organized.

4. Plastic pages for collecting cards of sports stars, like baseball cards, are already divided, and both sides of the card can be seen. The plant label tip may need trimming. An impressive folder with plastic sleeves works efficiently for some gardeners who use this method to document any losses. A tag helps back up a guarantee should the plant die. It is also convenient when reconciling purchases with charges.

5. Ziplock bags keep tags sorted either alphabetically or by flower bed.

6. Or you can do as my mother did and simply put them in a shoe box.

The answer to this question is to do what works for you. Any organization depends on time, space, and need. However, it's in a gardener's best interest to learn to utilize these mini masses of information.

Perovskia atriplicifolia
(PER-OFF-SKEE-UH)
RUSSIAN SAGE

SHAPE	Airy, shrub-like with spikes of blue flowers
HEIGHT	Three feet
WIDTH	Three feet
BLOOM TIME	Midsummer through late fall
COLORS	Lavender-blue lace
SITE	Fast-draining, dry, alkaline soil
LIGHT	Full sun
HARDINESS	Zones 4–9
COMMENTS	The large size and shape makes Russian sage valuable to a garden

Russian sage is one of the longest-blooming perennials, and it is easy to mix it with any color and size of flower.

Russian sage is a dependable, hardy perennial for a hot, dry environment on this busy street corner.

By July, this hose reel will be completely camouflaged with Russian sage's masses of tiny blue flowers.

Russian sage is an ideal background for shorter perennials like this petite monarda.

IF I WERE to attempt a greeting in Russian, you might doubt my sincerity, but never doubt my value in the perennial garden. I am *Perovskia atriplicifolia*, or Russian sage. Few perennials can compete with my huge size, unusual stem coloring, and light-blue, airy flowers. I serve many useful and positive purposes in the garden.

First, I take the place of a regular shrub without the tedious waiting for a traditional shrub to grow. I obtain my size by the second summer, returning each spring bigger and better. I'm also an excellent perennial for commercial landscapes, without requiring the constant maintenance of pruning. I go dormant and die back to the ground in wintertime, so I bypass the damage of broken limbs and burned foliage that is part of the care of most shrubs, especially conifers. There is an added bonus of using me as a shrub. I bloom a good fifteen weeks. Most shrubs bloom one or maybe two weeks at the most. This adds to my value as a foundation planting.

My second garden purpose is that I'm valuable as a background perennial. In midsummer, my upright, silvery-white stems covered with lacy, narrow leaves burst forth with a froth that act not only as a background for other perennials but also as a cooling element for the garden. My loose branching adds to this relaxed feel, but it is the masses of hazy blue flowers that cool the shimmering heat of summer. My twelve-inch flower sprays seem to float over the foliage with their two-lipped tubular blooms. My pleasant smell also creates a relaxed feeling. My fragrance gives me deer resistance, and I have zero pest and disease problems. I remind a gardener of the smell of salvia, or sage. Like salvia, I'm a member of the square-stemmed mint family. However, even if I'm called Russian sage, I'm not a sage.

An often-forgotten garden consideration is my third function in the garden. I grow the perfect size and shape to provide a natural seasonal screen in the garden. I'm beautifully effective planted as a hedge along a hot cement sidewalk to block unwanted viewers or along a fence line as a divider between properties. Used as a patio screen, I give enclosure and privacy in summer, and when I go dormant in the winter after the first frosty morning, the yard is opened up for a surreal winter landscape.

Fourth, I am useful as a filler plant between and on the back row of the garden. The lacy texture of my wispy stem-spikes stands attractively giving a contrasting background to shorter, coarser foliaged perennials. Pair me with the ball-shaped blooms of *Sedum* 'Autumn Joy' or with the rounded hot colors of tall garden phlox. I make the strappy leaves of daylilies look fuller, more grounded, and less coarse. Combine me with the flat-topped daisy blooms of *Echinacea,* or coneflower, and *Rudbeckia* 'Black-Eyed Susan'. The long-blooming *Achillea* 'Moonshine' also has flat-topped flowers and gives the classic blue and yellow combination that is so satisfying in the garden. In fall, I'm a fine companion for the intense rust, gold, and purple colors of late-season-blooming perennials. My silvery branches add interest to the winter landscape, so hold off pruning me until spring. Cut my stems to about six inches or even to the ground if the stems seem damaged. Be assured that this is the only pruning I'll ever need.

The only caution when planting me is matching the soil environment of these perennials with my requirements. If I receive too much water, fertility, or shade, I flop and will not bloom. Infertile soil is the same as poor or lean soil. Well-drained soil is a sandy or rocky loam that lets the water drain through quickly to prevent rot, and a full-sun garden spot with over six hours of sunshine is where I bloom best. To better understand these requirements, let me explain my origins. My name Russian sage probably came about because southern Russia, Afghanistan, Iran, Pakistan, and Tibet are my native homes. Visualize the rocky, dry terrains of these countries, and compare them with the North American Rocky Mountains. There is a physical resemblance between the areas. The main difference is the colder winter temperatures of a North American winter without snowfall. In this scenario, I can be marginally hardy. Fall irrigation and a very light mulching will help my root system get through winter. A covering of evergreen boughs, perhaps from a Christmas tree, can also make wintering easier.

I rarely need division, and my woody base is not comfortable with being dug and divided. I never quite find the time to self-sow in the early winters of the higher elevations, so the best methods of propagation are cuttings or layering. Take stem cutting in spring before I bloom. Snip off the top five-inches of the plant stock, remove the lower leaves and stick me into a pot of well-drained soil. A plastic tent in a warm spot that gets sun but no hot, very direct sun will encourage me to root in about a month. Layering has higher odds of success. Pull some of my bottom stems to the ground and cover them with soil. As soon as the stems form roots, the new plants can be planted about eighteen inches apart.

I serve other flowers in the garden. I'm a plant for the future!

FALL'S FAVORITE FLOWERS

RUSSIAN SAGE BRIDGES the gap between the July perennials and the fall bloomers. Fall is a favorite time of year for most gardeners. At last they have time to sit on the porch and watch their flowers grow. The early-blooming perennials are all cut back. The cooler temperatures have slowed the watering time. The lower slant of the sun seems to send a signal to the gardens and gardeners that the spring-growth frenzy has slowed and moved into a more sedate old-age period of rest and relaxation.

Fall enjoyment of the gardens depends on whether late-season perennials have been incorporated into the flower beds. If you're like many spring plant shoppers, the budget gets shot on the spring perennials that are in full bloom. They are just so desirable and pretty, and there is such a hunger and yearning for color in our gardens that we can't resist. Now that fall has arrived and a gardener really has time to enjoy the plentiful color filling the garden, there isn't any color! After one flowerless fall, a gardener starts to plan ahead for this special time of year. Below are a few fall favorites that deserve to be in your garden.

ACONITUM (SEE PAGE 10)

ASTER

Asters are valuable in the fall garden for the masses of rosy-colored pinks, fuchsias and purples they provide. The shorter days of fall trigger the formation of aster buds.

Asters grow in all sizes. The original natives were huge, but most of the asters now are a form of a hybrid. The tall ones grow up to four feet with twice that in width, so when planting asters, leave them plenty of space and plant them at the back of the garden border. The medium-tall asters can be anywhere from two to three feet in height, and the compacts form mounds that are around twelve to fifteen inches tall.

All asters prefer sun and thrive in cool, moist, well-drained soils, but they are not drought tolerant. Allowing asters to get too dry may result in powdery mildew on the lower stems. The mildew will not kill the plant but will definitely make it look unattractive. Fortunately, asters are at their most hardy when grown in the cool temperatures like those of the western Rocky Mountains. Asters are a hardy Zone 3 perennial, and they will survive to a -40°F.

CERATOSTIGMA PLUMBAGINOIDES, PLUMBAGO

Ceratostigma, or plumbago or leadwort, is a creeping perennial that blooms midsummer through fall and is attractively evergreen in winter when the leaves turn red or orange. After frost, the flower calyx, a tight group of center sepals—turns darker rusty-red, which persists and adds another distinctive touch to the reddened foliage. Plumbago is noted for its bright-blue, five-petaled one-inch flower clusters. The blue is so sensationally blue, without a trace of the usual tints of lavender, it creates an immediate love affair with a gardener. Added to this, plumbago provides shrubby evergreen foliage with red leaves that stays tidy and attractive all winter. All of this causes a gardener to question why it is so underused. The answer is that plumbago is fairly nondescript in the spring, when many gardeners are shopping for perennials, and it requires mowing as spring approaches, so it is far different in the garden from how it will look later on. It is sort of like the fairy tale ugly duckling. Plumbago is shade tolerant and will bloom in areas that receive only a touch of sunlight daily but will also perform in some sun. It is drought tolerant and requires only occasional watering once it is established, so it is a valuable ground cover for a xeriscape garden. *Almost perfection!* you're thinking, but this plant is a Zone 5 perennial and needs a moderate winter or deep snow cover to survive.

CHRYSANTHEMUM OR DENDRANTHEMA (A NEW NAME)

All too often a gardener will purchase potted, full-bloom chrysanthemums to place in the garden for fall color. These flowers have been overbred and overfed and do not come back as the perennials they should be. Memorial Day chrysanthemums experience the same expendable scenario that says they are not important to the garden or pocketbook and end up in the compost heap. One of the reasons is that chrysanthemums are not really hardy in the western Rockies, and the other is that they are a late-season perennial, and by the time they decide to bloom, our gardening days are all but over.

All is not lost, for there is a very hardy earlier-blooming chrysanthemum, rubellum, which grows and performs excellently. Rubellum, sometimes called a Korean daisy, is so easy to grow. Their blooms are highly substantial single daisy-ray florets around a central disk.

These chrysanthemums do not require the regular pinching that forces a late-season bloom. They are not the frilled, uptight, fancier forms but are more natural in appearance. Their names are 'Mary Stoker', with primrose flowers tinted pink, and 'Clara Curtis', deep rose flowers with a fine white band around their yellow eyes. These may need to be hunted down, but adding them to the fall garden will be worth it.

EUPATORIUM (SEE PAGE 208)

GAILLARDIA (SEE PAGE 78)

GAURA LINDHEIMERI

Gaura, or apple blossom grass, has all of the attributes of a drought-tolerant perennial. It is a US native that is deer and pest resistant. This erect, graceful, slender-stemmed beauty likes high levels of sunlight and well-drained soils, and it blooms summer to fall frost. Sounds like a perfect plant for our climate? Not quite. This plant would be ideal but is not quite hardy enough because it needs the warmer winter temperatures of a Zone 5 or a Zone 6, which is in the vicinity of a -10°F. In the North, it will live maybe two seasons, but in the warmer lower elevations, like the foothills of Colorado; southern Utah; or Boise, Idaho, it's worth growing. The original white apple blossom grass seems to be more hardy.

Nonetheless, with its continuous flowering performance of over two months and its long upright wands with whirling blushed-rosy butterfly blooms on arching stem ends, gaura is such a different perennial that a gardener can hardly pass it by. Its clean, tidy, solid-colored foliage with the new growth showing a burgundy color is dense and often winds through other plants and structures. But it never requires staking. What's not to love?

GRASSES (ORNAMENTAL)

The year-round interest of ornamental grasses has made them very popular in western gardens. Grasses have an elegant, tall structure that performs a seasonal show of uninhibited fountain-like texture by autumn. It can reach six to eight feet in height. The feather reed grasses and the switchgrasses are the hardiest for the intermountain West.

Feather reed grasses, or *Calamagrostis acutiflora* 'Karl Foerster' and 'Overdam' are excellent. 'Karl Foerster' is the taller and skinnier, growing to five feet. It is sterile, meaning it does not reseed. 'Overdam' is only three feet tall and gets even wider, but its variegated leaves give it a silvery beauty.

The switchgrass, or *Panicum virgatum,* has a finer texture than the feather reeds. They grow in a narrow clump with rust-colored blooms in fall. Their foliage tends toward the blue shades. They reseed so will need deadheading in fall. Many states such as Idaho have added grasses to the invasive plant list, so check with the extension service of your state to make sure any grass planted is legal.

GRASSES (SHORT)

All of the shorter bunch grasses are natives and can be found naturally in desert locations. The short *Festuca* grasses like 'Elijah Blue', with their fine-textured blue foliage and golden seedheads in fall, are dependable additions to any drought-tolerant garden. *Festuca* has a tendency to eventually die down to a scruff in the middle of the plant. However, the taller short grasses are more attractive and do not start looking rough so quickly. *Festuca idahoensis* 'Siskiyou Blue' and 'Blaze', which turns orange and red in fall, grows taller. It is one of the finest medium-height grasses. The shorter grasses are exceptional when planted solo in a container or pot and are hardy enough to overwinter.

HELENIUM

Helenium is a rugged North American native that flowers in autumn hues for up to ten weeks in the fall garden. Growing to about three-and-a-half-feet tall, Helenium is a perennial for the back of the border.

It's a dramatic sight when the daisy-like two-inch flowers bloom in all their brilliant reds, golds, rusts, and yellows above the other perennials. Then the gardener scratches his or her head, wondering where all that color came from because this plant is so low-key that it is not really noticed until it blooms, an important trait for a fall-blooming perennial.

These plants are sun lovers, but they also require regular moisture or even wet soils. They attract birds and butterflies but not deer and other pests. With their thick strong stems, they never need staking, and they make excellent cut flowers. Helenium is so attractive that it is referred to as *Helen's plant* and named after the famed beauty Helen of Troy. Helen's plant is a hardy Zone 3 perennial and thrives in western gardens as long as it gets enough water.

PHYSOSTEGIA VIRGINIANA, FALSE DRAGONHEAD OR OBEDIENT PLANT (SEE PAGE 172)

SEDUM 'AUTUMN JOY' (SEE PAGE 54)

SOLIDAGO, GOLDENROD

Solidago deserves respect. Native goldenrods were so prolific, spreading everywhere and not standing up on their own, that they were considered too common for a cultivated garden. Times have changed. Solidago is now used as a brilliant yellow-gold color contrast with the rich purples and soft lavenders of fall-blooming asters in flower gardens everywhere. Goldenrods are especially attractive when paired with the lavender-blue wands of Russian sage or the bronze-red blooms of helenium. Goldenrods have come into their own as one of the most glorious flowers in the late-summer and fall gardens.

This new respect of this plant has come about because of the superb new hybrids that have been cultivated. Now it comes in all sizes, from the tiny ten-inch long-blooming 'Little Lemon', which is a pale gold, to the two-foot-tall sizes of 'Baby Gold', 'Cloth of Gold', 'Crown of Rays', and 'Goldenmoss', which all bloom with large gold flower clusters. Many new solidagos are midborder size or up to two feet in height. *Goldenrod* 'Canadensis' has one-sided, plum-shaped, wide bright flowers, while another solidago, 'Zigzag', has wiry stems and cascades. There is even a creeping goldenrod that explodes in a rock garden like fireworks. It is an exciting time to garden when varieties of an old-fashioned native like goldenrod are available to gardeners in all types and sizes. Goldenrods prefer average, moist but well-drained soil in full sun or partial shade. They are a hardy to a -40°F.

Every color of flower is available for the fall garden, and there are tall, medium, and short perennials to fit any location. There are late-blooming perennials for drought situations, wet spots, and warmer climates. There are grasses that add movement and sound to the garden. There are even perennials that add to the winter landscape. In fact, there is a fall-blooming perennial to satisfy any gardener's wish and environment.

Here's hoping there will be no more flowerless falls in your garden.

Phlox subulata
(flocks)
CREEPING PHLOX

SHAPE	Ground cover with clusters of filler flowers
HEIGHT	Four to six inches
WIDTH	Fifteen to twenty inches
BLOOM TIME	Early spring
COLORS	Shades of mauve, pink, rose, lavender, blue, and white
SITE	Perfect drainage, alkaline soil
LIGHT	Full sun
HARDINESS	Zones 3–9
COMMENTS	Needle-like foliage, stays evergreen, excellent lawn substitute

Creeping phlox grows best in a hot spot like this with a rock highlight and sidewalk that provides mineral limestone or alkaline.

Creeping phlox, with its drought tolerance and evergreen foliage, makes a perfect container plant.

White *P.* 'Snowflake' creates the traditional eye-popping white color attraction in the garden that all white flowers add.

P. 'Candy Stripe', named after the pink-and-white-striped uniforms worn by hospital volunteers, is unique among phlox but appears as plain pink when viewed at a distance in the garden.

IF YOU HAVE a well-drained planting spot next to a warm sidewalk or concrete step, you are in luck. I am *Phlox subulata*, or creeping phlox. Occasionally a gardener will say I'm difficult to grow, but there are simple steps to growing me.

The first is a well-drained planting spot. I thrive as a walkway planting because walks are usually a dry, hot planting spot, and the lime from the cement adds a touch of alkaline that my roots appreciate. Being planted in a rock garden or being covered with rocky mulch is also to my liking, for rocks are made up of mineral limestone. Leave my crown above ground to prevent root rot, but add manure into the soil before planting for moisture retention and nutrition. Keep my crown dry and my roots moist.

The second pointer is to give my foliage two trimmings a year. Remove any dried or scruffy-looking stems that are hidden under my crown in early spring. Winter sun and winds are damaging and will bleach my evergreen needles.

My foliage is at its most perfect when it has wintered under a thick blanket of snow. The snow will melt, and my foliage will shine and soon be covered with a profusion of colorful, five-petaled, rosy-shaded blooms. The flowers will last for well up to a month, in cooler springs longer, but must be trimmed again after the blooming stops. Many gardeners are uncomfortable with cutting me back almost to the ground, but don't be! I'm not a reblooming perennial. My new green growth will develop from the crown and will hold attractively the rest of the season.

PRUNING CREEPING PHLOX

My dead needles can feel prickly, so use a pair of bypass pruners or scissors when trimming. Late winter or early spring, as soon as a gardener can get outside, is when to tidy me. I grow in three layers. Leave the excellent green growth that shows on top untouched unless it has snow burn. This is where my flowers will bloom. It's the lower layer of foliage that will look ratty. Lift the entire mat of foliage and remove the brown dead stems and needles that have accumulated underneath. This is a good time to aerate by loosening the soil around my roots, which will help with good drainage. Cut the scruffy stems out.

After I'm through blooming, trim each flower stem individually so I look natural. Removal of spent flowers improves my health and appearance by channeling my resources away from seed production into vegetative growth. After my spent flowers are cut, trim or shear the entire plant diameter back to almost half of my size, This will keep me dense and full and close to the ground for the season.

PROPAGATION OF CREEPING PHLOX

Dividing me is tricky. My crowns are small and woody and are hard to split. Unless the center has died out, don't try to divide my crowns, for success will be limited. Layering is a more natural method of reproducing me, and I often do the layering without any intervention from the gardener. You can often find a rooted stem when you remove the bottom layer of scruffy foliage. This can be potted up or moved to a nursery bed and will be ready to plant into the garden in late summer. Scoop or scratch out shallow holes under my foliage and tuck some of the stems into the holes. Cover the stems with soil using a garden pin or rock to make sure the stems stay buried. Forget them until spring. Wait until my flowers have finished blooming, and then remove the layered rooted starts. The roots may need severing from the mother plant. These can be planted right in the garden or gifted to neighbors.

Cuttings are slow and undependable to root. They need to be taken early, before I bloom. Personally I feel most gardeners would be better off not bothering with cuttings and instead enjoy my flowers.

Be wary of purchasing full-blooming potted perennials early in the season. My attractive flowers have been forced into bloom by artificial means: grow-lights, frequent fertilizers, and specialized greenhouse temperatures. After I'm planted outside, I'll have to deal with transplant shock, early freezing temperatures that destroy my buds, fewer fertilizer feedings, and a more normal growing cycle.

USING CREEPING PHLOX

I am a low-growing, ground-hugging carpet that forms mats and tumbles over rocks in rock gardens. Planting me on hillsides and banks will also stop erosion. Plant me as a substitute for grass in a narrow, hard-to-water part of the garden, and I'll save water, time, and money.

PLANTING SPOTS FOR SUCCESS

I'm an excellent substitute for thirsty turf areas and will cut back the water used by about 50 percent. I do not require the constant fertilizer that lawns do, nor do I need a weekly mowing with pollution-prone lawn mowers. My carpet of foliage looks luscious in bloom, but its slow-spreading reliability will hold its own after blooming has ceased.

I hope by now that a gardener realizes my value in the garden and not just as a rock-garden perennial.

WATER-WISE GARDENS

IN THE DRYNESS of the American West, the dream of a wide-open, spacious, verdant lawn is costly! Summer watering bills easily exceed the costs for winter heat. Are there areas of lawn that always shows stress and will not stay green no matter how much water is provided? This is the place to start removing turf and replacing it with water-wise perennials!

METHODS FOR GRASS REMOVAL FROM STRESSED LAWN AREAS

Using herbicides like Glyphosate or Roundup would probably work, but most gardeners shy away from the use of herbicides. Also two or sometimes three sprayings are necessary before the grass dies, so this process can be very expensive. If the decision is made to use herbicide to kill the grass, a fall spray job just before freezing will give the most complete removal of the turf. Bermuda grass is the most difficult to remove because even one blade or root will regrow.

Sheet mulching or "lasagna layering" takes longer and is not workable on slopes. The steps are as follows: Cut the grass as short as possible. Cover the entire area with cardboard or newspaper layers, making sure no sunlight can penetrate. Water the paper, and then cover the paper with compost or mulch at least five inches thick. Paper deteriorates quickly in the garden, so we like to use old paperwork that has been put through the shredder in our "lasagna layering" compost. Grass clippings, yard trimmings, fallen leaves, or household scraps like potato peelings can be added while the lawn dies. The positives of using this method are that it requires minimal labor and the area where the grass was removed will end up with plenty of organic materials to start a new drought-tolerant perennial bed. The negatives are that it takes all summer and winter and looks dreadful.

Physical removal of grass does not take as long, and it looks better than allowing the grass to die. Renting a sod-cutting machine is the fastest removal method, but it is hard physical labor. The machine is heavy, and it cuts the sod into strips. These strips can be hauled away or left to compost. In my personal experience, some grass will always regrow.

A flat shovel can also cut out the sod, but again the grass returned. I'm not sure if it was roots that were left or grass seeds.

Sterilization of the soil using the sun and black plastic is another method of sod removal. Hot summer temperatures will cook the grass and kill both good and bad insects. Cut the grass as short as possible and water well. Cover the area with sturdy black polyethylene held tight in place by heavy rocks or bricks. The heat from the sun will be trapped in the soil, where it will cook the top level. Leave the plastic in place until the sod is dead. Remove the plastic and leave the dead grass to compost.

WATER-WISE "WALK-ON-ME" SUN PERENNIALS

The entire group of perennials called alpines introduced with creeping phlox are appropriate low-water, turf-replacing perennials that thrive in hot, sunny gardens. Another group of perennial ground covers referred to as "walk-on-me" plants can be placed around stepping stones and paths that wind through flower beds. A few of these perennials are highlighted below.

Antennaria, pussytoes, bloom on a tiny mat of miniature-leafed silvery foliage. Pussytoes bloom in spring through summer as a native wildflower all over the Rocky Mountains. This miniscule, Zone 4 perennial spreads by reseeding.

Callirhoe, wine cups, has a deeply cut leaf that sprawls on a stem along with bright magenta flowers with white-eyed centers. Its deep taproot gives the plant drought tolerance and is zoned a 5, so it does better in the warmer areas.

Delosperma, ice plant, is a Zone 5 perennial more suited to the lower elevations of the Rocky Mountains. Breeding has developed all colors of ice plant, including yellow, pink, red, orange, wine, white, salmon, fuchsia, and lavender. The succulent foliage is very drought tolerant and turns maroon in winter.

Gypsophila, creeping baby's breath, blooms in trailing masses of white or in light pink clouds of starry flowers. The flowers bloom constantly and are fragrant. Creeping baby's breath is a hardy Zone 3 perennial.

Potentilla cinquefoil and *P. nepalensis* 'Miss Willmott', with its red-centered, rich salmon flowers, blooms on a cascading low-growing plant that resembles strawberry plant foliage. This hardy Zone 4 ground cover grows great in walls and containers.

Thymus or any of the low-growing thymes like the red creeping thyme, the variegated 'Highland Cream', or the 'Silver Thyme' are excellent and sturdy "walk-on-me" perennials. Mow or shear thyme, which has a tendency to become woody, to keep the plant rejuvenated.

The tiny-foliaged *Veronicas* 'Waterperry Blue', 'Sunshine' or 'Heavenly Blue' are dense, mat-forming blue-blooming, "walk-on-me" perennials.

WATER-WISE SHADE PERENNIALS

Ajuga reptans, bugleweed, blooms in spring with handsome blue or pink spikes. The colorful leaves of purple-blue to chocolate-bronze (plus some are variegated) gives a gardener a choice of favored varieties. Bugleweed grows to only six inches, can be mowed and is a hardy Zone 4 ground cover.

Ceratostigma, snow-in-summer, is a slow-growing ground cover with deep blue blossoms. Its dark green leaves turn glowing red in the fall. The foliage reaches about nine inches in height and is a Zone 5, or hardy to -20°F, perennial.

Galium, sweet woodruff, is a "walk-on-me" ground cover for shade that may require a touch more water. The fragrant whorled waxy green leaves are covered with small, brilliant-white flowers in early summer. Sweet woodruff grows to only eight inches in height and is hardy to a Zone 4.

Hedera, English ivy, makes wonderful ground covers for shade gardens. 'Thorndale' is Zone 4, so it is one of the best for western gardens. The dark-green small heart-shaped leaves are lustrous on this evergreen vine. English ivy doesn't play well with other perennials and performs best as a solo planting.

Lamiastrum 'Herman's Pride', with its striking green and silver variegated leaves on compact, mounding plants, has small, yellow, pearl-like blooms. The drier 'Herman's Pride' gets, the more perfect the plant grows, making it an attractive Zone 3 dry-shade perennial.

Lamium, spotted dead nettle, has silver, tricolor, or variegated foliage that shines in a shady garden. It blooms in clusters of pink, lavender, rose, or white flowers that will provide ground cover even under a pine tree. Spotted dead nettle is a hardy Zone 3 perennial that doesn't always grow a level height, so it looks better with mowing after blooming stops.

Liriope, lilyturf, is an evergreen, grasslike, twelve-to-fifteen-inch tufted foliage plant for shade. 'Big Blue', a Zone 5 hardy perennial, grows well in the warmer elevations of the Rockies. Lilyturf foliage is consistently attractive with the exception of early spring when it requires cutting out any dead stocks.

Lysimachia, moneywort, is a fast-growing ground cover for shade that is a "walk-on-me" perennial. This hardy Zone 3 ground cover will light up any shady spot with its bright-yellow flowers and glossy, round yellow-green leaves.

Pachysandra, Japanese spurge, forms a dense, slow-growing evergreen carpet of shiny foliage that will eventually carpet a shady area. The flowers bloom white in early summer. It is an excellent ground cover for under trees, and it adapts to alkaline soils and is hardy to a Zone 4.

Primula, primrose, is an early-spring-blooming perennial that will not perform in warm winter locations and prefers a Zone 3 environment. Balls of clustered flowers in reds, blues, lavenders, lilacs, and whites are right at home in a shady garden. Many varieties are annuals in the West, so stick with the old-fashioned cowslips.

Pulmonaria, lungwort, with its apple-green, pointy, elegant leaves spotted with silver, is the perfect plant for a shady garden. Brilliant blue-violet flowers appear in early spring on this clump-forming perennial for shade.

Vinca, periwinkle, grows spreading horizontal stems that will cover and root a large area. Grow it as a solo plant in a specific section and let it fill the area with its dark-green-foliaged runner stems. Periwinkle has bright blue blooms in late spring, is a Zone 4, and stays evergreen.

Water-wise perennials are an easy, attractive answer to the problem of water waste and turf.

Vinca, or periwinkle, grows spreading horizontal stems that will cover and root a large area.

Sempervivum tectorum
(sem-purr-VEE-vuhm)
HENS AND CHICKS

SHAPE	Mat-forming, flat-shaped rosettes
HEIGHT	Six inches
WIDTH	Six inches
BLOOM TIME	An occasional stem will rise up and bloom
COLORS	Foliage is every shade of green
SITE	Well-drained soil
LIGHT	High sun
HARDINESS	Zone 3
COMMENTS	An amusing, fun favorite

A sempervivum baby chick was dropped along this gravelly-soil sidewalk and liked the spot so much that in a single year formed this tight colorful planting.

S. 'Rocknoll Rosette' is a colorful selection of sempervivum that offsets freely with new chicks.

The colorful foliage of this unique variety of hens and chicks S. 'Sanford Hybrid' changes from gray-green to deep bronze and is a source of surprise and delight in the garden.

S. 'Ruby Heart' hens and chicks has silvery to blue-green sharply pointed leaves flushed red at the base.

I'M THE ONE perennial that thrives on neglect! Just plunk me onto any gravelly hot spot, and I'll make myself at home and proceed to raise a brood of chicks. In Latin, I'm *Sempervivum tectorum*, but you'll be more likely to know me by my common name, hens and chicks. Don't try to bury me in potting soil. My leaves will start to fall off, indicating that I'm buried too deep and getting too much water. Place me on the ground, and give me a little press. I'll root. Regular rainfall, even in the dry West is usually adequate to keep me happy. Less is more when it comes to growing me.

These independent qualities and the uniqueness of my mathematical-precision rosettes make me an interesting perennial for children to grow or to grow in pots and containers in the garden. I'm fail-proof as long as I'm planted in gritty soil, such as packaged cactus soil or builder's sand, which can be purchased at most box-store nurseries or construction sites. Many gravel companies will never say no to a gardener's request for a bucket of coarse sand. Adding organic compost or manure to the bottom half of the pot will help retain moisture, for I'm not completely without a need for water, even with my succulent, meaning "water filled," leaves. Good drainage is my most important need, so keep me somewhat moist, especially until I'm established.

I'm a natural plant for children to grow. Not only am I fail-proof, but it also delights them to watch me develop tiny buds of offspring close under my protective pointed petals. In less than a month, these buds or chicks, which look like rubbery roses, will grow an elongated stolon that will move the chicks to reside outside my protection. Our family will gradually colonize and fill the container with the most fascinating foliage available. I grow well as a houseplant, so I can be moved inside for the winter. But I stay healthier if I get some cold vernalization time, so move me outside the first part of March.

My colors are elegantly subtle, with soft porcelain greens and grays. Shadings of plum, pink, or bronze wash over my thick leaves, leaving the tips a deep bronze or a reddish work of art. In full sun, my foliage is more richly colored than when planted in shade.

My family will quickly fill the container to capacity, causing crowding and stress. This is when I usually bloom. My blooms will cover the tips of a stem that rises from the center of my rosette and grow to about six inches. The flowers are star-shaped, frilly-pink with red or lavender touches, but it's not really a time to celebrate. My flowers are a marker that my job is complete, and as the blooms fade so do I. Nature has provided, by my death, a natural cycle that gives more room for my offspring to grow and propagate a new generation.

I also like to grow in many areas of the garden. I'm completely happy tucked into nooks and crannies of rock walls or stonework. It's so simple to indent some soil in a small space, press me in and watch me secure a toehold. Place small rocks or pebbles around my rosette as an anchor so I won't fall out. Soon a whole colony of hens and chicks will be massed around me, filling up gaps with a tight tapestry of evergreen color. With my spreading habit, I'm a natural ground cover for filling areas along the front of a sunny border foundation planting or a narrow strip along a paving or fence line. For as long as I can remember, I've been used as a roof-garden perennial, and I acquired the common name of "houseleek" because of this. I will thrive in these areas even better if they are located in the lean soil, high-sun area of a western mountain garden.

To propagate me, cut the main, "umbilical cord" stolon from the mother hen. Take these offsets and press them into the soil just as if they are cuttings. They will grow! If a large area would look fantastic massed with a carpet of my richly colored leaves, a gardener can dig and replant my chicks as soon as they appear, ensuring multiplication. I never interfere in the new chick's independence and promiscuity, so frequently they change foliage color, which creates a unique mosaic in the garden. My genealogy is impossible to sort out, with one main difference—the spiderweb or cobweb side of the family is draped with silky hairs that connect to each other, forming a web so they are easy to recognize. They grow in a smaller ball shape and bloom red.

S. 'Purple Beauty' is a popular favorite, with a more open rosette and captivating blood-red leaf tips. Its winter foliage turns a deep bronze, and summer colors may vary from season to season. Sometimes it's hard to foretell what we will do. Growing us brings an intriguing surprise and element of fun.

In the past, we were used on rooftops to deflect lightning and prevent fires. Legends say that we were a gift from Jupiter for protection from these elements. Today, we are are used in fire-wise gardens due to the water that is stored in our fleshy leaves. With the worry of wildfires in the West, it makes sense that we should be planted in every western garden and perhaps on every roof too!

FIRE-RESISTANT PERENNIALS

A PLUME OF SMOKE rising from a distant mountain peak is one of the most gut-wrenching sights. Most of these fires are lightning caused. The summer heat and dryness of the West contributes to the uncontrollable rage of a wildfire, but so do some of the plants that are native to the mountains. Resinous plants such as spruce, pine, juniper, and fir explode in a fire, and so does the waxy, terpene, oil-filled wood of plants like sagebrush and greasewood. These are plants that inhabit our mountains along with the ground-spreading "fire starter" called cheatgrass.

The number of people who are moving into mountainous areas is rising, and protecting life and property from a wildfire is all but impossible. Fires in Utah in one year alone destroyed over a half a million acres, at the cost of fifty million dollars to fight the fires and eight million to reseed the scorched areas. Other western states reported similar statistics. Homeowners can obey the fire restrictions put in place when fire conditions are hazardous: no open fires, no smoking, no fireworks or discharging ammunition. For the protection of our own homes and surrounding environment there are things that we must do.

LANDSCAPING FOR FIRE SAFETY

1. REMOVE FUEL

Homes can be protected through a buffer zone of trimmed or cleared plants. The first thirty feet are the most critical and need to be defensible space around the house or structure. Many mountain cabin owners prefer a thick stand of trees and wildflowers around their cabins because it's a big part of the beauty of living in the mountains, but that is not defendable space, and firefighters will often pass over a property they can't get into with their equipment. Clearing the next one hundred feet from the house will slow or stop a ground fire. All vegetation, including ornamental plants, are potential wildfire fuel. Adding the protection of fuel breaks, like cement or gravel drives, walkways, parking areas, or irrigated lawns are effective fire-wise features. An outdoor source of water in the form of a sprinkling system or hose can save a property.

2. REDUCE FUEL

Yard maintenance with regular irrigation and well-trimmed and mulched plants is effective in slowing a fire. Mulch reduces water loss, making plants less flammable. Plus it reduces weeds and ambient temperatures. Keep weeds and litter removed and trees and shrubs well pruned. Remove any limbs of trees extending over buildings or within ten feet of a chimney. Reduce ladder fuels from shrubs that help fire leap from shrubs to trees by minimizing overlapping branches between trees and shrubs. It's an additional safety feature to prune the bottom ten feet of tree branches.

3. PLANT A FIRE-RESISTANT LANDSCAPE

Many plants with the following characteristics have a natural ability to resist burning.

- low stature
- high moisture content
- no volatile oils
- high salt content
- minimal production of dry, twiggy material
- slow growing and well adapted to the site

PERENNIALS FOR FIRE-WISE LANDSCAPES

The following huge list of perennials with fire resistance gives any landscape all-season color, excellent foliage, cold hardiness, and drought tolerance. The gardens may not be as lush and full, but they will look neat and tidy. The payoff is that at least a gardener still has a garden at the end of the fire season.

GROUND COVERS

- *Ajuga reptans*, bugleweed
- *Antennaria*, pussytoes
- *Bergenia cordifolia*, heartleaf bergenia
- *Cerastium*, snow-in-summer
- *Convallaria*, lily-of-the-valley
- *Delosperma*, hardy ice plant
- *Festuca*, fescue varieties
- *Heuchera sanguinea*, coral bells
- *Iberis sempervirens*, candytuft
- *Lysimachia nummularia*, creeping Jenny
- *Pachysandra terminalis*, Japanese spurge
- *Phlox subulata*, creeping phlox
- *Potentilla* spp. varieties
- *Sedum*, stonecrop

- *Sempervivum*, hens and chicks
- *Tulipa*, tulip
- *Veronica*, speedwell
- *Vinca minor*, periwinkle

HERBACIOUS PERENNIALS

- *Achillea*, or yarrow
- *Aquilegia*, columbine
- *Centranthus ruber*, red valerian
- *Coreopsis*, tickseed
- *Echinacea purpurea*, purple coneflower
- *Erigeron* hybrids, fleabane
- Ferns, native and non-native
- *Gaillardia*, blanket flower
- *Geranium*, cranesbill
- *Hemerocallis*, daylily
- *Iris*, flag
- *Kniphofia uvaria*, red hot poker
- *Lupinus*, lupine
- *Oenothera*, evening primrose
- *Penstemon*, beardtongue
- *Polemonium*, Jacob's ladder
- *Salvia*, sage
- *Stachys*, lamb's ears
- *Yucca*, Adam's needle

Ground crews, often called "Hotshots" or Smoke Jumpers, move into the burning inferno to cut firebreaks by removing fuel from the wildfires path.

A thank you should be given to Montana State University Extension for compiling parts of the above list of fire-resistant perennials. For additional listing of fire-resistant trees and shrubs, go ahead and visit www.msuextension.org.

The summer monsoon season brings a thunder and lightning firework show to the Rocky Mountains. Residents wait for the much-needed moisture the monsoon brings, but the lightning that dances from mountaintop to mountaintop and the gusty winds that accompany it are a time of worry about wildfires. The usual prevailing winds over the Rockies are from the Pacific West. When the monsoon occurs, the summer heat evaporates water from the southern gulfs, and the moisture-laden clouds move north. As the monsoon air lifts above our mountains, the clouds collide, causing a summertime light show that can cause fires but can also quench and restore the parched earth.

Next year may bring new calamities. That is the nature of the Earth and gardeners. We'll remove and haul away the burnt ashes and till the soil. We'll plant the seed, always having a vision of perfection in our gardens. Disasters humble us but will *never make us quit.*

Every summer, thousands of square miles of the western US is scorched and damaged by lightning-sparked fires during the summer monsoon.

This BLM Firewise Garden in Idaho demonstrates fire resistance with over 300 species of both native and non-native plants. The garden is located in the Idaho Botanical Gardens in Boise.

Yucca filamentosa
(YUK-uh)
ADAM'S NEEDLE

SHAPE	Vase-shaped with cup-shaped plumes of flowers
HEIGHT	Leaves to two feet, flower stems to six feet
WIDTH	The older, the bigger—up to two feet around
BLOOM TIME	Mid-June
COLORS	Cream
SITE	Well drained
LIGHT	Full sun
HARDINESS	Zone 4
COMMENTS	Strong focal point

Yucca in bloom is hard to beat for stunning looks. The height and delicate creamy-white colored bells are eye catching.

Yucca is such a dramatic, rugged perennial that it creates an architectural focal point wherever it grows.

Yucca's name is the Caribbean name for cassava. Yucca is the state flower of New Mexico and gives a distinct southwestern feel to gardens.

The heavy thick roots of yucca are all but impossible to remove. The ends break off, leaving root pieces in the ground that will develop into new yuccas by next spring.

YO! MY NAME is *Yucca*, and I'm as different as my name. First off, I give a crisp architectural focal point to any garden and will make it look dramatic. My dark-green, vase-shaped clump of evergreen leaves look excellent in every season. My thick, tough, swordlike leaves radiate out from an often-hidden basal rosette. They then reach upward to two feet in height. My shape is softened by a slight bending of my outer rim of leaves, almost as if they are bowing to the new center growth. Each leaf has a sharp end on its rigid spine that is edged with long filaments of thread along the margins. These filaments are why my second adjective name is *filamentosa*. As I mature year after year, I'll widen, creating larger even more dramatic focal points. I improve with old age. It may take several years after I'm first planted before I decide to bloom, and then perhaps several years before I bloom again. Each of my rosettes only blooms once and then dies, so don't get impatient. Each crown produces multiple rosette centers, so my blooming will soon occur annually. I promise, I'm well worth the wait!

In early summer, a thick stalk rises from my middle rosette and reaches majestically up to five or six feet in the air. By July, long panicles of nodding creamy-white bells open and completely fill my stalks. The flowers bloom individually and hang downward, opening from the bottom to the top on my semiwoody stem. My look is so ultra modern with a definite Southwestern, desert-xeriscape look that I've become very popular for these types of gardens. I've also become popular for landscaping around restaurants that want this type of dramatic look along with my indestructible constitution.

I'm a cinch to care for. My best performance is in well-drained soil, but I'm so adaptable that I grow in a variety of soils. To top this off, I'm also wind and fire resistant. Plant me in any problematic spots in the garden, even those that seem too dry for most plants, and I'll grow. Pollution doesn't faze me either, making me a top choice for urban roadsides and highway medium plantings. Once I'm in the ground, I'm all but signed in cement and will grow in the same spot for decades, never needing to be removed. I even grow well in part shade but may not bloom as much. However, with foliage as nice as mine, I can still be used as a specimen plant in a partial-shade garden. However, too much water will rot my roots.

The only real care I need is removal of my stem after flowering stops and trimming off my bottom foliage after winter. My flower stem is so tough that if it is left on, it will persist sometimes for a couple of years and is very unsightly. Cut or prune the stem right down to the base of my rosette. I stay nicely evergreen, even through the coldest of Zone 4 winters, but the bottom layer of my leaves will show discoloration after winter, so I'll look nicer with those leaves removed. Be sure to wear gloves and use a sharp knife or scissors because my foliage is impossible to pull by hand. Each browned leaf will need to be cut individually and placed in the garbage can. My leaves do not compost well and will turn stringy. On occasion, I have ended up looking like a miniature Joshua tree after pruning, but new shoots around my base will fill in nicely before the season is over.

I'm a rabbit-resistant perennial, probably because of the sharpness of my leaf margins, but I serve as a staple food for the western mule deer—especially in the spring. Earwigs like to hide in my thick foliage, but they are never damaging. Butterflies and hummingbirds are attracted to me, but it is the night moths that do most of my pollinating, because my fragrance is richer at night. In return, I feed the moth's larvae.

Propagating me is not an easy task. My roots grow so long and deep that it's almost impossible to dig me for division without leaving broken root segments. Taproots and lateral roots of mine have been found deeper than twenty feet. Any pieces of roots left in the soil will eventually grow into miniature yuccas, and this may be the easiest way to obtain new starts. Trying to germinate seeds gathered from my stems is rather thankless and can take three to four years or longer. The bottom line on propagation is to harvest my offshoots pulled from the base of the mother plant and plant these.

I'm a native plant of southeastern North America, but I have naturalized north. A close relative called *Y. glauca,* or soapweed yucca, is a true native Zone 3 plant and can be found north through Canada and south to Texas. Soapweed yucca can be a tenacious weed in many areas, but it adds a nice desert touch to a garden.

Modern science is now finding all kinds of uses for me, but the Native Americans have always used me as a source of healing. My leaves were used to treat skin lesions, inflammation, and sprains. I was also used as food, especially in winter when there was a shortage. My buds, flowers, fruits, seedpods, and stems are all edible. It's cool that not only am I ornamental for the garden, but I have also been of service to Native Americans and will probably serve more people in the future.

METAL ART AS GARDEN FOCAL POINTS

GARDEN ART CREATED out of metal simply had to originate in Rocky Mountain gardens. Our need for durable art that would stand up to the elements of hot and cold temperatures led naturally to using metal. A swing or gate made with metal will not deteriorate or require constant upkeep. A metal garden bench will not get ruined by water from sprinklers or winter snow. Metal garden furniture can be set solidly in cement and left outside through the seasons. Our desire for garden focal points year-round and not just during the summer gardening season found an outlet by using metal sculptures. Recycled cast-off farm equipment is always available on our ranches and farmyards, so why not use it in unconventional but affordable ways?

Metal artwork can be bold and daring or modern and contemporary. It can also be vintage like a bicycle or functional like a gate and bridge. Wherever it is placed, metal art adds a new fresh dimension and a strong focal point to its garden surroundings.

A small green gecko can be tucked almost anywhere in a garden. Small metal objects are just as delightful as larger sculptures.

These garden benches welcome a gardener to take a break, but more important they are indestructible art work—no matter how many years they sit out in the weather.

The metal roadrunner sculpture looks so natural that a gardener waits to hear its "beep-beep" any minute.

This steep hill would never grow an appropriate lawn, so the homeowner filled it with rock mulch and displayed an ancient treasure. Much better than grass!

Plants are not really necessary with this personable, hardworking rock-carrying man, who furnishes a focal point all by himself.

Gardens are being used as outdoor rooms, and no room is complete without art on the wall like the beauty of this bicycle.

A dog made of angle iron, flat steel plate, and sheet metal trimmings holds a colorful bouquet of flowers, which welcomes visitors to the garden.

DROUGHT-TOLERANT PERENNIALS SUMMARY

WATER HAS BECOME expensive and limited and may be considered a luxury item in the years to come. Growers have been lucky so far, but it's time to pull our heads out and face this reality. Gardeners can be the movers and pushers for good in the environment, and its time to face this challenge! How? Start with a hot, sun-filled area in your yard that shows stress and requires more frequent watering, and create a drought-tolerant garden. Check out the following list of attractive, easy-to-grow, drought perennials that will thrive from north to south in our mountain gardens. Any color, height, or growing season is available in these carefree flowers. Plant them in your garden as an experiment to see if they are enjoyable, and if they are, rally to spread the word. Just try it. You might like it! Perhaps as gardeners we can help sustain our most valuable resource—water. Without it, there would be no gardens and no gardeners.

POINTS TO REMEMBER

- Remember the three C's: compost, compost, and compost. Compost or mulch has the ability to cool the soil and help the plants retain moisture. Two inches at a time is adequate, and no other fertilizer will be needed.

- Remember, drought perennials' foliage can be fine and lacy, thick, succulent, or waxy and can have hairy or fuzzy leaves. These are the foliage traits of water-wise perennials.

- Remembering to loosen the soil in a drought-tolerant garden, for drainage is crucial. With aeration of the soil around the perennials, their roots will grow deep into the soil where the moisture is held.

- Water tips: Until perennials are established, they will need supplemental watering. Water deep and infrequently. Gradually lessen the amount of water. This will coax and train the roots to move deeper into the soil for water.

- Perennials are like children and do not always grow the way you think they will. Monitor and care for them until you become better acquainted.

- Drought-tolerant perennials are sustainable, rarely need division, and will reseed naturally.

Annuals are not recommended for drought-tolerant landscapes, but most gardeners need a few for more color, especially in the fall. So if you find you feel strongly about adding in a few annuals, choose from this list. They require half an inch to an inch of additional water per week. Happy water-wise gardening!

SPRING-TO-SUMMER-BLOOMING PERENNIALS

SHORT–MEDIUM

Ajuga, bugleweed

Alchemilla, lady's mantle

Antennaria, pussytoes

Arabis, rock cress

Arenaria, mountain sandwort

Armeria, thrift

Artemisia, wormwood

Asters, alpine asters

Cerastium, snow-in-summer

Coreopsis, tickseed

Delosperma, hardy ice plant

Dianthus, pinks

Erigeron, fleabane

Euphorbia, cushion spurge

Festuca, blue fescue grass

Geranium sanguineum, cranesbill

Helleborus, Lenten rose

Iberis, candytuft

Lamium, dead nettle

Nepeta, catmint

Phlox, creeping phlox

Poppies nudicaule, Iceland poppies

Pulsatilla, pasqueflower

Saponaria, rock soapwort

MEDIUM–TALL

Anthemis, golden marguerite

Aquilegia, columbine

Hesperis, sweet rocket

Iris

Lychnis, rose campion

Nepeta, catmint

Papaver orientale, poppy

Penstemon, beardtongue

Tanacetum, painted daisy

SUMMER-TO-FALL-BLOOMING PERENNIALS

SHORT–MEDIUM

Artemisia

Callirhoe, wine cups

Centaurea, mountain bluet

Gaillardia, blanket flower

Gypsophila, creeping baby's breath

Hedera, English ivy

Lavandula, lavender

Oenothera, evening primrose

Sedum, stonecrop

Sempervivum, hens and chicks

Veronica repens

Thymus, creeping thyme

MEDIUM–TALL

Achillea, yarrow

Alcea rosea, hollyhock

Centranthus ruber, red valerian

Echinacea, coneflower

Grasses, tall

Hemerocallis, daylily

Kniphofia, red hot poker

Liatris, gayfeather

Limonium, sea lavender

Linum, blue flax

Rudbeckia, black-eyed Susan

Salvia nemerosa, sage

Stachys, lamb's ears

Verbascum, mullein

Veronica

Yucca, Adam's needle

FALL-BLOOMING PERENNIALS

SHORT–MEDIUM

Ceratostigma, plumbago

Gaura, whirling butterflies

Liriope, lilyturf

Schizachyrium, little bluestem

Sedum, stonecrop

MEDIUM–TALL

Grasses, ornamental

Perovskia, Russian sage

Sedum, stonecrop

Solidago, goldenrod

WATER-WISE ANNUALS

Artemesia, dusty miller

Calendula, marigold

Centaurea, bachelor's button

Cosmos

Dianthus

Fountain grass

Gazania

Lantana

Lobularia, alyssum

Mexican sunflower

Mirabilis

Nasturtium

Osteospermum

Pentas

Petunia

Portulaca

Rudbeckia hirta

Salvia

Scavola

Verbena

Zinnia

THE DOE

Early morn
Power walking
I chanced upon a deer.
Soft eyes met mine.
I smiled!

Summer
Thru fall we met,
From tall grass she greeted.
I had a friend.
I laughed!

Deep snow
Was my doe all right?
Spring brought joy and two fawns.
Recognition.
I thanked!

Hard hit
A speeding car
Left her as roadkill.
A magpie's feast.
I cried!

WILDLIFE-RESISTANT PERENNIALS

WHERE I LIVE, I have to be aware of local garden pests and how to keep them out of my garden. The Rocky Mountains are the backbone of the West. They stretch more than 3,000 miles from Canada to New Mexico, and every mile is deer habitat. Rocky Mountain deer are called mule deer because of their big, mule-like ears. Mule deer are large. Mature bucks weigh from one hundred to over four hundred pounds and need a lot of food. In the bitter cold of winter, the deer require over five pounds of food per day. During spring birthing, females need more than ten pounds of new green sprouts per day. In early spring, they browse our lawns, pawing out huge circles of snow in order to find food. The lawn will always recover, but flower beds may take longer. The best way to protect your garden is to plant deciduous perennials, or plants that go underground in winter. Evergreen perennials such as ajuga, bergenia, lavender, or creeping phlox all have a reputation for being deer resistant, but when it's a matter of life or death, deer will consume these and anything else that is evergreen.

When we first started gardening at Bear Lake in Idaho, the deer dilemma was an eye-opening experience. The previous spring, we had planted our total income tax return in trees and shrubs. By the end of that next winter, our entire investment was decimated by deer, and we were devastated. We tried a multitude of deer repellent techniques that never worked. One of the funniest was playing an all-night talk show on the radio. The talk shows were effective until the guardian buck, who watches the herd from the hill, decided that the radio was not a threat. Then with only a simple nod or lifting of his head, the herd moved down into the garden to graze. Without a sound, the buck would again lift his head and the entire herd would evacuate in an instant.

Deer adapt quickly, so a change of tactics was needed. Electromagnetic or ultrasound devices were useless. We'd heard of some chemical and natural repellents being advertised, so we tried Irish Spring soaps, human hair collected from a beauty parlor, rotten eggs, hot sauce, and even bobcat urine sprays. The philosophy is that the more pungent the odor, the more the deer will avoid the plant. This concept is true up to a point. Artificial smells dissipate, so an egg and hot sauce spray that will only last until the next watering is ridiculous.

About this time, we started to relax with the wildlife and let the old adage "If you can't beat them, join them" kick in. So many of our special memories—like the time we watched and guarded a herd of elk swimming across the lake on the first day of deer hunting season or the time our beach became the home for twin moose calves—come from that time and are still talked about. A sighting of a pure-white albino doe and two fawns started our grandsons on their photography craze. By rethinking the wildlife situation, we have made some planting adjustments, and the gardens remain full, lush, and worry-free.

You may also find that your garden is overrun by hungry wildlife, whether that wildlife takes the form of deer or something else. If so, then let me recommend a few adjustments you can make to your garden.

ADJUSTMENT # 1 PLANT PERENNIALS THAT ARE UNAPPEALING TO WILDLIFE

- Plant deciduous perennials that go underground in winter.
- Do not plant any perennial that stays evergreen in winter.
- Do not plant perennials that invite animals like deer into the garden, such as tulips. My neighbors said they enjoyed watching the deer so much they put a salt lick in their yard. Now they wonder why the deer won't leave.

Several winters ago, gardeners in the West were blessed with a long winter of deep snow. My gardening friend Janet, from across the lake, took pity on a hungry moose that lived near her yard. She would travel to the Brigham City fruit stands and beg for their withered old apples. She fed the hungry moose as long as she was able to keep bringing apples but was greatly relieved when a spring thaw opened up some grazing space for her moose. She forgot about that incident until the next winter when her moose and a hungry calf showed up on her porch again, begging for apples.

A doe and two fawns took up residence in our yard that same winter. Our four– and five-year-old granddaughters were playing on the sun porch when the fawns moved right up to the sliding glass doors and pressed their leathery noses against the windows. Maybe they were attracted by the girls' giggling? My granddaughters still talk about this fond memory.

- When deer browse gardens all summer, they destroy vegetable and flower gardens. We are fortunate in the Rockies that our "mulies" move to the more private dining spot of the cooler higher mountain ranges. The following deer-repellent recipe was given to me by a gardener who swears it stinks and works: one egg to a cup of water. If the gardens are large or the sprayer holds more liquid, add eggs and water in the same ratio to fill the sprayer. Add hot sauce for stink and dish soap to make it stick. Spray when needed.

- Plant annuals in accent container pots. The small wildlife such as rabbits love annuals, but they never seem to bother the containers. One of our first experiences planting annuals at the lake was a dismal failure. Two flats of pansies were consumed in an overnight raid of the garden.

- Know that a hungry animal will eat almost anything, and regional differences play a part. What works in one area may not work in other places.

- *The most important adjustment is planting wildlife-resistant perennials.* It is the smell, taste, and texture of a perennial that makes it deer resistant. Strong, spicy, or scented plants with soft, hairy, or spiky-foliage will be scorned by deer. Planting a row of stinky, spiky chives along the edges of our vegetable gardens protects the plants from deer and rabbits. Cilantro is also a deterrent and keeps fresh lettuce and vegetables safe from rabbits.

ADJUSTMENT # 2 INSTALL A FENCE

When we first started gardening at Bear Lake, my need for a clean, green piece of lawn was overwhelming. On the Fourth of July holiday, while everyone was at the beach swimming, boating, waterskiing, and fishing, I worked at clearing sagebrush and hand-turning the soil. In the last few minutes of vacation, the grass seed was spread, and a sprinkler was set. Great discipline was required to leave the new lawn and return to the workweek.

The following weekend, instead of my imagined picture of germinating green grass . . . I got a big shock! Every cow on the east side of Bear Lake was wallowing in our mud puddle of supposed lawn. Now we laugh at having provided the cattle with a free spa mud bath. We really needed a basic knowledge of the environment in our new gardening situation. Knowledge is a first priority to success in landscaping.

In the West, only about 4 percent of the mountain ranges are under cultivation, but 35 percent of the land is utilized for livestock grazing purposes. Livestock represents the largest portion of farm income within the states. Idaho is an open-range state, meaning cattle are fenced out. Utah's range cattle law is to fence in. Fence in or fence out, a fence was needed!

Fencing the property was not an option but a necessity. The standard requirement for a deer fence is that it be over seven feet in height with a capacity for an electric shock system. The mule deer's stiff-legged gait bounces them right over a shorter fence. Invisible deer fencing was also available at an enormous cost, far over our budget.

We wanted a more decorative type fence than an invisible or electric one. With the constant flow of family and friends in and out and on their way to the beach, there were not satisfying alternatives. What we ended up installing was a black metal pipe fence that also serves as a sprinkler system. This fence not only keeps out the cattle, but it also waters the gardens. The deer can still easily jump over this fence, but they seem to have chosen not to anymore.

ADJUSTMENT # 3 GET A LARGE DOG OR CAT OR BOTH

A large dog will almost always keep wildlife away. Even the scent of a dog is a deterrent to deer and other animals. Our golden lab, Drake, does an amazing job of keeping the Bear Lake gardens deer-free. Fortunately, Drake's fine puppies have continued this service.

Rabbits and other small pests are in many ways more destructive than deer. Our rabbits live across the road and like to play what we call "the go-out game." First, they sneak across the road. Then they look around and hop to the lawn where they wait, frozen to see if we notice them. If we do, they hustle into the flower beds to hide. Most of the deer-resistant perennials are also rabbit resistant, and soon they return to the grass to help us cut and fertilize the lawn.

The entire Rocky Mountain range is a habitat for ground squirrels that we call "potguts." The potguts emerge from their tunnels in early spring to gather food storage for their expected offspring. They stand up on hind legs and chatter as if laughing while they fill their cheeks as full as possible before returning to their tunnels to pack all the food into storage areas. This is where their babies are born. Before it gets hot, the fat little fur balls settle into their burrows, not to be seen until the next spring.

There are a variety of removal methods for these ground squirrels from electromagnetic or vibration devices to mothballs in the tunnels. None of these made any difference. However, when we bring the cats to the lake for the summer, the small wildlife pests seem to evaporate.

Outside pets can solve wildlife problems but are frowned at for bringing their own bathroom usage problems into the garden. Cleaning up after a dog is a regular chore, but cats can be encouraged to use only a certain area for their business. Bare soil attracts a cat because they have natural scratching instincts to dig a hole. The same plants that repel other wildlife will repel cats, especially lavender and *Melissa officinalis*, or lemon balm. Add these perennials to your garden. The shade areas under pine trees are also avoided by cats because the fallen pinecones are prickly to their feet. Coffee grounds scattered in a problem area will also stop a cat and so will citrus peelings left under bushes.

ADJUSTMENT # 4 INSTALL A MOTION SENSOR OR NIGHT LIGHT

At Bear Lake, all electric power is buried underground along the east side of the lake. Black light or star-filled nights are a value treasured by homeowners, but the number of deer getting hit on the highway, especially through winter, was heart wrenching. A solution was to have the power company install a light pole with an electric eye that comes on after dark. We paid for this service, and it is just one of a few night lights located along this entire side of the lake.

Now the number of deer hit by cars in front of our cabin has dropped to nearly nothing. Nighttime drivers can now see that deer are crossing the road and can stop for them.

A surprising new benefit of the installation of the streetlight was an eye-opening shocker. Deer are very savvy! After the streetlight was installed, the deer changed their route to the lake by crossing the highway under the lights. They then followed a new, deer-created, well-packed, well-worn trail behind the greenhouses. Deer are so shy that the greenhouse walls must have made them feel more safe and comfortable.

We rewarded them by leaving huge piles of harvested trimmings along their trail. This must serve them as winter food, because they will have pawed through and sorted out what they liked to eat by spring. They reward us by consuming the trimmings and leaving a calling card of deer droppings, which helps accelerate the composting action of what is left. It makes

Hunting is a great way to practice garden conservation and provide food for a family simultaneously.

a gardener stop to ponder—could the streetlight and compost food serve as a training tool to help eliminate damage in the garden? Or is it just that deer randomly changed to another path? I don't think so, and here is another reason: year after year, as soon as the first fall freeze occurs, the deer will move into the garden and start stripping everything. They seem to know it's okay now. Mutual respect and appreciation flows toward and from the deer. With a little thought and effort, interacting with nature is surprisingly enlightening and rewarding.

ADJUSTMENT # 5 APPRECIATE THE HELPFUL BENEFITS WILDLIFE PROVIDE

Deer and other wildlife animals are helpful in cleaning the yard. Tons of *Hemerocallis*, or daylilies, are grown in our gardens, and fall cleanup of these tough, hard-to-pull leaves is both time consuming and nearly impossible. We leave the daylilies untouched in fall, and by spring the tough, strap-like leaves remove easily. I suppose the deer discovered this also because when I get to the lake in spring, the daylilies are completely cleaned right to the ground. Also, a nice deposit of organic deer pellets surrounds the daylilies to help them grow and bloom better through summer.

Elk and deer venison are food for a family. Wild game is an excellent nutritional source. A mature buck will yield 150 pounds of meat, while a mature elk will provide over 600 pounds.

Alchemilla mollis
(al-keh-MILL-uh)
LADY'S MANTLE

SHAPE	Mound, flowers are clusters
HEIGHT	Twelve inches
WIDTH	Fifteen inches
BLOOM TIME	Early summer
COLORS	Chartreuse
SITE	Alkaline soils
LIGHT	Shade or partial shade
HARDINESS	Zones 3–8
COMMENTS	No serious problems

The fuzzy leaves of lady's mantle catch the tiny dew droplets that glimmer in the morning sun. Alchemilla also produces airy sprays of tiny yellow flowers in the spring.

The lacy sprays of alchemilla are a perfect edger to enhance the blue-green foliage of *Sedum* 'Sunset Cloud'. Both plants are deer resistant and do well in this Idaho garden.

Lady's mantle's foliage is so extraordinary that no garden should be without this fine perennial. The Royal Horticulture Society awarded it the Award of Garden Merit.

Alchemilla's compact mound of lime-green flowers is so unique that it draws attention no matter where it blooms.

I'M KNOWN IN horticultural circles as *Alchemilla mollis*, but you can call me lady's mantle. I'm a small, low-growing perennial with a nicely rounded form that grows a mere twelve inches tall and spreads to about fifteen inches. My flowers are soft, chartreuse sprays that bloom on stems above the foliage, creating a nice airy look.

My most unique trait is my hairy foliage that looks and feels like velvet. It also gives me resistance to marauding wildlife. These gray-green, nearly round leaves have deep pleated lobes, and with one trim after blooming, I will look pleasing all season. My foliage is so different that I'm a good candidate for a container or edging plant in a shady area of the garden. In the heat of the summer, I prefer being planted in partial shade and given a little extra water. I even grow well under the protection of pine trees.

My unusual flowers will brighten a shady garden spot. Most shade perennials bloom white so they show up, but my unique color of chartreuse lights up the garden as if yard lights had been placed along the path or walkway. Include several plantings along borders to encourage visitors' eyes to follow my bright colors. Sprinkled around in the shade, my tiny star flowers will perk up the entire shady area.

I'm a really easy perennial to multiply because I self-seed. A direct sow in the fall will ensure my seeds get the vernalization they require. For my seedlings to germinate around me, allow the seed pods to dry on the plant and fall at my feet. If they fall in an optimal-growing condition, I have been known to become invasive. Should my dappled, sun-like flowers and my neatly pleated foliage be needed in another area of the garden, bag my seed heads to capture the ripening seeds. I can also be sown directly into the spring garden after the last frost.

I'm so well-mannered that it's an uncomplicated process to dig and divide my root ball. First, cut me back hard, dig, and split me into three or more pieces. Then plant me wherever airy clouds of delicate lemon froth are needed.

The origin of my common name came about because of two well-known folklore concepts. Lady's mantle was the flower used to adorn the neck of the Virgin Mary when she entered Jerusalem with Jesus before His Crucifixion. I was also named for the pleated ruffs worn around the necklines of fourteenth-century Spaniards. All of this came about because of my beautifully lobed foliage.

I'm helpful when I'm planted to soften pathways and edges in the shade garden or to anchor the feet of bigger plants. Use my graceful foliage in front of the tall, vertical spikes of spuria iris for a satisfying combination. For a unique look, mix my lime-green, lacy foliage with the huge lime-colored leaves of *Hosta* 'Sum and Substance'. I break dormancy earlier than hosta, so I fill in the blank spring garden spot until the hosta develops more fully. By the time I bloom, the lime hosta leaves are just unfolding, giving the garden a real wow factor. I really stand out when planted in the middle of a flat-growing blue-green foliaged perennial like ajuga, or any blue flower for that matter.

I'm small, so planting me with a vigorous spreading ground cover like *Galium*, or sweet woodruff, would give both of us the look of a no-identity or a mish-mass mess. Keep the edges of the garden where I'm planted simple to suit how simple, neat, and tidy I am.

My foliage is my most remarkable feature and adds a touch of magic to a garden. After watering or a rainstorm, water sparkles on my pleated surface like diamonds. This is due to my leaves remarkable water-resistant abilities. The contact force between the water and the leaf is so incompatible that a layer of air penetrates the solid-liquid interface. These beads of water were considered by alchemists as the purest form of water. They utilized this water in their quest to turn base metal into gold. That is how I became know as alchemilla. My Latin name is derived from Arabic, meaning "alchemy," or "little magical one."

SOFTENING GARDEN EDGES WITH PERENNIALS

SMALL, COMPACT PERENNIALS that can be planted on the front edge of flower beds, paths, driveways, raised beds, and lawns are important to the garden because they act as a picture frame or finishing touch to the flower bed. Planting small perennial clumps along the front edge of a garden hides any inconsistencies in cement, edgings, or rock work, and furnishes a finished, neat appearance.

Not only do these small plants improve a garden's appearance, but they also form an attractive weed barrier by blocking seeds from blowing into the garden and germinating.

Tiarella's delicate spikes are secondary to the colorful foliage of this excellent shade plant edger.

EDGING PERENNIALS FOR A SHADED AREA

- *Aquilegia* 'Winky Double' is a short twelve-inch columbine for partial-shade gardens. The size and long-blooming ability of 'Winky Double' make it a choice perennial to grow in pots or containers.

- *Bergenia*, heartleaf, is an evergreen edger with such excellent foliage that it can be used along a walkway in wintertime and look superb!

- *Campanula carpatica* 'Blue Clips' or 'White Clips' has a long-blooming season of delicate blue and white bells. The flowers only reach eight inches tall but will spill over rocks to soften edges.

- *Corydalis lutea*, yellow corydalis, is considered a Zone 5 perennial, but it winters reliably. It forms fernlike green leaves and produces masses of golden-yellow flowers from late spring through summer.

- *Helleborus,* Lenten rose, is an excellent choice for an edger because of its leathery evergreen foliage and nodding, cup-shaped, early-spring flowers.

- *Heuchera*, coral bells, is an excellent edger due to its compact size, colorful foliage, long bloom time, and tendency to stay evergreen.

- *Heucherella*, foamy bells, is a hybrid cross between heuchera and tiarella. The foliage stays attractive throughout the season, making it an excellent candidate for containers or pots.

- *Hosta* 'June' is just one of many dwarf hostas. 'June' has colorful turquoise-edged leaves with a golden center.

- *Iberis* (See page 34)

- *Lamiastrum,* Herman's pride, has unique, dark green foliage that is marbled in silver. Each stem is topped with pale yellow, pearl-shaped blooms. This fine perennial only grows twelve inches tall and holds a compact mound shape all year.

- *Tiarella*, foamflower, is a clump-forming, fragrant, native perennial. The foliage leaves are glossy with prominent markings in the middle.

Hosta 'June' is just one of many newly developed dwarf hostas. Edging a shady flower bed without using annuals can be a smart, economical solution. The dwarf hostas, just like other hostas, are dependable and reliable, meaning they return year after year, are consistent in size, and their unique colored foliage adds class to a shady garden.

EDGING PERENNIALS FOR SUN

The edges around areas like lawns, sidewalks, or driveways usually require a perennial that grows in sunshine. The following is a sampling of deer-resistant, sun-loving alpine edgers.

- *Armeria*, thrift, blooms early and sporadically throughout the summer months. The blooms are traditionally ball-shaped flowers in rose shades.

- *Artemisia* 'Silver Mound' (See page 66)

Campanula carpatica 'Blue Clips' or 'White Clips' are considered late-breaking perennials. Plants that fit into this category usually need longer daylight hours before breaking dormancy.

- *Aster dumosus* 'Wood's' are small, compact fall bloomers. The 'Wood's' series, with their abundant clusters of purple, pink and blue, are indestructible plants for the front border of a garden.

- *Dianthus,* pinks, has low blue-green mats of evergreen foliage that grows seven to eight inches tall. (See page 74)

- *Coreopsis verticillata,* threadleaf coreopsis, has bright, lemon-colored flowers that bloom midsummer through fall. It forms an airy clump of fine, needlelike foliage on bushy, fifteen-inch perennials.

- *Gaillardia aristata,* 'Arizona' series, or blanket flower, offers a shorter, more compact and uniform blanket flower for edging.

- *Geranium sanguineum,* little-leafed cranesbill, is an especially strong grower but stays in a compact mound. Brilliant, red-colored foliage gives this low-growing geranium a winter season of color.

- *Lychnis arkwrightii* 'Orange Gnome' and 'Lumina' are a surprising new spring-blooming duo that brings orange and red to the early summer garden.

- *Monarda* or bee balm (See page 160)

- *Nepeta* 'Little Trudy', or catmint, is tiny—only ten to twelve inches tall. Shearing 'Little Trudy' after its first bloom will guarantee it will bloom again.

- *Oenothera missouries,* evening primrose, is an attractive, short edger but will also cascade. Evening primrose's pale yellow blooms appear new each morning and won't stop blooming from early summer through fall.

- *Platycodon* 'Astra', balloon flower, has interesting buds that burst open into bell-shaped violet, pink, or white flowers. The 'Astra' series has exceptional branching and a uniform, compact habit. They grow to only eight inches tall.

- *Sedum,* stonecrop, forms low, compact clumps of silvery, smokey-green or even cherry-red-tinted foliage.

- *Veronica spicata* 'Royal Candles' grows spikes of violet-blue flowers that bloom all summer. 'Royal Candles' will reach fifteen inches tall and is nicely compact.

Gardeners who plant a few of these short, compact perennials will have attractive, colorful, finished edges in their gardens. They might choose to forfeit planting expensive annuals. This one simple planting technique moves way out in front in creating gorgeous, sustainable gardens that are easy to care for, have all-season color, and return bigger and better the next year.

Dianthus blooms in late spring or early summer, just when its masses of hot-pink, red, rose, and white colors are enjoyed the most. By deadheading the first season of bloom, this perennial will bloom again off and on all summer.

Pictured here are two 'Wood's Pink' asters. They are very neat and tidy, but best of all they add color to the fall perennial garden.

Allium
(al-EE-uhm)
'PURPLE SENSATION'

SHAPE	Tall stems, globe flower
HEIGHT	Twenty-five inches
WIDTH	Single stem and bloom
BLOOM TIME	Late spring to early summer
COLORS	Purples
SITE	Slight alkaline, well drained
LIGHT	Sun or partial sun
HARDINESS	Zones 4–8
COMMENTS	Adds interest; goes dormant in summer

'Purple Sensation' is my favorite allium. It is just the right size in the garden; it grows tall enough to be showy and short enough not to topple.

Stacking 1: These pink and red 'Darwin Impression' tulips are planted over the lilium and allium bulbs.

Stacking 2: Allium in bloom. Notice the lilium foliage emerging around it.

Stacking 3: Lilium is now blooming, hiding any remains of the yellowing tulip or allium foliage.

ANY FLOWER THAT earns the prestigious European Gardening Award of Merit might deserve to be proud, but vanity isn't necessary because Mother Nature has already crowned me—literally. I'm *Allium* 'Purple Sensation', and I'm not only beautiful, I'm also strong and versatile. I'm tall enough to be showy and short enough not to topple over, with an intense purple "crown" of flowers that forms into a colorful, perfectly rounded bloom that perches on the top of my single, tubular stalk—almost like a fancy headdress on a Las Vegas showgirl.

I've not always been so gorgeous. I started out as a lowly onion, grown in the vegetable garden, but now I've been moved to the perennial bed or border with the other flowers. Cultivation has turned me into a novelty plant, so spotlight me in full or partial sun. I may have evolved from an onion, but I have still retained my marvelous health-giving properties.

For a late-spring performance, plant my bulbs during the fall in average soil with my point side up. The Latin root of onion is *unio,* meaning one. I grow from a single bulb, and when I break dormancy in the spring, I send up one stock. I bloom only once a year, so I suppose I could be considered a one-show stand . . . but what pizzazz I add to the flower garden!

I even add pizzazz to floral arrangements, especially contemporary designs, and I have been painted by artists such as Rembrandt and Baker, who immortalized me in works of art. I also dry nicely, so I'm an ideal choice for dried arrangements.

I'm a deterrent to aphids, apple scab, and mildew in the garden. I chase away ants, Japanese beetles, and deer. I can even be poisonous to cats and dogs, so don't let them consume my foliage. I contain some iron, vitamins, and even a mild antibiotic. I think science would be wise to explore my healing abilities.

For a full-season of color, plant me in the fall with other perennial bulbs by stacking. Depending on the size of the planting spot, use about seven or eight liliums, five to seven alliums, twelve daffodils, or twelve tulips. Remove soil from a five-to-six-foot oval in a full-sun or partial-shade area of the garden. Plant the liliums first, twelve inches deep. Cover them lightly with soil that has been enriched with manure or compost and phosphorous. The deeper stacking method of these bulbs will need phosphorous for root development, and the phosphorous on the surface may never reach the depth of my bulbs, so mix a handful into the soil. Place my allium bulbs in next, but stagger me, and don't set me right on top of the lilium bulbs. I multiply slower when planted deeper, so place me at about a ten-inch depth and cover lightly. Next, push in your choice of either daffodils or tulips, and fill up the planting hole. If tulips are used, be sure to use the Darwin tulips, which are more perennial than other types. Now wait for the next season's performance.

In spring, the daffodils or tulips will bloom first. If you garden in a deer-free area, you should have no worries with growing tulips. But if you don't, then use deer-resistant daffodils. I make my spectacular entry next in late spring. I'm followed by the grand finale of the midsummer-blooming lilium. That's a pretty amazing production for a five-foot section of garden area! Bulbs really know how to put on a show.

I'm a strong, Zone 4, long-lived perennial. I'll live even longer if I'm divided about every four years. My offspring can be dug and divided and planted or shared with other gardeners. All bulbs prefer a dry period after blooming, so remember that overwatering can weaken us.

If my flower spheres are left to dry on my stem, they look very interesting, but the seeds will drop and I'll reseed like grass. Just let the seedlings grow or weed them out. It will take years for the seeds to be ready for an audition.

PERENNIAL BULBS

PERENNIAL BULBS LIKE allium add excitement to the garden. Its unusual look probably came about naturally by the bulb's need to accommodate pollinators. Over the 3,500 years that these flowers have been noted, a vast array of unique sizes, shapes, and colors have evolved. When lumping all of these different varieties and characteristics together, one trait stays common. All have a highly developed, miraculous underground food storage system called a bulb. Having their own food storage makes bulbs the easiest perennials to grow.

When outside conditions become favorable or spring arrives, the bulbs start to grow rapidly. As the plant expands and blooms, the bulb's food reserves are depleted. The plant must work to build next year's provisions. Using the magic of photosynthesis and the yellowing foliage left after the plant stops blooming, bulbs convert water and nutrients into stored energy for next year's growth. Incredibly, the bulb storage container becomes filled by just waiting and resting until the next year.

WHAT IS A BULB?

Bulbs have four distinct types of storage systems: true bulbs, corms, rhizomes, and tubers. All four types of bulbs consist of fleshy tissue where nutrients and moisture are stored. However, each bulb type has a different way to accomplish this storage.

TRUE BULBS

True bulbs are modified buds with fleshy scales. Shoots emerge from the top, and roots grow from a basal plate. A true bulb has a covering and often has scales that look as if they could be peeled. A few of the true bulbs are *Allium, Amaryllis, Chionodoxa* (glory-of-the-snow), *Fritillaria, Galanthus* (snowdrop), *Hyacinthus* (hyacinth), *Lilium, Narcissus* (daffodil), and *Tulipa* (tulip).

PROPAGATING TRUE BULBS

After the foliage has turned brown, dig the clumps of bulbs. Carefully brush away soil and discard any injured, diseased, or rotten bulbs. Divide the bulb by easing the daughter bulb away from the mother bulb. Make sure each includes a portion of the basal plate. If they do not separate easily, leave them for another year.

CORMS

Corm bulbs are similar to true bulbs but are more solid and lack scales. A corm's food supply is the big difference. The stems are packed with nutrients. Small corms are perfect for naturalizing. As the corm gathers nourishment for the next season, infant corms (called *cormels*) develop on top of the dying mother corm. These new cormels will be ready to bloom the next season.

PROPAGATING CORMS

Obtain cormels by lifting the plant when the foliage has withered but is still visible. Remove the cormels that have formed above or around the mother corm and replant.

RHIZOMES

The rhizome's food storage units are underground stems. This type of bulb structure is planted near the soil surface. Examples of rhizome bulbs are *Agapanthus, Anemone, Canna, Convallaria* (lily-of-the-valley), and *Iris*. Shown below is the process of growing canna lilies.

Canna lilies are not hardy perennials in cold climates and have to be lifted and stored after frost.

If cannas are lifted, they will have multiplied three times for every rhizome planted. This is a great investment for a little bit of elbow grease and time.

Daffodil bulb in fall (true bulb)

Crocus corm

Canna rhizome in spring

Dahlia tubers in spring

PROPAGATING CANNA RHIZOMES

After a frost turns the canna lily's leaves to a papery brown, cut off the stock with pruners.

Dig up the clump carefully, lifting the canna from underneath. The lifted roots will often separate naturally while shaking off the soil. Leave any soil that remains, because it will help the rhizomes winter better. The final division is done in the spring.

- Box up the cannas: The lifted roots are packed in a medium-sized cardboard container lined with a plastic garbage bag. Fill the voids in the box between the cannas with a dry, neutral medium like perlite or peatmoss.

  The boxed cannas are then moved into a dark, cool area that does not freeze. Old potato cellars are an ideal storage area with their consistent humidity. Check them midwinter for moisture. If the surrounding media feels dry, either sprinkle with water or push an extra-small paper cup filled one-third full of water into the media and fold the plastic bag closed again. The natural evaporation process will restore the humidity.

- In spring, Unpack and clean the cannas: Clean and discard any withered or damaged rhizomes. Save only firm, crisp, white-fleshed bulbs that are showing new growth. Most of the Cannas will divide naturally, but extra-large ones will need to be cut with sterilized pruners or a knife.

- Plant the cannas: Pot rhizomes or plant them into the garden depending on outside temperatures. Water initially and then withhold water until green foliage is visible. Too much water at first is much worse than too little. They grow in hot sun, and both leaves and blooms will not perform up to expectations in a shaded area. They are heavy feeders, so at the initial planting give each a double feeding of timed-release plant fertilizer (such as Osmocote 18-6-12) and mix it into the soil.

GROWING CANNA LILIES

Cannas at one time were called swamp lilies because they adore water. They will even grow in water features or ponds, so give these beauties plenty of water to keep them happy. Deadheading the spent blooms as well as removal of the wart-covered seedpods will keep the lilies in full bloom. Adding manure to their planting area the fall before also helps the flowers perform at peak potential.

TUBERS

Tubers have enlarged portions of underground stem storage units that form chubby bulbs. A potato is a tuber type of plant. Tubers have eyes from which sprouts grow. Many of a gardener's favorite plants are grown from tubers. For example, *Anemone spp.*, *Begonias*, *Caladium*, *Corydalis*, *Dahlias*, *Eranthis*, and *Eremurus* (foxtail lillies). Many of these tuberous type plants are not winter-hardy perennials in the West but can be harvested and stored inside during winter. Dahlias, probably the most recognized of the tuber family, are shown below.

PROPAGATING DAHLIA TUBERS

With a big shovel, carefully lift dahlia clumps at least a week after the plants have been frozen. This gives time for any nutrition in the stems to move down into the tuber's storage bulb. Trim off the flower stems, leaving at least a two-inch stem on top. Leaving a stem is an important step because the stem contains an enzyme that triggers germination in the spring. Wait until spring to divide the clumps. Cutting the clumps in fall seems to weaken the tubers, making them more likely to deteriorate and go mushy during storage.

- Box up the dahlias: Pack the tubers into a box lined with a plastic bag. Black plastic bags store the tubers better than white or clear colors. Cover the tubers with perlite or peatmoss and place in a freeze-free storage area for the winter. In midwinter, check the box for moisture. If the medium surrounding the tubers is dry, add moisture by a light sprinkling or push an extra-small paper cup filled one-third full of water into the media.

- In spring, unpack and clean the dahlias: Divide the tubers by cutting with a sterilized knife. Make sure each tuber has a stem and a growth bud to trigger germination. Each stem requires three attached tubers. The growth bud or eyes often have sprouted during storage, so do not tear these from the tuber. Trim the stems enough for easier planting. Clean and inspect the tubers, discarding any that are damaged.

- Plant the dahlias: These can be potted early and placed in a warm, protected area like a southern exposure foundation for a head start on blooming. Be prepared to wrap the pots in a frost cloth if temperatures suddenly dip down into freezing. Planting dahlias into the garden should wait for nonfreezing temperatures. Follow the same procedure as the lily preparation. Add an 18-6-12, doubled feeding of fertilizer to the soil at the time of planting. Osmocote is good brand because it is a timed-release, safe fertilizer. Water well and then withhold water until green growth appears. Dahlias overwatered at this vulnerable point can easily rot.

GROWING DAHLIAS

After the dahlia develops four full leaves, pinch out the center leaf. This promotes a bushier stock. Dahlias have hollow stems, so they require staking. Use an upside-down tomato basket that is secured with wire pins in the ground for a sturdier stake. When they set buds, they are normally in sets of three. Remove the center bud. This will enlarge the size of the blooms and perhaps curb the tendency for it to tip. Deadheading the spent flowers will keep these incredibly beautiful flowers blooming until frost. Different sizes, colors, and styles of dahlias are available.

Convallaria majalis
(kon-val-AIR-ee-uh)
LILY-OF-THE-VALLEY

SHAPE	Spreading ground cover, cup-shaped flower
HEIGHT	Short, about six inches
WIDTH	Spreads to over twenty-four inches
BLOOM TIME	June
COLORS	Delicate white bells
SITE	Normal
LIGHT	Shade or partial shade
HARDINESS	Zones 2–7
COMMENTS	All parts are poisonous

The perfume of lily-of-the-valley is used worldwide in fragrances and essential oils.

Tiny, nodding white bells cuddled inside tulip-shaped leaves look so delicate that this flower is a popular choice for weddings.

Lily-of-the-valley is one of the few perennials that will grow in the dry shade of a pine tree.

Lily-of-the-valley's delicate beauty contradicts its steely constitution.

WITH ALL THE genetics going on in the perennial world right now, I'm happy to say I haven't changed a bit. I am *Convallaria,* or lily-of-the-valley, and I'm exactly the same as when the early colonists found me in the Appalachian Mountains and took me home to sweetly perfume their cabins. After all these years, I'm still perfuming cabins, homes, and (of course) gardens just as I did back then. I'm much too shy to brag, but I must be all right if I'm still loved and appreciated the way I am without any genetic "improvements."

I'm a hardy little thing, surviving extreme Zone 2 (-40°F) temperatures. My looks are deceiving. I look so demure and sweet with my tiny little bells that my toughness is surprising. I may be an old-fashioned, delicate-looking perennial, but I've been around for a long time, and I'm certainly a survivor. Plant me where winters are cold, in a shaded area, and where my underground stems (called rhizomes) have room to spread, and I'll stay there forever. Be warned though, if I don't like where I'm planted, I'll pout and refuse to grow.

The two things about me that are special are my diminutive beauty and my exquisite fragrance. I grow to only six inches in height, but my tulip-shaped leaves will spread and form a wide mass of dark-green ground cover. In June, tiny nodding white bells are cradled protectively inside my foliage carpet bloom. I'm so pretty that I'm a favorite in bridal bouquets. I even played a prominent role in the royal wedding of William and Catherine, Duke and Duchess of Cambridge. Her bridal bouquet and the maid of honor's headband were adorned with my blooms. I symbolize a return to happiness, purity of heart, sweetness, humility, and love's good fortune—all the ingredients for a successful marriage.

Few flowers can equal the intensity of my perfume, which smells faintly of jasmine. My perfume is used worldwide in fragrances and essential oils. The roster of designer labels containing my fragrance reads like a who's who in the fashion world. I'm the perfume basis for so many perfumes from *a* for "Avon" on down to Gucci's "Envy," then through "Lily Dior" by Dior, and Estee Lauder's "Pleasures" straight through to *z* for "Zara." I'm in them all!

These are just a few of the reasons why brides like to twine me in their hair and mothers plant me a year in advance in pots for wedding decorations. Surrounding a June wedding with my fragrance will heighten the feelings of love.

To keep me content, plant me in a shaded garden where I'll get regular water. I have been categorized with dry-shade plants, but that's not entirely true. With regular water, my foliage stays nicer longer into the season. Cover me from time to time with a blanket of compost. Then I'll reward a gardener with my fragrance and a carpet of green, even in difficult areas like under a pine tree. When planted on a steep shady slope, my dense root structure will hold the soil in place.

When my plants stop producing flowers, it's a sign that I need to be divided. Wait until late summer when my little unique berries are formed and my leaves start to go dormant. My berries have an interesting history and have been called the tears of Eve when she was forced to leave the Garden of Eden and the tears of the Virgin Mary as she viewed Jesus hanging on the cross. One thing for sure about my berries is that they are poison! If ingested, all of my parts cause abdominal pain, vomiting, and a reduced heart rate. This slowing of the pace of a heart has proven to be much safer than *Digitalis,* or foxglove, as a heart medication.

My smell and toxicity have certainly given me deer-resistant qualities, but now back to division. The first thing a gardener needs to divide me is a sharp shovel. Thrust the shovel down through my mass of dense roots (or *pips* as they are called) and carve away. Pips are new shoots that form underground but remain connected to the mother plant. This would be an ideal time to plant a few containers for spring.

Now that we have become acquainted, let me share one last thing. I was presented the Royal Horticulture Society Award of Merit! That is pretty darn good for such a demure, shy little thing like me!

SHOVEL SAVVY: CHOOSING GREAT GARDENING TOOLS

THE TOUGH, DENSE root mat of lily-of-the-valley is nearly impossible to divide. There is only one gardening tool that is equal to this job: a sharp shovel. When I pick up my shovel to garden, it transports me to a place of peaceful, creative pleasure. It tills the soil, removes the weeds, plants the flowers, and heals any emotional hurts. Throughout our sixty years together, my husband and I have raised an incredible family and had fulfilling careers, but in the background, we have always gardened.

I garden with a lightweight shovel because my legs are stronger than my arms. To me, a trowel is useless; it always bends, is way too slow, and just doesn't match the quality and quantity of work that can be accomplished with a shovel.

My preferred shovel design is a lightweight, small irrigation shovel. The blade is thick enough that a lip along the top edge isn't needed, and the stomping edge easily fits my foot. The well-worn handle is made of ash that has stayed smooth to the touch for years. The only problem with my shovel is that anyone who tries it even once rarely wants any other shovel, so I spend lots of time retrieving it after it's been borrowed.

My husband prefers a big shovel. For planting, leveling, and harvesting his cannas and dahlias, he uses a heavy, number-four blade irrigation shovel. The large blade can get beneath the huge clumps of tubers and lift them without damaging or cutting them off. His handle of choice is a seasoned handle made of ash.

The point is that a shovel is as individualized as the gardener who uses it. Make sure you test your tools before taking them home. Is the length of the handle comfortable? The weight is important. Lift the shovel. Does it feel comfortable? Your tools should be considered investments. Replacement parts are important to Donrey, and for that reason, he will never consider any tool made outside of the US. That may be something you want to consider too as you make a purchase.

This traditional pose of us as two old farmers made us laugh because our lifestyle is often so similar to old farmers. Working with the earth keeps both the body and spirit very much alive!

Purchase wisely, which means price should never be the only consideration, nor the most important. My shovel will probably outlive me!

GARDENER'S GUIDE TO GARDEN TOOLS

1. Is there storage for this new tool?

2. Is this built to last?

3. Is this tool necessary?

4. Will I actually use this tool?

HIS AND HERS GARDENING TOOLS

My husband, Donrey, and I often have our own tastes and opinions about gardening tools. You may find that one suits your taste better than another. Here are a few "his and hers" ideas to help you decide which tools you might like best.

PRUNERS

His: Donrey uses two sizes of pruners—one long-handled pruner, or lopper, and a bypass, or hand pruner, which accomplishes most any trimming needed in the garden. The loppers are good for inaccessible areas where reaching is necessary. These can reach to remove damaged tree or shrub limbs up to one-and-one-half inches in diameter. Hand pruners (bypass pruners) are used for trimming or shaping. Look for a comfort grip and nonstick blades that give an easy, clean cut.

Hers: I use short stainless steel bypass pruners and a short-blade (seven-inch) handheld hedge shear for cutback and fall cleanup of stems less than three-quarter inches in diameter. I also use a cheap, convenient pair of large scissors that fit comfortably in my back pocket for quick tasks. My pruners are made with one-piece forged steel handles and blades. They are easy to clean with steel wool and sharpen with a diamond file.

SAWS

His: Donrey uses two gas-engine chainsaws—one for extensive trimming of trees and shrubs up to three inches. The other saw is extremely powerful and can cut large limbs and trees for fireplace logs. He also uses a pruning saw for high tree limbs.

Hers: When I purchased my small electric "space-age" chainsaw, I held it up over my head for at least a minute to make sure I could handle the saw easily. I also have an old hand-curved pruning saw that belonged to Grandma Louise. This old-fashioned saw cuts close to trunks and will saw apart thick clumps of perennials like lily-of-the-valley.

HOES

His: Donrey has precision-cut long-handled and short-handled hoes that have been sharpened like razors. Age, use, and a grinder have custom-shaped these tools until the blades are only about four inches wide and two inches deep. The handles are of ash. Even when weeds try to hide within a perennial, these blades will seek them out for removal without damage to the flower.

Hers: A good hoe lays out rows and furrows while easing bending and backaches. It cultivates around plants, making short work of the tenacious weeds while I remain standing. Hand weeding or pulling of weeds is not recommended, because it is so easy to break off weed tops without removing roots.

RAKES

His: Donrey uses a bow rake for heavy work. The bow rake, with its shorter and thicker heavy-steel tines, is excellent for clearing clods of dirt and grading soil until it's level. By reversing the rake with its teeth in the air, the heaviness of the rake levels soil to perfection, getting it ready for grass seed. The bow rake can damage close-to-the-surface perennials in flower beds like coral bells and irises, so refrain from using a heavy bow rake for cleanup.

Hers: Whenever there is a mess in the yard, I run and get my leaf rake. I've found that the metal rake tines are actually gentler than the plastic broom tines, but the plastic cleans much better. A leaf rake is absolutely necessary for raking up fall leaves and cleaning out ground cover beds. A regular straw broom to sweep sidewalks or driveways keeps them looking clean.

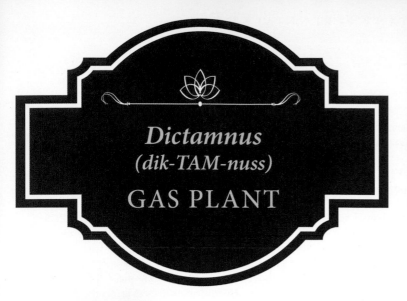

Dictamnus
(dik-TAM-nuss)
GAS PLANT

SHAPE	Shrub, mound; Flower, a trumpet cup
HEIGHT	Twenty-four to thirty inches
WIDTH	Twenty-four inches around
BLOOM TIME	Early June
COLORS	White or mauve with contrasting veins
SITE	Normal, composted clay
LIGHT	Sun or partial sun
HARDINESS	Zones 3–8
COMMENTS	Long life and pest-free

Dictamnus is a shrub-like perennial that is very slow growing, but once it's in your garden, you'll love it forever.

When in bloom, dictamnus, with its curled tongue, has a childlike frivolousness that is delightful.

These *D. albus 'Purpureus'* are in their third year in the garden and are still small and puny. Having patience is easier said than done.

The unique striping and coloring of *D. albus* flowers adds a rare treasure to the garden.

YOU MAY HAVE heard me introduced as a gas plant, but the title is absurd! I am *Dictamnus*. I do have a small chamber behind my petal lips where a fragrant, citrus-like oil is produced, and if you ignite this flammable substance with a match, it actually expels a small *whoosh* sound. However, the pungent oil is more effective in chasing away deer and pests than starting a fire.

More important than my flame-throwing abilities is my toughness and hardiness. My stout, shrub-like stems grow to about twenty-four inches and are sturdy enough to be sheared into a thick hedge. I'm a neat grower and am well mannered, giving a strong focal point or anchor to the garden. My stems are covered with dark glossy-green rounded leaves that stay attractive all season. Seldom can a gardener find a flowering shrub that stays small, goes dormant in winter, and doesn't require any care with the exception of being left unbothered.

My flowers of mauve or white blooms are exquisite and bloom with small orchid-like flowers on the ends of my stems. The star-shaped, five-petaled blooms are unusual and veined with a darker color. The unfurled petals are intertwined with long, skinny, almost eyelash looking male reproduction stamens that seem to play tag with my flowers. My blooms are self-cleaning and do not require deadheading.

My seed heads are also attractive and provide interest to the late-summer or fall garden or can be added to dried arrangements. Allow the seed pods to dry on the plant. I'm never invasive and am actually quite valuable. The pods can be opened to collect the seeds or they can be allowed to drop and self-sow. Self-sowing is the most reliable method of propagating new starts, which may or may not appear until the next spring.

Hopefully, these starts will be left right where they germinate to grow. Moving my seedlings often means sudden death to me. An attempt to divide a mature plant will set me back for at least three years, and the success rate is very low.

I may be slow to establish, but that doesn't mean I'm not hardy. I grow carefree in cold, dry, alkaline soil. Wind doesn't really bother me because of my sturdiness. I'm dependable in both sun and partial shade areas as long as I don't sit in soggy soils. Also, I tolerate growing under walnut trees, which few perennials do. Plant me in a permanent home where I can get established, and I will live a long and vigorous life, giving many years of pleasure to the garden. My longevity almost equals that of peonies. Perennials that are good companions for me are campanula, hemerocallis, iris, monarda and veronica.

I better mention an odd characteristic. It's the same reason I'm named gas plant. The lemon-smelling citrus oil I produce can cause fairly severe skin irritation in people who have an allergic reaction to it, so be cautious when working around me in the garden.

I break dormancy in late spring, so a tag or label of some kind to mark where I'm planted would signal a gardener to not mistakenly dig me up. One gardener I know uses old blind slats that are cut into smaller pieces and sticks them by my roots during fall cleanup to mark my spot. As valuable and rare as I am, it would be a shame to unknowingly dig me up. I don't start easy, move easy, or seed easy, so all that is required of gardeners is to wait, proving they have the patience to grow a remarkable fine plant like me!

Purchasing bare roots is one way to get me started, but be prepared—I will look like a stick with roots. It's better to purchase potted starts from another grower. I look so little and puny on the nursery display shelf that gardeners pass me by for a faster-growing perennial that will not equal my remarkable beauty and long-lived qualities. Rare perennials like me are slower to establish and are quite expensive because we take more time to grow; but we are worth the wait. This is one time when patience is truly a virtue!

ALL IN GOOD TIME

GARDENING AND PATIENCE are natural synonyms, and plants like dictamnus reenforce that concept. Gardeners must need a lesson in patience, because it seems that they always must wait. Patiently they wait for the long-lived perennials to become established, forgetting that those are plants that will bloom even after the gardener is gone.

Gardeners are always waiting. First, they wait for the freezing temperatures of winter to creep upward. Then they wait for the first spring buds to open. It seems as if gardeners are always waiting for the new perennial bed to sleep, creep, and leap to maturity finally after its third year. The hardest wait of all is for the late-season perennials to slowly emerge in the spring.

Many of the late-summer and fall perennials are not visible in April and May. These perennials wait until the days are longer, the soil is warmer, and the freezing nighttime temperatures are over. In the inter-mountain area, hosta does not break dormancy until some time in May—even later in the higher elevations. It is wiser than many gardeners and doesn't want its gorgeous foliage damaged.

For an excellent gauge to planting annuals, watch the hosta. When the leaves unfurl it's safe to plant geraniums, though maybe not yet safe for coleus, sweet potato vine, or zinnias.

As soon as the hosta breaks through, the ferns unfurl. Next the red, pointy echinacea and rudbeckia's small, tight, dark-green crowns will show. A spade or finger probed into the garden soil will find monarda, oenothera, and coreopsis right where they were planted and will bring a sigh of relief from the gardener who hoped that an early turning of the soil didn't destroy these favorites. When the late-blooming tall garden phlox finally peaks through, it's time to celebrate. Finally the platycodon, eupatorium, and of course the sign of traditional fall color—asters—appear. All of these wonderful late-season perennials have survived another winter.

Wait! There is one more perennial to be patient for: hibicus is usually the last to appear. Then the waiting is over, and once again the gardener is taught patience!

When shopping for perennials for your garden, it's easy to pass by the later-season-blooming plants. If the nursery grows its perennials naturally and has wintered the plants, fall-blooming perennials will appear small and not look as vigorous as the spring bloomers. Think patience. No garden is complete without late-summer and fall color.

Be sure to add these perennial favorites; they may look small in the spring, but the roots are what tell the real story!

Shown on the opposite page are a few of the perennials that do not break dormancy or start to grow until temperatures reach 60 to 70°F. At spring nursery sales, these plants should be small, like they are pictured. If these perennials are for sale and they are big and bushy, it is an indication that they were grown in a heated greenhouse on a rich diet of fertilizer. Stay away from perennials that are not grown naturally, no matter how pretty they look, especially if they are blooming out of season. With flowers, as with all things, there is a season.

Hibiscus is usually the last perennial to break dormancy in the spring. During fall cutback time, leave enough stems above ground to be able to recognize the plant. It's not until almost Memorial Day that it will start to grow.

The *Matteuccia*, or ostrich fern, waits until the days are long and the sun is warmer to break dormancy. These distinctive shade plants send up very unique-looking fronds as they start to unfurl.

LATE-BREAKING PERENNIALS

Aster

Echinacea

Monarda

Campanula

Helenium

Phlox

Coreopsis

Sedum

Rudbeckia

Euphorbia polychroma
(yew-FOR-bee-uh)
CUSHION SPURGE

SHAPE	Half-round mound, flowers are filler bracts on stem tips
HEIGHT	Fifteen inches
WIDTH	Fifteen inches
BLOOM TIME	Early to late spring
COLORS	Fluorescent yellow
SITE	Alkaline, sand, clay
LIGHT	Full sun or partial sun
HARDINESS	Zones 4–10
COMMENTS	No pest or disease problems

The bright glow of *E. polychroma* contrasts with the dark purple rock cress in this early spring rock garden.

Cushion spurge can be relied on to give spring gardens a much-needed mass of bright yellow color.

'E. Bonfire' is one of the new colorful-foliaged euphorbia hybrids. The leaves emerge green but turn red all summer. New hybrids often lose their hardiness. *E.* 'Bonfire' is a Zone 5 perennial.

The brilliant radiance of a close-up of a euphorbia flower displays how unique the foliage and blooms of perennials can really be.

WITH A NAME like *Euphorbia polychroma*, it is expected that I'll bring a burst of brightness to spring gardens, and I do! I'm one of the earliest perennials to bring showstopping color to the landscape. The spring bulbs are okay, but they fade, and their foliage gets ratty. My foliage stays nice all season. My flowers bloom in the brightest yellow imaginable as soon as the weather permits. I'm sure this is how I got the adjective part of my name, *polychroma*, for I truly shine in the garden. My flowers are interesting bracts on the ends of my stems. I develop into a brilliant clump of yellow in spring that lasts well over a month. As my flowers start to fade, they turn green and become part of the stem. Technically, my flowers are not really flowers but a tip of the foliage that turns yellow in spring.

My best features are my small size and neat shape. I start out in spring at about twelve inches tall. After my flowers morph into my foliage, I grow taller. I become a lime-green dome that sits about fifteen by fifteen inches. I hold my shape throughout the season, and toward fall, my foliage takes on a tawny-bronze color. My all-season holding power, shape, and size are reasons why I'm an excellent perennial for a container. At the end of the season, I'll start to cascade over the edge of the pot, but otherwise I stay in a nice, tight mound.

After blooming, I assume a low-key shape in the garden and can almost be forgotten. There isn't really a need to deadhead unless you don't want more of me all over the garden; I reseed easily.

A red fruit is produced in late summer, which then pops off, and I proceed to propel these seeds several feet to self-sow. My growth rate is medium to slow, but in a couple of years, these baby euphorbias can be moved to other areas. If you're feeling generous, they can also be gifted to neighbors who will appreciate both the gift and the giver each spring when I bloom. My long taproots resent being moved, so plant me while I'm still young where I can stay.

I'm an easy perennial to grow and am enjoyably long-lived. I bloom brighter in the sun, but my seedlings grow anywhere they land, be it sun or shade, and they bloom satisfactorily. My natural habitat is the rocky hillsides of southern Europe and Turkey, so I feel right at home in the western mountains, with their extreme climate and rocky conditions. I'm considered a Zone 4 perennial, but I'm so comfortable in this area that I never winter-kill. I'm drought tolerant due to my taproot, a trait that perennials planted in container pots must have in order to perform.

Often gardeners will plant me at the front of the flower bed, but I'm far more pleasing when planted in the middle. Planting long-blooming dark-blue sage alongside me and short purple rock cresses or blue veronicas in front of me will look delightful because their cool shades contrast nicely. For fall, the taller burgundy sedums will give a dissimilar, pleasant look, and the lower sedums in front of me will complete an all-season display. I'm a natural rock garden perennial, blending well with all alpines and enjoying alkaline soils.

Many fancy-colored new hybrids have come out lately. Be cautious. Just because I'm such a reliable, easy plant doesn't mean they will be. With names like 'Ruby Glow', 'Blackbird', 'Glacier Blue', and 'Bonfire', it's obvious that horticulturists are breeding my excellent foliage to have unique colors of leaves. These new hybrids may be attractive, but their hardiness is at Zone 5 or above, and they are not reliably hardy like I am. *E. myrsinites*, or donkey tail, is a spreader and is banned in many western states.

Because we are related to the poinsettia family, we inherited a white, milky sap. This sap drips out of my stems when they are cut, so always wear gloves if you decide to deadhead me. My sap can irritate your skin, especially the sap of donkey tail, which has been known to burn a child's eyes. This sap is why deer and other pests ignore me.

Choose me for your garden; I'm a solid performer, and I'm absolutely reliable.

CONTAINER GARDENING WITH PERENNIALS

HERE ARE A few rules for planting decorative pots:

- Use a group of three in your design: tall and strong, medium and full, and short and cascading. Using a plant from each group will give a container a designed, professional look.
- Avoid plants that only bloom in spring.
- Choose interesting foliage: striped, variegated, burgundy, chartreuse, or silvery.
- Aim for drought-tolerant plants that can withstand a little neglect on days you forget to water.
- A timed-release fertilizer will be adequate for perennial container gardening.
- Determine the location of the container and then plant shade-loving or sun-loving plants accordingly.
- Annuals can be added to your perennial pots the first year but will probably not be needed the second year.

Aannuals are safer in containers from the foraging of hungry deer and wildlife. This container is set on top of a water valve box where plants won't grow.

Plant perennials for containers in reuseable plastic nursery pots so they can be exchanged from season to season.

Whether to spend a small fortune each spring for annuals is a question only a gardener can answer. However, using perennials and adding just a few annuals will create much more attractive flowerpots simply because of the additional height and structure. Another benefit is being able to enjoy the containers a month earlier because perennials are tougher against cold temperatures. A container gives a gardener the best of both worlds; flowers won't need to be weeded, and deer and wildlife won't bother the pots. These are valid reasons, but our real reason for loving potted containers in the garden is because they are beautiful. The focal point containers add to the landscape just can't be achieved any other way!

Wintering perennial containers can be a problem. They will need protection from the extremes of winter weather, and the freeze-thaw cycles in springtime are damaging. Placing your pots in the shade or against a north fence or building will slow the thawing if the weather warms up. Wrapping containers with bagged raked leaves or bubble wrap is an option. Another good idea to lay the pot on its side. Less moisture will stay in the pot. Pressure from frozen soil can crack containers. And more plants are killed in winter by too much moisture than not enough. Check during winter to make sure the container's soil stays moist not wet, and you'll have much larger, healthier perennials ready to perform for next year!

HARDY SHADE-CONTAINER PERENNIALS

Tall	Polemonium, Jacob's ladder
Medium	Alchemilla, lady's mantle
Short	Ajuga

Tall	Eupatorium 'Chocolate'
Medium	Bergenia
Short	Lamium

Tall	Iris spuria, Turkish iris
Medium	Hosta
Short	Campanula 'Blue Waterfall'

Tall	Dwarf Aruncus
Medium	Brunnera
Short	Iberis

Tall	Physostegia 'Miss Manners' series
Medium	Heuchera
Short	Campanula carpatica

Tall	Filipendula vulgaris
Medium	Hosta 'Blue Mouse Ears'
Short	Pachysandra 'Green Sheen'

Tall	Hosta 'Francee'
Medium	Tiarella wherryi
Short	Silene 'Druett's variegated

Tall	Iris spuria
Medium	Anemone 'Rubra' or 'Snowdrops'
Short	Ceratostigma, plumbago

HARDY SUN-CONTAINER PERENNIALS

Tall	Scabosia, pincushion
Medium	Anthemus 'Charm'
Short	Aurinia 'Gold Dust'

Tall	Echinacea, coneflower
Medium	Salvia 'May Night'
Short	Oenothera missouri, evening primrose

Tall	Yucca, Adam's needle
Medium	Gaillardia, 'Arizona Sun' series
Short	Aubrieta, rock cress

Tall	Liatris 'Kobold'
Medium	Sedum 'Voodoo'
Short	Sedum 'Tri-color'

Tall	Hemerocallis 'Daring Deception'
Medium	Phlox 'Pink Flame' series
Short	Saponaria, soapwort

Tall	Rudbeckia fulgida 'Goldstrum'
Medium	Lavandula 'Munstead'
Short	Dianthus deltoides

Tall	Iris pallida variegata, striped iris
Medium	Aster 'Red Alert'
Short	Veronica 'Crater Lake Blue'

Tall	Sedum 'Xenox'
Medium	Leucanthemum 'Snow Cap'
Short	Thymus, mother of thyme

Most potting soil mixes shrink in volume. It's smart to add to or replace the old potting soil with new soil each spring. The perennials will have formed a root ball, so changing out the soil should not be a problem. Add the used soil to a garden area.

For ease of planting and wintering, plant your container plants in a similar-sized separate pot or liner. This creates less trouble for relocating or wintering the container. Many planters formed out of ceramic or cement have a tendency to crack in winter and are way too heavy to move around the garden, so a liner makes it easier to change out a pot.

If sunlight in your area is very intense, many of the sun containers will do better in partial shade. This is the beauty of containers—they can be moved at the whim of the gardener unless they weigh a ton. (Then it may be wise to use a moving dolly.) All of these hardy perennials can be interchanged as a gardener chooses, so being creative will naturally happen.

Geranium
(juh-RAN-ee-um)
'Johnson's Blue'
CRANESBILL

SHAPE	Low spreader, cup flower
HEIGHT	Twelve inches
WIDTH	Twenty-four inches
BLOOM TIME	Late spring through early summer
COLORS	Shades of blue
SITE	Most types, even alkaline
LIGHT	Full sun through shade
HARDINESS	Zones 2–9
COMMENTS	No serious problems

Gardeners should not confuse this hardy, adaptable perennial with the popular annual geranium, which is really *Pelargonium*. The word *wild* is often added to the perennial geranium's name; *wild geranium* means that the plant being discussed is a perennial.

Cranesbill will happily weave through other garden perennials like this hosta and will cover spent poppies.

Wild geranium is highly deer resistant due to the plant's strong astringent smell. It will cascade nicely over a rock wall.

The cranesbill's beak on the wild geranium is the seed pod. Wild geraniums, with their cranesbill beaks, have a seed-dispensing germination system that is one of nature's marvels.

NO DOUBT YOU are familiar with my regal cousin, an annual geranium who adorns tidy flower boxes and planters all summer and then winter-kills to nothing but dead, brown sticks at almost the first sign of a frost. By contrast, I'm a choice perennial called wild geranium or big-leaf cranesbill, which fills natural or cottage gardens across the United States. Because of my hardiness, I really thrive in areas where the garden is covered with a blanket of snow in winter and cooled by mountain air in summer. Here are some other reasons that gardeners will appreciate getting acquainted with me:

- I'm long-lived and can be divided each spring for more new starts. With one established planting, a gardener will always have new plants available.

- I'm related to the native geranium wildflowers but have been upgraded to a larger size with longer blooming power and more colorful flowers.

- I'm easy to grow and am not fussy about soils, water, light, or anything else for that matter. I bloom where I am planted!

- I received the Royal Horticulture Society Award of Garden Merit. This prestigious award is given only to the best.

- I'm so pretty that gardeners forget I'm a tightly knit, weed-smothering ground cover.

I may only be a foot tall, but I'm a great spreader. My bright-blue flowers are funnel-shaped and rise open-faced above my foliage on wiry stems. My rounded leaves are lobed, toothed, and divided to resemble a hand. Not only are they attractive, but they are also fragrant with a citrus-astringent smell. My smell, taste, and fuzzy stems give me wildlife resistance. Even if pests don't like my taste, gardeners do sometimes add my edible leaves to their salads.

I bloom from spring into summer, and with shearing I will thicken and bloom again later in the season. Beak-shaped seed-pods form after flowering (thus my nickname, *cranesbill*). My seed pods are so interesting. They seem to take on a life of their own when dispensing seed. The seed pods will dry, curl, and then open, propelling my seeds into the air and all over the garden. The seeds then start their own journey. The tail or awn of my seed curls when dry and straightens out when wet. These two motions allow me to creep until I find a hole or crack to burrow into where I will germinate.

My pollen is also interestingly unique because, unlike most yellow, orange, or white pollens, if I'm viewed under a microscope, my color is a brilliant blue. Insects are especially attracted to blue and will come to pollinate.

My rootstock grows long and skinny and is rarely success-ful at propagating unless the plants are dug in early spring when my roots are still relatively short and more manageable for potting. I send my roots deeper into the ground as summer heats up, and these long roots give me my ability to perform well in dry shade. The inside of my rootstock is white and fleshy, with a strong astringent taste. The main ingredients in my roots are tannic acid, starch, sugar, gum, and pectin, and I am still used medicinally today, just as I was used long ago. My powdered rootstock mixed with liquid will make a mouth-puckering wash for treating canker sores and toothaches. Made into a paste, I'm effective at stopping bleeding and hemorrhag-ing on wounds or sores. The paste adheres to the membrane, causing it to pucker, shrink, and constrict.

I'm so adaptable that I can be planted anywhere. I grow in sun, partial sun, and shade. I will thrive when planted in rocks, under trees, over walls, and among larger perennials, where I'll magically weave through them and smother weeds as I grow. Soils aren't a problem. Wet, dry, alkaline, rocky, sandy, and even salty soils are fine with me. My short stature works easily into any section of a garden. My reputation for being a perennial that fits wherever I'm planted is well deserved. Gardeners are aware that if they can't find just the right perennial for a certain spot, plant a wild geranium! I'll never cease to please.

Ajuga reptans, bugleweed

Convallaria, lily-of-the-valley

Helleborus, Lenten rose

DRY-SHADE PERENNIALS: DRY, DARK, AND DIFFICULT

GARDENS EVOLVE. WHEN gardens are first started, the perennial choices are often the plants that grow well in the sun. As time passes, the trees mature and the shrubs fill out, shading the garden. Now the perennial choices have evolved to shade-loving perennials. Few perennials are as adaptive as the wild geraniums, which will grow where they are planted even if the area is sunny, partially sunny, shady, or—the trickiest spot to grow anything in—dry and shady.

My first attempt at planting under a huge pine tree was a serious failure. A neighbor brought me a piece of ground cover called bishop's weed, which grew rampantly. On the day I found a huge rattlesnake nesting in it, I decided to eliminate this obnoxious, detested weed, but it took two years of digging and straining the soil to remove all of the roots. Unfortunately, the ground still refused to grow anything until I hauled in a truckload of manure and compost and spread it under the pine tree. To my joy, when I dug my shovel into this dry-shade area the next spring, the ground was full of earthworms—an indicator of nutritious soil!

Due to using dry-shade perennials like *Geranium* 'Johnson's Blue', this area is now quite respectable. Add a few early bulbs and plant the following perennials in your garden for an attractive, wildlife-resistant garden that will thrive in dry shade.

- *Ajuga reptans*, bugleweed: This is a blue-leafed ground cover that likes acidic soil, so it seems to be comfortable beneath a pine tree where needles drop and keep it healthy. In western gardens, bugleweed is a slow spreader and does not have the eastern reputation of being a weed.
- *Convallaria*, lily-of-the-valley: In spring, lily-of-the-valley pushes up under the dry shade of the pine trees and spreads to form a lovely carpet. (See page 136)
- *Helleborus*, Lenten rose: Planted under the eaves of the house or along a porch or walkway, this fine perennial will stay evergreen and impress guests. Winner of the prestigious Perennial Plant of the Year Award, Lenten rose is not bothered by wildlife, probably due to its smell, which earned it the nickname of "Stinking Hellebore."
- *Hemerocallis* 'Stella de Oro': This is a dwarf daylily that surprisingly grows nicely in a dry-shade area. (See page 82)
- *Hosta*: Shade-loving hosta is very drought tolerant. After the dry-shade area under a pine tree was filled with manure and compost, this plant thrived. The height and lime-yellow colors of hosta's beautiful foliage really light up a dry-shade garden. It is extremely adaptable as long as the area is shaded and it gets an occasional drink.

- *Lamium,* dead nettle: This makes an excellent ground cover for dry shade. These perennials spread, root solidly, and their silvery or stripped foliage stands out in shade. As they age, the silver on the leaves of 'Beacon's Silver' or 'White Nancy' can revert and change their coloring, turning green with a white stripe in the middle.

- *Lamiastrum* 'Herman's Pride': This is a fabulous perennial for dry shade. It grows into a perfect mound of deep-green leaves marbled with silver. It blooms in late spring and covers itself with pale yellow, pearl-like flowers.

- *Liriope,* lily turf and big blue: Lily turf is an evergreen spike for dry shade. Big blue performs nicely as a border plant where nothing else seems to want to grow. Planting liriope in the warmer, Zone 5 areas without a huge deer population is best.

- *Tiarella,* foamflower: Tiarella is a native perennial that blooms in late spring. The foamflower foliage is an interesting, heart-shaped leaf that often has intricate patterns. The bottle-brush flower stalks of foamy white or pink are unique and add distinctive color to a dry-shade garden.

Solving problem areas like dry shade in the garden is a test to every gardener's creativity. Adding manure or compost will completely change the soil and help dry shade hold moisture. In addition, give dry-shade perennials an occasional watering because, as hard as dry-shade plants must work to live, they certainly deserve a drink.

Lamium, dead nettle

Lamiastrum 'Herman's Pride'

Hemerocallis 'Stella de Oro'

Tiarella, foamflower

Hesperis matronalis
(HESS-per-iss)
SWEET ROCKET OR DAME'S ROCKET

SHAPE	Bushy spike, clustered flowers
HEIGHT	Thirty inches tall
WIDTH	Fifteen to twenty inches
BLOOM TIME	Spring and early summer
COLORS	Shades of mauve, pink, white, and purple
SITE	Any soil, even alkaline
LIGHT	Sun or partial sun
HARDINESS	Very hardy, Zone 2
COMMENTS	Short-live perennial or biennial

Sweet rocket self-sows the first year, germinates the next, and blooms the third year.

The thin, long seeds of sweet rocket shoot out to reseed even before the flowers are through blooming.

Sweet rocket will quickly take over the forest floor and crowd out other plants, including tree saplings.

This close-up of sweet rocket shows its distinctive four-petaled floret. The mixture of lilac and white is eye-catching.

I'M KNOWN AS *Hesperis* (more commonly called dame's rocket or sweet rocket). The genus name *Hesperis* is Greek, meaning "evening," while the Latin word means "vespers." My flowers are more strongly scented in the evening, and I'm often referred to as a night-blooming perennial. Thus I'm named *Hesperis*.

The second part of my name, *matronalis,* is derived from the mother figure in Greek mythology, Hesperis. Atlas, who supported the world on his broad shoulders, and Hesperis, the western evening star, parented three daughters they called the Hesperides. These three daughters became gardeners and tended the garden of the golden apples. *Matronalis* could signify that I'm prolific, producing hundreds of seeds per plant. I even rocket them out while I'm blooming!

Brassicaceae, or mustard weeds, are my close relatives. Gardeners in the West are continually trying to eradicate this bright yellow spreader. Scout troops, grade school groups, and park service employees will hike the mountains in June, stuffing the seed-filled plants into great huge plastic bags for disposal.

I was introduced from Eurasia for ornamental purposes in the 1700s, and when brought here, I made myself at home. I now cover all parts of North America except the Deep South. I'm usually included in wildflower seed packets. This, coupled with my prolific seed production, has helped me escape from gardens and establish my plants wherever I choose. In Connecticut and Massachusetts, I'm rudely outlawed and have been legally put on the invasive weed list. Rocky Mountain gardeners don't seem to find me as big a threat, probably because their soil is so lean, dry, and barren.

I admit, I'm really easy to grow. My seeds germinate and can be sown in July, or you can let the seeds land and self-germinate.

I'll show up the next spring in the form of an attractive rosette at ground level. I often stay evergreen all winter under the snow.

In the spring, my rosettes send up an erect two-to-four foot-tall flower stem. My leaves are pointy and are six inches long, like a lance. I'm almost the tallest plant in the late-spring garden, so I'm quite valuable. As my flower clusters branch out, they grow extensions that keep my gorgeous flowers blooming. The fragrance and rich colors of my flowers are breathtaking.

It is my slightly sweet scent of cloves that makes me attractive to butterflies, which is why my seeds are also used for the production of essential oils for aromatherapy. My seeds are cold-pressed into a liquid that uses natural botanical smells to improve psychological and physical well-being.

All parts of me—leaves, oil, and seeds—are edible. My leaves are rich in vitamin C and can be eaten raw like watercress. They will give a sharp tang to salads but need to be picked and used before I flower. Germinated seed sprouts can be added to the salad also.

After my thin, oblong seeds germinate, I'm easy to grow. I send a long taproot into the soil, so I'm relatively drought tolerant. Warm weather will shorten the duration of my bloom time, so growing me in cooler climates gives me a longer blooming window.

My only problem is I'm a short-lived perennial or biennial, so divisions or trying to propagate me by cuttings is not worthwhile. Just let me reseed in your garden, and I'll surprise you wherever I pop up. I promise to do everything in my power to be so outstanding that you would never consider removing me. I'll make your garden breathtakingly fragrant.

ROCKY MOUNTAIN WILDFLOWERS

HESPERIS, OR SWEET ROCKET, naturalizes so easily that if it escapes into our mountains, it will compete with the native wildflowers for light, moisture and nutrients. It spreads so readily that it inhibits tree seedling germination and growth. Part of the reason sweet rocket has spread is because of its widespread distribution in wildflower seed mixes. It also spreads via vehicle tires, clothing, and animal fur. To prevent invasion of our forested areas, think twice about using wildflower seed mixes.

If a natural-looking wildflower garden is the heart's desire of a gardener, it can be better achieved by a careful choice of a gardener's favorite perennials. Harvest the seed as soon as the perennial stops blooming. Let the seed dry and shuck off the duff. Add in a few annual seeds like poppies or cosmos, then mix the seeds into sand for a more uniform application. Leave out the grasses that are pictured in natural wildflower gardens. There are few grasses that do not cause problems, so be cautious. Spread the seeds on disturbed soil and then water.

Once the seeds germinate and start blooming, repeat the procedure. A thick stand of wildflowers usually requires at least two seasons of seeding. Snip the dried stems and place them back in the flower bed to reseed for the next season. Gradually the bed will fill. Note: Stored seed has a tendency to rot or mildew, so let the seeds self-sow and have Mother Nature do the germinating.

These are quick suggestions for a wildflower garden, but now let's get to the real reason for this side sketch. Wildflowers in our acres and acres of national forest lands are just that, wildflowers, and are perfect in everyway. Interference by well-meaning gardeners, unaware that introducing a new plant or weed into these forested areas, is infringing on perfection and could start an invasion of a weed. Most mountain wildflowers are delicate but tough perennials that have adapted to the areas.

Our wildflowers grow in the meadows or higher elevation snowfields. When the snow is deep that year, the wildflower display is glorious! If a winter is dry, these amazing plants conserve energy by with sparser appearance. In the West, all living things perform according to the water they get.

Another factor is that wildflowers grow on their own without interference or cultivation. Native wildflowers are indigenous to the area they grow in. In other words, they have picked where they'll grow. Others, like the beautiful invasive *Hesperis matronalis*, have been introduced and are referred to as naturalized. Both types are self-equipped to grow in nature.

A look at the following wildflower profiles will show how fragile yet tenacious native wildflowers really are. It is interesting that all of these perennials hold the title of a state flower.

After getting acquainted with these five unique native perennial wildflowers, how can any gardener consider competing with Mother Nature to grow a wildflower garden? Just the addition of the wild grasses that act as stabilizers for the wildflowers would overtake any urban cultivated flower bed. The moral of the story is *let wildflowers be wildflowers, and allow the tenacious little darlings to be who they are and grow where they belong.* Using more cultivated perennials in urban gardens gives gardeners more time to smell the flowers.

Mountain valleys are filled with wildflowers in late spring. The blue and yellow color scheme done by Mother Nature is a favorite for gardeners everywhere.

COLORADO

The state flower of Colorado is a blue-and-white native columbine. The blue is the symbol of the sky, the white represents snow, and the flower's golden centers symbolize Colorado's gold mining industry. The plants are even called Rocky Mountain columbines. The best time to view these exceptional flowers in their natural habitat is in spring after a deep snow. Columbine's comfort zone is in partially shaded pine or aspen groves, and it will easily bloom into late summer in the mountains. There are seventy species of columbine, and only a third of those are native to North America. The botanical name for columbine is *Aqulegia*. *Aquila* is Latin for "eagle" and refers to the long eagle-like spurs on the backside of the bloom. These unique spurs are designed like straws that are full of rich nectar that furnish the bees, hummingbirds, and butterflies all the energy they need to pollinate the wildflower-carpeted forest floor.

IDAHO

The next native wildflower plant profile is called mock orange. The botanical name is *Philadelphus*, but sometimes it's called *Syringa*, which actually is a lilac. Mock orange is shrub-like and covered with elegant, white waxy flowers in springtime. The shrubs fill in along Idaho's numerous waterways and stabilize the banks with their tough root structures. Mock orange also grows in dry ravines, rocky areas, and canyons, so it's not fussy about water requirements. Its blooms, which are similar to orange blossoms, are hard to forget. Also, its intoxicating fragrance smells like citrus combined with jasmine, so the name mock orange came about due to the plant's exquisite fragrance. Idaho residents show up in droves for the spring bloom time of the mock orange. (The Chinook salmon migrates upstream at the same time, which is probably the real reason they come.) Native Americans used the mock orange's straight and strong branches for arrows, pipes, and combs because the inside of the wood is pithy and easily hollowed out.

MONTANA

The state flower of Montana was found by the explorers Lewis and Clark. The name bitterroot was given the plant due to its location along the Bitterroot Mountains, and its botanical name is *Lewisia rediviva* to honor Meriwether Lewis for discovering it. However, the Native Americans had been using this plant for trade and food way before Lewis came along. They mixed the perennial's roots with berries or meat after carefully removing the small red cone in the upper taproot. This they put into their medicine bag to ward off bear attacks. Bitterroot is so small that it is camouflaged unless it's blooming. Then the exceptionally beautiful flower and buds are standouts. Their fleshy taproot holds the flowers snugly into gravelly scree areas of sagebrush plains or foothill areas. Bitterroot is native to all areas of Montana, east to Colorado, and south to Arizona. Bitterroot survives in such inhospitable circumstances and apparently does well in taking care of itself.

UTAH

Next is the state flower of Utah, the sego lily. This little wildflower was instrumental in saving the lives of the state's first settlers. The pioneers struggled to get across the plains and over the Rockies to reach Utah, and once there they struggled valiantly to plant a crop of food so they would not starve to death. Just as the crop reached prime, hoards of crickets banded together, migrating a mile a day, destroying everything in their path. All would have been totally lost if the seagulls living around the Great Salt Lake had not swooped down at the last minute and devoured the greedy insects. Fortunately, the Native Americans also came to the rescue of the starving settlers and shared with them a great delicacy, a bulb that they dug from the ground, now called a sego lily. Sego lilies are a small single stem perennial bulb, having only one single three-inch terminal flower. They make up in beauty what they don't have in size. Their flowers are goblet-shaped with wine-red and yellow watermarks around the inside base of the petals. Sadly, the sego lily is only conspicuous while it is flowering, and the plant dries up after blossoming. It grows in the semi-desert and open sagebrush foothills, as well as in pine stands at moderate elevations. It thrives in dry sandy soil. Sego lilies balk and refuse to grow in cultivated gardens.

WYOMING

Wyoming's state flower, *Castilleja linariaefolia,* is well known in the West as Indian paintbrush or prairie fire. Indian paintbrush is a native perennial in all states west of the great divide and from Alaska south to the Andes Mountains. This obstinate, red-tipped brush grows on rocky slopes and arid plains, mixing in with sagebrush, scrub, pinion, juniper pines, and with the grasses, which are the protectors of all of the wildflowers. Sagebrush acts as a host plant for the semi-parasitic paintbrush. The plant sends up a cluster of stems, and the tip ends of the stems turn red or orange. The legend of how Indian paintbrush got its name is the story of a young Indian boy who wanted to paint great pictures of the world around him. In a vision, the boy was directed to a place where many brushes of vibrant colors awaited him. Soon his masterpiece was complete, and he slept. In the morning, he found that all of his paint brushes have taken root, and this is why the magnificent Indian paintbrush is so widespread in the West.

Iris
(EYE-ris)
BEARDED IRIS

SHAPE	Tall, swordlike leaves and a trumpet-like cup of flowers
HEIGHT	Thirty-six inches
WIDTH	About fifteen inches
BLOOM TIME	May to June
COLORS	Every color of the rainbow
SITE	Well-drained soil
LIGHT	Full sun
HARDINESS	Zones 3–9
COMMENTS	No problems in western soils

The unique patterns and coloration of each iris makes it a easy perennial to use for hybrids.

The colors of this strip of iris resemble a rainbow.

The royal symbol of the *fleur-de-lis* comes from the iris. Irises are a gorgeous and regal addition to any garden.

Irises are in full bloom by Memorial Day and are used as flags to decorate graves. This is how their common name of flag was derived.

MY NAME IS *Iris*, and you'll be interested to know that, statistically speaking, I'm the most popular perennial on the planet! Like all bearded irises, I'm gorgeous. With my tall, thin, and graceful shape, I really stand out. My blooms have three petals up and three petals down. The upright petals, located in the center of my flowers, are called standards. These are ringed by three falls, or downward-extending petals. At the base of my falls, I have a funny fuzzy spot. This is why I'm called a bearded iris.

My flowers may sound complicated, but it is my colors that are complex. I can be one color or a blend of different colors. Some are even striped or spotted. Often my top petals are in contrast to my falls. I bloom in every shade of the rainbow except red. My name was given to me by a beautiful Greek goddess named Iris, who traveled over a rainbow to reach Earth. As she danced over the terrain, every delicate footprint left a rainbow-colored flower. Those flowers are now called irises. The name is suitable, for the word *iris* in Greek means "rainbow." My flowers, with their rainbow colors, are so lovely they had to be a gift from the gods.

A major reason I'm so popular is because of my long history of being passed from gardener to gardener. The best way to get more irises is to trade rhizomes or roots with a neighbor, or to ask your grandmother for a start of her most treasured iris.

My popularity could be because I'm an easy perennial to divide. I can be divided every four years. Divide me when I'm through blooming or wait until late summer when my foliage is at its worst. Dig up my rhizomes and pull the plants apart. Discard the oldest, for each rhizome only blooms once. These are usually in the center and may look diseased. To avoid spreading disease, use a sharp knife dipped in rubbing alcohol or a bleach solution to cut the rhizomes. To prevent further problems, the cut rhizomes can be dusted with powdered sulfur. In arid western gardens, a fungicide isn't usually needed. Trim the foliage, making sure each section has a fan of trimmed leaves. This is a good time to write the iris's name or color on the leaves in magic marker. Allow the iris to dry for at least a day before planting.

When replanting me, think of me as a child that is being put to bed. My foliage fan is the child's head and the long rhizome is the body. Lay my rhizome in the shallow soil bed lying horizontally. Cover me lightly, leaving my fan head above ground. Remember, my head needs to breathe. Planting me too deep can cause root rot. I appreciate the dry climate of the western mountains because I stay healthier and seldom suffer root rot, which is my worst enemy in wetter and warmer regions.

Bearded irises are also popular because if a gardener craves a new or different iris variety, my blooms can be cross-pollinated. Irises are the easiest perennials to cross-pollinate. Choose beautiful and vigorous irises from the garden for the parents. My sex organs are inside my upper petals. The stamen could be called the male part, and it carries the pollen. The stigmatic lip, or female part, is where the pollen will be received.

When my flowers are in full bloom, collect the pollen-dusted stamen with tweezers or forceps. Then rub the pollen on the stigmatic lip of every flower on the mother plant. Congratulations, you just cross-pollinated! Then wait. When I finish blooming, a seed pod will form below the drying flower. This seed pod—if the pollination was successful—holds the seeds for a new hybrid iris. Let the pod dry on the stem until it cracks and starts to break open. Remove the seed pod and plant the seeds.

Iris seeds, like many perennials, require a vernalization period, or chilling, before they will germinate, so a cold winter climate is an asset. It won't be until spring when the baby iris breaks through the ground. Two years later, you'll be able to celebrate a first bloom.

Successful hybridizing of irises is so popular that iris societies have been formed. The American Iris Society has a website where a successful gardener can register amazing new iris hybrids. The AIS does evaluations only in gardens, not using cut flowers. At present, the AIS is trying to publish a complete encyclopedia of registered new irises. They now have 52,663 cataloged varieties and figure they are at about 75 percent.

The Dykes Medal Award is the Nobel Prize for irises. The awards first started in 1927 and have been given only seventy-seven times because some years the irises were not deemed worthy.

The *fleur-de-lis* is a traditional symbol for my bloom. The French word *fleur,* meaning "flower," and *lis,* meaning "lily," has been used through recorded history as a royal symbol. I suppose this indicates that I have always been a popular perennial.

All of the excitement and drama that surrounds me is well deserved. I'm a hardy, Zone 4 perennial that provides a flamboyant flower show full of beauty and drama in late spring. I think I've earned the title of the most popular perennial.

FLOWER BED DESIGN: CONGENIAL COMPANIONS

TRADITIONALLY, IRISES ARE planted in beds filled with as many plants as the grower was able to stuff in. This is due to the ease of growing, propagating, and spreading ability of bearded irises. Planting irises in clumps of only five or seven starts is more design appropriate than planting them in huge masses. After irises bloom, there will be no color in the garden, and their foliage will look exhausted by fall, with dried leaves falling off. To remedy these problems, a gardener can plant companion plants with bearded iris. To do this painlessly, a gardener needs to use the four common design rules that not only help irises look attractive but also improve any garden.

1. PLANT PERENNIALS WITH THE SAME GROWING REQUIREMENTS TOGETHER

Irises like full sun and well-drained soil. The list of perennials that grow in this environment is endless.

2. PLANT PERENNIALS IN TIERS

Place plants according to height. Planting small plants in the front of the bed, medium-sized plants in the middle, and tall plants in the back will show off the perennials to their best advantage.

The leaves of bearded iris plants will fill the criteria for the medium-sized perennials, so companion plants need to be short or tall. A common design mistake is using plants of all the same size. Visualize some of the well-known skylines of the United States, like the famous view of New York City or Seattle. These skylines, with their variety of heights and sizes of buildings, are remembered because they look exciting and dramatic. A garden is the same way. Companion plants need to not only be planted in tiers for easier viewing, but they also need to grow at different heights and shapes.

3. MIX PLANTS FOR CONTRAST AND DRAMA

A perennial bed should always include plants that vary and contrast sharply in height, color, texture, or shape. Achieve this in three ways:

A. FOLIAGE SIZE, SHAPE, AND COLOR

Bearded irises—with their large, flat leaves—would look excellent with ferny-, lacy-, or rounded-leaf companions. The foliage could also be coarse, furry, hairy, shiny, leathery, or smooth. Including plants with colorful leaves such as *Artemisia* 'Silver Mound' or with variegated and bronze foliage would add garden color the entire season. The trick is to choose leaves that differ from iris leaves in several ways. Daylilies and red hot pokers would have to be eliminated as companion plants for iris because of similar foliage, while late-season-blooming asters, with their shrub-like rounded shapes, would be a better choice.

B. FLOWER COLOR, SHAPE, AND SIZE

Iris blooms really cannot be equaled in beauty, so use companion plants that do not bloom the same time as them. Allium's flower size, shape, color size, and late spring blooming time would be ignored if it had to compete with iris. Color needs to balance between unity and boredom. For example, red and green or blue and yellow are energetic, and lively contrasting colors are never boring. Warm colors appear closer, while cool colors look farther away, so balance color to suit yourself. Plant flowers with irises that contrast in shape, bloom time, or color.

C. OVERALL SHAPE OF THE PERENNIAL

Some plants grow into mounded globes. Some grow tall and narrow, while others are short and will creep or cascade along the front of the flower border. There are perennials that climb walls like the hardy clematis or the malva, which creates a huge bush and blooms all summer. Look carefully at a bed of iris. What types and sizes of perennials would make attractive companions?

4. PLANT FOR COLOR WAVES OR DRIFTS OF FLOWERS SPRING THROUGH FALL

A well-designed flower bed will display waves of color, not the dizzying look of everything blooming at once. Use plants that have different bloom periods. Start with the bulbs of spring. As they start to fade, the columbines step up with color. When the columbines finish, the lilies bloom. Next is the garden phlox for summer, and the procession continues throughout the season. The grand finale is the fall asters and sedums.

Flowers planted in waves or drifts, meaning groups of three or more plants of one species, produce a sense of movement and generally have a more pleasing visual effect than individual flowers. Planting in horizontal lines or drifts tends to give a more graceful feeling, especially when the drifts overlap each other slightly and bloom in gentle succession.

A PICTORAL DEMONSTRATION SHOWING HOW COMPANION PLANTS WORK TOGETHER

- All grow well in a full-sun watered flower bed, so the environments are similar.

- The perennials are grown in tiers from high to low for better viewing but not in strict rows.

- The perennials are planted in clumps or drifts for maximum impact.

- The foliage and flowers vary in size, shape, and color. Notice the variety of different foliage, like the spiky daylilies, the round clumps of sweet William, and the cascading *Lobelia* 'Techno Heat' in front of the spikes.

- The berm is planted for flower color from spring through fall, starting out with daffodils. Then the striped iris, sweet William, and cranesbill bloom. Dark-red liliums bloom in huge clumps of five

or six lilies, which gives height to the upper corner sections in midsummer. The middle section or saddle of the berm is planted with blue and white salvia for spring and everblooming red *Daylily* 'Pardon Me' for late summer. The red dwarf gallery *Dahlia* 'Singer' blooms next and will keep blooming until frost. For height, the handsome *Heliopsis* 'Summer Sun' opens in June and provides masses of golden-yellow color until Labor Day. Drifts of canna lilies furnish height and a focal point. There is not a season when the berm is not packed with color. Just like the Seattle skyline or Teton Mountain range, the berm has every shape and size of perennial. This garden will never be static or boring to look at.

Monarda didyma
(mow-NAR-duh)
BEE BALM

SHAPE	Huge clump with clustered flower heads
HEIGHT	Thirty inches
WIDTH	Two feet around
BLOOM TIME	Midsummer
COLORS	All shades of red, wine, rose, pink, and lavender
SITE	Alkaline soils with constant moisture
LIGHT	Full sun or partial shade
HARDINESS	Zones 3–8
COMMENTS	No serious problems

M. 'Pink Lace' has large, colorful three-inch blooms.

M. 'Violet Queen' has consistent height and a huge size, which gives it presence in the garden.

M. 'Raspberry Wine' fills a bed or border with intense color and huge size, adding summer drama.

M. 'Petite Delight' is a dwarf monarda that works well along the front edge of the garden.

LET'S GET ACQUAINTED. I'm *Monarda*, but I go by several common names, including bee balm and bergamot. But whatever I'm called, it's important to me that you remember that I'm all-American. Grown from species native to the American continent, my ancestors originally had scarlet-red flower heads arrayed in loose clusters that looked like fireworks. I'm often called "fireworks," and I like my nickname. Admit it. There is nothing more American than the Fourth of July and red fireworks!

I'm so American that after the Boston Tea Party in 1773, when the early colonists broke their ties with England, we monarda plants were substituted for their tea. The Osweg Indians taught the New Englanders how to simmer my leaves in an enamel saucepan, pour this into a cup, and add a new leaf for trim. I taste just like Earl Grey tea. I also smell like it because I contain oil of bergamot.

Just like other American native plants, I'm easy to grow, and I'm deer resistant. My distinct square stems indicate that I'm a member of the vigorous mint family. I prefer to grow in full sun when I'm planted in the coolness of the high elevations. But in the valley afternoon, partial shade is good. It's important that I get consistent moisture. If I'm planted in full shade, do not expect flowers.

I'm adaptable to a variety of soils but appreciate a covering of fine leaf mulch before winter. I'm considered to be winter-hardy and am a Zone 4 perennial, but injuries caused during winter result in shorter stems or spot die out for the next season. These are easy to repair, for my running rhizome rootstocks make large clumps that are easy to divide in spring. I am a late-breaking perennial, so don't expect me to peek through the soil until the weather warms up.

Divide my expanding clumps every three years, or just dig sections from my outer edges to transplant elsewhere. When transplanting my starts, leave me plenty of room to spread; I'm a big guy. Go easy on the fertilizer. Too much nitrogen can make me lanky and prone to disease. Cut me to the ground when I finish my parade of flowers. This keeps me healthy, and might even spark another bloom.

I'm undeniably one of the showiest perennials in the summer garden. My large clumps of strong stems are clothed in aromatic dark-green leaves that grow to a relatively consistent height of three feet. My flowers bloom all at the same time, creating a month-long mass of color, which is positively captivating. My spiky blooms are tubular, two-layered blooms that crowd into terminal clusters. My basic color is still the original red color of the first native monardas, but cultivars have been bred to bloom in not only rich shades of red but also violet, purple, pink, and white. We are a little wacky looking with our two-layered clusters, but we are impossible to ignore. Even butterflies and hummingbirds can't ignore us. We are nectar-producing machines! When we bloom in our patriotic red colors, it's parade time.

My only problem is a tendency to get mildew damage on my leaves. The arid western mountains help curb this because mildew is caused by humid weather, but if I get too wet, too dense, or too dry, white spots will show up on my leaves. Plants that receive consistent moisture and never wilt are less susceptible to this fungus. A homemade spray that works wonders on me is one teaspoon of baking soda mixed with one quart of water. Add a few drops of either dish soap or cooking oil to help the spray adhere, and spray it on my leaves.

Gardeners often find themselves wishing for the good old days when they grew a garden of native perennials that were untroubled, hardy, carefree, and drought tolerant. Gardeners also forget that problems like mildew on monarda or flopping asters were the norm. Fortunately for gardeners, horticulturists are now breeding mildew-resistant varieties of monarda.

The following are some of the highest rated mildew-resistant monarda: 'Colrain Red' is a deep purplish red with three-inch blooms. 'Gardenview Scarlet' is red with big blooms and rarely shows winter die out. 'Marshall's Delight' is purple-pink and has good winter survival skills. 'Raspberry Wine' has intensely colored purple-red medium-sized blooms. 'Violet Queen' is a strong purple and has smaller blooms.

The breeding of native plants into well-behaved cultivars has given me mildew resistance, so I have become a popular perennial again. I bring the best of both worlds to the garden. I'm a native North American species, but I'm also a North American native cultivar.

Antennaria, a native cultivar, is so small it disappears in a flower garden.

The cultivated native aruncus opens a garden spot with white lace flowers and green foliage.

Echinacea purpurea is a native cultivar that grows to about thirty inches and blooms from late summer through fall. Their flowers are pink with large copper cones.

NATIVE PLANTS IN THE GARDEN

NATIVE PLANT SPECIES of perennials are defined as plants growing naturally in a particular geographic area prior to European settlement. Plants that are common to our area, but not indigenous or native to North America, are referred to as "naturalized natives" and grow well here also.

These plants have adapted to local conditions for thousands of years. They have survived the cold and heat, are resistant to drought, and are not bothered by pests and diseases. Native plants provide a habitat for birds, butterflies, and wildlife. Native plants and naturalized native cultivars require less of everything. They have adapted so they need less water, fewer chemicals, and less long-term maintenance. Their résumé reads like a perfect perennial.

My personal experience with native perennials in my garden was far from the ideal of the unspoiled American frontier. My failures were probably due to a sprinkling system and amended clay soil. The reality was some native species in my garden were wild, weedy, and unattractive. They just weren't hardy as a native plant would be expected to be, and I was glad when they were removed to the compost heap!

Cultivars are more easily available at nurseries everywhere, so look for both native and native cultivars to grow in your garden.

The bottom line is native plants are just like all perennials. When they are grown in their comfort zone similar to where they gained their native status, they perform. Mistakes are excellent teachers, so when growing natives, a reasonable expectation and evaluation is needed on how and where the natives will be used.

Epilobium, fireweed, is hardy to a Zone 3 and grows all over Alaska. Pictured is fireweed blooming on the Klondike Highway near the Alaskan border.

Heuchera, a low-clumping native perennial, has moved up to the big time as a hybrid of numerous colors of foliage.

Sphaeralcea is a native shrub with apricot flowers on the end of long silver-leafed, hairy stems.

Eupatorium, Joe-pye weed, has pale mauve-pinkish blooms that are huge (up to eight inches in diameter). The striking perennial is six feet tall.

Liatris has hardly changed from when it was first discovered in North America.

Solidago, golden rod, is a drought-tolerant fall-blooming perennial.

Geum, prairie smoke, is a high-elevation perennial that looked dried up and insignificant in my garden.

Polemonium, Jacob's ladder, is a native perennial that is still delivering its distinct foliage and blue flowers to shade gardens.

Thalictrum, meadow rue, adds height to a shady spring garden.

163

Narcissus
(nahr-SIS-uhs)
DAFFODIL

SHAPE	V-shaped with strap-like leaves, flowers are trumpets
HEIGHT	Twelve inches
WIDTH	Twelve inches
BLOOM TIME	Early spring
COLORS	Typically yellow
SITE	Normal alkaline, enjoys clay
LIGHT	Partial sun
HARDINESS	Zones 3–9
COMMENTS	Removing yellow foliage too soon weakens the bulb

The brilliant sunshine yellow of the early-spring daffodils are the messengers trumpeting that the garden is new again.

The common names of daffodil, narcissus, and jonquil are used interchangeably among the species, but narcissus usually has a shorter cup.

Daffodils may be self-colored like this pure-white one, or their colors may differ widely.

Planting daffodil bulbs in drifts, half-circles, or teardrops give the flowers a natural appearance. When landscaping, throw a mixture of bulbs over your shoulder and plant them in freeform clusters wherever they drop.

IF YOU KNOW your Greek mythology, you'll recognize my name—*Narcissus*. And if you love spring, you'll also recognize my second name—daffodil. I love both names, and I love telling the tale of how I received the Greek version of my name. A vain young man gazed at his reflection in a pool of water until he became so obsessed by his own beauty that he fell into the pool and drowned. Another version of the same story is that Narcissus died of starvation and thirst while transfixed by his own reflection in the water. But in both versions, a beautiful blossom sprang from the ground where he died. As a result, I'm the symbol of unrequited love. But I'm sure any young lady would be delighted to get a bouquet of daffodils—despite the symbolic meaning!

I believe I'm also the symbol of spring when the garden is new again. Why else would my perfect, five-petaled flowers with fringed golden trumpets be shaped as if they are heralding in the season of spring? Why else would I be the welcoming committee or first major showstopping color to eliminate the drabness of winter with the colors of sunshine? For what other reason would I be such a popular subject in poetry or festivals and even be the flower that symbolizes the month of May? I'm also totally weatherproof in the finicky season of springtime. It's obviously true—I am the symbol of spring! Even my favorite name of daffodil, or "daffydowndilly," sounds like spring!

There are many other reasons I'm such a springtime delight. The first is my hardiness. I'm a Zone 3, long-lived perennial. But more than that, I grow from a bulb. All gardeners know that bulbs are the easiest flowers to grow because of their internal storage systems. If my storage system refills after I bloom, I'll be there to brighten the colorless landscapes of many late winters. This is done by leaving my foliage intact after it yellows and not overwatering my dormant bulbs.

The second reason I'm a springtime delight is that I'm easy to grow. Soils are not a big deal to me. If a garden has clay soil, just add compost or some other type of organic mulch. A 10–10–10 fertilizer applied in early spring and early fall at the same time lawns are fertilized is more than adequate. Applying fertilizer after I've started blooming encourages bulb rot and sometimes shortens my life.

Another reason I'm popular is that I grow almost anywhere. I can be planted in the sun or partial shade. My bulbs originated in the forests of Northern Africa and Europe, so woodland-type areas in partial shade areas are my natural home.

A little shade is why I'm best planted under deciduous shrubs or perennials like daylilies where I'll finish blooming before the larger plants leaf out. Here, I get the cool spring sunshine, but when summer heats up, I'm shaded. Also, front-row planting of my bulbs will leave colorless, ratty-looking leaves when I finish blooming. No gardener wants dying foliage where it shows, but if I'm removed early, I'll lose the energy for next year's blooms. Wait until my foliage pulls or twists and can be detached easily, or better yet, plant me so I'll be hidden under another perennial's foliage.

I'm an autumn planting item. If it is imperative I be moved in the spring, lift me green and replant my bulb deep (leaves and all), so I'll have nutrition for next year's bloom. Deep planting slows the formation of small daughter bulbs so I stay stronger, especially my older, standard varieties like golden 'King Alfred' and white 'Ice Follies' that will colonize in the same spot for years and years.

My deer resistance is legendary, even as far back as Pliny, who wrote of my numbing qualities. The numbness I cause is the alkaloid poison lycorine that is in both my bulbs and flowers. Cooks at a primary school once confused me with an onion bulb and added me to the soup. A number of the children fell ill. My poison is why I'm deer resistant and appreciated by gardeners.

I produce galantamine, a drug used to combat Alzheimer's. The Cancer Society also uses bouquets of me as a fundraising symbol. I'm just happy that I can bring joy to spring gardens with my irresistible brightness that a late-season snow or freeze can't thwart!

SEDUCED BY THE SEED CATALOGS

D AFFODILS MAY BE considered the first official start of spring, but in January, when the freezing cold, snow, sleet, and fog inversions tighten their grip, it's really the arrival of the seed and plant catalogs that announce spring's arrival. Gardeners gazing out at the colorless landscape and fighting the furnace for air feel like they are in a straight jacket. But when the catalogs come in the mail, the winter confinements start to loosen. There, on the color-enhanced, airbrushed catalog pages is every conceivable perennial, each in full bloom! Gardeners find themselves falling, willingly and swiftly into a state of bliss that will ultimately cause a huge hole in their pocketbook.

How do the catalogs do it? How do they cause gardeners to come alive and realize that spring is coming and that they soon will be able to breathe again? Is it just that the catalogs arrive at the dreariest time of year when gardeners are in their weakest state? Could it be because the desire for green and the hope for spring are so overwhelming? The pictorial miracles of gigantic-sized blooms displayed on the catalog pages, without a trace of weeds, are enough to cause any gardener to drool. Or perhaps it's the special discounts and free shipping?

The attention-getting markings of starburst icons on certain flower pictures signal a gardener that here on these pages is where new and improved hybrids (which no other gardener in your neighborhood has grown or even seen) can be found. And these are the exceptional new perennials that a gardener simply cannot live without! (Or resist . . .)

How do your gardening taste buds resist a flower named 'Persian Chocolate', 'Meringue', or 'Raspberry Swirl'? And if they can't get you by going after your sense of taste, advertisers can always appeal to your passionate side. Delphiniums have both 'Blushing Bride' and 'Double Innocence'. Echinacea will lure a gardener with names like 'Fatal Attraction' and 'Irresistible'. *Hemerocallis* 'Spell Binder' and 'Wedding Band' along with *Gaura* 'Passionate Blush' and *Hibiscus* 'Sultry Kiss' really set a romantic mood for gardening. Not to be left out, hosta offers a 'Seducer', a 'Striptease', and finally 'Satisfaction'. Salvia's pink and blue 'Endless Love', tidies up the romance so everything turns out appropriate.

Flower seduction at 0°F in January sounds close to impossible, but the seed and plant catalogs manage just fine. With catalog illustrations so exceptionally beautiful and names of perennials that appeal subconsciously, gardeners are at the mercy of nursery growers. Unless, of course, they really like being seduced!

When the seed and plant catalogs arrive, it's like opening your mailbox to spring, summer, and fall in bloom all at the same time.

Catalogs will seduce your taste buds with flower names like *Hemerocallis* 'Strawberry Candy'.

How will you resist *Hibiscus* 'Sultry Kiss' and its appeal to your romantic side?

Trollus 'Golden Queen' is named for royalty to appeal to your sense of aristocratic pride.

Brunnera 'Jack Frost' sounds like it would be cold to touch.

Helleborus 'Red Racer' is named to evoke youthfulness and adventure—which should help the seed catalog convince you to purchase it.

Hosta 'Patriot' has a name that creates feelings of loyalty to your country.

Mother Nature created color to seduce bees, but the seed catalogs will seduce the gardener's sense of sight with names like *Geum* 'Totally Tangerine'.

While searching the catalogs in January, you won't be able to resist *Papaver* 'Summer Breeze'.

Aquilegia 'Granny's Rose Bonnet' will evoke a sense of family and nostalgia, which will also cause you to open your pocketbook.

Nepeta
(NEP-uh-tuh)
'Sweet Dreams'
CATMINT

SHAPE	Tall spikes, with spike flowers
HEIGHT	Thirty-inch tall clumps
WIDTH	Twenty-four inches
BLOOM TIME	Late spring to late summer
COLORS	Pink with wine bracts
SITE	Well-drained alkaline, sand, or clay
LIGHT	Full sun or partial sun
HARDINESS	Zones 4–10
COMMENTS	No pest or disease problems

N. 'Sweet Dreams' mixes well with any other flowers in the border.

Colorful spires of N. 'Sweet Dreams' light up this shade garden.

The attractiveness of nepeta's flowers can be observed in this close-up photo.

The fragrant sweet mint smell of N. 'Sweet Dreams' foliage causes deer to shy away.

THIS MAY SOUND stuck-up, but I have a right to feel a little superior. You'll agree when you see how I stack up against my relatives, the common blue catmint perennials. I'm *Nepeta* 'Sweet Dreams', and the reason most gardeners prefer me is that I'm a hybrid! Also, I'm sterile and will not set all that messy seed. I can only be propagated by being dug and divided into starts. You'd better believe starts are important, because there can never be enough of me in the garden. That's how marvelous I am.

Like all nepetas, I'm really hardy. Winter suits me well, and I fit into the Zone 4 or -30°F cold slot. I also like the lean, alkaline, and rocky soils of the West. Unlike my blue relatives, however, I expect a touch more shade and water. I'm sure that gardeners will appreciate a catmint that is happy in partial shade rather than the heat of full sun.

I grow to an imposing, strong thirty-six inches. Never would I consider flopping. I'm far too good for that. In the garden, I'll expect plenty of space to have room for my vigorous clump to fill a two-foot area. With such imposing qualities, I need to be planted in the middle or back sections of the flower border, where I'll bloom most of the summer.

Because I'm a hybrid, I'm a sterile perennial and do not use my energy to set seed. Instead, I use it to bloom and bloom and bloom. A sterile hybrid does not have the ability to reproduce itself. I was probably hybridized naturally by cross pollination. I don't think anyone knows for sure. A bird or insect could have crossed my pollen with another variety of catmint species, and I'm the result.

I do know that people are creating hybrids in their laboratories, trying to improve a perennial by taking qualities of two different varieties, such as a longer bloom time or perhaps larger, flashier blooms.

My sterility is worrisome because it's the result of abnormal cell division and results in uneven numbers of chromosome pairs in the cells of the hybrid offspring. Not all is lost though. I can still be reproduced asexually or through vegetative propagation. Just like tubers, rhizomes, stolons, or bulbs (which reproduce from their roots), I reproduce from my roots. That's why I said I have to be dug and divided to get more starts. By now you should be agreeing that I'm uncommon, and I have every right to be a little stuck-up.

Just look at my elegant pink flowers that sit on the tips of burgundy bracts, creating a two-toned, eye-catching display, which really stands out in the garden. Every spike is loaded with long-lasting, pink trumpet-shaped florets that mass on the top third of my stem. Planting a clump of two or more of me will endow the garden with a dazzling mass of summer color.

Nepetas are part of the fragrant mint family, but my rich green foliage is minty and more sweetly scented than regular catmint. Maybe this is how I got my 'Sweet Dreams' name. I smell so sweet. Touching my soft, felt-lobed leaves will cloud the air with my perfume. My leaves also contain vitamin C, so a hot cup of my minty tea will relieve a cold or fever. For a refreshing summer afternoon break, use my mint leaves with a tall, ice-filled glass of tea. My pretty green leaves on the rim of the glass will give the tea an appetizing look.

Placing my freshly picked leaves on a bruise on your arm or leg will hasten healing and ease the pain because my leaves have mild sedative qualities.

Hummingbirds, butterflies, and bees flock to my fragrance, but rodents, rabbits, and deer avoid me. They dislike my smell and my soft leaves. This is just one more reason that I'm so incredible. I chase away a gardener's enemies.

HYBRIDIZING PERENNIALS

NEPETA 'SWEET DREAMS' is a newly discovered perennial, and no one seems to know where it came from. 'Sweet Dreams' could possibly be a natural mutation, a cross-pollinated plant, or a hybrid perennial. Traditional propagation of plants since the dawn of gardening began has been done by the saving of seeds. Through the simple selection of seeds year after year from plants that were hardier, more attractive, or had traits the gardeners desired, a higher quality of perennials evolved.

Occasionally, a perennial comes about by **natural mutations**. Gardeners can't be certain, but it seems that mutations occur when a spontaneous disruption or a mistake in DNA replication occurs. That mistake can be passed down to subsequent generations through seed for a different perennial if that mutation yields desirable traits. Many of our favorite variegated perennials are the result of naturally occurring mutations.

Cross pollination is another method of creating new perennials that can be patented. Cross pollination is the transference of the pollen of one flower to the stigma of another. The pollination is successful if the plant sets a viable offspring seed that exhibits beneficial traits. Cross pollination is a long, painstaking process much more difficult than the traditional saving of seeds. In cross-pollination, the plants need to be the same species or compatible. This is the way most amateur plant breeders or gardeners create new varieties.

The next step breeders used to develop new or better perennials is **hybridization**. If hybridization was used to create a new plant like 'Sweet Dreams' that blooms pink, grows in partial shade, and is sterile, then a process called *hybridization* was probably used. In hybridizing, the first step is having two pure strains of compatible plants that can be repeatedly inbred until a stable strain is attained.

The new plants are then cross-pollinated until seeds that grow are uniform with predictable results. Hybrids are usually stronger, shorter, and longer blooming with more spectacular flowers and colors. This sounds good, right? It's questionable. Buying hybrid varieties is a double-edged sword because it's only fair that perennial breeders are compensated. This makes the perennials more costly to gardeners who pay patent charges.

A PPAF on a perennial tag stands for US "Plant Patent Applied For." Once the patent has been granted, it is assigned a PP#, or a patented plant number. Propagation is not allowed on patented plants, and purchasing patented perennials does not automatically mean they are better.

Another major drawback is that sterile seeds will not reproduce. Gardeners who grow hybrids need to know that these hybrid plants kill their own embryos. Seeds and children are the future. What will our future as gardeners look like if we can't propagate and start seeds? Gardeners need to ask themselves these questions.

Now breeders have expanded perennials by creating **genetically modified organisms,** or **GMOs**. Plant material from one organism can be inserted into the DNA of a completely unrelated organization, even a non-plant series. This breakthrough is the only method for plant breeders to obtain beneficial traits between unrelated species. For example, breeders may decide to breed perennials that are resistant to weed killer, so they insert a soil bacteria gene that makes the plant tolerant. Gardeners can spray the weeds without damaging their resistant perennials. Sounds good! Or are monsters being created that have hidden biological effects, and pollen drift could contaminate or overtake?

It's foolish to try to mess with Mother Nature. She has a way of teaching valuable lessons. Not being allowed to propagate seeds or perennials takes a big hunk of the joy out of gardening. But the tried-and-true plant characteristics of the old-time perennials can be trusted. They have proven their worth generation after generation.

NATURAL PERENNIALS TO HYBRIDS

The bright golden flowers of *Heliopsis* 'Summer Sun' should already be enough for any gardener, but the long-blooming hardiness of this fine perennial makes it exceptional.

Heliopsis 'Loraine Sunshine' is a newly patented hybrid with variegated foliage. When I tried to grow these in my garden, they did not grow as vigorously as the picture to the left, *Heliopsis* 'Summer Sun'.

The tried-and-true native echinacea are also very attractive and will not winter-kill.

Echinacea 'Pink Double Delight', a new hybrid, is certainly different in appearance and hardiness from regular coneflowers.

Physosomegia virginiana
(fie-so-STEE-gee-uh)

OBEDIENT PLANT

SHAPE	Upright spikes
HEIGHT	Thirty inches
WIDTH	Twenty inches
BLOOM TIME	Early fall to frost
COLORS	Lilac, pink, and white
SITE	Lean to average, even clay
LIGHT	Sun to partial, plus shade
HARDINESS	Zones 3–9
COMMENTS	No pests or disease

Physostegia is so tall and straight, it brings a sense of vitality and energy into the garden.

A Physostegia close-up shows the snapdragon-like blooms that look so delicate but are tough as nails. Obedient can even be bent and curved for cut-flower arrangements.

The pink 'Miss Manners' is not as mannerly as the white. The pink gets over two feet tall and is a pale (almost washed out) pink.

Obedience has been in my garden for almost sixty years.

I'M A NATIVE perennial called *Physostegia*. I originated in eastern North America, but I found my real home after moving west. The lean soil slows down the spreading of my roots. I stand thicker, shorter, straighter, and stronger in the West, and the cold winters invigorate rather than kill me.

Being a member of the mint family gives me my distinctive square-shaped stems. I have narrow lance-shaped leaves that march vertically up my thirty-inch tall handsome spires of rose or white flowers. I grow in impressive, dense clumps that supply masses of late-season color to the garden.

The name *obedience* came about because my tubular, two-lipped flowers can be rearranged on my stem. By twisting my blooms or bending a stem, I'll stay put for a superb accent in flower arrangements. I'm really not fond of being called obedient plant. The name *disobedient plant* suits my personality much better! I'm just not a stay-put type of perennial, and I prefer to multiply in the garden. I'm really not invasive, but it's really cool to send out my fibrous roots and proliferate.

It's interesting that my high-bred children are well behaved. They are even called 'Miss Manners' and do not spread in the garden. When the eldest, white 'Miss Manners' was introduced, she became so popular that the horticulturists realized that a pink 'Miss Manners' was required. So now, white 'Miss Manners' is not an only child. Pink 'Miss Manners' is more like me, taller and more disobedient.

My lovely daughters are smaller. In the West, they get about fifteen to twenty inches tall. Their compact forms of petite, strong stems stay neat and tidy. Their roots are smaller, and they bloom earlier and for a longer season in the year. Everything about them, from their fresh green foliage to their exquisite, frilly trumpet-shaped flowers is faultless. However, the poor things are hybrids and are not allowed to propagate. Now doesn't that just ruin everything!

Propagating is the easiest thing I do. When I outgrow my space, simply dig up my root clump with a shovel or spade. Pull my roots apart, making sure that each start has several (three or four) stems with roots. Keep my starts shaded with a wet newspaper until I get replanted, but don't mess around! The sooner I'm in the ground, the better. Water me until I become established. If I'm planted in the sun, I'll need more to drink, but in the shade it's okay if I dry out a little. I promise that in no time at all, I'll provide the garden with masses of my late-season color. After all, proliferating is what I do so well!

AUTHOR'S NOTE

My very first physostegia plant was presented to me from Grandma Louise, who was determined to turn me into a gardener. On early spring mornings, she would be at our door, holding a wrapped newspaper or paper cup. "Here," she would say. "I brought you a start." She knew that even a novice gardener such as I was could grow a vigorous perennial like obedience. She spoke truth, because after sixty years, that first plant has been divided year after year and is still providing masses of vivid color to the late-season garden. What Grandma didn't know was that clump perennials like obedient plant would eventually lead us to an enjoyable social retirement career called Secrist Gardens.

A highlight of spring gardening was finding an overgrown clump of perennials to dig up and divide. I never could discard a living gift from nature, and this type of perennial propagates so easily I just couldn't let them die. Every possible resource of finding these plants a home had been tapped. Neighbors, garden clubs, and even my kids would groan when I knocked on their door to present them with a container of freshly dug starts. So I potted them up.

On holiday weekends like Easter and Memorial Day, I advertised in the local paper, "A Real Yard Sale." Yard sales were still a new fad at this time, so imagine my surprise when customers happily took home these starts, and to this day they are still coming back for more. This started an enjoyable family business that is still growing (no pun intended).

PROPAGATING CLUMP-GROWING PERENNIALS

PERENNIALS LIKE THE obedient plant enthusiastically "proliferate" by spreading an underground root ball of new, fibrous roots. This type of root system is easily divided into starts. These can be replanted to expand your own garden, or they can be dug for the health of the perennial.

Early spring, just as the first tiny stems peek through the ground, is the time to divide perennials in the West. With our early winters, fall division does not give the plants time to establish.

The first step in division is to dig up the plant. A garden fork is less damaging to the roots than a shovel, but if the clump is huge, a shovel will be needed. Dig a trench at least six to twelve inches from the edge of the crown. Excavate a full circle around the plant before trying to lift it out. Lift the root ball out of the ground, and then shake or tease away the soil. If the plant is small, divisions can be pulled apart. A huge root ball may have to be sliced into manageable sections with a sharp shovel. My favorite dividing tool is a big old serrated bread knife that saws the root ball apart.

Clump divisions are so successful because the new plants are young already-rooted offshoots from a mature perennial. These offshoots, starts, or slips (as they are usually called), will be exact duplicates of the parent perennial. Slips establish themselves quickly, and they frequently bloom the first year.

Division of perennials is also done to keep the plants healthy and looking good. For example, asters, chrysanthemums, gaillardias, and leucanthemum will develop dead, woody centers in the middle of the plant. This could be because the plant is competing for nutrition, but it definitely means that it is time to divide. Other perennials like rudbeckia, monarda, and nepeta will need dividing because they outgrow their space and stop blooming. Plants that crowd their neighbors will stop flower production. Division will thin out the plants, and the perennials will start to bloom again.

Other plants need division to keep them from dying out. Dianthus, a short-lived perennial, is an example of this. Without division so new offspring can be replanted, this perennial has a tendency to disappear from the flower bed. Remove any dead or damaged roots and stems. Division is best done on cool, cloudy, or rainy days.

Once the perennial clump has been pried from the hole and divided, it's time to baby the babies. Handle them gently. Keep them shaded until planted and check the roots for disease or rot. This is the easiest time to remove weeds that have insinuated themselves into the clump. Slice or pull the perennial into sections, making sure each section has crowns or growing points on it. Replant at the same depth the plant was grown at originally. Have the soil where they are to be planted ready, and plant as fast as possible to reduce stress and shock.

After the babies are planted, water them to keep the soil moist at all times. Fertilizing is always beneficial but not absolutely necessary. Shade the babies from intense sun for several weeks. This is another reason that early, cooler spring division is beneficial. Soon they will be growing vigorously, and if they happen to be late-season bloomers, they will probably bloom the same year.

When dividing, always prune plants with larger crowns before planting (cut them back). Pruning gives the new roots less to nourish and reduces water loss through respiration. So baby your babies, and the reward will be more, healthier flowers.

Pulling a wagon around the yard, viewing the perennials that are growing in the flower beds, and choosing perennials to put on your wagon is more like child's play than shopping.

The following perennials are a few examples of fibrous root plants that can be regenerated by division. Flower production will improve, and vigorous plants will be kept within bounds. Never hesitate by worrying that dividing may damage the perennial. It will only improve the plant.

- *Achillea*, yarrow
- *Ajuga*, bugleweed
- *Alchemilla*, lady's mantle
- *Anchusa*, bugloss
- *Anemone*, windflower
- *Arabis*, rock cress
- *Armeria*, thrift
- *Artemisia*, wormwood
- *Aruncus*, goat's beard
- *Brunnera*, heartleaf
- *Campanula*, bellflower
- *Centaurea*, mountain bluet
- *Geranium*, cranesbill
- *Geum*, avens
- *Lamium*, dead nettle
- *Ligularia*, leopard plant
- *Limonium*, sea lavender
- *Lychnis*, campion
- *Oenothera*, evening primrose
- *Phlox*, garden phlox
- *Potentilla*, cinquefoil
- *Pulmonaria*, lungwort
- *Solidago*, goldenrod
- *Stachys*, lamb's ears
- *Thalictrum*, meadow rue
- *Trollius*, globeflower
- *Veronica*, speedwell

PERENNIALS THAT DIVIDE EASILY

Brunnera

Geum

Oenothera

Salvia nemorosa
(SAL-vee-uh)
SAGE

SHAPE	Shrub-like clump with spike flowers
HEIGHT	Fifteen inches
WIDTH	About fifteen inches
BLOOM TIME	Early to late summer
COLORS	Intense shades of blues, sometimes pink or white
SITE	Well-drained soil
LIGHT	Full sun
HARDINESS	Zones 3–9
COMMENTS	Foliage will flop in shade

With a little deadheading, salvias bloom all summer.

Salvia lives a long life, and age gives it a bigger, fuller, and more handsome appearance over the years.

Salvia's tight-lipped blooms resemble a mouth that is ready for the pollinators.

Salvia is so versatile that this fine perennial grows anywhere it's planted. Here, it's growing in front of shade-loving hosta.

I GET NO RESPECT! Before we get acquainted, there is a matter I would like to clear up. I find it very irritating that I am often considered a common perennial without a lot of class. It could be due to the fact that sagebrush completely carpets any uncultivated ground in the western US, and gardeners know that my common name is sage. If there is one thing western gardeners don't want, it is more sagebrush! I'm not sagebrush. I'm the very handsome perennial called *Salvia nemorosa*.

Or maybe I'm considered common because of my unfussiness. I grow in the hot, desertlike sections of the country, but I also grow in the colder, more northern gardens. I even perform along the coastlines where salt spray would be the death of many less-hardy perennials. In fact, I grow most anywhere in the United States, or anyplace I'm planted. If that makes me common, you're mistaken, and I'll prove it now!

First of all, I'm blue—deep blue—and sometimes pink or white. My flowers climb up fifteen-inch narrow spikes and are loaded with tons of tiny, tight-lipped flowers. These blooms have a unique pollinating system unlike any other flower. I have two stamens instead of the more common four of other flowers. My stamens are hinged like a lever. When the birds, bees, and butterflies that adore me visit, the lever opens almost like a mouth, and the pollen releases.

My foliage is also uncommon. I have soft, felted, two-sided leaves with fine hairs growing on the leaves, stems, and even on my flowers. The hair helps reduce water loss and gives me a drought tolerance that not many perennials have. My leaves are filled with an aromatic, herb-like scent that, when brushed against, release the smell. This is why deer and other animals avoid me. They don't like how I smell.

I even have a long history of healing. My name *Salvia* is from the Latin *salvere*, meaning "to be in good health, to cure, or to save." My herbal powers have been known to increase longevity,

and my other name *sage* means wisdom. When it comes to longevity, I'm noted because the older I get, the more attractive I become. My foliage gets thicker, my circumfence doubles, and my flowers cover more stem in brighter colors. This is one time that age improves beauty.

I start blooming in early summer on a tight mound of shrub-like foliage. Cold-hardy salvia is one of the showiest and longest-blooming perennials. I look stunning massed in either the middle or front of a flower bed. The red shades of Maltese cross or the gold colors of achillea planted behind me are strong attention-getters. Most any smaller-sized perennials look attractive growing beside me, and any short, flat ground covers will look nice around my feet. My blue colors are easy to pair with other perennials and will not clash with other flowers.

If I'm planted in shade or rich soils, I have a tendency to flop, but the lean mineral soils of the West keep me shorter and sturdier. I bloom heavier in full sun but will also provide color to a partially shaded area.

With a little deadheading, I bloom all summer. Shear me when I start to form seeds so I'll thicken and keep blooming until fall. If I don't get deadheaded, I'll stop blooming, and my energy will go into seed production. My seeds propagate easily, so if I'm deadheaded, it will cause the seed forming to terminate. I'll double my efforts to produce more of my amazing blooms. Then I can set seed later in the season. After all, even though I add so much richness to the garden, my real job in nature is to produce seeds so I can propagate.

When the center of my plant falls open, it's a signal that I need to be divided. Lift my root ball with a shovel and pull apart solid clumps of roots and replant. Spring is the best time to start divisions in the colder mountain areas.

As any gardener can now see, I am not common at all. For me, growing is easy, blooming is easy, propagation is easy, and reseeding is easy. I'm not common at all—only easy!

DEADHEADING PERENNIALS

IT'S MORNING, AND anticipation of a new summer day pops my eyes open. Forget household chores! Grabbing my big scissors that fit nicely in the back pocket of my jeans, I'm out the door to deadhead.

Deadheading sounds worse than it is. To deadhead, just snip or shear off the tops of perennials that have finished blooming. This simple task usually doesn't start until July, but it is critical because it prevents reseeding and encourages new flowers. To prevent weeding, prevent seeding.

Perennials, like most Earth species, have one major goal in life. Reproduction! In spring, the plant's cycle breaks dormancy, grows, blooms, and sets seeds to propagate. If the seed-setting process is terminated early, perennials will force a reblooming in order to set seed again. Seed and children are the future, and Mother Nature makes sure both stay strong.

Deadheading also diverts the plants' energy into root growth for next year's flowers. As a perennial's flowers fade, the plant is in a weakened stage. This is when diseases can gain a toehold.

My favorite deadheading tool is a ninety-nine cent pair of heavy scissors purchased at a war surplus store. I use the scissors mainly to remove fading blooms. The size is heavy enough to cut even thick stems but cheap enough that if I drop and lose a set when stooping to pull a weed, it's not a great loss. I buy them by the dozens.

For more intense deadheading, using a good pair of pruners or charged cordless trimmers is more efficient. The cordless trimmers snip the tops of spent perennials quickly and easily.

I love the solitude on these priceless summer mornings. Removing the spent flowers pulls me into the gardens for one-on-one time with my flowers. Flowers are like a gardener's own children. They need quality time, and they respond back positively to attention, love, and caring. Deadheading is a two-way street where both the gardener and flowers benefit. My soul feels restored and filled with such joy that I can hardly wait for tomorrow's deadheading.

DEADHEADING TIPS

REGULAR DEADHEADING

Regular deadheading is an ongoing summer activity that encourages perennials to keep blooming and not reseed. Deadheading is done by hand pinching, clipping with scissors to a leaf axle, or simply trimming up the plant. Perennials that respond best to this type of deadheading will often keep blooming until fall.

- Echinacea
- Gaillardia
- Helenium
- Leucanthemum
- Penstemon
- Rudbeckia
- Solidago
- Veronica

SHEARING

Shearing is a quicker, more efficient method of deadheading perennials. Perennials that need to be sheared have masses of tiny, dense flowers. Shearing is done with a short-handled pair of shears or with electric shears. Listed below are perennials that require shearing.

- *Centranthus ruber*
- *Coreopsis verticillata*
- Dianthus
- Iberis
- Nepeta
- Lavender
- Wild geraniums (Shear them to about five inches from the ground.)

STEM CUTTING

When the perennial has finished blooming, cut the stem or the stalk to just above the ground. This will promote new growth of the plant's rosettes or foliage. Stem cutting is done with hand pruners. For heavier stalks, use a lopper or larger pruners. For fall stem cutting after frost, a string trimmer makes the job quick and easy. Here are some examples of perennials that benefit from stem cutting to keep them from reseeding and looking unattractive or to encourage another blooming. Fall-blooming perennials do not apply.

- *Brunnera*: Cut only the stems that have flowered. This reveals brunnera's excellent heart-shaped foliage.
- *Campanula persicifolia*: Cut stems to the basal rosette when flowers finish. Sporadic reblooming is possible.
- *Delphinium*: Cut the finished flowering spikes to a lower leaf bud to encourage another blooming.
- *Lychnis*: Cut all stalks when the flowers are almost finished blooming. If the flowers are left to dry, lychnis will have already seeded everywhere.
- *Monarda*: Cut stems after blooming to promote healthy, neat mounds of foliage.
- *Phlox paniculata*: Cut stalk when flowers are finished, and do not let the plant go to seed. Seedlings will not resemble the parent plant and will probably return to a white, invasive form.
- *Tradescantia*: Cut back to half. It can look extremely ratty after blooming.

Deadheading is the number-one factor that affects the appearance of a perennial garden from late summer on. Without at least a small amount of deadheading, a garden can look messy!

If hybrid phlox is allowed to go to seed, the seedlings are usually a dirty, white-colored or pale mauve invasive form of phlox that is hard to eradicate from the garden.

Tradescantia begins looking shaggy after blooming and its seed flies all over.

These one-dollar scissors make a handy and convenient deadheading tool.

Dianthus 'Fire Witch' blooms in such profusion that shearing is a must.

Veronica spicata
(ver-ON-ih-kuh)
'ROYAL CANDLES'

SHAPE	Compact mound with spike flowers
HEIGHT	Twelve to fifteen inches
WIDTH	Twelve inches around
BLOOM TIME	Long blooming, all summer
COLORS	Deep blue
SITE	Average, fertile soil
LIGHT	Full sun or part sun
HARDINESS	Zones 3–8
COMMENTS	An excellent replacement for annuals

V. 'Royal Candles' planted along this cement driveway shows off the faultless look of this fine perennial.

The foliage of V. 'Royal Candles' is just about as perfect as the flowers.

The compact size and long blooming ability of V. 'Royal Candles' is attractive for bordering edges, filling planter containers, or decorating rock gardens.

V. 'Royal Candles' planted as a border along this curved fire pit provides season-long color. 'Royal Candles' acts more like an annual than a perennial.

IF YOU HAVEN'T discovered me yet, you are in for a treat. I'm *Veronica* 'Royal Candles', and I'm so extraordinary with my long bloom time (June through August), my dense compact size, and my upright shape that I could easily be mistaken for an annual. But I'm not an annual. I'm a hardy perennial.

Like all members of my family, I'm an easy, fuss-free perennial that is pleasant to grow. I'll bloom nonstop when living in the West where I'll get my required six-week winter cold treatment. When grown in warmer temperatures of higher Zone areas, my flowers will be smaller.

I'm not fussy about soil either. A neutral alkaline soil with a 7.0 pH is fine. I tolerate a wide variety of soils, but adding composted amendments to heavy clay will provide me a better comfort zone. In turn, I'll provide the gardener with a better plant and more flowers that will attract butterflies to the garden and send deer scurrying away.

Once established, I'm drought tolerant and grow nicely in rock gardens with their well-draining soils. Good drainage is important to me; however, I really need consistent moisture to look my best.

Another item I need is fertilizer. I'm a moderate feeder, but a constant liquid fertilizer similar to what annuals require will make certain that I'll bloom like an annual. Otherwise, just furnish me with a three-month control-release fertilizer in the spring. If I'm not fertilized, my foliage can look yellow, and I won't flower until later in the season.

My foliage is one my most distinguishing characteristics. It's clean and compact, growing in a dense mat of attractive two-inch-long leaves. My deep-green foliage reaches only twelve inches tall in bloom and is topped with numerous vertical flower spikes called candles. These blue flowers have purple undertones and start blooming in late spring, continuing until midsummer. Deadheading as the flower spikes start to brown will result in more candles. With regular deadheading, I will bloom until frost.

I serve important purposes in the garden. My size, shape, and blooming power arranged at the feet of taller perennials gives the flower beds a tasteful, finished appearance. Plant me as a front edger for *Hemerocallis* (daylilies). I'll make *Echinaceas* (coneflowers) in pink, white, or even the sister gold coneflower *Rudbeckia* 'Goldsturm' look sharp. I'll provide any taller, white perennials such as *Leucanthemum* (Shasta daisies) and even another *Veronica* called 'White Icicles' with the finishing touch they need.

I'm relatively disease-free; however, in late summer when the days are warm and the nights have cooled, I might show a powdery, mottled talcum on my leaves. This is mildew. The best control of mildew is to hard-cut me clear to the ground. Do not compost my removed foliage because most compost piles do not reach a high enough temperature to destroy the mildew spores. Fortunately I'm all but through blooming at this time, and late-season infections do not usually result in significant losses. Another good thing is that when I'm overwintered outdoors in the northern mountains, the fungus dies. If I get powdery mildew, it probably originated either in my seed or where I was initially grown before purchase. After cutting me to the ground, spray me with a mildew-destroying-soak as more insurance.

My history is interesting. I was discovered in an annual flower bed in Kent, England, by an avid gardener named Heather Philpott. While I belong to the huge veronica family, I'm considered a chance garden hybrid and have been patented. This means that propagation of me is prohibited without a license. This should give incentive to all gardeners who may discover unique flowers growing in their flower beds. Your perennials just may make you famous. Lucky me, I'm already famous! 'Royal Candles' is considered an outstanding perennial and one of the showiest hybrids in my genus. So think about planting me as a permanent plant in your garden, for I'll outperform any annual available!

Dragon wing begonias

Coleus

Dahlias

WILDLIFE-RESISTANT ANNUALS

GARDENERS LOVE ANNUALS. They love their constant color and dependable sizes. In fact, there isn't much about annuals that is not to love, except, of course, the yearly cost; annuals germinate, grow, bloom and die with the first frost. Annuals also require constant water and fertilizing.

Ageratum: Often called flossflower because of its soft, thread-like blooms, ageratum grows in compact mounds that reach about a foot tall and wide.

Alyssum: sweet alyssum is long-flowering, often still blooming after the first frost. It grows only a few inches high but will spread to a foot in diameter.

Artemisia 'Dusty Miller': The silvery, almost-white finely cut foliage of 'Dusty Miller' is an outstanding accent in gardens.

Begonias, dragon wing begonias: Often called wax-wings, these begonias are tough! They are undemanding. They grow well in alkaline soils in either sun or shade and can be saved as house plants in the winter.

Calibrachoa 'Million Bells': This is a tiny one-inch petunia that blooms from spring through summer. "Callies," as they are often called, are self-branching, self-cleaning, cascading, trailing plants. Their small stature—only five-to-eight inches tall—makes them valuable for growing in containers.

Cannas: Cannas add an elegant, exotic element to a garden. They also add much-needed height, so they are valuable as focal-point plantings. Cannas can be harvested after the first frost and stored in a freeze-free area to be planted for the next season.

Coleus: A foliage plant for shade, coleus is now offered in brilliant, colorful leaves that outdo flower blooms. It becomes well-branched after an initial pinch of its center stem. That stem can be rooted easily by placing it in water or soil. A huge pot of a variety of colorful coleuses brings more color into a shade garden than any other annual available.

Dahlia: The diversity of colors and sizes of dahlias, from short to medium and up to five feet in height, make them an attractive addition to any area of the garden. They must be planted each spring after danger of frost and then harvested in the fall. But they multiply, so growing dahlias is well worth the extra time and effort. After planting the tubers, water well, then hold off on watering until a sprout of green growth appears. Too much water will rot the tuber. Once growth occurs, water and fertilize on a regular basis. Dahlias will fill the garden with late-summer and fall color.

Datura, angel's trumpet: For an exotic, white accent in the garden, plant datura.

Euphorbia 'Diamond Frost': Most euphorbias are perennial, but 'Diamond Frost' is a new hybrid annual.

Geraniums: Zonal geraniums, or pelargoniums, are basically tropical plants with huge, ball-shaped blooms, which are popular for container planting and in bedding areas.

Helianthus annuus, sunflower: Helianthuses are perhaps called sunflowers because of the myth that their large, showy flower heads in sunny colors follow the sun throughout the day.

Lantana: Our hot, sunny summer, with its high-intensity light, alkaline soil, and arid climate are a natural home for this plant's drought-tolerant ability. Lantanas are Zone 7 perennials, so they can easily be potted before winter to be saved for bigger plants in next year's gardens.

Lobelia 'Techno Heat': This has medicinal qualities so it is not poisonous, but deer tend to ignore it. My 'Techno Heat' has bloomed through several early fall snowstorms and has proven to be cold resistant.

Morning Glory: A deer-resistant, vertical feature like *Morning Glory* 'Heavenly Blue' vine allows gardeners to utilize walls, trellises, and arbors as flower-planting spaces.

Snapdragons: These plants love alkaline soils and intense sunlight. Snapdragons are fail proof; they grow quickly, they bloom all summer with minimal care, and they reseed for the next season of color.

Verbena 'Homestead Purple': *Verbena* 'Homestead Purple' is a Zone 6 perennial, but gardeners use it as an annual because of its incredible bloom power.

Zinnia 'Profusion': This series of zinnias simply had to be bred especially for the western gardens. They love the West's alkaline soil and hot summers and are mildew- and deer-proof.

For annuals to turn out as expected in western gardens, they must:

- Be tough, dependable plants.
- Grow well in alkaline soil and water.
- Endure summer heat that ranges in the upper 80° to 100° temperatures.
- Have an element of deer resistance like scent, soft texture, hairy foliage, or poison. There are no deer-proof annual flowers, but there are annuals with deer resistance. Deer are regional in their choices of food, so what may be resistant in some gardens will be grazed in other areas. Annuals are also safer from hungry pests if they are planted in containers or decorative pots.
- Have regular fertilization. Annuals will not perform well without it. This means a minimum of watering every other week with a liquid fertilizer. Annuals are grown in a soilless mix type of potting soil. This soil has been sterilized, has no organic nutrition, and cannot support annual growth without fertilizing. This is why I grow the least number of annuals possible.
- Choose bright-colored annuals. For example, red is a rare color in perennials, so use red annuals to pull red into the garden. So many perennials are softer colors of violets, blues, yellows, and pinks that bright, hot-colored annuals make a strong color statement and add that eye-catching presence that gardeners want.
- Most annuals will stop blooming without regular deadheading or a haircut type of trim.

Sunflowers

Geraniums

Lantana

WILDLIFE-RESISTANT PERENNIALS SUMMARY

THERE IS A huge variety of wildlife-resistant perennials. The three main criteria that give a plant wildlife protection is the way it tastes, the way it smells, and the way it feels.

TASTE

- If a perennial is distasteful, it's unlikely that wildlife will bother it. Daffodils, for example, are poisonous. Deer seem to have an uncanny ability to know if a plant is poisonous or not.

SMELL

- Wildlife will be discouraged by perennials with strong smells. Lemon, mint, garlic, or any other strong herbal fragrances will be avoided.

FEEL

- Certain textures of foliages determine if wildlife will make shambles of a plant or leave it alone. Soft, felted leaves like lamb's ears are not appealing, nor do deer like hairy leaves or spike-like plants like festuca.

Any of these traits will give a perennial some wildlife resistance. The following tables list perennials that have a reputation for being wildlife resistant. Gardeners have reported success with them. However, regional wildlife have different taste buds, so be aware that a hungry deer will likely eat what is available.

SPRING-TO-SUMMER-BLOOMING PERENNIALS

SHORT–MEDIUM	MEDIUM–TALL
Achillea	Allium
Ajuga	Centaurea
Alchemilla	Columbine
Bergenia	Dicentra
Brunnera	Dictamnus
Campanula	Fritillaria
Columbine	Hesperis
Convallaria	Iris
Daffodil	Papaver
Euphorbia	Tanacetum
Fragaria	Thalictrum
Galium	Trollius
Geranium	Yucca
Gypsophila	
Helleborus	
Herb, chives	
Iceland poppies	
Lamiastrum	
Lamium	
Lychnis	
Myosotis	
Phlox subulata	
Potentilla	
Pulmonaria	
Saponaria	
Veronica	
Vinca	
Violets	

SUMMER-TO-FALL-BLOOMING PERENNIALS

SHORT–MEDIUM

Artemisia
Campanula
Cerastium
Ceratostigma
Coreopsis
Delosperma
Delphinium
Dianthus
Fern, *Matteuccia*
Festuca
Filipendula
Geum
Gypsophila
Houttunia
Lamistrum
Lavender
Lychnis
Lysimachia
Monarda
Myosotis
Nepeta
Oenothera
Pachysandra
Platycodon
Polemonium
Potentilla
Salvia
Stachys
Thymus
Tiarella
Veronica

MEDIUM–TALL

Achillea
Aruncus
Alcea
Campanula
Centranthus
Coreopsis
Delphinium
Digitalis
Echinacea
Fern
Filipendula
Grasses, tall
Gypsophila
Iris sibirica
Kniphofia
Lavender
Liatris
Ligularia
Lychnis
Lysimachia
Monarda
Malva
Nepeta
Papaver
Peonies
Phlox
Platycodon
Salvia
Solidago
Tanacetum
Veronica
Yucca

FALL-BLOOMING PERENNIALS

SHORT–MEDIUM

Artemisia
Aster
Ceratostigma
Chrysanthemum
Eupatorium
Gaillardia
Liriope
Sedum

MEDIUM–TALL

Aconitum
Alcea
Aster
Chrysanthemum
Cimicifuga
Eupatorium
Perovskia
Physostegia
Rudbeckia
Sedum
Veronica

DEER-RESISTANT ANNUALS

Alyssum
Artemisia 'Dusty Miller'
Begonias
Calibrachoa
Cannas
Coleus
Cosmos
Dahlia
Datura
Euphorbia
Helianthus
Lantana
Lobelia
Snapdragon
Verbena
Zinnia

PARDON OUR DIRT

Ancestral rocks upthrust
Violent volcanoes erupt.

Magma and lava release
Ash spills, layers deep.

Darkened skies
No sun can shine.

Glaciers grow
Melting in time.

Flood waters
Form inland seas.

Tropical landscapes
Cease to be.

Again earthquakes
Shake the ground.

Spewing ash
All around.

Repeated geology
Create western topography.

Eons of history
Explain the mystery

Why our soils
Are so problematic—

It's because of
Zero organic.

GARDENING IN DIFFICULT SOILS

TREMENDOUS GEOLOGICAL SEISMIC transformations had to occur to lift the magnificent Rocky Mountain range shown on the map. Heights of over fourteen thousand feet, like that of Mt. Elbert in Colorado, were shaped. To gardeners who know that soil is the structure that houses and holds plants, thinking about our topography is mind boggling. Eons and eons of time have helped to evolve the rocks, magma, and lava by weathering to create our modern day mineral-rich alkaline, clay, sand, and gravel soil. Understanding how the geological factors of volcanoes, earthquakes, sedimentary ash, glacial activity, floods, and lake-bottom soil meshed to create our western soils is both enlightening and entertaining.

The darker shades of browns are the mountaintops that were seismically lifted to form our soils where we garden.

SEISMIC ACTIVITY

We know that Rocky Mountain gardens sit on top of gigantic, rugged layers of rock produced by the initial uplifting of the clash of tectonic plates. The growth of our mountains is a perplexing geologic puzzle but was probably due to an

Twin Geysers is one geyser with two vents. The geyser is located along the edges of Yellowstone Lake and has short periods of dramatic eruptions and then goes dormant for a while.

unusual subduction slab. The flatter angle of the slab moved the mountain building from the oceanic plate farther inland, and volcanic arcs formed above the plate waiting for their chance to "blow off steam." Volcanoes erupted through openings or faults caused by earthquakes and ejected great conglomerates of molten rock, lava, and ash.

This simplified version is written in the rocks from which our soil evolved; however, the mountain building is never over. Bubbling seismic activity is still occurring, and steam-blowing thermal hot spots dot the states. Idaho has a naturally carbonated geyser in Soda Springs and Lava Hot Springs has river rapids running through walls of lava. Utah has so many thermal hot spots and pools that a map with red dots for each hot spot would look like it had measles. Gardeners will be interested in knowing that greenhouse heating for the production of plants is the number one use of geothermal resources in Utah.

The largest Rocky Mountain thermal hot spot is the Yellowstone Ecosystem that surrounds the Yellowstone Park. The park is located right in the middle of Wyoming, Idaho, and Montana and has over ten thousand thermal features. Yellowstone has over half of the world's geysers that are hot springs with some type of restriction that doesn't allow the hot steam to circulate until finally there is enough pressure for it to blow. A slumbering magma caldera, often called a supervolcano, rests a mere thirty miles beneath Yellowstone Lake and is rising at the rate of three inches per year. Should the

Devil's Slide in northern Utah.

caldera decide to blow, it would spew a cloud of plant-killing ash, ten feet deep, thousands of miles away.

Devil's Slide in northern Utah is a classic example of the mountain-building remnants of the rock's geologic past. The slide is several hundred feet in length with the limestone edges reaching forty feet in height. The twenty-five-foot wide middle section between the outer layers is composed of a softer limestone that has made it more susceptible to erosion and weathering, thus forming the chute of the slide.

Idaho's City of Rocks, called the weirdest place on earth, was formed by crustal stretching that produced steep abrupt faults, leaving great masses of rocks to erode.

Colorado's Bear Mountain is a multilayer formation of various colors and types of rock.

Wyoming is famous for its monolithic rock formation called Devil's Tower. The tower is 1,200 feet tall, with a top the size of a football field. The question of its creation has never been solved. These formations are symbols of our mountains' violent past.

SEDIMENTATION

Sediment accumulations have been estimated at spewing continually for over six million years. These deposits contain an assortment of gravel, sand, mud, volcanic ash, and limestone. Six million years of accumulation accounts for the West being blanketed deep in miles and miles of sedimentation. A sampler of the remains of the layers and layers of ash is revealed in areas like the Grand Staircase-Escalante National Monument in Colorado and Southern Utah. The name "staircase" was attached to these formations because of the alternating colors and textures of the various erosion materials that resemble stairs. The harder rock, such as sand and limestone, erodes slower while the shale and siltstone erode faster. Each layer has its distinct coloring, including buff, tan, and gray up through the brilliant shades of corals and reds.

Fossils abound in the West's sedimentation turned to stone. Wyoming's Fossil Butte National Monument, often called an ancient aquarium in stone, has a superb museum displaying fossilized fish, insects, plants, reptiles, birds, and mammals. Visitors can participate in fossil digging or explore the wide open spaces presently inhabited by antelope, elk, deer, and other wildlife.

I've heard Utah dubbed the dinosaur state, and within its layers of sedimentation lies a more complete record of prehistoric life than almost any other geographic location on the planet. New species are being discovered yearly.

Colorado's Florissant Fossil Beds National Monument is just one of several sites where ash from volcanic eruptions trapped and preserved an entire ecosystem. Dinosaur skeletons like the mother and child stegosauri on display at the Denver Museum of Nature and Science tell the story of Colorado being covered several times by shallow, subtropical, inland seas.

INLAND OCEANS AND SEAS

Inland oceans and seas of prehistoric time left soil accumulations of limestone, clay, silt, and shale, plus the dense vegetation that later became coal beds. The largest and most famous body of water that covered the West was the ancient Lake Bonneville that spread in the Great Basin bowl over the state of Utah. The lake's surface of twenty thousand square miles had a maximum depth of one thousand feet. The fresh water lake was derived from precipitation, rivers, streams, and melting glaciers. Three distinct lake elevations can be viewed today as mountain benches along the mountain ranges of the Wasatch Front. Today, these benches or terraces are rock and gravel pits, some eighty feet deep or deeper.

Subsurface leakage at the north end of Lake Bonneville's unstable gravel and limestone containment at Red Rock Pass caused a massive

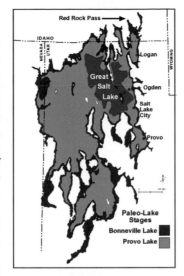

The huge freshwater Lake Bonneville drained, leaving beds of weathered alkaline clay, sand, and gravel that Utahns garden on today.

Today, Red Rock Pass (where Lake Bonneville broke through) sits on what is today huge buried peat fields. These organic remains now grow the virgin peat we grow our perennials in.

flood into the Snake River Valley. The southwestern Idaho landscape is strewn with granite and basalt boulders that were tossed and polished by the flood. The colossal amount of flooding was so powerful that it scoured the walls and beds of the Snake River drainage, cutting deep recesses, gouging holes, creating waterfalls, and leaving great deposits of sand and gravel as the lake moved relentlessly toward the Pacific Ocean.

As the Ice Age ended, the climate became warmer and what remained of the vast lake began to evaporate and retreat. The Great Salt Lake is all that is now left of this once-majestic body of water, but it explains why our soils are so salty and we are left with the Bonneville Salt Flats raceways and the Great Salt Lake Desert.

DESERTS

The Rocky Mountain West is home to a variety of regions where the wind deposits and rearranges the sand and salt. Many of the sand dunes are like the ones left along the Idaho Snake River by the flood of Lake Bonneville, and others are so dry that they are devoid of any soil-holding vegetation. Without ground cover in very dry climates, soil erodes rapidly. Some sand dunes are like those in Montana and Colorado that start out with a basin that holds the water of a shallow sea until the tropical period ends and a new dry period changes the terrain to an area much like the Sahara Desert. Wyoming's ecoregion is a veritable ocean of sagebrush and sand dunes sitting on top of sedimentary strata. The Great Sand Dunes National Park and Preserve of Colorado is what is left behind after the climate change reduced the shallow seas and left behind sheets of sand. The Sand Flats Recreation Area near Moab, Utah, is popular slickrock biking spots.

The Great Salt Lake Desert shows up white on satellite maps due to its high concentration of salt. This area may be called different names, but the sand and salt are part of the soil that western gardeners try to garden with, and this is one of the reasons that gardening in the West is such a challenge.

Salt content is a part of the soil left by the great flood and evaporation of Lake Bonneville. This is why today's gardeners need to learn how to deal with soil salinity.

GLACIERS

Glaciers are the finishers and polishers of the rough-hewn Rocky Mountains. They act as gigantic ice cream scoops that carve out centers in mountain valleys called cirques. As they move they flatten out mountain peaks and use their accumulation of till or debris frozen into the ice to cause abrasion, thus smoothing the land. During the ice ages, thick snow accumulated in the ridges or fissures left by the many volcanic actions. In protected areas, wind would blow extra snow into the ice bowls or cirques, and as long as the winter snowfall equaled more than the summer thawing, the ice sheets would grow. All of Canada was covered with an ice sheet similar to the ice in Antarctic regions now. When a mass of ice got large enough, it would start to move downhill. As this icy glacier moved, it plucked up boulders by freezing onto them and dragged them over the remaining rocks to grind and sand the surface.

This action of a glacier's debris, which were carried and deposited when thawing occurred, gives geologists the Earth's climate history and reveals the big picture of climate change. For example, according to the United States Geological Survey map, the twelve Teton Glaciers located below the north face in Grand Teton National Park in Wyoming are the largest remaining glaciers in the Rocky Mountains. Today the Teton Glaciers have lost twenty percent of their surface area.

Diminishing glaciers are a good argument in support of global warming. Gardeners would be happier if a new ice age started, bringing an increase in snowfall and rain along with cooler weather. Our gardens would flourish and so would agriculture crops. We might have to wear our jackets longer, but it would takes thousands of years before a glacier could grow large enough to intrude on communities or homes.

Remnants of the Earth's glacial activity are shown in the pristine beauty of our glacier lakes. Montana's glacier lake; Wyoming's Jenny's Lake, which nestles at the base of the Grand Teton Mountain range; and the Yellowstone Lake were all created by glaciers that gouged out the mountains. Today we live in a hotter period of time. Glaciers have retreated and many have dried up. It's all a process of billions of years of time.

Our mountains reflect these years of geologic history from the massive, gray metamorphic rock blocks that built the mountain peaks to the many colors of erosion in the Colorado Plateau. Our folded, faulted, complex landscape contains fossils that record life when areas were seas leaving sandy beach deposits. Western geology is fragile, and much of it is protected for future generations to enjoy. As gardeners, we are a part of this crusade. The past is a prelude to the future. An understanding of how our soils came to be leads to acceptance of what is. So we find out what type of plants do well in our environment and this is what we plant.

Of course, we add all the organic amendments we can get and end up with amazing gardens in an inhospitable but stunningly beautiful environment.

Happy poor-soils gardening!

Armeria
(ar-MAIR-ee-uh)
THRIFT

SHAPE	Low, grassy tufts of globe-shaped flowers
HEIGHT	Tiny, six to eight inches
WIDTH	Twelve inches
BLOOM TIME	May to June
COLORS	Rosy shades of pink and red
SITE	Well drained, tolerates salty soil
LIGHT	Full sun or light shade
HARDINESS	Zone 3
COMMENTS	An almost perfect plant for the West

Armeria, with its tiny tufts of grassy foliage, grows most anywhere, even in a cement walkway. More important, wherever it grows, it's just the right plant for the spot.

The rosette globes sit on top of six-inch stems and are very intricate when viewed up close.

Thrift usually blooms in every rosy shade of pink, but it sometimes surprises a gardener with lavender flowers.

Salty, alkaline soils grow nice, straight, strong armerias.

HEJ! THAT IS Iclandic for "Hello," and if you are looking for a "just right" perennial for a spot with difficult soil, look no further—I'm that plant, especially if a diminutive, good-looking plant to fill the front of a garden is needed. In spring, I'm covered in blooming colorful, globular flowers that bob on leafless slender stems for over a month and longer if I'm deadheaded. When I'm not flowering, my foliage is still a round-shaped, attractive, tidy grassy tuft. The bronzy color of my fall foliage often stays evergreen in milder winters, so I always look first rate.

I require a minimum of care and never need staking, trimming, or fussing over. I'm drought resistant and tolerate difficult salty-alkaline soils. I'm so easy to grow that a lot of fertilizers or added amendments to the soil aren't necessary. I behave well, slowly forming bigger clumps, but I will never spread out of control. I have no disease or pest problems—even deer avoid me. So if your garden needs a "just right" perennial for the rock garden or an edger, I'm that reliable perennial. If I haven't proven my point yet, take a closer look:

I'm a native perennial of coastal regions like Iceland, where I grow wild. My natural home was perched on a barren, windblown rocky cliff above the ocean where the salt spray from the waves was often the only moisture I received. With my second name, *maritima*, the adjective *maritime* means "of the sea." I'm very salt tolerant, so I will grow in the many salty soil areas in the West. I also grow well in the lean alkaline soil from weathered rock because of my origins. I'm totally drought tolerant, being used to the well-draining, poor soils of a hillside. Too much water has a tendency to rot my roots. Wind never bothers me either. This could be due to the small tightness of my size that hugs the rocks; or it could be due to my toughness. My flowers look dainty, but each small trumpet-shaped petal is hooked securely to the top of my stem. It should be plain to see that the environment of the West is my home away from home.

Plant me in problem areas, like along curbs or sidewalks, where the salt used for snow removal would harm many other perennials without my salt tolerance. My strong fibrous roots will secure soil in areas between rocks that can easily get washed out. With my drought tendencies and year-long excellent-looking foliage, I make an attractive perennial for pots or containers. My fine-stemmed grassy foliage grows from a center rosette that forms a round clump. I present a refreshing, simple look that adds a nice texture and contrast to the overblown foliage of some of the perennials or annuals that are often used in pots.

I'm a slow grower and never invasive, but if my clump spreads into a wider mat and looks untidy, it's time to propagate me. My fibrous root structure makes dividing me very successful. It's best to do early spring divisions when I'm still dormant, because my normal bloom time is late spring and I need to regroup before that high-energy time arrives. Fall division is too late in the higher elevation regions because I won't have time to set a root ball that will take me through the winter months. In the first days of spring, grab a shovel and dig my entire clump. Remove sections of the basal rosettes and plant. Keep the sections a good size because I'm slow to recover.

Starting me from seed is also an option, since I germinate readily. Soaking my seed helps if it is older. Seeds can be lightly covered or left exposed. Seedlings are quick to emerge, but my plants grow slowly. Even several months after sowing, I'll still only have a small tuft with shallow roots. Divisions of mature plants are a surer and safer way to propagate me.

My neat dense foliage makes me an excellent companion plant to place in front of taller perennials. Even after my flowers fade, I add an attractive season-long grassy accent. The silvery foliage of artemisias, aurinia, or aubrieta will be more attractive with my very different foliage next to them, or with me fronting for them, as will the blue colors of scabiosa and the golds of coreopsis.

When purchasing me from a nursery, be aware that the hybrid varieties like 'Ballerina', which are usually redder than pink and grow taller, may not be as hardy and are zoned higher. The 'Joystick' series of armeria are zoned a 4 and have taller, larger flowers. So purchase *Armeria maritime*—every gardener needs that "just right" perennial.

Asparagus

Digitalis, foxglove

SALINE OR SALTY SOILS

AN EXCESS OF salt in a gardener's soil prevents the plants from absorbing water properly—thus the first symptom of too-salty soil is wilting. The second symptom is leaf burn. The next is leaf drop, which leads to death. Here are a few pointers for gardeners with salty soils:

- Select plants rated as salt tolerant.
- Plant during a rainy or cool season.
- When planting, position the perennial's crown higher than the soil around it so the water will not pool.
- Instead of sprinklers in flower beds, use bubblers or drippers that will not cover the plant with salt.
- Drought-tolerant perennials in well-drained soils are very tolerant of salty soils.
- Have separate timers for sprinklers in flower beds. Turf requires more water. Also, Kentucky bluegrass is very drought tolerant and has a higher degree of salt tolerance than many other lawns.
- Some shade on hot afternoons helps plants conserve moisture.
- Mulch with organic material like compost, not rock, to increase water retention.
- Do not overfertilize. Fertilizers contain salt and will make a bad situation worse.

Here is a list of moderate salt-tolerant perennials that should survive a salty soil condition. The very short descriptive blurbs only mention the plants' best traits:

- *Achillea*, Yarrow—Medium height, blooms summer through fall
- *Alcea*, Hollyhocks—Tall height, blooms in summertime and will reseed
- *Antirrhinum*, Snapdragon (annual)—Plant as either seeds or bedding plants
- *Aquilegia*, Columbine—Short to medium height, spring blooming
- *Armeria*, Thrift—Spring blooming with all-season nice foliage
- *Artemisia*, Wormwood—Adds a short, all-season silvery color
- *Asparagus* (perennial vegetable)—Every garden needs asparagus
- *Calamagrostis*, Fountain Grass—An all-season tall focal point
- *Coreopsis grandiflora*—Short to medium height, blooms summer
- *Delosperma*, Ice Plant—Ground cover that turns red in winter
- *Dianthus*, Pinks—Short, June blooms in every shade of pink

- *Digitalis*, Foxglove—Tall elegant spike, summer blooming
- *Echinops*, Globe Thistle—Flowers resemble Canadian Thistle
- *Euphorbia*, Cushion Spurge—Spring blooming, short round mound
- *Gaillardia*, Blanket flower—Adds hot colors to the garden
- *Geranium*, Cranesbill—Spreads or mounds, blooms early summer
- *Hemerocallis*, Daylily—Long-living, long-blooming, classic flower
- *Heuchera*, Coral Bells—Late spring blooms, evergreen foliage
- *Iberis*, Candytuft—White spring bloomer with perfect foliage
- *Iris*, Flag—Tall, skinny late spring bloomer, likes water
- *Iris ensata*, Japanese Iris—Slender, attractive, all-season foliage
- *Iris sibirica*, Siberian Iris—Tall and slender with purple, blue, or white flowers
- *Lamium*, Archangel—Dry shade, a silvery leafy mound
- *Lantana* (annual in cold zones)—Purchase as bedding plants
- *Lathyrus*, Sweet Pea—Best used to cover chain link fencing
- Lavender—Long-blooming fragrant flowers
- *Monarda*, Bee Balm—Mid-summer color, tall height
- *Nepeta*, Catmint—Sky blue, long-blooming flowers
- *Oenothera*, Evening Primrose—Yellow cascading trumpets all summer
- *Penstemon*, Beardtongue—Tall spike, attracts hummingbirds
- *Petunia* (annual)—Purchase as bedding plants
- *Physostegia*, Obedience—Fall, partial-shade bloomer in pink or white
- *Portulaca*, Moss Rose (annual)—Purchase bedding plants or sow seed
- *Salvia*, Sage—Blooms late spring and fall in blue colors
- *Sedum*, Stonecrop—Reliable, attractive, all-season foliage
- *Stachys*, Lamb's Ears—Soft silver foliage, medium height
- *Tradescantia*, Spiderwort—Medium tall, bright blue shades of flowers
- *Vinca*, Periwinkle—Ground cover for under trees
- *Yucca* or Adam's Needle—Evergreen shrub focal point

Learning to work with what we have is a slogan most gardeners live by; however a few knowledge tools to help solve problems can save time, money, and stress. Hopefully some tidbit of this information on salty soil gardening will ease working with these difficult soils.

Monarda, bee balm

Stachys, lamb's ears

Yucca, Adam's needle

Calamagrostis
(Kal-ah-mah-GROS-tis)
'KARL FOERSTER'

SHAPE	Tall, compact column with wheat-like spiked heads
HEIGHT	Five feet, up to six feet in bloom
WIDTH	Two feet around when mature
BLOOM TIME	All four seasons
COLORS	Bright green, with beige seed heads in fall and winter
SITE	Tolerates alkaline clay well
LIGHT	Full sun with water or part shade
HARDINESS	Zones 3–8
COMMENTS	Focal point in gardens

How boring this bermed flower bed would be without the dramatic height and structure of C. 'Karl Foerster'.

Native fountain grass grows wild along the canyon highways in the Rocky Mountains.

Calamagrostis is so adaptable that it grows in hot sun on the top of an Idaho mountain and in the deep shade along north-facing buildings in lower valleys.

Calamagrostis snuggled up against this heat-sink boulder breaks dormancy earlier, turning a bright green while in other spots it may still be dormant.

I'M 'KARL FOERSTER' a very well-known, popular fountain grass for the western Rockies. I'm such a superb specimen that I was awarded the 2001 Perennial Plant of the Year Award. The reasons for this prestigious award are many: first is my erect, narrow stature with its tall vertical lines that add such a unique focal point and rhythm to a garden. My more modernistic-looking foliage adds movement, bringing a dynamic life to landscapes. More than any other type of perennial, I look different, and wherever I'm planted, a young freshness is added to the shorter spikes and rounded shapes of most other perennials.

Second is that I'm a low-maintenance perennial with few demands for a year-long four-season performance. C. 'Karl Foerster' is a sterile hybrid, so there is never a problem with me reseeding in other places. I'm also a clumping type of grass that stays put, not a spreader that will run rampant in the yard. My only need is the spring "chop job" of cutting my stems almost to the ground. Wrapping my stems with duct tape and cutting me with a hedge trimmer makes even this maintenance a simple task. My trimmings can be used as mulch for the gardens and nesting material for the many birds I've fed throughout the winter.

Because of my tall, slender height, I make a graceful backup to other perennials. Plant me with other moisture lovers like *Eupatorium* 'Gateway' (or Joe-pye weed), hibiscus, ligularia, monarda, and cannas. The clay soils of the Intermountain area provide moisture because the molecules are so small they hold on to water.

I can be planted in a dense row as an inexpensive, trouble-free hedge. Each season I will thicken, and over time I'll become a living screen. My stiff erect clumps will not topple with snow buildup and will ensure privacy even through wintertime. Blowing wind, which will wreak havoc for most tall perennials, only gives me a perpetual motion that is charmingly graceful. Also, I'm pollinated by the wind, so for me, wind is a good thing. For hedges, plant me at least three feet apart. Planting me as a focal point requires much more space, equal at least to my six-foot height. This wide spacing will only look naked for awhile, since I will quickly fill in the voids.

I fit nicely in narrow spaces in the landscape. My height, carefree nature, and wind resistance will turn a strip of unattractive parking lot dividers into an eye-catching work of art. The installation of a dripper at my roots for water will keep me happy and healthy. I'm so versatile that I'm often considered a drought-tolerant perennial because I grow well in these types of difficult spots. However, my leaves will signal my need for water by rolling inward, so a drip watering system is necessary.

My foliage of stiff spikes turns bright green in spring. By late summer, purplish-pink wheat-like sheaves form on the tips and then turn golden in late fall and beige through winter.

I'm considered a cool-season grass, which really doesn't mean that I'm a cold-climate perennial even with my Zone 3 hardiness. What *cool season* means is that I perform better in cooler temperatures and do most of my growing before the hot summer weather arrives. The higher elevations of the Rockies with their low temperatures are a year-round cool summer climate so this is another reason why I thrive here. The lean soils are also to my liking. Only fertilize me at the same time as turf—in early spring and fall. Fertilizer can promote floppy, soft growth, which will defeat my vertical accent or the real reason I was planted in the first place. Grasses as a whole have no serious insect or disease problems and are very deer resistant—another reason to add me to your garden.

I'm lucky to have two variegated siblings that have the same allure in the garden as I do. 'Avalanche' has deep green leaves with a white stripe down the center, and 'Overdam' has spikes that are highlighted by white margins and adds a silvery look to the same environment I grow in. 'Overdam' seems to think that because she is smaller that makes her more refined than her big brother.

So, if a gardener wants a different look in the garden or carefree perennials, the calamagrostis grasses are the answer.

The excruciating trek of the early pioneers who settled the Rocky Mountains is dramatically portrayed in this thought-provoking statuary.

This family of bears is welcoming visitors to a Bear Lake cabin.

This garden art sea monster, pattenered after the legendary Bear Lake monster, seems to hold no fear for the children.

GARDEN ART TELLS YOUR HISTORY

WESTERN ROCKY MOUNTAIN art is just as unique and provides the same excellent focal points in the garden as the calamagrostis grasses do. However, western art is like the West, completely different and tells a story about us. Including Afton, Wyoming's, largest arch in the world made of elk antlers, Colorado's Monte Vista Crane Festival, and Montana's Whitefish celebration with its parade of torches, we acknowledge these local lifestyles through statues, paintings, signs, or billboards, and if they are pictorial in nature they are considered garden art. Often, art in the garden retells or symbolizes a story or legend about the area.

How to display garden art is a gardener's choice. Sometimes statues are tucked into the greenery, but antique farm equipment often takes a large center stage in western gardens. The first decision of the gardener will usually be based on the available room and areas to display. Next, a gardener should decide on what kind of feel he or she wants to give a yard. If you are into antiques, use a shabby chic look with an ancient wooden chair with a hole cut into the seat for a flower pot. If you like a more modernistic feel, use a garden sculpture. Sometimes a whimsical garden with fairy-filled fanciful items gives gardeners the feel they want. Of course, for a more masculine feel, use the farm equipment or tools that create fun animals. The art in your garden tells who you are!

A few cautions:

- Try to keep garden art items along the same theme.
- Use items that are weatherproof. Plastic is more for children's toys than artwork.
- Keep the look simple. Too much stuff can detract from an artistic look and instead look messy. The old rule of "simplicity is elegance" holds solid with any art.
- Eliminate the use of toilets. Flowers stuck in a john is not necessarily attractive to your neighbors.
- Above all, remember that garden art is the result of a thoughtful partnership between art, nature, and the gardener.

Strong and proud stands this elk in a sea of blue salvia.

Clematis
(KLEM-at-is)
'JACKMANII'

SHAPE	Vine that twines, with trumpet cups of flowers
HEIGHT	Varieties twine six to thirty feet high
WIDTH	Three feet around
BLOOM TIME	Depends on variety; early-flowering clematis blooms on old wood, midseason-to-fall-flowering blooms on new wood
COLORS	Purples, blues, reds, pinks, and whites
SITE	Well-drained alkaline soil
LIGHT	Feet in shade, head in sun
HARDINESS	Zone 4
COMMENTS	Hardiest of all clematis plants

The vertical accent created by climbing vines makes clematis a much-needed, valuable garden perennial.

C. 'Jackmanii' has huge four-inch blooms in a deep reddish, velvety purple that are spectacular!

C. 'Niobe' is just as fabulous as 'Jackmanii' but has deep red, almost burgundy, flowers and only grows to eight feet in height.

C. 'Nelly Moser' has attractive stripes of pink and pale mauve on its petals and grows to ten feet.

I'M SO PLEASED to introduce myself. I'm *Clematis*, and I'm valuable in the garden as a hard–to-come-by verti-cal accent. I scamper and trail over walls and trellises, following wire frames or fences. I can enclose an arbor and thread myself through trees and climbing roses while cover-ing all of them with a colored extravagance of flowers.

I'm also valuable because there is no other plant as spectacu-lar as I am. I bloom in rich purple colors that look like velvet. At the center of my blooms is a smaller flower with creamy feath-ery spikes and fuzzy yellow centers. Even as my blooms fade in fall, these centers expand to form fascinating, spidery seed heads for another season of interest.

I'm valuable as a good-looking foliage backdrop for my flow-ers. My glossy heart-shaped leaves unfold from my vines and wind tightly around, forming a mass of foliage that holds my profusion of flowers. To keep this backdrop full and lush look-ing, I need a seasonal cutback. Pruning needs to be done in early spring, because I start to set buds in March. Otherwise, my old wood forms an unruly mess of tangled stems that will not leaf out properly or have blooms. I am a late-flowering clematis, which means I bloom on new wood shoots beginning in midsummer and through fall. The late blooming on new wood makes me very easy to prune. Wait until spring, and then cut back all shoots to the main stem to about two feet above the base of the plant.

As soon as I'm trimmed is the only time I'll need fertilizer. An all-purpose granulated fertilizer with equal percentages of nitrogen, phosphorus, and potassium or a 10-10-10 keeps my foliage lush and green. The nitrogen is for producing foliage. The phosphorus helps both my roots and flowers to grow and the last number, or potassium, aids in the coloring and size of my blooms.

I often hear complaints that I'm difficult to grow, but it's not true. The Rocky Mountains' alkaline soil and cool summertime temperatures fill my biggest basic needs. Another requirement is to set me low in the planting hole, at least eighteen inches deep. Work moisture-holding compost into the soil around my root ball and mulch the ground above me so my roots stay cool. This deep planting encourages thicker stem development as well as protecting me from clematis wilt. Wilt is rare in the Rockies, but should it occur, remove the infected branch at ground level, and dispose of it in the trash—not the compost heap.

My roots will stay cooler with a small perennial like ever-green *Iberis,* or candytuft, planted at my feet. If there is a deer problem where you're planting, substitute 'Petite Monarda' or some other deer-resistant perennial for the iberis. Deer think I'm tasty and will prune my bottom stems, leaving the higher ones they can't reach. Let the deer prune the bottom part of me but finish the upper part of the job in early spring.

Other clematis are not this fortunate, and the early-flowering ones bloom on old growth, requiring trimming a month after they bloom. The deer would really ruin these. The midseason clematis blooms on both old and new growth, so rather than figure that out, just plant me, 'Jackmanii', the best of the rest. I'm still the hardiest and easiest to grow out of over three thousand other available varieties!

Keeping the soil moist helps keep me attractive. Ants dislike wet soil and won't try to live under me. I'm a big plant with a huge mass of foliage so I require a lot of water when I'm blooming.

When installing a trellis or arch for me to grow on, make sure it has small enough rungs that I can curl and wrap my petioles (or leaf stems) around it. Anything over three-fourths of an inch in diameter is too large for me to grasp. I really don't find metal arches to my liking either; they get too hot in summer. A grape vine or mesh wire wrap twined around and into a metal arch will make it much more comfortable and easy for me to climb. I grow best when I have a strong support for my heavy, abundant flowers. Try to erect a structure that will support my weight and attach it firmly to a base or background wall. I think this is why I scramble so carefree when I find a tree or rosebush to twine into. It gives me the best of both worlds: my feet in the shade, my head in the sun, and plenty of space to roam.

Another fine, hardy clematis I recommend is the beautiful *C.* 'Niobe', which has deep, rich red flowers that can look almost black. A neon bluish stripe in the petals intensifies the color. Like me, *C.* 'Niobe' is an easy-care clematis but grows much shorter, only climbing to eight feet. 'Niobe' has the reputation of being hardier than me and is considered a Zone 3 perennial. Trim 'Niobe' the same as me by pruning the plant back to its lowest pair of healthy buds. *C.* 'Nelly Moser' is another popular hardy variety for those gardeners who like the way pink stands out in their yards. *C.* 'Nelly Moser' has pink and light mauve stripes on her more pointed petals and is stunning. She can cover a ten-foot tall structure.

It's obvious for all these reasons I'm valuable in the garden, but my most important service is providing a vertical statement that adds more dimension and class to wherever I call home.

VERTICAL ELEMENTS IN THE GARDEN: THE ONLY PLACE LEFT TO PLANT IS UP

Clematis in bloom is spectacular! No other perennial can equal the breathtaking splender of a trellis wound with the gigantic blooms of deep purple *C.* 'Jackmanii'.

An arch looks attractive even on the coldest winter day because it adds a vertical element to the garden.

VERTICAL ACCENTS ARE everywhere in a community, and we often get so used to seeing them that we almost don't notice how they upgrade an area. Clock towers, decorative lights, statues honoring our troops who fought in wars, or arches that enclose a cemetery entrance are all around us.

After paying attention and noticing the impact provided by vertical architectural elements in your own community, look at your own garden and visualize how a vertical accent or two would "uplift" your whole backyard. If your garden has an unattractive view or area that needs to be disguised, a vertical element can block this.

Upright structures furnish winter interest in the garden (as do column-shaped evergreens). Narrow spaces that cause gardeners to scratch their heads, wondering what to do with such a hard to landscape spot, can become remarkable with the addition of an upright arch or trellis. If your garden has a narrow space, the only way to go is up. These vertical-type structures can also change a boring flower bed into a valuable element in the garden. The varieties of methods for adding tall elements are many and not limited to a trellis.

ARBORS OR ARCHES

A well-placed arbor or arch in a garden can serve as an entryway, frame a focal point or take your spectacular *C.* 'Jackmanii' to new heights. An arbor gives dimension or closure to a much-too-open space. It may even form a tunnel covered with clematis or roses over a pathway leading to a peaceful retreat. Arbors or arches can be ornate or simple. They can be built with recyclable materials, such as a set of used French doors serving as vertical supports for the curved upper portion, or can be purchased ready to install.

BIRDHOUSES

Place your birdhouse close to shrubbery to give the birds a hiding place. Available water also attracts birds. Install birdhouses eight to twelve feet above the ground in a wind-protected spot. If bird feeders are incorporated with the birdhouse, they need to be set lower so they can be reached for maintenance. A tube-type container for birdseed that can be opened at the top for filling and at the bottom for cleaning is more convenient. Clean the birdhouses in February with a one-part bleach to ten-parts water solution. A birdhouse provides winter vertical interest and all-season enjoyment of watching birds.

CONTAINER PLANTERS

Container planters can be used to line pathways, hang from vertical shepherd's hooks, fill shelves in walls or garden screens, or simply be elevated to add a tall focal point in the garden. Placing large containers in garden beds breaks up the usual garden horizontal rut. A divider screen with walls of shelves for potted plants adds an attractive architectural privacy screen for a patio or deck. Placing container plants on top of posts or half walls that allows vines to cascade down is not only stunning but softens a structure.

PERGOLAS AND GAZEBOS

Pergolas and gazebos provide outdoor living at its very best. A gardener can sit in the middle of the garden, protected and sheltered from sun and wind, and still smell the flowers. Pergolas are freestanding wood or plastic wood structures that can shade walkways, pools, or provide a hideaway sitting area in the garden. Pergolas and gazebos not only furnish a place to relax but also a place to plant spectacular vines.

WALL GARDENS

A wall garden will dress up an unsightly blank wall, or create extra gardening "real estate" when space is limited. Urban living often doesn't provide gardening space, so wall gardening can give a terrace or balcony a spot to grow plants.

TRELLISES

Clematis, with its twining ability, adds a dramatic effect when growing on a trellis. Most trellises are constructed with a lattice type of structure that can be simple or elegant in design.

ESPALIER

Espalier is the term used to describe the process of training plants against a flat surface like a wall. The process requires constant trimming of wayward stems to keep then in the required design. Usually espalier walls are grown on wires attached to a wall.

PLANTS GROWN ON WALLS

Sheets of fabric or plastic with sturdy pockets to hold soil or potted plants are attached to walls. Annuals, vegetables, and succulents can be planted in the pockets. A sprinkling type of watering system needs to be addressed as well as a drain system. Wall gardens have become very popular in warmer regions.

Vertical elements are everywhere. As gardeners become more aware of these, they will start adding trellises, arbors, birdhouses, planting screens, and gazebos to lift up their own gardens.

Birds make themselves at home in these rustic birdhouses due to the height of the houses and the protection of the pine tree.

Vertical elements in the garden can be as simple as this rustic trellis or as complicated as an enormous arch that reaches across a main street, welcoming guests to a community.

Coreopsis
(core-ee-OP-sis)
TICKSEED

SHAPE	Average, compact mound
HEIGHT	About fifteen inches
WIDTH	About fifteen inches
BLOOM TIME	June to August
COLORS	Vivid gold and yellow
SITE	Average pH, well draining
LIGHT	Full sun
HARDINESS	Questionable Zone 4, 'Early Sunrise' hardy to -20 degrees, 'Zangreb' to -30 degrees
COMMENTS	Exceptionally long blooming

C. grandiflora 'Early Sunrise', or big-leaf coreopsis grows best in my personal garden. The long-season and high-performance blooming power of its cheerful golden flowers give this fine perennial priority in the summer garden.

The long stems of *C.* 'Early Sunrise' make excellent cut flowers.

When *C.* 'Moonbeam' was first introduced to gardeners, it was in so much demand that it was difficult to find.

C. verticillata or threadleaf coreopsis produces starlike, one-inch blooms on short spreading mounds.

I'M *COREOPSIS, AND* I'd like to show you why I'm a good choice for a gardener who struggles with difficult soils. I'm so low-key that I only grow to an average fifteen-inch height and width. Even my preferred soil is average, ranging in the middle of the pH scale of 5.0 acidic to 7.0 alkaline. I grow well in almost any soil from poor soil to average, sandy, and even dense clay as long as it drains, plus I tolerate salt. I even favor soils of low-to-medium fertility, so all I need is an early spring fertilizing to keep my underground roots healthy. Rich, fertile, moist soils are not for me—I'll grow long, leggy and sprawl. My water needs are low to average and I tolerate short droughts, heat, and humidity. My flowers are members of the native, very hardy aster species and have the most common type of daisy-shaped blooms. Even my common name, tickseed, has an ordinary feel about it. I'm named after my small dark seeds that resemble ticks. Because I'm a native North American perennial, I grow most anywhere, even in the Rocky Mountains. Like most natives, butterflies love me and deer ignore me. You can tell I'm just an average sort of plant that's easy to grow, so it's time to get acquainted with two of my special cultivars, *C. grandiflora* 'Early Sunrise' and *C. verticillata* 'Zangreb'.

C. GRANDIFLORA

My *C. grandiflora* flowers are large, two-inch, semi-double blooms that make beautiful cut flowers. I also grow as a native, reseeding wildflower in the high Rocky Mountains. In cultivated gardens, I'm not as reliably winter hardy because I don't have sense enough to know when to stop blooming, and I almost bloom myself to death. The self-sowing establishes me in the garden for future years, but the June through September blooming puts so much energy into flower production that it weakens me. It would help if gardeners cut me back the first of September to prevent any more blooming so my crown could toughen and I could rest before winter. Mulch for protection would also help ward off the susceptible frosts of the high elevation climate. Division of my clumps every two or three years also increases my chances of winter survival because it revives me.

Seed is the easiest propagation method for me. Other cultivars, like *C.* 'Sunray' or *C.* 'Sunburst', will not bloom their first year. With me, March sowings transplanted into the garden in May will flower the rest of the summer. I only need one hundred days between germination and a full flowering season. This reason, and because I'm longer lived than other *grandifloras*, is probably why I received the very prestigious award of the 1989 All-American Gold Medal.

I make an excellent companion to any blue perennial that blooms in early summer, such as salvia. The tall *Veronica* 'Sunny Border Blue' and I team up for a later summer combo. Perennials with a natural wildflower appearance and seeding ability like coneflowers, daisies, and gaillardia will bring unity and nonstop color to the garden.

My long bloom time, compact shape, and drought tolerance are reasons I'm an excellent choice for containers. I can't guarantee I'll winter well in a pot, but I'll do better than any annual for sure.

C. VERTICILLATA 'ZANGREB'

My *C.* 'Zangreb' flowers are a foolproof perennial with masses of starry-shaped true yellow daisies. They're not the pale-yellow of my sister *C.* 'Moonbeam', but I have a denser mass of flowers that envelops my entire bush while 'Moonbeam' only blooms on the ends of her foliage. I bloom earlier and longer, even into late fall, and I keep blooming without deadheading. Once 'Moonbeam' stops flowering, usually in August, and sets her sterile seeds that won't multiply, her plant is through blooming, but I'm not. Best of all, my *C.* 'Zangreb' is hardy and will survive Zone 3 while 'Moonbeam' struggles in Zone 5. In the higher elevations of western gardens, 'Moonbeam' should be considered an annual.

Our sizes are similar, but my 'Zangreb' grows somewhat cleaner, tighter, and more upright. I'm also more vigorous. I will reseed gently and my thick rhizome roots can easily be divided on a regular three- or four-year basis. I have better drought tolerance than 'Moonbeam' and my foliage will yellow if I get too much water. This makes me a good choice for poor-soil rock gardens and hard-to-water planters. My excellent consistency and the contrast of my fine, feathery, fern-like foliage is especially attractive in containers. I'm more adaptable to locations than 'Moonbeam' and will bloom sporadically in partial shade. I also grow well in dense clay soils as long as I don't get overwatered. Oh, and before I forget, I also won an award! The Royal Horticultural Society's Award of Garden Merit was given to me for my outstanding excellence!

COMPOST, COMPOST, COMPOST

Recycling programs are an efficient and economical way to turn yard waste into dark, rich, velvety compost.

The finished compost results in a rich black soil that looks attractive on flower beds, but more important, the compost is conditioning the soil so gardeners can turn poor soils into excellent soils.

T HE THREE MOST important words in real estate are, "location, location, location," but in gardening they are, "compost, compost, compost."

Compost or mulch is organic material that can change the poor western soils that will not grow much of anything into excellent soil. Compost helps release minerals that are tightly locked into the fine particles that make up clay soil. Compost added to sandy soil will provide moisture-holding elements so water and nutrients won't drain quickly through the sand. Compost, with its organic origins, will cool the soil to help perennials get through drought and summer heat. Compost will create soil in rocky ground just through the simple procedure of adding organic materials to the scree soil. These are the reasons compost is the answer to successful gardening in poor-soil locations like the Rocky Mountains.

Nothing is quite as attractive as rich black soil on flower beds, but even more important are the many studies that say using compost or mulch will cut fertilizer usage by half. Other studies have found that synthetic nitrogen fertilizers speed up the decay process of organic matter so that it is released into the air as carbon dioxide rather than stored in the soil as carbon, so it is wasted.

An obsessed gardener I know jumps on every bandwagon that sounds good for the environment or "green." In the early days of composting, a magical compost tumbler that could "spin straw into gold" came onto the market. The gardener was the first to purchase it and change all of her yard waste to "black gold."

As soon as the compost tumbler was constructed, she exuberantly filled the four-foot-wide by five-foot-tall tumbler full of the stinking bags of green waste she had been saving. She was happy that she could finally start "spinning," since a spoonful of compost contains a few dormant weed seeds, hundreds of microscopic worms, literally thousands of fungal spores, millions of miniature insects, and five billion or so bacteria. She wanted all of these biodiverse organisms working frantically to make her soil more hospitable to her plants. The advertisement promised she would have this compost in about eighteen days.

When her husband arrived home that evening, all he could do was hold his nose at the smell and ask, "Why is this thing sitting in the middle of our nice patio?" (He had planned to grill some nice steaks.) Additional equipment began to multiply: a probe to test moisture content, a new chipper/shredder to break down larger limbs and twigs, and a heat thermometer to make sure the compost was warm enough to kill weed seeds. Even the greenish juice that leaked from the drum was saved as a "super garden nutrition elixir."

After three long months, the gardener opened the drum in great anticipation to find . . . about two inches of usable compost. Her patient husband observed that she would have to make her own compost for two hundred years to pay for her investment.

WHAT NOT TO COMPOST

- Animal products like fats, oils, or meats

- Pet and human waste

- Diseased plants

- Yard trimmings treated with herbicides: When communities recycle, if weed killer–treated grass clippings get composted, they could wind up back in your own garden and destroy plants. Bag "weed and feed" sprayed grass clippings and place them in the regular garbage can, not the green waste container.

- Yard trimmings treated with pesticides can reduce the number of microorganisms that do the decomposing in the soil.

- Black walnut leaves and nuts: Black walnut leaves release a chemical called juglone that can be damaging to many plants. Other types of nut shells make excellent compost by adding the bulk necessary for oxygen.

- Pine needles (use a minimum): They add much-needed acidity to the compost but are heavy and decompose slowly, so go easy on pine needles.

Healthy soil grows healthy plants and compost gives both. It helps soil stay moist and drain well. Along with that miracle, compost adds air to the soil to keep the plant's roots healthy and feeds the plants. Compost as a soil conditioner improves every type of soil and grows more healthy and beautiful perennials.

THE DIRT ON WORMS

The most accurate, "down to earth" soil test on the quality of garden soil is earthworm activity. The hardworking earthworms tunnel underground as natural "tillers" to aerate the soil. As they penetrate the ground by eating organic matter, the digested matter turns to a nutrient-rich soil excrement called castings. Not only do they create an aerated drainage system allowing water and air into the ground but their castings are fertilizer food for plant roots.

The efficiency of the worm production cycle is so competent that many gardeners are setting up worm farms in a corner of their gardens where citrus peelings, food leftovers, and biodegradable paper scraps can be turned into the marvelous worm casting compost. The worms are so industrious that there are many commercial worm farms available that sell worms or compost bins. The worm business is so fruitful that information on how to farm worms is also offered online.

My personal worm farm is created by spreading mulch or compost on the surface of the ground in the fall. I'll run trimmings through the shredder and chop and gather the leaves with the lawnmower. These are spread over the surface of the flower gardens, and by spring, the mulch will have all but disappeared and the flower beds rarely need raking. Over the winter months, greedy worms have been busy consuming and turning the mulch into their nutrient-rich castings. When digging or planting in springtime, I bury any biodegradable material I can find in the planting holes. The worms are so competent that they find the materials almost immediately and start working their magical science. When a gardener feeds the worms with compost, the worms return the service by feeding the garden.

Anxious to be a "green" gardener, I purchased a magic garden tumbler that was supposed to "turn straw to gold." I recommend supporting community recycling programs as a more effective option.

The activity of the earthworms in your garden is the most reliable test of the quality of your garden soil.

Eupatorium
(you-puh-TOR-ee-um)
E. PURPUREUM, JOE-PYE WEED, AND E. RUGOSUM 'CHOCOLATE'

SHAPE	Tall, erect clump with huge flower clusters
HEIGHT	Joe-pye weed, five feet; 'Chocolate', three feet
WIDTH	Two feet around
BLOOM TIME	Late-season perennial
COLORS	Joe-pye weed, dusty rose/mauve; 'Chocolate', creamy white
SITE	Moist alkaline clay soil
LIGHT	Joe-pye weed, full sun; 'Chocolate', shade
HARDINESS	Joe-pye weed, questionable Zone 3; 'Chocolate' Zone 5
COMMENTS	Eupatorium is often called invasive in the midsection of the United States, but in the Rockies, gardeners celebrate when it survives winter.

E. 'Chocolate' is medium sized with elegant dark bronze foliage that contrasts nicely with other shade-loving perennials. *E.* 'Chocolate' blooms with lacy white clusters in late fall.

Eupatorium, or Joe-pye weed, is a huge perennial with long, narrow, serrated dark-green foliage and enormous, globe-shaped mauve flower clusters.

The huge size of Joe-pye weed's leaves is healthy and vigorously attractive. Growing alongside a creek or pond in full sun is a natural place to plant this stunning perennial.

The fine foliage of *E.* 'Chocolate' is superb.

I'M EUPATORIUM PURPUREUM, also known as Joe-pye weed, and I'd also like to introduce you to my cousin, *Eupatorium rugosum*, better known as *E*. 'Chocolate'. We are both so different but in many ways are so alike. Our differences are mainly due to appearance and constitution. I'm much bigger, stronger, and hardier. I also stand taller than 'Chocolate'. Our foliage grows in attractive whorls on sturdy stems. However, my long, narrow leaves can extend out eight or ten inches and have coarse serrated edges, and the leaves of *E*. 'Chocolate' are round and bronze. Both of us grow straight strong clumps that will never need staking. With my height, I give a magnificent presence to the back of a flower border and will compensate for other perennials that have completed their blooming earlier in the season. Plant me with other late-season flowering perennials like golden rudbeckia and solidago for a contrasting, eye-catching focal point. Rugosum's foliage is fine-looking and is often considered more handsome than its flowers, so it makes an excellent accent in shade plantings of lime and yellow hostas or alchemilla (lady's mantle).

Our flowers are also very different. Again, mine are big and coarse, while the flowers of *E*. 'Chocolate' are more delicate and lacy. I bloom in clusters of rosy-mauve florets. The florets are composed of tiny trumpets that birds, bees, and butterflies, especially the Tiger Swallowtails, find ideal for sipping my vanilla-scented nectar. My size, and especially my large foliage, provide a multipurpose habitat for pollinators where they can hide or lay their eggs. We are far superior as shrubs in the gardens rather than butterfly bushes that require constant trimming and invariably succumb to the early frost-freeze cycles in western spring seasons. The flowers of *E*. 'Chocolate' are fluffy creamy-white florets and grow more in a plume cluster that stands out nicely in a shady garden. We both bloom toward the end of summer, but our heaviest blooming occurs in September and October. We will literally be covered with flowers, furnishing a very important element to the fall landscape.

Eupatoriums are native wildflowers, and in the eastern areas of the United States where water is plentiful, we are frequently called a roadside weed and considered invasive. I can't recall ever reseeding when planted in the aridness of the West, but removing my abundant seed heads after my flowers freeze will help control any unwanted spring germinators. I do not break dormancy in springtime until almost the end of May. This can cause two problems: first, a gardener may forget over winter where I was planted and perhaps dig me up while grooming the flower beds; and second, any divisions will have to wait to be divided until I show life.

I'm easy to divide with my fibrous shallow root system, so dig, divide, and replant for more starts. Cuttings can be taken when I reach six inches. Stick these in starter pots and keep them damp. These vegetative starts will be identical to the parent plant whereas *E*. 'Chocolate' seedlings will never have the richness of their parent's chocolate foliage. My cuttings need the winter protection of an unheated greenhouse or a protected, heavily mulched area for me to be ready to plant in the garden the next spring. A quick cut of the first leaves that poke through will really thicken the number of stems.

We are both considered herbs, and I was named after a famous North American Indian herbalist named Joe-Pye. The herbalist crushed my wet hay–smelling dried roots and boiled them in an infusion that he used to cure typhus. Drinking the tonic induced profuse sweating, and the typhus fever would break. The Latin name, *Eupatorium*, was derived from an early herbalist, a Roman king named Mithridates Eupator. In the king's zeal to aid his subjects, Eupator grew many herbs. I was the most successful healing herb in his garden and was named in his honor. I'm also called gravel root because, when used as a tonic cleanser of the urinary tract or kidneys, I act as a diuretic that will increase the flow of urine.

E. 'Chocolate' has a common nickname of snakeroot that came about when grazing cattle mistakenly ate excessive amounts of euportium they mistook for nettle, a look-alike favorite pasture food. Native *E*. 'Chocolate' was allowed to reseed in the damp woodland gardens and pastures of the East. The cattle would graze the snakeroot and never show any problems. It was the nursing calves and lambs who would get the "tremors" and die. The cows' contaminated milk caused the tremors, so the illness was named the "milk sickness." Abraham Lincoln's mother is a well-documented case of a person who died from this sickness. Now gardeners know not to grow eupatorium as pasture for cattle. I can be poisonous when ingested, unless I'm used with the expertise of experienced herbalists!

Perennials like us prove the point that there are perennials for every garden situation; shade, sun, drought, wildlife, cold, and of course poor soils. So plant me in my comfort zone with plenty of moisture and alkaline-dense clay soil, and I'll become a gorgeous focal point in your garden.

THE ROCKY MOUNTAIN HYDROLOGIC CYCLE

MANY OF OUR high mountain streams gradually work their way downhill until they eventually reach the valley and reservoirs below, where we live and garden.

Showing appreciation for yet another gift from our mountains can be demonstrated in how we care for our water. Our goal should be to conserve by evaluating how we use our water. We also need to address management of our water quality, protecting public health and wildlife, and giving consideration to economic impact. This is how we can show gratitude!

EVALUATE WATER USAGE

To wise up about the water used in your own space, evaluate how you are watering. The biggest user of water in most homes is the landscaping, and westerners love greenness in their yards. Using less water in our yards will not only conserve water but also save "green" for our wallets.

EVALUATE PERSONAL NEEDS

- Use a commercial car wash for washing your car. Waste water from these businesses does not enter storm drains and is sent to a water treatment facility for recycling.

- Pull your car onto the grass when washing it at home. This will help water the lawn, and soapy water isn't usually damaging to a lawn.

- Use plastic milk jugs for watering the vegetable garden. Cut off the bottom. Leave the lid on, but punch some small holes for slow drainage in that section, and plant the jug neck down next to the vegetable. Fill the container with water in the morning and let gravity do a slow soak.

- Pour boiling water, left after boiling eggs or potatoes, on weeds. Even the toughest weeds, like those that grow in driveways or sidewalk cracks, will die instantly.

BE CAUTIOUS ABOUT POLLUTANTS

- **Overfertilizing** both in home gardening and agriculture causes nitrate runoff into groundwater. If contamination reaches drinking water, fertilizers can cause serious health risks, especially to infants and livestock. Our desert climate has limited water supplies that are compounded by urban development. Most wetlands are in public ownership, but the water supply is not. It is crucial that we keep this runoff groundwater pollutant-free not only for man but also for our wildlife. We all live downhill!

- **Pesticide** spills can lead to contamination of groundwater. Managing pesticides to reduce the risk of water contamination is a responsibility every water consumer needs to assume. Licenses are required, by law, to buy and apply dangerous pesticides and herbicides.

- **Household chemicals** can be hazardous wastes if they are toxic, corrosive, or flammable. Even a small amount of these materials carried into our ground- or surface water can be difficult to clean up. Solvents, oil-based paint supplies, cleaners, and of course, asbestos

are just a few of over five hundred specific government-identified products that must not reach our water supply. Never pour these chemicals into storm drains or the next rain will move them directly into our local water systems.

- **Oil and fuel spills** pose a serious threat to human health and environmental quality. One gallon of gasoline can contaminate a million gallons of water, and cleanup is expensive.

- **Pet waste** can carry disease organisms and contribute to nutrient pollution, so never wash it downstream. Our water goes places we may never have been. Burying the waste about five inches deep or putting it in the trash are the best disposal methods.

- **Construction debris** needs to be picked up, cleaned properly, and disposed of so as not to flow into storm drains. When starting a project, locate the nearest storm drains and protect them from building materials like concrete or mortar.

The important role our wetlands serve in natural water purification is often misunderstood. Not only are wetlands home to wildlife, but they also improve watershed quality by their capacity to process pollutants. Microorganisms in barrier riparian areas that border and protect bodies of water either utilize or break down numerous chemical and biological contaminants in water.

THE ROCKY MOUNTAINS PROVIDE AN EFFICIENT HYDROLOGICAL CYCLE

Most of our water is derived from winter snow. Snow is more pure since it falls from the sky and isn't as contaminated as frozen ice. Small lakes are collection systems for saving snowmelt and runoff.

In spring, catch ponds form in high mountain valleys. These ponds hold water for a slow, deep ground percolation that fills subsurface reservoirs.

- Runoff water gradually makes its way downhill into rivers and streams, filtering impurities as it meanders.

- Rivers remove microscopic colloidal particles from water as it transports it and filters it through sand, soil, and rock. Rapids move quickly and add air to oxygenate the water.

- Waterfalls clean water through spray evaporation and the addition of oxygen, which purifies water.

- Western reservoirs fill with snowmelt if the winter had the necessary snowfall. By fall the reservoirs are almost empty.

- Glacial lakes and trees play an important role in protecting and purifying our water sources. They slow the rain, prevent soil erosion, reduce storm water runoff, and lessen flood damage.

- Snow dusts peaks and we wait for mountain ponds, rivers, lakes, waterfalls, and springs to be refilled with much appreciated snow.

Gypsophila
(jip-SOF-i-la)
G. PANICULATA AND G. REPENS
BABY'S BREATH

SHAPE	Paniculata, tall shrub with flower clusters; Repens, creeping ground cover with flower clusters
HEIGHT	Paniculata, three feet; Repens, six inches
WIDTH	Paniculata, three to four feet; Repens, eight to fifteen inches
BLOOM TIME	Summer
COLORS	White or light pink
SITE	Well-drained, sandy alkaline soil
LIGHT	Full sun
HARDINESS	Zone 3
COMMENTS	The common name, baby's breath, describes the delicate flowers.

G. paniculata is an airy, blooming perennial with shrub-like proportions. Clouds of delicate, tiny white or pink flowers smother the shrub in summertime.

G. repens is a low-growing, alpine ground cover that spreads to form leafy mats covered with sprays of small, graceful, starry flowers that spill and cascade.

G. paniculata bears a profusion of tiny white or pink flowers.

Baby's breath, *G. paniculata*, planted solo is not the most attractive perennial in the garden, but planting it as a filler, backing other perennials, is splendid.

I'M KNOWN AS baby's breath, and the name is an apt description of my lacy, delicate pink or white flowers. You may question how a perennial as exquisite as I am can survive poor soils, but I do! The Latin name *Gypsophila* literally means "a lime or chalk soil lover." Western gardens have plenty of lime, but it will need to be added in areas with acidic soils or I will not grow. "Sandy Soil Gardening" tackles gardening on sandy soils that drain way too fast to hold water or nutrients (see page 214); so, another reason I'm here is because of my huge taproot that holds on to both those water and nutrients. My foliage helps me retain water also. My masses of small grayish-green leaves have the waxy shine that signals I'm a drought-tolerant perennial. This seems to be why an exquisite flower such as myself ended up in a unit on impossible soils.

G. paniculata is the shrub-sized baby's breath, and I'm used as fillers both in the garden and in dried arrangements. My foliage before blooming has an ungainly look rather like an overgrown weed, but in bloom I'm transformed by a multitude of one-sixteenth-inch flowers appearing in open sprays, covering me completely. If I'm a hybrid baby's breath, I can bloom with double petals, but other than that, I have single flowers. Planted with spiky-shaped perennials, such as iris, liatris, lilium, or veronica, I'm gloriously invaluable. I also work miraculous "makeovers" on perennials with large blooms or big foliage such as echinaceas, delphiniums, and leucanthemums.

I provide the same incredible service when mixed with cut flower arrangements. A prime example is Valentine's or Mother's Day roses that look almost boring until my splendid sprays of lace are added; then the arrangement becomes a work of art. The roses will fade and crumble, but my lacy sprays will keep looking fresh for a long time. One note: florist baby's breath is usually in the annual form and cannot be dried. I'm not only one of the best perennials for drying, but I'm also probably the easiest. I can be air-dried right in a vase and do not require special drying materials or being hung from the ceiling in a dark, warm place. Taking my fifteen-inch stem cuttings at dawn and leaving me standing in a vase with about an inch of water is all that is necessary for dried baby's breath. Let the water evaporate as my flowers dry. When the water is gone, test my stem. If it snaps and breaks, I'm dried. If not, repeat the procedure. It's interesting that my appearance will hardly change whether I'm fresh or dried, and I'll be the favorite filler for crafts, floral arrangements, wreaths, hat decorations, and other endless projects. This is a prime reason that I should be planted in every perennial garden.

On the other hand, short *G. repens* really doesn't act as a filler for other flowers but is a wonderful mat-forming ground cover that starts blooming in June and flowers all summer. It's now her turn to tell about herself:

I may be smaller than *G. paniculata*, but I still add the same exquisite white froth of lace to wherever I'm planted, making me every bit as valuable. I perform excellently as a well-behaved, border edger in a sunny garden or as a cascading flower that hangs over a rock wall. Any place, such as a rock garden, that a smaller pink or white, alpine perennial is needed is where I'll do an outstanding job. With my drought-tolerant huge taproot and almost evergreen foliage, I complete a look in container pots better than most white annuals. Every gardener knows that planters with a lacy touch of white are more stunning. All I require is a little deadheading, and then I'll never stop blooming.

We are impossible to move or divide unless we are seedlings. Our taproot resents transplanting, and cuttings are primarily done by hybridizers, so the best way to propagate us is by seed sowing. Our seeds will emerge in about a week at seventy-degree temperatures, and we do not require covering. Seed varieties are somewhat inferior to vegetative varieties and usually do not bloom until the second year. I self-seed sporadically in the garden but can be easily moved in early spring to a different location.

Our history is as uncomplicated as we are, but it's our ability as tall fillers and short spillers that really make us famous.

This colorless pile of sandy soil has been weathered by the eons of waves licking a shoreline of rocks. Amend sandy soil by mixing in grass clippings, mulch, and manure.

Achillea millefolium will add color and ferny foliage to a summer garden.

Alcea rosea, better known as hollyhocks, grows tall and reseeds in sandy soil.

SANDY SOIL GARDENING

SAND DUNES ARE located in every western state. Colorado's Great Sand Dunes National Park and Preserve has the tallest dune in North America.

Dig up a shovel full of dirt from your garden and squeeze some in your hand. Does it sift like sand through your fingers? If it does, you are trying to garden on sandy soil where water and nutrients slip through the soil just as sand did in your hand. Sand has the coarsest active particles and feels gritty when rubbed. Sandy soils usually have rapid water intake and aeration but low holding and nutrient storage capacity. How can a gardener plant something in soil that is so porous that water and nutrients run right through it? How can a gardener plant a garden in soil that is too weak and flimsy to even provide structure to the plants?

Organisms eventually produce humus or decomposition of vegetable or animal matter. As the organic matter decomposes, it starts to build substance to the sand. Organic substance material holds both water and nutrients in soil. Once a stand of plants are growing and organic mulch or compost is added regularly, the bed will gradually change to sandy loam. Sandy loam is every gardener's dream soil, so sand is not hopeless. Peat moss is a water-retaining soil additive and will help sandy soil retain water.

Here are a few options for planting in sandy soil:

PERENNIALS THAT TOLERATE SANDY SOILS

- *Achillea*, yarrow, (see page 6) grows in several sizes (tall, medium, or short) and blooms in several colors most of the summer. While your yarrow is growing and blooming, keep adding organic materials to the soil. By the time you are ready to get rid of the yarrow, your soil will be ready for any perennial you choose to plant.

- *Aquilegia* (see page 18) grows in sand, especially seedlings from the mother plant that seems stronger and more vigorous. A partial-shade environment helps columbine bloom better and longer.

- *Catananche*, Cupid's dart, is an everlasting flower that blooms in summer in blue, lavender, or white. The daisy-like flowers stand about twenty inches tall in clumps of grassy gray-green foliage.

- *Coreopsis* (see page 204)

- *Euphorbia* (see page 144)

- *Gaillardia* (see page 78)

- Hollyhocks (see page 14)

- *Miscanthus* grass is very drought tolerant and grows well in sandy, well-drained soil. The grass forms an impressive, handsome giant that might eventually have to be removed with a backhoe. The seed heads bloom late in the season, and it seeds way too easily.
- *Nepeta* (see pages 94 and 168) is a dependable, long-blooming, carefree perennial for a sandy soil garden.
- *Oenothera* (see page 98) is very hardy when growing in soil like sand that drains well. The large flowers, resembling poppy parachutes, are yellow, pink, or white. They bloom most of the summer.
- *Potentilla*, often called "five fingers" because of its hand-shaped foliage, will perform admirably anywhere in the sandy soil of the West. Potentilla grows as a shrub, a mound, a sprawler, or a low, dense ground cover. The perennial blooms in yellow, apricot, coral, and white.
- *Rudbeckia* (see page 240) is a dark-center-eyed beauty that is outstanding!
- *Salvia* (see page 176) spikes will bloom most of the season with deadheading. The gray-green, almost rough foliage has the smell of sage and grows in a compact mound.
- *Tanacetum* (see page 244) sometimes has silvery foliage and other times has dark-green foliage, but it is always fern-like and lacy. Tanacetum is valuable because of its adaptability to various soils and conditions.
- *Thymus*, thyme, forms a cushion or mat of wooly-gray, sweetly fragrant, walk-on-me foliage. Thyme grows best in the difficult garden areas of rock gardens, wall plantings, ground cover, or between stepping stones. The mats will color in late spring with lavender, rose, carmine-pink, or purple flowers.

The above selection gives a few choices as to season of bloom, height, and shape of perennials to plant in sandy soil. It's wise to keep building the organic into this kind of soil. The more compost and peat moss added, the better the flowers will grow and perform, and the less water they will need.

Coreopsis grandiflora's sunshine-golden flowers will bloom wherever a garden needs a long season of color.

Euphorbia polychroma has a long, thick taproot that gives it drought tolerance in sand.

Salvia is a fine perennial that is dependable year after year. With salvia's long bloom time and longevity, it's a keeper in the garden.

215

Heliopsis helianthoides
(hee-lee-OP-sis)
'SUMMER SUN'
FALSE SUNFLOWER

SHAPE	Upright branching clump, daisy-shaped flowers
HEIGHT	Three feet tall
WIDTH	Twenty or more inches
BLOOM TIME	Midsummer to fall
COLORS	Golden yellow
SITE	Well-drained soil
LIGHT	Full sun
HARDINESS	Zone 3
COMMENTS	Self-supporting, wind-resistant stems

H. 'Summer Sun', with its attractive height and huge size, looks surprisingly appealing as an edger because it always stays nice, requires little to no staking, and always ignores the wind.

A windblown seedling of *H.* 'Summer Sun' found a home tucked among delphiniums, sedums, and striped iris in a partial shade garden.

H. 'Summer Sun' attracts nectar-seeking pollinators for twelve long weeks of the midsummer blooming season.

The flowers of *H.* 'Summer Sun' may be in the sunflower family, but they look more like a double golden daisy.

I'M SUNSHINE AND simplicity all wrapped up into one attractive package. My name is *Heliopsis,* or false sunflower, and I'm so adaptable that a gardener can plant me and forget about me. Nothing—not even being completely ignored—slows down my blooming power, which starts in June and continues through July, August, and into September. My compact, clump-forming tall stems will be covered with double golden-yellow daisies with deep orange-yellow centers, and that's when a gardener will finally notice what a fantastic perennial I am.

My stature helps me stand out, and it's hard to miss a perennial as big, bushy, colorful, and long-blooming as I am. My productive strong stems also make me eye-catching, for each one holds as many as ten smaller stems that produce a canopy of golden daisy flowers. Being covered from head to toe with three-inch blooms that look like sunshine has a tendency to be conspicuous. Even my dark-green leaves with their somewhat coarse, lance-shaped serrated edges are an attention-grabbing complement to my never-ending supply of flowers. It's a good thing I'm so showy or my carefree, undemanding adaptability would be taken for granted.

Part of my adaptable nature is due to my being a native perennial that grows everywhere in the United States. I grow well in damp moist meadows or in hot, dry mountains, producing plenty of flowers wherever I'm planted. I'm not at all fussy about soils; normal, sandy, or clay work for me, and I never complain about poor, neutral, alkaline, or acid soils either. I prefer well-drained soil but I will do fine in moist or average sites. Full sun is my first choice but I tolerate partial shade. I'm fast growing, a trait that usually contradicts longevity, but I will stick around the garden for many years, especially with regular division. My height usually dictates a back-of-the-border placement that is used to hide utility boxes or compost piles, but I'm so compliant and tidy that I also look great along the edges of a walkway or front border. I'm never even bothered by pests or diseases or anything else for that matter. I'm a perennial that in every way is effortless to grow.

I'm also easy to propagate. I can be started from seed, cuttings, or divisions. Self-seeding in the fall as I finish blooming will produce seedlings for the next year that truly resemble my mother. If my overabundant seeding is worrisome, cut off my blooms. Narrow, dark seeds form in my center disks but also grow in my ray petals, so if self-seeding isn't an option, then cut me back to ground level. Just remember that starts of H. 'Summer Sun' can end up almost anywhere. I bloom the first year with flowers that may be too big and heavy for unestablished roots, so I might need cutting back or staking my first summer.

Any cuttings need to be snipped from mature plants in spring before any buds are set. The starts can be stuck in pots for growing. This could very easily be an economical method of producing enough H. 'Summer Sun' for a hedge, for I do a fine job at enclosing a property or giving privacy to a garden or patio. In wintertime I'm deciduous and will conveniently die back to the ground and come back in springtime thicker and better for many years to come.

Divisions are a win-win because I root easily. For division, wait to dig my root ball until I just start to break dormancy, for I'm a sun lover that likes to wait for heat before I start to grow. Split the ball, leaving at least two or three stems per division, and replant me. If you would prefer me to fill out and look more attractive the first year, then cut my stems back to keep me shorter and fuller.

Because I'm so adaptable, I can companion up with a big variety of other perennials. *Monarda* (bee balm), with its tall spiky red flowers, and I are natural go-to-together plants, and I'll even tolerate the same moist soil that monarda prefers. The long strappy foliage of daylilies and I are attractive because of the sharp contrast they create with my roundness. The dark blue spikes of 'Sunny Border Blue' or mixed colors of 'Sightseeing' are *Veronicas* that look outstanding with my golden daisies. Purple *Liatris,* tall fountain grass, and the lacy blueness of Russian sage will be showier when grown next to my golden blooms.

Grasses

Gaillardia

WORRISOME WIND

WHY SHOULD A gardener worry about wind? Perhaps it is because wind really messes up a yard by all the debris it blows in. It seems like every time the lawn looks pristine right after a fresh mowing, the wind will come up during the night and the grass will be littered with leaves and twigs the next morning. Not all plants are as sturdy as *Heliopsis* 'Summer Sun', so the wind is worrisome when it snaps off our perfect delphiniums or dahlias just as they set buds. The wind can also ruin a garden party or outdoor wedding, not only by toppling flowers but also by making the garden a very uncomfortable place to be.

Wind is a fact of life and an interesting part of nature because our winds are influenced by the sun's heating and cooling of the Earth's surfaces. As long as the sun shines and temperatures change, the wind will continue to blow. So as long as there is sun, we can grow a garden and as long as there is sun, wind will irritate the flora, fauna, and gardeners of the Earth.

BECOME FAMILIAR WITH CLIMATE CONDITIONS IN YOUR SPACE

Every yard has microclimates. One side of your property can be sunny and warm and the other side might be cool and windy. Knowing these microclimates can make a difference in effective landscaping, making your yard and home a more comfortable place, but it will also save energy and fuel costs. Planning a yard with an understanding of the wind's airflow, summer solar paths, and winter solar paths will certainly make outdoor living more comfortable. Knowing what direction the winter wind comes from as well as the summer breeze needs addressing before planning a patio. Landscaping, especially trees and shrubs, should be orientated at right angles to the winter and summer prevailing winds.

WINDBREAK BENEFITS

Windbreaks can be planted to slow down winds with a row of trees interspaced with shrubs. Trees are the very best wind deflectors. Pine trees with their thick density and shade trees with their free summer air conditioning planted in a corner or berm that is at right angles to the wind will slow down wind blasts. In a hilly area, locate windbreaks on the crest of the hill for the greatest benefit. If a fence is used as a windbreak, it should slow the airflow down without completely blocking it. Solid fences act similar to Denver's mountains and foothills, causing a downdraft on the side of the fence where airflow is first pushed up to go over the fence then drawn down into the garden. These downdrafts, with their winter snow deposits, can damage plants more than the original wind problem, so ensure that your fence lets the wind sneak through. Eliminate wind erosion by providing at least a minimum of vegetative cover to reduce wind velocity.

For help in creating a windbreak, sometimes called Oasis agriculture, where several layers of vegetation are used as shelter belts; go to any website of your University Extension programs to find individual information. Not only will windbreak plans be offered, but lists of trees and shrubs for both local homes and agriculture will also be listed.

PLANT WIND-RESISTANT PERENNIALS

Wind in a garden provides the basic requirement of circulation and helps prevent mildew and plant diseases that can flourish in damp, overly protected gardens. But too much wind can strip or break plants, dry out soil, and destroy new starts.

Gardeners can select perennials that can withstand prevailing winds. All of the short, ground-hugging alpines with their aggressive root structures are wind resistant. Native and drought-tolerant perennials with small, narrow, waxy, or hairy leaves are impervious to wind. Grasses with their nature of swaying and bending in the wind are wind resistant.

WIND RESISTANT PERENNIALS

- *Alchemilla*, lady's mantle
- *Coreopsis*
- *Dictamnus*, gas plant
- *Echinacea*, coneflower
- Grasses both short and tall
- *Hemerocallis* or daylily
- Lavender
- *Linum*, flax
- *Leucanthemum*, Shasta daisy
- *Nepeta*
- *Perovskia*
- *Sedum*

Without winds, clouds would not make it to our gardens to deliver the much-needed rain or snow. Wind is nature's delivery system. The trick is learning how to work with it rather than be controlled by it.

Lavender

Alchemilla, lady's mantle

Iris spuria
(EYE-ris)
WHITE SPURIA IRIS OR TURKISH IRIS

SHAPE	Tall, grasslike
HEIGHT	Two to three feet tall
WIDTH	Nine-inch clump
BLOOM TIME	June
COLORS	White with a yellow stripe
SITE	Clay, alkaline, and saline soils
LIGHT	Partial shade
HARDINESS	Zone 2–3
COMMENTS	Rare to the United States

The foliage of *I. spuria* looks better than any grass or spikes available with its tall, straight, standing clumps that grow well in any western environment.

Turkish iris stays upright and could be likened to the sturdy bulb foliage of gladiolus.

I. ensata, Japanese iris, with their huge blooms of variegated flowers, have a rounder, more flat profile than the lovely Turkish *I. spuria*.

The *I. spuria* flower blooms low on the foliage and almost hides. The flowers are natural and understated, adding a quiet elegance.

WHEN GENETIC PARENTAGE is so mixed by the thousands of available iris plants, it's a little mind boggling to still be a native species perennial iris that hasn't changed. I wondered if I was like a variety of other irises, but I couldn't match myself to many of them. Finally I've found out about me.

I'm a little-known, rare native heirloom-species iris and not readily available on the green market. My grasslike foliage is better than any annual spike, and I'm a long, long-lived, hardy perennial so gardeners need to get acquainted with me. My green, swordlike leaves are somewhat thicker and sturdier than my look-alike, *I. siberica*'s, foliage, so I stay more upright and attractive all season and often stay evergreen through mild winters. I also grow in shade or partial shade, which none of the other irises do.

I grow tall and provide a perfect background for the ferny-lace leaves of filipendulas or the round colorful leaves of hostas, and lady's mantle. I back up the unique bronze-foliaged bergenia, lacy-leafed corydalis, and cranesbill in partial shade. Actually, I do well when planted most any place except the hot baking sun. My excellence in western gardens is because of my drought tolerance and my preference to clay, alkaline, and even salty or sandy soils. The arid environments of the West are so similar to my origins in Asia that I'm totally at home and need little care to maintain the fresh greenness of my impressive good looks.

My flowers bloom in late May or June in white with a blotch of yellow. They have a subtle quiet style that grows on a gardener, unlike the gaudy blooms of bearded iris. I've been told we look exotic and resemble orchid blooms, but I think we are simpler than orchids. My bloom grows about four inches in diameter with falls that are more pointed than other irises, almost clawlike. Our vanilla scent and the yellow blotches on our falls are a beacon to attract pollinators.

Because of my rareness, propagation needs to be considered. I never really require division. My clump slowly increases in size but keeps looking better year after year; however, if more starts are desired, my bulbs can be dug in August. Most iris roots are elongated rhizomes, but mine stay in a rounded, one-and-one-half-inch, bulb-type rhizome. It's called a rhizome because the stem actually forms the bulb. Offsets will be produced and can be pulled apart quite easily. Replant these offsets or clumps but make sure it is in a permanent position. I resent division and will take several years before I will look up to standard. Plant me at the same depth I was growing (I like to be planted a little deeper than other iris plants). Other forms of propagation are almost a waste of time because starting my offsets or clumps is so efficient, although I'll take my time to reestablish myself.

Seed propagation is possible and I self-seed occasionally, but if seed is a gardener's only method of acquiring a rare iris like myself, then give it a try. Seed exchanges are available online, but so many of the irises have been crossbred that it may be difficult to get true species seed.

My ripened seed pods or fruit capsules can be harvested for seed in late summer. Break the pod open and plant my round, smooth, dark-brown seeds immediately. Holding my seed until spring will decrease any odds of me germinating. Sown in pots of a standard commercial seed mix that are fully topped off with sand, I can be left outside to winter or placed in the protection of a cold frame. By spring I should start to sprout but will need another year before my rhizomes form. Grow me until I'm well rooted before planting me outside. My offspring from seed, unlike many hybrid irises that will not provide viable seed, will be true. The second year after seeding, I will start to form clumps but may take my own sweet time before I bloom nicely.

Like most native plants, I have no disease or pest problems. And like most species plants, I'm tough, adaptable, and dependable. In so many important ways (like being easy to grow, never needing division, and seeds that grow true) I'm superior to hybrid iris. About the only thing I don't have that they have is huge gaudy flowers. I hope there has been value in getting acquainted with me, even if it's only to realize how great native heirloom species really are.

GARDENING IN CLAY SOIL

CLAY SOIL IS weathered rock. Rock is full of minerals; therefore, clay soil is full of plant-loving minerals, right? Not entirely. The minerals are there, but the particles in clay are so miniscule that the clay holds tight to the minerals and can't release them as nutrients. Clay soil is so heavy and dense that water cannot drain well, so water just sits there and saturates the soil or runs off the top. Every gardener knows that about ninety percent of the thousands of perennials they plant prefer well-drained soil. Inorganic clay soil isn't gardener approved.

Clay soil also doesn't breathe because of the heavy density that provides no pore space for air. Clay particles are attracted to each other when wet and stick together. When the clay particles are dry, they adhere, forming a crust without pores for breathing, so wet or dry clay sticks together.

DRIED CLAY PARTICLES TURN EITHER INTO TALCUM POWDER OR CEMENT CLODS

The particles in dry clay adhere so there is no space for water to drain, release nutrients, and *breathe*! The air in soil is where beneficial organisms live and is required to manufacture the nitrogen compounds that feed the plant roots. If soil doesn't breathe, plants are suffocated, because their roots cannot get the air they need. Trying to water this talcum powder clay or rock-like clods results in water runoff because the water can't penetrate. A clay layer deeper in the soil, called hardpan, can also form that prevents all water drainage.

Water and air are required for all living things on earth, so what is a gardener to do so they are able to grow perennials in clay soil? The answer is to change the soil structure so water and air can penetrate.

HOW TO CHANGE THE STRUCTURE

1. EVALUATE THE SOIL

• A. Soil tests to evaluate the soil can be as simple as a DIY project where you take a ball of soil in your hand. Squeeze the ball and release it. If the ball crumbles, breathe a sigh of relief—you have balanced, textured soil. If the soil feels gritty and slips through your fingers, your soil is sandy. If the ball holds its shape and can be rolled as if you were playing with modeling school clay, your soil has clay.

• B. Percolation tests in the yard or lawn can show water drainage. Dig a hole one foot across and one foot deep. Fill the hole with water and let it drain. When the hole is empty, fill it again and keep track of how long it takes to drain. If the water has not drained out in eight hours, you have a clay drainage problem.

- C. The local extension service can do a laboratory test on your soil that will cover a full spectrum from soil pH to nutrient levels. Contact them for a kit and directions for sending a sample.

2. RAISE YOUR FLOWER BEDS

Clay soil is richer in mineral nutrients than any other soil type so it is an advantage to keep it. By raising flower beds, the soil can be aerated with organic matter as the beds are refilled so it can drain and breathe. Flowers will benefit from the rock minerals that only clay soil provides.

3. ADD ORGANIC MATERIALS

The addition of organic materials will add structure to clay, allowing it to breathe and drain water plus bring in all the microscopic elements that make dirt into soil. Perlite will increase aeration.

With the addition of organic material, clay soil grows plants that are not bothered by wind, rain, hail, or diseases. Perennials grown in amended clay are shorter and stronger, and their flowers are more numerous with richer colors. Sedums planted in my amended, gravelly loam soil in Brigham have a tendency to open in the center and flop. Sedums planted in the amended clay soil of Bear Lake never flop. Be prepared; trying to change clay soil will probably be the most difficult, time-consuming, backbreaking labor imaginable. I hauled truckloads of manure to amend the clay soil when we built our home. I strongly recommend having your soil tested. Extension office tests are very reasonable, charging a bare minimum for the service.

HOW MANURE CHANGED THE CLAY'S SOIL STRUCTURE

Adding organic matter in the form of manure to the dense clay soil was like a miracle.

- Manure improves the soil structure and thus improves the biological activity of the bacteria and other organisms that help create a vital and productive soil. Manure increases the ability of the soil to drain by changing how the soil particles clump together. Pore space needs to be up to fifty percent in excellent garden soil.

- Manure increases the ability of the soil to retain moisture and air. It also makes nutrients available for plant use. Plant roots use water as a coolant as well as the carrier of nutrition. Air allows plants to breathe for proper development.

A wide selection of perennials that tolerate clay soil is often the same selection as perennials for moist soils. See page 208 (*Eupatorium*) for a list of these plants.

When excavating for our cabin, the construction equipment hit hardpan and could dig no deeper. This old photograph shows the white inorganic, sticky soil that surrounded the foundation.

Sand, clay, and amended soil.

If fighting the sticky, water-holding clay soil is overwhelming, cover it with a rock or a cement hardscape like this driveway.

Liatris spicata
(ly-AY-tris)
'KOBOLD'
BOTTLE BRUSH

SHAPE	Tall, upright spikes; fluffy flowers
HEIGHT	Two feet
WIDTH	One-foot clump
BLOOM TIME	Midsummer through early fall
COLORS	Magenta
SITE	Well drained, do not overwater
LIGHT	Full sun
HARDINESS	Zone 3
COMMENTS	Resembles a bottle brush

Liatris, or bottle brush, with its erect wands of grasslike foliage topped with intricate fluffy flowers, is so unusual; it adds an exclamatory dramatic touch to the late-summer garden.

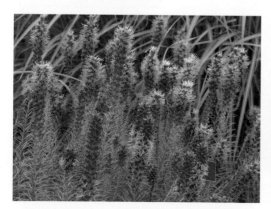

L. 'Floristan Violet' grows three feet tall, is propagated by seed, and likes extra water. The fluffy flowers look like feather dusters.

The creamy-white spire-like spikes of *L.* 'Floristan White' seldom need division and will bloom in partial shade and perform better with more water.

L. 'Kobold' has masses of tiny, compact, feathery clusters of magenta-to-violet florets that bloom generously.

I'M A LITTLE bit quirky looking, but I'm a carefree, American native perennial that prefers poor soils that drain freely. Amended gravelly soils give me good drainage, and the addition of mulch will help hold any moisture I need. Planted in rich, moist soil, I have a tendency to flop. Clay soils or any soil that holds onto moisture will cause crown rot that blackens my foliage, especially in a wet winter. So if your garden needs the upright durable drama of a vertical accent in the late summer garden, and the soil is amended gravel, then I'm the perennial that will perform.

I'm proud to be *L*. 'Kobold', the shortest, strongest, most compact of the liatris family. I am a neat and tidy vegetative-produced perennial.

Vegetative production protects my superior genetic integrity. My flowers are more striking when planted in a dense clump and will look puny if not grown in a group of at least five corms. In time the clump will multiply, filling out and getting more and more beautiful year after year. A fall self-seeding will result in new liatris, but they may not be as predictably dependable in stature or have my lovely distinct color of flowers. For a guaranteed expected outcome, grow me from a corm rather than a seed. Corms are underground modified stem tissue sometimes called rhizomes but are rounder instead of elongated, so the term *corm* is more descriptive.

Corms are easy to send for and transport (not needing sunlight or water or being bothered by freezing temperatures). The cost of shipping corms is much like that of bulbs, so it is very reasonable—much less than shipping live plants. These can go in the ground as soon as the ground can be worked. I'm very savvy weather-wise and will not break dormancy until I know the conditions are safe from freezing. This trait often makes me prone to being dug up when early spring grooming is being done, and a gardener may think I've been winter-killed.

When purchasing live pots of *L*. 'Kobold' from a nursery, check the tag to make certain that it isn't another form of liatris and that it says 'Kobold'. Other liatris plants can be tall, up to three feet, and gangly with sparse and more faded colors of flowers. I'm a lovely, well-known variety, so I've become favored for many uses: the floral, cut-flower trade finds me indispensible for funeral baskets, and my medium height adds a classy spiky accent to perennial decorative containers. It's another plus that I'm hardy enough to live over and multiply easily in decorative containers. My flowers dry well and will add the same spike accent to dried flower arrangements. If a gardener wants richer, darker-colored flowers with a more uniform appearance that never need staking, choose me, *L*. 'Kobold'.

I'm also easy to divide and transplant. My corm clusters put down deep roots that readily pull apart when dug. They also form offshoot bulbs that can be pulled and then planted for extra propagation. These can be taken in either spring or autumn. When dug and replanted in March, I will flower in July. Maturing slowly, I become more indestructible and striking every year. My need of infrequent division allows me to stay put and looking lovely for a very long time. When my dense, colorful flower heads bloom, they are quite attractive to bees and butterflies. Leave my stems after I finish blooming if feeding birds is a priority, but know that I reseed easily. Less seeding means less weeding.

Plant me with any companion that grows well with sun and good drainage such as artemisias. Their silver foliage is really startling mixed with my magenta colors. I add a lovely accent to the entire round, daisy-shaped family such as echinaceas, leucanthemums, rudbeckias, and heliopsis. Here's hoping I'll be in your garden!

The wise owners of this home have used the rocks found on their property to create a lovely rock garden area.

These superb examples of what can be done with an over abundance of rocks in the soil are Historic Homes from Centerville, Utah.

GARDENING IN ROCKY OR GRAVELLY SOIL

ONCE UPON A time, a long, long time ago, a pure pristine lake called Lake Bonneville filled what is now Utah. Lakes such as Bonneville covered huge sections of all the Rocky Mountain states. These lakes left massive accumulations of rocky gravel along their shorelines. The hills on the sides of valleys, mouths of canyons, and waterways are all composed of this rocky gravel or light soil. Gardening on this type of soil is very limiting, requiring truckloads of rocks to be removed before grass or flower beds can be installed or planted. Removing rocks is not one of the more pleasant parts of gardening!

Rock work is a trademark in western homes and gardens. The stability of rock houses and churches built by early settlers is timeless, and many such buildings are still standing. The inside of the buildings may deteriorate, but the outside rock walls are strong and attractive. Rock fireplaces, chimneys, and outdoor barbeques are a big part of western lifestyles. Many garden flower beds are structured with rock walls. Raising the elevation of these rock-walled gardens makes adding amendments to the gravelly soil an easier task and the gardens have more area to hold compost.

TECHNIQUES FOR GROWING GARDENS IN ROCK AND GRAVEL SOIL

Incorporating basic gardening techniques when attempting to landscape a mountainside home (situated in the harsh soil environment of rocks or gravel called scree), is more challenging than gardening in other soils. Most of the sand, silt, or clay particles may be blown or washed away, leaving only pockets of thin soil beneath the scree.

START FROM THE GROUND UP

Healthy gardens equal healthy soil. The quality of gravel soil can easily be increased by first removing enough of the huge rocks to make the soil workable. Truckloads of expensive topsoil are often the best and most time-saving solution. Add compost and organic matter to the soil on a regular basis. This step will always be a part of this type of gardening because rocks seem to have an innate ability to grow and grow and grow. Recycle every blade of grass or fallen leaf for compost. Peat moss, manure, or compost will improve the soil and hold water. For a large area of poor soil, if it is tillable, cover crops can be planted and tilled back in the soil before they set seed. Winter cover crops, often called green manure, with their nitrogen-fixing ability, can be planted in fall and allowed to grow until the next spring. A few suggestions are as follows:

- Red clover (short-lived, drought and shade tolerant) is very cheap in cost and effective at building soil.
- Annual oats and rye are cost effective and add a lot of humus to soil.
- Austrian winter peas are an annual with nitrogen-fixing legumes.
- Note: Alfalfa is a perennial and the seed is very expensive. Allowing alfalfa roots to get established may cause as much work as getting rid of rocks.

SELECT PLANTS SUITED TO YOUR GROWING CONDITIONS

Cold-hardy plants that thrive in the West's intense sunlight, arid growing conditions, and poor soils will be more resistant to stress and require less care. Drought-tolerant perennials with long deep roots and native plants already adapted to unmodified soil are good candidates.

The small, tough alpines will grow in natural scree, but other perennials like daylilies and peonies will need to be planted in amended soil and will need to be watered. Regional gardening books and extension services are the best resources for finding out which plants will thrive, so check these out to help make the right choices.

SIMPLIFY YOUR PLANT CARE

Look at your plants to see if they look healthy. Keep plant care simple. Way too many gardeners kill their plants with kindness by overwatering, overfertilizing, overspraying, or overpruning. Weeds compete for water and nutrients, so stay on top of the weeding. If you are monitoring your plants, early detection of insect or pest problems can be solved, and often just a strong blast of water is all that is needed. For example, a yellow bowl with soapy water will attract aphids and beer-filled troughs will control slugs. Nature has an army of pest-controlling help in the form of birds and insects. Use organic alternatives for pest problems to reduce pesticide use. This promotes pollinators that eat the pests.

When it comes to rocky or gravelly soil, use it as much as possible to your advantage, but most important, choose what works for you in your garden.

Rocks have many uses, but often they are simply too huge for landscaping. Many home owners, ranchers and home-building companies are forced to utilize rock removing equipment.

Many uses of rocks, such as this attractive dry creek bed, will add special landscaping elements to a garden.

227

Linum lewisii
(LY-num loo-ISS-ee-eye)
'Sapphire Blue'
BLUE FLAX

SHAPE	Fountain- or vase-shaped small, five-petal cluster flowers
HEIGHT	fifteen-inch-tall foliage
WIDTH	Narrow, upright vase
BLOOM TIME	Springtime
COLORS	True blue
SITE	Light soil, well drained
LIGHT	Full sun
HARDINESS	Zone 3
COMMENTS	Easily naturalized

Flax's appearance looks so simple and pretty, but its fire and drought resistance make it much more than just a pretty face.

Flax is so hardy and versatile it is used as for fire suppression, erosion control, reclamation, and beautification by the forest service and state road construction crews in the West.

Five true-blue flower petals with tiny yellow centers are held gracefully above clusters of ten flowers per stem.

The rare blue of my sapphire flowers should be adequate to make me popular, but my other talents make me valuable.

I'M A NORTH AMERICAN native perennial that was discovered by the early explorer Meriwether Lewis on the Lewis and Clark Expedition. You may know me as *Linium lewisii*. The *lewisii* part of my name is a tribute to Meriwether Lewis and, as I'm about to explain, is also a tribute to how valuable his discovery really was.

My bragging rights are earned because of my unique, hard-to-find true-blue flower color. They have a special aesthetic showiness and I'm sure it's because my color matches the summer sky. I flower for a six-week period starting in spring, depending on the elevation where I am growing (the higher the better, and the later and longer I'll bloom). My satiny, shimmery blooms are rather ephemeral, opening and lasting only one day. They open to greet the sun and rotate so as to face the sun as it moves across the sky. At sunset, my petals fall, covering the ground with delicate blue confetti. I repeat the same sun worship scenario the next morning and will close my petals in rainy weather. Wind or excessive heat can shorten my blooming season, but when I grow in the coolness of the high elevation mountains I flower longer.

Next is my amazing foliage. I have needlelike wisps of stems that may look delicate but are as strong as steel and are very difficult to break. I am often considered a semievergreen subshrub, and I provide forage for wildlife and livestock. My silvery leaves are simple and narrow, and they spiral up slender stems. These stems and my taproot retain a high moisture content that gives me drought tolerance and fire resistance. These are the reasons I'm seeded along stretches of highways in the western mountains. I don't require watering and I won't burn. The other reason I'm planted in this difficult environmental situation is because I furnish both erosion control and reclamation. In my opinion, the real reason the highway department plants me there is my beauty. I'm a natural at beautification.

My common name, flax, explains my medicinal qualities. Flax oil is a good vegetarian substitute for fish oil. Experiments and studies are now being conducted that attribute *L. perenne* with a wide variety of beneficial qualities, including modifying cardiovascular risks and controlling hyperactivity.

Traditionally, I have been used as a home remedy for a multitude of internal ailments, but my raw seeds contain a cyanide-related compound that can be toxic if eaten, so I must be cooked first. The Native Americans roasted my seeds as a nutty treat that tasted similar to pistachio nuts. Added to baked goods and health products, my delicious flavor and flax oil qualities are known to produce a healthy glycemic response.

Flax fibers obtained from my delicate-looking but strong stems have been used by humans since primitive times. The fibers are used for string or cords and for weaving cloth called linen. My Latin genus name, *Linum*, is the origin of the common name, linen. I am also grown commercially and harvested for products like paper, cosmetics, artist's paints, linseed oil, and varnishes.

I reproduce by reseeding. My taproot is almost impossible to split, and because I'm considered a short-lived perennial, division would not be worth it. Allowing me to reseed myself will create dense populations of linum that are dispersed by the wind and small wild bees and flies. My flowers form a dry, hard, dark-colored capsule that shatters and frees my seed once I'm through blooming. It takes the winter's snow to chill my seeds so I'll germinate. Not all of my seeds will germinate the first year. Some will leave what is called a viable seed bank for the future. Often I'm considered a biennial and not a perennial, because I usually bloom the second year after germinating.

By this time it's easy to understand why I have bragging rights. My rare blue color is the number one reason, but my fiber foliage that's fire resistant, feeds livestock, and provides both erosion control and reclamation is a close second. Adding in my healing properties and common household uses shows how really valuable I am.

Brunnera macrophylla

Iris

BLUES ARE COOL

BLUE COMES FROM the cool side of the color wheel and seems to be everyone's favorite color. Is this why flax is a favorite of western gardeners? Is blue a favorite color of yours in the garden? Why? Answer the following quiz for your personal reaction to blue.

Q: Does the endless space of a blue summer sky make you smile?
Fact: Blue has been proven to calm, sedate, and gives depth and space to any setting.

Q: Does blue, especially when mixed with white, look clean and fresh?
Fact: Blue is the highest selling color of toothbrushes.

Q: When you step into yesterday's soil-stained blue jeans, do the jeans feel dependable and comfortable?
Fact: Blue is perceived as a constant in our lives and seen as trustworthy and committed.

Q: Do those same gardening jeans look well with any color of shirt in your closet?
Fact: Notice that every flower in the garden looks attractive with blue.

Q: Is blue the least gender-specific color?
Fact: Blue has equal appeal to both males and females.

Q: Does gazing at the wide spectrum of blues in a lake or ocean help you reflect on the important qualities of life?
Fact: Blue seems to aid intuition.

Now we understand why gardeners like blue in their gardens. But the real blue color, like the color of *Linum*, or flax, is rare. Most flowers touted as blue usually end up blooming lavender or violet. Even photographs struggle at capturing a true-blue color. But there are flowers that bloom in the true-blue colors, and here are a few of the hardiest perennials for our western gardens:

SPRING

- *Brunnera macrophylla* is the original and most vigorous *Brunnera* available. Heart-shaped leaves produce mounds of lacy panicles of baby-blue flowers most of the spring. As the flowers fade, the elegant foliage will wind through other perennials, becoming larger as the season moves on.

- Iris blooms in late spring, and blue is its original basic color, giving it a preference for blooming in blues or blue-and-white combinations.

- *Pulmonaria*, lungworts, bloom in a light blue but start out with pink tints on their buds. Wait until the flowers open for the real-blue color of this flower.

Campanula persicifolia

- *Veronica* 'Crater Lake Blue' is a medium-height full-sun perennial that is long-living, vigorous, and blooms in an absolutely true-, gentian-blue color. Plant *V.* 'Crater Lake Blue' along the front of late-spring flower beds so their beautiful colors will show off front stage in the garden.
- *Veronica* 'Reavis' Crystal River, or *Veronica liwanensis*, grows with vigor, flat to the ground, and will spread nicely in the garden or into the crevasses of rocks. Tiny, bright, true-blue flowers open in midspring on lush semievergreen foliage.

SUMMER

- *Campanula persicifolia*, the tall, peach-leaf variety of bellflowers have several sky-blue, tall perennials, such as 'Telham Beauty' and 'Takion Blue', that bloom in china-blue flower bells in late spring or early summer. Peach-leaf varieties prefer partial shade.
- Delphiniums steal the summer show when it comes to the true-blue shades of flowers. Some of the blues are so delectable that they seem too beautiful to be real, but they are!
- *Delphinium grandiflorum* are short, bushy, well-branched members of the delphinium family, and this explains their glorious baby-blue colors. *D.* 'Summer Blues', a true baby-blue color, will self-sow if the seeds are allowed to drop on the ground.
- Ornamental grasses with their blue spikes of foliage add a quiet calmness to a garden all season long. They are available in short to medium heights and some even bloom.
- Hosta, the finest shade perennial available, has many varieties of blue-leafed foliage.
- *Lobelia* 'Techno Heat Dark Blue' is an annual that no gardener should ever pass up. The masses of baby-blue blooms that this plant provides throughout the season and even after several fall frosts have occurred are incredible. *L.* 'Techno Heat Dark Blue' grows in mounds or cascades.

Delphinium grandiflorum

FALL

- *Aconitum*, monkshood, is a tall, fall-blooming perennial.
- *Carmichaelii* has the finest foliage and the bluest flowers imaginable.
- *Ceratostigma plumbaginoides*, plumbago, is a short evergreen ground cover with foliage that turns burgundy in winter. Intense sky-blue flowers sit nestled in glossy green foliage.
- *Gentiana* is a little-used perennial because it takes a long time to get it established. When this alkaline soil–loving plant blooms in its brilliant gentian-blue flowers, a gardener knows it was well worth waiting for.

One last note: planting a blue spruce pine tree in the corner or perimeter of a garden gives a sense of space and makes the garden look larger. The addition of the color blue not only enhances its beauty but also brings a sense of quiet calm that feeds the spirit. It's cool to use blue!

Blue hosta

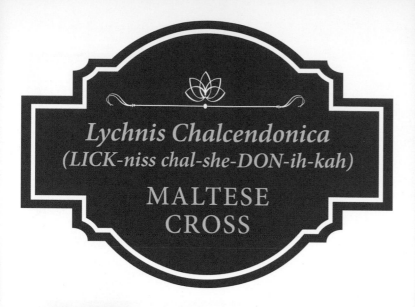

Lychnis Chalcendonica
(LICK-niss chal-she-DON-ih-kah)
MALTESE CROSS

SHAPE	Upright clump with flower clusters on stem tips
HEIGHT	Two to three feet tall
WIDTH	Narrow, round clump, about ten inches around
BLOOM TIME	Early to midsummer
COLORS	Brilliant scarlet
SITE	Average alkaline soil
LIGHT	Full sun to partial shade
HARDINESS	Often a Zone 2 but in reality considered 3
COMMENTS	Underused perennial

The notched, five-petaled blooms of *L. chalcedonica* form rounded clusters that sit on top of its tall stems, giving the garden an eye-catching, red-orange accent.

The excellent height and early blooming of Maltese cross's scarlet flowers adds specialness to any other flower colors in the garden.

The excellent height and early blooming of Maltese cross's scarlet flowers add specialness to any other colors of flowers in the garden.

Lychnis has self-seeded here to form a solid hedge of bright-scarlet, full-sun, summer-blooming color.

I'M SO PLEASED to meet you! I'm *Lychnis chalcen-donica*, a world traveler and international old-fashioned favorite for the few who are acquainted with me. My origins started in Russia, Mongolia, and northwestern China. Gradually I moved into Alaska and Canada, across the northern United States, and south to the western Rocky Mountains. I even inhabit gardens in the high elevations of the Teton Mountains and Jackson Hole, Wyoming. I've been around for ages and have certainly proven my value, so it's not necessary for me to brag. I only wish gardeners were more aware of me. I suppose I'll just tell about my brilliant, scarlet flowers that reside on lanky stems of bright-green foliage and how much they light up a summer garden. Then perhaps I'll become more popular.

My flowers are arranged in four-inch round clusters of many small blooms. Each three-fourth-inch flower has five petals that are deeply notched on the tip. The notched petals resemble the symmetrical Maltese cross, symbol for the order of the Knights of Malta and today's symbol on the badge of firefighters. My name has both past and present prestige and stands for a badge of honor. Now, if only my flower had more prestige, I wouldn't feel so left out.

In bloom, my startling scarlet colors are attention grabbers as the clusters perch on the tip of each individual tall stem. My upright stems are mostly three feet tall, but side-shoots will be shorter. Opposite pairs of light-green, pointed leaves accent my flower's scarlet colors, creating an attractive garden combination. I'm an early bird in springtime, breaking dormancy as soon as the ground warms. This is the best time to pinch back my stems, but if tall perennials for the back of the border are needed, then leave my stems to provide the height. In western gardens, I rarely need staking, for I grow shorter and sturdier in their arid, poor soils.

My foliage looks ratty after my flowers are through blooming, so cutting me back almost to the ground will keep the garden looking neat. Not to worry, after blooming, I'm ready to rest. Sometimes I'll revive for another sporadic blooming session but I'll stay short. Plant tall, late-blooming companions around me to hide the blank space I've left. Perennials like asters, Joe-pye weed, helenium, and *H.* 'Summer Sun', along with tall garden phlox and hibiscus will fill in nicely for me.

When my showy flowers bloom in midsummer, they stimulate the colors of other companion flowers. Mixed with yellow or golden *Achillea* and *Anthemis* (golden marguerite), I cause a sensation. White Shasta daisies, with their huge yellow centers, and I are garden soul mates. Planting the blues of tall nepetas, veronicas, and delphiniums around me gives a satisfying, showstopping display. Shorter perennials, such as the tall sedums or hemerocallis, with their nice strap-like foliage, look excellent both before and after I bloom.

It's pleasing to be a world traveler, and my ability to reseed has a lot to do with it. All of the lychnis family, including Maltese cross, self-seed with abandon, and we are easily propagated. My dry-capsule flower seeds are geared for germination even before they are through blooming, and the blooms can be cut for collecting seed early. If gardners wait too long for harvest, they may find I have already spilled my seeds. Shake the cut blooms over a container and the seeds will fall, ready to be sown. These seeds can be planted, stored, or bottled for a later propagation. I stay viable and germinate year-round. Enough seeds to scatter over a pasture can be collected from one season of my blooms. If self-sowing is acceptable, allow the seeds to fall from the blooms, and in three to four weeks, little seedlings will have germinated. Many of these new starts will not survive winter, but with how readily I reseed, this might prove to be a positive garden ploy. I'm so easy to seed that I need no pretreatments and no coverings. With summer's warm temperatures, I can be transplanted in as little as three weeks after germination. The wind also helps disperse my seed, and Maltese cross will germinate in the most surprising places, sometimes right inside other perennial clumps. I think I add a touch of excitement to these plantings.

Propagation by dividing is difficult. I send down masses of thin, fibrous roots that grow deep, thick, and dense. My flowers also grow from a single basal rosette that resents splitting. I perform reliably year after year without division, so allowing me to reseed is the best way to propagate me.

Other members in the lychnis family are noted for their intense colors and short-flowering span. Rose campion has silvery-gray foliage in sharp contrast to magenta flowers and may need to be paired with artemisias or blue nepeta to tone it down. *L. viscaria* 'Splendens Plena' has lovely, deep-pink flowers that are very showy. Other hybrids are also showy but tend to be less hardy than myself. I'm adaptable when planted, enjoying alkaline as well as average soils. I bloom in full sun, but my flower colors seem brighter in partial shade. I'm still that old-fashioned, tried-and-true perennial that is underused but so hardy that I perform where many other perennials dare not!

Doronicum

Hibiscus

Lamium

GARDENING IN ALKALINE SOIL

IN THE MIDDLE of a colder-than-usual March. We stopped at one of the big-box stores to purchase a new sprayer and were awed by their entrance display. It was decorated like a posh, red-carpet walkway with a double row of the most beautiful blueberry bushes lining the sides. The stunning bushes were leafed out in all their glory and were on sale.

I stopped, dumbfounded, and gazed at the gorgeous bushes, mesmerized by their perfection and beauty. As I picked up one of the packages to place it in my cart, my husband firmly took hold of my elbow and pulled me away.

As soon as I moved far enough away for the spell of the blueberry bushes to be broken, reality kicked in. I knew we couldn't grow blueberries here! Blueberries are relatives of the Deep South garden favorites rhododendron and azaleas that only grow in the mineral-leached acidic soil of the rainy Eastern and Northwest coasts of the United States. Rocky Mountain soils were created from weathered rocks. Rocks are composed of minerals, meaning our soils are mineral rich or alkaline, a soil blueberries won't tolerate.

ALKALINE SOIL AND WATER

The Rocky Mountain water is alkaline and so are our soils! In way of explanation, allow me to again use examples from where I garden: Bear Lake, Idaho. All western bodies of water, be it from Montana to Colorado, originate in the mountainous rocks. Bear Lake is a natural freshwater lake divided by the Utah–Idaho border. The Lake is fed by springs and the Bear River. Bear Lake has been called the "Caribbean of the Rockies" for its deep turquoise-blue color that is a result of the suspended limestone or high concentrations of the mineral calcium carbonate deposits in the water. Most of the precious lake water is provided by high mountain snow that melts into springs and works its way down, washing through layers of rich mineral grains that are part of the shale, sandstone, and compacted quartz that compose the mountains. We occasionally have the lake water pH tested along with our well tests, and the pH levels in the water are 8.0. This level has remained consistent for years.

So what is alkaline? What is acidic soil? The terms alkaline and acid refer to the pH measurement of soil, but what does that really mean? If the soil is acid like vinegar or lemon juice, it's considered sour. If the soil is alkaline like baking soda, it is considered sweet. The pH of the soil influences how effectively plants can take up nutrients from the soil. A grid of a pH scale for acid moves from 1.0, strongly acid, where not much can grow, to 5.0, moderately acid. The neutral range, which is, fortunately, where most perennials grow well, is the middle area, in the 6.0 to

7.0 range. The moderately alkaline soil range is below 8.0, because it is eighty times more alkaline than the 7.0 level. Above 9.0 is so strongly alkaline that not much can grow.

Many growers recommend adding mineral amendments like lime to acidic and sulfur to alkaline, but adding compost, manure, and other organic elements is a more reasonable method and can change the pH somewhat. The problem is when the water, like that in our mountains, has a high pH level. Trying to change what nature has delivered requires special consideration. Knowing the plants' preferences and utilizing the perennials that are adapted to your soil is a more effective approach to gardening no matter what the pH level. Alkaline and acidic perennial preferences are not common knowledge, even with growers, local nurseries, and gardening books.

Many of the flower varieties mentioned in earlier chapters will do well in alkaline soils. Here are a few additional varieties for you to consider:

Lysimachia

- *Anthemis*, golden marguerites, are medium tall and reseed yearly.
- *Delosperma*, ice plant, is a walk-on-me garden perennial with succulent flowers.
- *Doronicum*, leopard's bane, blooms spring with a double set of golden petals.
- *Geum*, avens, are bright orange or scarlet flowers that bloom on wiry stems in spring.
- Grasses, tall varieties, with their narrow blades and height, add excitement to the garden.
- *Hibiscus*, rose mallow, blooms in late summer with dinner plate–sized flowers.
- *Lamium*, deadnettle, is a spreading, silver-foliaged ground cover for shade.
- *Ligularia*, leopard plant, has red-purple foliage and yellow spike blooms.
- *Lysimachia*, loosestrife, blooms on tall spikes or short ground covers.
- *Sedum* grows low as a ground cover or medium high for the middle of the garden.
- *Sidalcea*, minature hollyhocks, bloom in hot pinks or fuchsia spikes.
- *Solidago*, goldenrod, blooms in dense, golden-yellow sprays in fall.
- *Tradescantia*, spiderwort, has striking, strap-shaped foliage with blue flowers.
- *Trollius*, globeflower, adapts to either soil and blooms gold or orange in shade.

Sedum

Alkaline plants are abounding, with a wide variety of shapes, sizes, and colors. If acid-loving perennials are planted, they may survive in our gardens but never really grow and bloom well. They will never show the vigor they have in acidic gardens. This could be a part of the reason that western gardeners assume incorrectly that perennials are just not as vigorous when planted in western soils.

Papaver, Iceland poppies

235

Phlox paniculata
(FLOCKS)
TALL GARDEN PHLOX

SHAPE	Clumps of spikes with ball-shaped floret clusters terminating on the stem tip
HEIGHT	Twenty-four to thirty inches
WIDTH	Twelve- to fifteen-inch clump
BLOOM TIME	Midsummer through fall
COLORS	Wide color range of rosy shades and white.
SITE	Amended clay that drains but stays consistently moist
LIGHT	Full sun or partial shade
HARDINESS	Zone 4, often 3
COMMENTS	Garden phlox are the most beautifully colored of any summer flower

The rich intensity of this violet phlox adds an instant, eye-catching element to any summer garden.

P. 'Flame Pink' has an alphabet soup list of patent numbers (CPBR #1094, USPP #11804) that make it like royalty and not reproducible without a license.

The soft, rosy colors and fragrance of P. 'Coral Flame' add romance to the garden.

The colors and fragrance from the huge, round-shaped flowers of garden phlox creates a dreamy feeling of tender intimacy in the summer evening garden.

SUMMER IS OFTEN defined by "the rockets' red glare and bombs bursting in air," but in the garden I make even better fireworks. I am *Phlox paniculata*, and my bursting bombs are very different from the ones spoken of in the national anthem. My bombs create fireworks in the garden but with the softest, most colorfully romantic flowers of tall garden phlox.

Summer wouldn't be summer without the rosy colors of my family of tall garden phlox. Many western gardeners shy away from me because they think I'm simply too elegant and fussy for their gardens, but I enjoy growing in the West. The well-drained, amended gravelly soil that provides good drainage is preferred because sitting in excessive saturated soil will be the death of me. The amended clay soil with a pH of 7.4, or slightly alkaline, suits me fine, probably because it holds consistent summer moisture and has lots of yummy minerals. I seem to adapt to any western soil. I form clumps of rigid stems that produce huge, colorful clusters of small florets on their tips. I'm not prone to needing staking, for my stature in western gardens is shorter and sturdier, and the rich minerals in western soils add to that stable stance.

I especially enjoy the summer warmth and dryness of the West, but at the same time, the cooler evening temperatures of higher elevation gardens help me bloom better and longer into fall. It could be because I'm a native wildflower in the western mountain forests, so I could say the Rocky Mountains are my origins (which make me even more adaptable to the area). My wildflowers have a well-developed, slender trumpet that flares open into five-petaled, one-half-inch florets that invite hummingbirds to sip. The flowers bloom in shades of magenta and pink but mainly white. They only grow to about four-inch-tall clusters and can be found in rocky openings. Native Americans used this phlox to help build blood in anemic children as well as an eyewash.

Another reason I'm well suited to western gardens is the arid climate that discourages mildew. In many of the areas where I'm planted, the constant humidity plays havoc on my appearance, causing mildew. The fungus starts out as spots on my leaves that absorb nutrients and will cause my leaves to yellow. The hybridizing of phlox has given gardeners many phlox that are mildew resistant, but in hybridizers' zeal for more and newer colors, we phlox seem to have lost our fragrance and ease of care. Planting mildew-resistant varieties that are often bred from old-fashioned, untouched healthy stock seem to give less disease-prone plants. The reds, oranges, and salmons seem to have a stronger tendency to mildew and don't really have the romantic, heady scents of some of the older varieties. Variegated *P.* 'Norah Leigh' is a good example of what overbreeding does. 'Norah Leigh' was the rage until gardeners watched it die a slow death due to the variegation having less photosynthetic abilities. As a phlox, I can caution gardeners who are anxiously waiting to grow me in their western gardens to never purchase phlox that is not mildew resistant and fragrant. The delightful smell of garden phlox seems to be the important trait that signals that I come from old-fashioned carefree stock. *P.* 'David' won the Perennial Plant of the Year Award and smells romantically intoxicating. *P.* 'Bright Eyes', with enormous pink blooms and a scarlet center, is fragrant and one of the oldest phlox available. Both of these cultivars are very mildew resistant.

My hardiness, a Zone 3 or 4, is one more reason to consider phlox in western gardens. We survive even the bitterest of winters. A late-breaking dormancy helps us circumvent the spring freeze-frost cycles that damage so many other perennials.

My siblings and I prefer not to be babied. We don't require fertilizer or spray for insect or disease problems. We are water-wise in a way but not extremely drought tolerant. Excessive drought might weaken us to the point where spider mites will attack and turn our foliage yellow. Plant us and forget us with only a cut-back and cleaning up of seeds in fall. Our seeds are not desirable for self-sowing because we can revert to an invasive form of phlox. If germination of seeds is desirable to a gardener, prepare to use your refrigerator for a six-week cold treatment after the seeds are sown into a tray. When the tray is removed from the fridge, it must be kept in the dark until seedlings emerge. This might take a month or longer. Then move the baby starts into the light. Even after all of this waiting, my seeds will only germinate sporadically. Divisions or vegetatively propagated starts will stay true to the parent plant and can be dug or taken successfully in spring, even before I break dormancy. Cut the crown into sections, each having three or more stems and a nice rootball. If the center of the plant has turned woody, send it to the compost heap.

Western gardeners are encouraged to add me to their gardens. I'll provide the brightest, most colorful flowers to their late-summer gardens without any worry that I'm simply too fancy, hard to grow, or romantic to grow in the West.

An ancient birdhouse chair with its welcoming ears of corn nestles nicely in *Aster* 'Purple Dome'.

Two little farm animals filled with hens and chicks add extra color and fun imagination to any garden

WHIMSY IN THE GARDEN

WHIMSY IS A lighthearted, playful way for gardeners to express themselves in their gardens. Whimsy decorates a garden in an artistic way that will never resemble another neighbor's yard. It's a delightful way to add color, texture, or focal points that will certainly outlast flowers. Whimsy is the lighter side of gardening, often using American folk art or vintage items that have been recycled. Bicycle baskets, tool boxes, jugs, galvanized buckets, old shutters, chandeliers, signs, or trellises can be tucked around the garden for adding a playful expression. Neon bright funky colors can embellish the garden every bit as well as annuals.

Gardens are never a place to be serious, so cheerful creatures can appear from hidden planting spots that will be sure to tickle the garden visitor's funny bone. Wall hangings in the folk art, vintage collectibles, creatures, signs, or birdhouse styles can adorn a porch with timeless elegance or with bits and pieces of color or fun that will greet guests with appealing warmth. Also, whimsy never has to be situated in any special spot or soil. These art objects like hot sun or shaded areas and don't mind drought or cold. Salty, clay, rocky, or alkaline soil make no difference to their performance. Plus, they never need to be watered.

The hand-painted treasure trunk and folk art tiles give the front of this plain cream house character.

Rudbeckia
(rud-BEK-ee-uh)
BLACK-EYED SUSAN

SHAPE	Broad clump, daisy-shaped flowers
HEIGHT	Twenty inches
WIDTH	Fifteen inches around
BLOOM TIME	Mid to late summer
COLORS	Golden-yellow with brown, cone-like centers
SITE	Neutral, alkaline, acid, sand, or clay
LIGHT	Full sun or partial sun
HARDINESS	Zone 4
COMMENTS	Most recognizable plant

A very popular perennial, black-eyed Susan's long-blooming flowers can be found everywhere in the US.

Shown above is the annual *R. hirta* 'Denver Daisy'.

R. hirta 'Cherry Brandy' has rich burgundy-colored blooms that grow shorter and reseed nicely in the garden.

R. fulgida 'Goldstrum' blooms with such an abundance of flowers that it could easily be called a golden storm, which is what the German name *goldsturm* means.

IT IS IMPOSSIBLE to find a perennial, or even an annual for that matter, that can equal my profusion of golden blooms in midsummer. My colors (a contrast of gold with chocolate-brown centers) are so floriferous and distinctive that most gardeners recognize me as black-eyed Susan, but my Latin name is *Rudbeckia fulgida*. As a native North American perennial, I can be found in gardens all across the United States and I grow well everywhere. Different soil types of normal, sandy, or clay, as well as a variety of pH levels from neutral, alkaline, and even acid, are considered optimal growing conditions for *R.* 'Goldsturm'. Each daisy-shaped flower is up to two or three inches in diameter, and when my drifts and masses of golden flowers bloom, I supply the garden with a steady color intensity that cannot be equaled by any other flower. In addition, my showy flowers bloom for most of the summer, from late July through August and September. When left standing, I also provide winter interest by attracting hungry birds to seeds located inside my dark cones. Is there any wonder why I'm such a popular and well-known perennial? I even won the Perennial Plant of the Year Award in 1999.

There is no mistaking me for another perennial, unless it is my relative, Gloriosa daisies, which are also called rudbeckia. Gloriosas are not perennials but annuals or short-lived perennials. This is confusing for a gardener who assumes they have purchased a perennial and will be disappointed when their Rudbeckia doesn't return after winter. *R. fulgida* is the only true perennial. The other look-alikes are called *R. hirta* and bloom in a variety of bold, bicolored autumn yellows, bronzes and mahoganies. The centers are usually darker than the outer petal rays. The word *hirta*, meaning "hairy," was tagged on these for the short bristles that cover their flowers, leaves, and stems. These bristles, a trait of drought tolerance, can cause fungal problems by holding too much water against the stems in wetter regions. Plants are healthier and bloom longer during dry summers in cooler climates like the Rocky Mountains. Gloriosa daisies are the self-sowing rudbeckias that are seen in western gardens, pastures, and range lands and are good forage for cattle. Having stands of Gloriosas on a property is a sign of a healthy environment.

Some of the more popular *R. hirta*, Gloriosa daisies, are the following:

R. 'Prairie Sun' and *R.* 'Tiger Eye', which do not have the traditional cone-shaped blooms of *R. fulgida* and are larger and more open. The flower colors are soft yellow with orange shaded centers. *R.* 'Prairie Sun' has lime-colored centers, as does another very popular *R. hirta* called 'Irish Eyes'. *R.* 'Indian Summer', a taller hirta with dark centers, has huge flowers that are more open without the traditional cone-shaped blooms. *R.* 'Indian Summer' is a very garden-worthy annual. *R.* 'Cherokee Sunset' is double petaled with multicolored rays and polished button noses and continues flowering unabated well into late fall. These are only a sampling of the many Gloriosa daisies available. All of the *R. hirtas* are self-sowing. The original species natives show consistency by staying true from seed, but the hybrid cultivars may revert back to the original species form. Purchase seeds and sow in the garden in early spring.

I'm only propagated vegetatively by taking cuttings or digging divisions when clumps get overcrowded. Seeded *R. fulgida* is not really a true rudbeckia. Most other traits of the annual *R. hirta* and I are similar. We both fill in empty garden gaps left by earlier blooming perennials and are very attractive to butterflies, both for nectar and as a larval host. We both make excellent cut and dried flowers. We both thrive in the dry West, which eliminates any disease problems, and we are not attractive to deer or rabbits. I'm much more drought tolerant than the hirta types, which prefer a touch more moisture. I'm also hardier, a solid Zone 3 while hirta is higher, a Zone 4.

Our flat, yellow, daisy-like blooms are especially attractive in mass plantings beside the blue lace of *Perovskia*, Russian sage. None of the fall asters, with their rosy to purple colors, are golden, so I help intensify the garden by adding this contrasting color. The softness of the *Sedum* 'Autumn Joy' and the tall Joe-pye weed or fountain grasses, such as *Calimagrostis* 'Karl Foerster', are natural companions. We add zing to the fall garden and to other perennials.

FERTILIZERS IN THE GARDEN

Using too much fertilizer is worse than none at all for both plants and the environment. A timed-release fertilizer is a good option for perennials.

Minimize the label usage amount for water-soluble fertilizers to prevent damage.

ORGANIC

- Organic fertilizers include composts, mulches, and manures. They improve soil and feed plants.
- Organic fertilizers are nonburning and slow-feeding, often taking months or years to decay.
- Most organic fertilizers are low in nitrogen, which is the missing element in most Rocky Mountain gardens. Nitrogen is the necessary ingredient for rapid, greener growth.
- Manures often contain excessive amounts of salts and must be thoroughly leached.
- Dried alfalfa pellets, bone meal, coffee grounds, grass clippings, peat moss, and worm castings are common organic fertilizers for the West.

CHEMICAL

- Chemical fertilizers contain mineral salts that furnish a quick fix for plants.
- The salts do not provide a food source for soil microorganisms and earthworms, and over time, the soil will lose the living organisms that are found in quality soil. Eventually soil will require increasing amounts of chemicals to stimulate growth as soil structure and water-holding capacity declines.
- Many chemical fertilizers are made from nonrenewable resources like coal and natural gas.
- Granulated fertilizers are easy to broadcast on lawns.
- These fertilizers need moisture to activate and so must be applied right before a rainstorm or watering. Granules can burn leaves and roots if left on soil without watering.

There are pros and cons of either type of fertilizer. Choices should be made from results of a soil test and the gardener's preference. I use organic on gardens and chemical on lawns. Numbered labels on the bag tell the concentrations of the numbered ingredients.

1. **Nitrogen** content is listed as the first of the nutrients:
Nitrogen is absorbed in the greatest quantity and is the most important ingredient in fertilizers in the western mountains because soil suffers from iron chlorosis or iron deficiency.

Our soils require nitrogen, but not to exceed the average recommended one pound of nitrogen per one thousand square feet for lawns, ornamentals, or flower beds. When fertilizing twice a year, split the nitrogen fertilizer into two parts. Always minimize the amount recommended on the label. Less is better.

2. **Phosphorus** is the second number listed:

Phosphorus is essential for crop maturity, meaning flowers, seeds, or fruit development. Phosphorus also produces a strong root system.

3. **Potassium** is the third number listed:

Potassium is used by plants in the development of flowers. Their size and color depends on the availability of potassium to the plant. This is why Miracle-Gro is so popular for flower gardens. Their engineered formula for western gardens with high alkalinity is 21-5-20, or potassium levels almost equal to the nitrogen level.

Application of organic fertilizers and chemical fertilizers is the same. The granular form is broadcast with a rotary or drop spreader on the soil surface then tilled or watered into soil. The spreaders are efficient as long as they are calibrated properly and the directions are followed.

Foliar fertilization is done with water-soluble products that are sprayed. In plants that hold moisture, such as sedums, which have curved leaves, damage can happen, so follow directions carefully. For safety, always reduce the label usage amount. Two tablespoons of fertilizer per gallon of water is safe. Apply foliar sprays early in the morning or late in the evening to curb leaf burning. Perennials react to foliar fertilization faster than granular, but granulars can last longer, especially if the fertilizer is a timed-release one. Timed release fertilizers rarely burn plants, and they reduce the environmental impact.

I learned a hard lesson one year when I purchased ten new hosta plants that mesmerized me when I passed them at the grocery store. Within ten days, several of the hostas turned yellow and the tops flattened. In the next week, all but two of the plants had collapsed. In frustration at my inability to keep a hosta alive, I turned for help to the local extension office.

After examining them, he was able to identify the problem: "These hosta have no roots. They have been forced, living on the fertilizer they were receiving in a nursery greenhouse." He went onto explain that fertilizing every time a plant is watered is similar to a human using steroids. It helps the plant bulk up and grow faster, but doesn't promote the development of a strong root system.

Buyer beware: when you are tempted to buy a huge perennial with enormous blooms that may be blooming out of season, realize that it may be on steroids!

Perennial plants are a permanent part of a landscape, so when you purchase your first perennials, keep this advice in mind:

- The first year they sleep
- The second year they creep
- The third year they leap
- And the fourth year, a gardener reaps a harvest, and they can be divided.

Tanacetum coccineum
(tan-uh-SEE-tum)
'Robinson's Crimson'
PAINTED DAISY

SHAPE	Short, mounding perennial, daisy-shaped flowers
HEIGHT	Twenty inches
WIDTH	Fifteen inches around
BLOOM TIME	Late spring, early summer
COLORS	Dark, rich red with huge golden centers
SITE	Well drained, neutral alkaline
LIGHT	Full sun or partial shade
HARDINESS	Zone 3
COMMENTS	A natural insecticide

A flower so precision-perfect in color and form belongs in every garden.

T. 'Robinson's Red' will bloom twice or three times, depending on the length of the season, by cutting back the flower stems.

T. coccineum may be the most important perennial available, due to its sharp medicinal fragrance that acts as a natural organic insecticide to control pests.

Tanacetum blooms in lovely soft pinks, rose shades, reds, crimsons, and whites.

TALK ABOUT CONFUSION! I was once called a chrysanthemum, and now I have the entirely different nomenclature of *Pyrethrum* and *Tanacetum*. Botanists must have reevaluated my classification and assigned me to a new genus. I suppose this is because one of my names, *Pyrethrum*, is a natural insecticide made by crushing my dried flowers into an oil, so I figure *Pyrethrum* is my product name. When my flower heads are dried, pulverized, and mixed with water, they are commercially sold as safe, organic, natural insecticides. I think my commercial name is *Pyrethrum* and my home gardening name is *Tanacetum coccineum*, which is a synonym for *Chrysanthemum*.

My insecticidal properties were first used centuries ago as a lice remedy inside mattress ticking. This led to the discovery that I am a natural source of insecticides. Pyrethrin oils, which are the product derived from pyrethrum flowers, attack the nervous systems of insects and inhibit female mosquitoes from biting. My spray must drive insects crazy because they come out of hiding and scurry around in the open, making them easy targets. Even when I'm not fatal to insects, I still have an insect repellent effect. Add to this that I'm biodegradable, nonpersistent, and decompose when exposed to sunlight, so I'm a safe, important element in organic gardening.

My naturally effective insecticides are concentrated in the oil glands of my tightly packed seed surfaces and this has led to pyrethrum being grown commercially in huge operations in East Africa and Australia. A white version of tanacetum called Dalmatian *P. cinerariifolium* that looks somewhat like a common daisy is used in these agricultural harvests. *P. cinerariifolium* produces a more potent strain of the insecticide pyrethrin. It's interesting that hybridizers, in trying to clone and breed a painted daisy with increased yields of pyrethrin, have found that the natural seed of pyrethrum cannot be equaled. I'm also a convenient crop in that my picked flower heads can be dried and stored without losing potency. The miles and miles of these lovely white painted daisies in full bloom have become tourist attractions. More important is that pyrethrum grows naturally in our Rocky Mountain environment, which is very similar to where it has become a cash crop. All a gardener needs to do is plant the herbaceous perennial, dalmatian pyrethrum in their own gardens and harvest, dry, and crush the flowers to create a spray that discourages all kinds of insects like aphids, ticks, wasps, whiteflies, and spider mites.

There are little known curative properties in my fern-like foliage. Three or four of my fresh leaves eaten daily have been noted by herbalist healers as an effective aid in relieving migraines. Besides being a medicinal herb, my finely cut foliage, which resembles the greenery of carrots, is beautiful with an appealing pungent smell.

I stand erect—two feet tall—on lush bushy stems with dissected fern-like foliage that accents my deep, rich red daisies. *T.* 'Robinson's Red' is the most admired of all painted daisies because of my striking color and size of blooms that surround my huge golden disk centers. I also bloom in pink, rose, crimson, and white. These colors are offered in a 'Robinson's Mix' seed or nursery plants. I flower in late spring or early summer and by removing my stem before I start to form seed, I'll bloom repeatedly later in the summer.

I naturalize and reseed readily without cover or pretreatments, so this is the easiest method for propagation. I can be sown directly into the garden in early spring and often flower that same year. The 'Robinson' series of tanacetum bloom with double rows of three-inch, daisy-like petals but will not reliably reseed double. Self-seeding starts usually revert back to single-row petals, which are still very attractive. I germinate quickly, in about fourteen to twenty-one days, and can be transplanted to another garden spot. I'm considered a short lived perennial, so allowing me to reseed will ensure an adequate supply of my remarkable red blooms in the garden.

Plant me in a well-drained location with my crown above the soil. I grow well in full or partial sun. I thrive in the high altitudes, volcanic-rocky soils, and warmth of the Rocky Mountain West's summers. I have excellent drought tolerance but will look better with regular watering, so soil amendments are appreciated, since they help me retain the moisture that keeps my foliage looking fresh and lush. Clay soil is not my first choice for growing in, but with my strong fibrous root system, I can actually tunnel in and improve clay soil.

Preparation of my planting spot by loosening and amending the soil will result in fuller foliage and more flowers. Fertilizer does the same for me, so an application of a timed-release fertilizer will keep me looking good all summer.

I'm very hardy and thrive under a layer of snow, but if no snow has fallen by December and the ground has frozen, it would be beneficial to add a layer of mulch to insulate my roots.

I present excellently as a cut flower because of my long-lasting blooms and strong stems. I outlast roses in vases, plus my petals furnish a fun "love me, love me not" entertainment when given to a special friend.

INSECTICIDES AND HERBICIDES

Snails are newcomers to the Rocky Mountains and have moved into our gardens through plant material brought or sent from warmer areas.

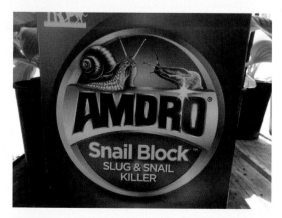

Always follow label instructions precisely or damage to beneficial worms, butterflies, bees, and other insects may result.

NOWHERE IS THE arrogant attitude of man more prevalent than in his thinking that he can subdue nature and use Earth for his own benefit by trying to tame it with insecticides and herbicides! *Crop production is much more than chemistry.*

The rewards of organic gardening are so positive, but it's still not easy to rely solely on organic yard helpers, so there has to be a trade-off. Chemical pesticides and herbicides can become necessary in situations where a gardener becomes infirm through an accident or age and is no longer able to do the heavy work of moving compost or manures. Time is also a factor. Organic gardening is more time consuming because nature amends the soil using its own time schedule, and some gardeners live in urban settings where it is more difficult to acquire organic products.

Many good chemical products are available that make gardening more satisfying and enjoyable, but *less is best* is a sound gardening method. Here is a look at a sampling of well-known organic and chemical pesticides and herbicides, so gardeners can make their own choices. They are sequenced from mild-organic to the stronger chemical killers, and these are but a tiny handful of what is available. All have cautions and warnings, and it's imperative that directions are followed exactly.

PESTICIDES

- **Vacuum:** Your neighbors may think you are crazy, but infestations of many types of bugs can be controlled with a handheld vacuum. Simply suck the insects away from plants and dispose of them.

- **Copper:** Copper tubing placed along the perimeter of our property keeps the neighbor's mollusks or snails on their side of the fence. The copper pipe causes an electric charge that shocks the snails and slugs as they secrete slime when crossing the pipe. Hand-picking is the best way to control snails, since baits will also kill earthworms. Be sure to bag snails in a plastic ziplock bag for disposal, since smashing them does not halt snail reproduction.

- **Pyrethrum:** The natural insecticide Pyrethum affects the central nervous system of all types of flying and crawling insects and paralyzes them on contact. The main advantage of pyrethrums is their low toxicity to animals and humans. They are considered the safest insecticide for use around food production, such as in dairy barns.

- **Insecticidal Soap:** The active insecticidal ingredient in these products is potassium salt of fatty acids. The alkaline hard water of the Rocky Mountains can cause a decrease in control of the product. Soap pesticides must contact the insect and are applied as diluted sprays.

- **Diazinon:** Diazinon is a synthetic chemical used to kill insects that was created as a replacement for DDT. It quickly became an all-purpose pest control product . . . and it works! It contains an aromatic sticking petroleum distillate that damages a pest's nervous system. Diazinon is being phased out due to health concerns.

HERBICIDES

- **Vinegar:** Vinegar can function as a natural weed killer due to the acetic acid it contains. Saturate weeds by painting or nozzle-to-weed spraying the vinegar directly. Repeated application may be required. Vinegar as a weed killer is non-selective and will damage lawns.
- **Boiling Water:** Boiling water kills any plant and any seeds.
- **Rubbing Alcohol:** Rubbing alcohol herbicide spray is as effective at destroying weeds as many chemical sprays and rarely needs a second application. Mix your own using one quart water to one tablespoon rubbing alcohol.
- **Corn Gluten Meal:** Corn gluten meal acts as a pre-emergent and works best when applied to bare ground before the weed seed sprouts (apply in early spring when bright yellow forsythia are blooming). It is a byproduct of corn and is yellow powdered or pelletized in form.

Fall, when the perennial weeds start moving nutrition into their roots for winter, is the most effective time to spray and rid yards of weed problems. The best part of using these naturally organic products is that they pose no risk to bees.

- **Roundup:** Roundup or glyphosate is a broad-spectrum, systemic herbicide used to kill weeds by inhibiting an enzyme that is found only in plants. The weed killer is absorbed through live foliage, stems, or tree trunks, so it is effective only on growing plants. When glyphosate comes into contact with the soil it becomes inactive and can be degraded by bacteria. Roundup is one of the most popular herbicides, commonly used by agriculture, horticulture, and home-use garden maintenance. The EPA, FDA, EU (European Union), and WHO (World Health Organization) have all sanctioned Roundup in various ways, but some research indicates that herbicides are contributing to a new population of "superweeds" in agriculture.
- **2,4-D:** 2,4-D is the most widely used weed killer in the world. 2,4-D is an herbicide that is selective and manages broadleaf weed control in wheat, corn, and rice crops but will not damage grasses. It must be used responsibly to prevent pollution of waterways and surface water.

Online information for gardeners needing more in-depth knowledge of chemicals being sold for pesticides and herbicides can check out the many excellent resources supplied by extension offices and universities. *Act sustainably; dig the weeds, collect the snails, and plant tanacetum in your gardens!*

It is interesting that both fertilizers and weed killers contain phosphorus. Does that mean Roundup kills weeds with extra strong fertilizers?

When applied to a lawn, 2,4-D will volatize and change into a gas when temperatures reach 70°F. The 2,4-D gas can be carried with the wind and will kill plants like tomatoes or grapes that are blocks away. Never spray 2,4-D with the wind blowing!

This dairy cow cleaner contains 25 percent pyrethum and keeps the cows free of flies and insects. It is also used to wash down the cows udders and backsides.

SUMMARY

THE PERENNIALS HAVE SPOKEN. They have introduced themselves in this book and have proven their diversity, adaptability, and beauty.

Gardening in arid desert climates, in cold climates, with poor soils, and with hungry wildlife can be challenging, but gardeners love a challenge! We garden to beautify our homes and satisfy our souls. Perennials help us do both.

These perennials with their versatility bloom early for spring, stay late in fall, and can be counted on for summer's in-between times. Year after year, they provide the structure for the landscape and furnish an unending option of attractive choices for any climate. There is a perennial that will manage to make a comfortable home in your garden.

Getting acquainted with perennials is what *Powerful Perennials* is about. It's questionable that anyone would want to spend the rest of their life with a person they just saw on the Internet based solely on that person's good looks. This principle also applies to perennials. If the plant looks pretty in a catalog picture or at a nursery, look closer and find out the same information that you would seek if you were choosing a permanent partner. After all, perennials are very permanent parts of a garden, and just like an individual, they are much more than a pretty picture. Any investment in perennials is an investment in the future.

ENVIRONMENTAL NOTES

Your climate and environment is not negotiable. Western gardens will never be the moisture-laden gardens of England or the fertile fields of Holland. Gardeners need to accept their limitations and grow perennials that will thrive where they live.

A plant's origins are fascinating and enlightening, for they tell where it will perform best.

A plant's cold hardiness needs to match the area where the plant will find a home. Zone maps that show the lowest possible temperatures a perennial can survive are helpful, but a gardener's knowledge is far more valuable, so discover what other local gardeners are growing when choosing your own perennials.

Is the planting site in hot, all-day sun or in a more protected spot of partial shade or full shade? Any sun perennial planted in shade will rarely bloom and just get long and lanky as it reaches for sunlight. Shade perennials will end up with burned leaves and continue to go downhill when planted in hot sun. Being aware of the plant's needs and your space constraints will assist in choosing the right perennial for the right spot.

How much water does the perennial you have chosen require? Matching the water needs for perennials planted in a certain environment will make watering easier and plants healthier. Mulched gardens hold moisture longer and will save a grower costly water.

What type of soil does the perennial prefer? The chapter on soils has provided examples of perennials for a variety of soils. Knowing the type of soil your garden sits in will simplify perennial choices.

DESIGN NOTES

The shape of a flower bed is an indicator of the garden style of the landscaper. Curved edges can indicate a relaxed, informal cottage or country garden. Curves might also indicate a line for the eye to follow to see a display of remarkable splendor. Straight edges and box shapes in the landscape are the markers of formal gardens, with their precision-trimmed plants.

Planting perennials for every season, spring through fall, will ensure constant color. Start the garden out in early spring with the "ice breaker" bulbs followed by midspring blooms of perennials like basket-of-gold, columbine, rock cress, bleeding hearts, candytuft, and geum.

Summer perennials are numerous with abundant choices, such as coreopsis, coneflowers, daylilies, delphinium, haillardia, heliopsis, iris, peonies, and phlox.

Fall-to-frost perennials include asters, chrysanthemum, hibiscus, obedience, Russian sage, and sedums. The seasons of bloom is a gardener's most creative challenge.

Colors of perennials often provide the framework of accent, rhythm, repetition, and balance in the garden. A different main and secondary color for each season often simplifies this artistic endeavor, but using drifts or triangles (never rows) of one plant color each season avoids a hodgepodge look in the garden. Drifts are usually a trio or more of one perennial that highlights a particular season. Perennials, on average, bloom three to four weeks, so choose a favorite to accomplish this type of professional-looking structure.

The height of a perennial is important, and staggering their heights helps showcase the flowers. To gracefully achieve the tapering of heights in flower beds, plan borders at least four or more feet deep. The backs of the borders or the centers of island beds are prime spots for tall perennials. The midsection of a flower bed is where medium-height perennials provide bulk and fullness, and the very front edges need the finishing touches of the short perennials. Fortunately, perennials like the taller columbine are infamous for popping up in unplanned spots in gardens, softening or rupturing the tall, medium, and short pattern. Including a few spots with height variations gives interest and attention-getting character to a garden.

The huge variety of shapes and foliage of perennials adds another structural element to the garden. Perennials spill or grow flat, become tall, or form clumps or mounded mats. The plants may develop spikes, clusters, or daisy-shaped blooms. Perennial foliage is as varied as its shapes, often adding unique silver, blue, or burgundy colors with small and delicate or thick and coarse leaves to the garden. Their foliage may be rounded, lacy, flat, or even glossy, and no two perennials are exactly alike.

CARE OF PERENNIALS NOTES

Perennials like long-lived peonies, aconitums, daylilies, and poppies can grow in the same spot for many years. Soil preparation with the addition of amendments such as manure, compost, or peat moss is a key nourishment factor for these long-living perennials. A garden can never get too much of a good thing, like amendments that lighten clay or help sandy soil retain moisture and nutrients.

Planting perennials is fairly simple. Plant flowers at the same depth shown on the plant's label. Give the perennial room to spread its roots by digging the planting hole larger than the root ball. Space between plants provides air circulation, reduces risks of diseases like mildew, and gives the plant room to breathe. Allow plenty of room so perennials do not have to compete for water and food. An average space allowance is one small perennial for a square foot of flower bed and fifteen inches for larger plants. However, the size of the plant at maturity is also a factor.

Little gardening jobs like labeling perennials or keeping records of plant locations is information that is as necessary as the act of keeping income tax receipts and can prove to be valuable later on.

Staking tall perennials is also important and will keep flower faces out of the mud, so do it early in the season.

Many perennials perform better if they are not allowed to get too tall and leggy. Pinch or snip the tops of extra-tall perennials like asters, delphiniums, or lychnis early so they will bush and produce strong stems with plentiful flowers.

Watering is necessary when growing perennials in dry climates. Aridness often dictates the installation of a sprinkler system to keep the soil moist. An efficient timing device on the watering system will save dollars and plants. New perennials are killed more often by overwatering than by cold, so use sprinklers sparingly.

Too much fertilizer will weaken a plant, giving it a rank look and making it difficult for it to withstand the cold dormancy of winter. All perennials really need is an all-purpose fertilizer in spring. Iron deficiency in lean soils dictates that a high-nitrogen number like a 10 as the first number on the fertilizer bag be used. Perennials really perk up if a water-soluble plant food is sprayed on the plants when they are blooming.

Weeding has been mandated since the Garden of Eden. The best defense against weeds is to not allow them to go to seed. Once a weed has set seed, the seeds will remain viable for seven years, so stop them by weeding regularly and cover flower beds with several inches of mulch. Mulch forms a weed barrier that will eventually decay, becoming part of the soil. Apply a new layer of mulch as needed.

PERENNIAL PROPAGATION NOTES

Perennial propagation using division, seed, or cuttings varies for perennials. Half the fun of gardening is the involvement and success in multiplying plants.

One of the easiest and most successful methods of propagation is perennial division. Dig the root, lift, and wash the soil from the roots. Split the root into sections by pulling or cutting with a sharp knife. Plant the perennial immediately, keeping it moist. Spring is the best times to divide perennials unless they are early-season bloomers. Then wait until after the plant finishes blooming.

Seed can be dispensed by nature or sown by gardeners. Using a pointed tool like a chopstick that has been dipped in water makes seed easy to pick up and move to a prepared garden spot or tray. If seeds are too tiny for this method, mix them with fine sand and spread them from a salt shaker. Germination by seed is the most time-consuming method of propagation.

Many perennials, especially those with woody stems, can only be started by cuttings. Snip the tip end of a three-to-five-inch new growth of a plant like Russian sage. Remove any leaf foliage that could be covered by soil, and stick the cutting into the ground or tray. Many gardeners set aside an area, called a nursery bed, of their gardens for new starts. A cold frame or plastic-covered box is valuable for getting new plants up to size and for wintering new cuttings.

The techniques for propagation differ, so knowledge—as in all things—will furnish a higher success rate. Discovering the ways to start seed and propagate plants will become more and more valuable in the future. Our Earth with its soil and water is the only real value in life.

Meanwhile, keep taking care of our Earth by gardening, especially with perennials, and acknowledge how Mother Nature provides much-loved recreation for gardeners. We are certainly blessed.

Happy gardening!

ACKNOWLEDGMENTS

THANKS TO MY mate, who tried to understand the hibernation and early morning hours at the computer. Thank you very sincerely to the Extension Department of Utah State University and their fine Master Gardening program, which still welcomed us after four years of training.

Thanks to Ken Sutton and to my niece Cassie Holbrok and grand-daughter Megan Sorenson, who suffered through helping me conquer my fear of computers and kept mine productive.

And thanks to my wonderful family, whose pictures, experiences, and laughter have shown that they've made gardening a part of their lives.

THANKS TO THE FOLLOWING SOURCES OF PHOTOGRAPHS

First and foremost: a strong thank you to Walters Gardens Inc. for access to their website of outstanding flower photos.

Second, thank you to the national park service and their public domain policy of using their pictures so I was able to show nature's glorious gardens in the Rocky Mountains.

Third, thank you to national and state geological surveys and to Wikipedia for both information and guidance in finding maps and resources.

Thanks to the many gardeners who sent pictures of their gardens for use in *Powerful Perennials*—Marsha Fryer for the downtown Salt Lake City pictures, and Jeannie Gamble and Karen Matthews for mountain scenes. Also thank you to my friends and neighbors who allowed me to photograph their gardens. Most of all, thank you to my family for allowing me to use children to show the softer side of gardening. Photos without credits are the author's.

PHOTO SOURCES

INTRODUCTION PHOTO SOURCES

Page v, Betty Ford Alpine Gardens, Dan Sweeny.

Page xi, Idaho Botanical Garden, Ranae White.

COLD-HARDY PHOTO SOURCES

Rocky Mountain, United States Zone Map, USDA, United States Geological Survey.

Average Snowfall Map, Wikipedia, Alex Matus.

United States Frost Areas map, reprinted with permission from *Compton's by Britannica*, ©2011 by Encyclopaedia Britannica, Inc.

Page x, Image courtesy of Nick Mealey.

Page 10, Bottom three photos courtesy of Walters Gardens.

Page 33, Image courtesy of Vince.

Page 34, 'Absolutely Amethyst' the bowl of candytuft courtesy of Walters Gardens.

Page 37, Hens and chicks courtesy of Walters Gardens.

Page 39, 'Sarah Bernhardt' and 'Karl Rosenfield' courtesy of Walters Gardens.

Page 50, "Butterflies are good indicators . . . ," 'Fama', and the flower profile image are courtesy of Benary Catalogue, 2011.

Page 50, "A side view of scabiosa's . . ." image courtsey of Donna Dickson.

Page 57, Conference Center roof gardens, Peter Eckert.

DROUGHT-TOLERANT PHOTO SOURCES

Page 66, Flower profile image courtesy of Walters Gardens.

Page 70, "The rosy-colored, lacy . . ." image courtesy of Walters Gardens.

Page 73, Genista image courtesy of Scott Drissel-Martin.

Page 75, 'Firewitch', 'Frosty Fire', and 'Eastern Star' courtesy of Walters Gardens.

Page 78, 'Arizona Apricot' courtesy of Walters Gardens.

Page 84, 'Always Afternoon', 'Apricot Sparkles', and 'Round Midnight' courtesy of Walters Gardens.

Page 86, Flower profile image and Veronica 'Royal Candles' courtesy of Walters Gardens.

Pages 96–97, all images courtesy of Walters Gardens.

Page 106, "Russian sage is an ideal . . ." image courtesy of Walters Gardens.

Page 110, Bottom three images courtesy of Walters Gardens.

Page 114, Bottom three images courtesy of Walters Gardens.

Page 117 "Every summer, thousands . . ." image courtesy of NFS.

WILDLIFE-RESISTANT PHOTO SOURCES

Page 127, Image courtesy of Derick Secrist.

Page 129, Flower profile image courtesy of Walters Gardens.

Page 136, "Tiny, nodding white bells . . ." and "Lily-of-the-valley's delicate . . ." images courtesy of Walters Gardens.

Page 144, 'Bonfire' and "The brilliant radiance of . . ." images courtesy of Walters Gardens.

Page 150, Bugleweed, lily-of-the-valley, and Lenten rose courtesy of Walters Gardens.

Page 154, Image courtesy of NPS.

Page 155, Montana image courtesy of NPS.

Page 155, Utah image courtesy of Sego Lily Gardens.

Page 155, Wyoming image courtesy of Cheyenne Botanical Gardens.

Page 160, all images courtesy of Walters Gardens.

Page 162, "The cultivated native aruncus . . ." and "Echinacea purpurea is a native . . ." images courtesy of Walters Gardens.

Page 163 (left to right), Row one: Fireweed, Media Commons; Heuchera, Walters Gardens; Sphaeralcea, John Lance; Row two: Eupatorium, Walters Gardens; Liatris, Walters Gardens; Row three: Geum, Prairie Moon Nursery; Jacob's ladder and Thalictrum, Walters Gardens.

Page 167, All images courtesy of Walters Gardens.

Page 168, "The attractiveness of nepeta's . . ." image courtesy of Walters Gardens.

Page 171, 'Lorain Sunshine' and 'Pink Double Delight' courtesy of Walters Gardens.

Page 172, 'Miss Manners' image courtesy of Walters Gardens.

Page 173, Physostegia image courtesy of Walters Gardens.

Page 176, Flower profile image, "Salvia's tight-lipped . . . ," and "Salvia is so versatile . . ." images courtesy of Walters Gardens.

DIFFICULT-SOILS PHOTO SOURCES

Page 187, topographical map, geology.com.

Page 188, Twin geysers image is courtesy of NPS.

Page 189, Lake Bonneville Map, USGS.

Page 192, Flower profile image and three bottom images are courtesy of Walters Gardens.

Page 201, 'Niobe' and 'Nelly Moser' courtesy of Walters Gardens.

Page 205, 'Early Sunrise' and Coreopsis verticillata courtesy of Walters Gardens.

Page 207, Top image courtesy of Walters Gardens.

Page 211, Water image courtesy of Jeannie Gamble.

Page 212, All images courtesy of Walters Gardens.

Page 214, Achillea millefolium and Alcea rosea courtesy of Walters Gardens.

Page 218, Grasses and gaillardia images courtesy of Walters Gardens.

Page 222, *Iris ensata* courtesy of Walters Gardens.

Page 225, Both 'Floristan Violet' images courtesy of Walters Gardens.

Page 230, *Brunnera macrophylla* courtesy of Walters Gardens.

Page 234, Hibiscus courtesy of Walters Gardens.

Page 250, 'Denver Daisy' courtesy of Walters Gardens.

INDEX

ABOUT THE AUTHOR

NEDRA SECRIST is a retired schoolteacher who teaches gardening seminars at libraries, churches, garden clubs, and civic groups. She has been growing perennials for over fifty years. She and her husband own Secrist Gardens, a home-based perennial nursery with locations in Brigham City, Utah, and St. Charles, Idaho. She uses "green" gardening methods and hands-on training courses to help gardeners succeed.